Palatable Poison

WITHDRAWN

TURE

(K. Miller, Editors

GENDER & CULTURE
A series of Columbia University Press
Edited by Carolyn G. Heilbrun and Nancy K. Miller

In Dora's Case: Freud, Hysteria, Feminism
  Edited by Charles Bernheimer and Claire Kahane
Breaking the Chain: Women, Theory, and French Realist Fiction
  Naomi Schor
Between Men: English Literature and Male Homosocial Desire
  Eve Kosofsky Sedgwick
Romantic Imprisonment: Women and Other Glorified Outcasts
  Nina Auerbach
The Poetics of Gender
  Edited by Nancy K. Miller
Reading Woman: Essays in Feminist Criticism
  Mary Jacobus
Honey-Mad Women: Emancipatory Strategies in Women's Writing
  Patricia Yaeger
Subject to Change: Reading Feminist Writing
  Nancy K. Miller
Thinking Through the Body
  Jane Gallop
Gender and the Politics of History
  Joan Wallach Scott
The Dialogic and Difference: "An/Other Woman" in Virginia Woolf and Christa Wolf
  Anne Herrmann
Plotting Women: Gender and Representation in Mexico
  Jean Franco
Inspiriting Influences: Tradition, Revision, and Afro-American Women's Novels
  Michael Awkward
Hamlet's Mother and Other Women
  Carolyn G. Heilbrun
Rape and Representation
  Edited by Lynn A. Higgins and Brenda R. Silver
Shifting Scenes: Interviews on Women, Writing, and Politics in Post-68 France
  Edited by Alice A. Jardine and Anne M. Menke

Tender Geographies: Women and the Origins of the Novel in France
    Joan DeJean
Modern Feminisms: Political, Literary, Cultural
    Maggie Humm
Unbecoming Women: British Women Writers and the Novel of Development
    Susan Fraiman
The Apparitional Lesbian: Female Homosexuality and Modern Culture
    Terry Castle
George Sand and Idealism
    Naomi Schor
Becoming a Heroine: Reading About Women in Novels
    Rachel M. Brownstein
*Nomadic Subjects: Embodiment and Sexual Difference in
    Contemporary Feminist Theory*
    Rosi Braidotti
Engaging with Irigaray: Feminist Philosophy and Modern European Thought
    Edited by Carolyn Burke, Naomi Schor, and Margaret Whitford
A Certain Age: Reflecting on Menopause
    Edited by Joanna Goldsworthy
Second Skins: The Body Narratives of Transsexuality
    Jay Prosser
Mothers in Law: Feminist Theory and the Legal Regulation of Motherhood
    Edited by Martha Albertson Fineman and Isabelle Karpin
Critical Condition: Feminism at the Turn of the Century
        Susan Gubar
Feminist Consequences: Theory for the New Century
    Edited by Elisabeth Bronfen and Misha Kavka
Simone de Beauvoir, Philosophy, and Feminism
        Nancy Bauer
Pursuing Privacy in Cold War America
    Deborah Nelson

Gender and Culture Readers

Modern Feminisms: Political, Literary, Cultural
    Edited by Maggie Humm
Feminism and Sexuality: A Reader
    Edited by Stevi Jackson and Sue Scott
Writing on the Body: Female Embodiment and Feminist Theory
    Edited by Katie Conboy, Nadia Medina, and Sarah Stanbury

Palatable Poison

CRITICAL PERSPECTIVES ON
THE WELL OF LONELINESS

EDITED BY

LAURA DOAN & JAY PROSSER

COLUMBIA UNIVERSITY PRESS
NEW YORK

COLUMBIA UNIVERSITY PRESS
Publishers Since 1893
New York Chichester, West Sussex
Copyright © 2001 Columbia University Press
All rights reserved

Library of Congress Cataloging-in-Publication Data
Palatable Poison : critical perspectives on The well of loneliness /
edited by Laura Doan and Jay Prosser.
   p. cm.—(Gender and culture)
   Includes bibliographical references and index.
   ISBN 0-231-11874-0 (cloth : alk. paper — ISBN 0-231-11875-9
(pbk. : alk. paper)
   1. Hall, Radclyffe. Well of loneliness.   2. Lesbians in literature.
I. Doan, Laura L., 1951–   . II. Prosser, Jay. III. Series.
PR6015.A33 W57 2001
823'.912—dc21

2001028992

∞

Casebound editions of Columbia University Press books are printed
on permanent and durable acid-free paper.
Printed in the United States of America
Designed by Lisa Hamm
c 10 9 8 7 6 5 4 3 2 1
p 10 9 8 7 6 5 4 3 2 1

Contents

Acknowledgments xi

Introduction: Critical Perspectives Past and Present
LAURA DOAN AND JAY PROSSER 1

PART ONE / PERSPECTIVES PAST

The First Wave

1. Commentary (1928)
HAVELOCK ELLIS 35
2. "A Book That Must Be Suppressed" (1928)
JAMES DOUGLAS 36
3. Judgment (1928)
SIR CHARTRES BIRON 39
4. A Selection of Early Reviews 50

The Second Wave

5. "Radclyffe Hall" (1975)
JANE RULE 77
6. "The Mythic Mannish Lesbian:
Radclyffe Hall and the New Woman" (1989)
ESTHER NEWTON 89
7. "Perverse Desire: The Lure of the Mannish Lesbian" (1991)
TERESA DE LAURETIS 109

PART TWO / PERSPECTIVES PRESENT
New Sexual Inversions

8. "Some Primitive Thing Conceived in a Turbulent Age
of Transition": The Transsexual Emerging from *The Well*
JAY PROSSER 129

9. "A Writer of Misfits": "John" Radclyffe Hall
and the Discourse of Inversion
JUDITH HALBERSTAM 145

10. "The Outcast of One Age Is the Hero of Another":
Radclyffe Hall, Edward Carpenter and the Intermediate Sex
LAURA DOAN 162

11. "All My Life I've Been Waiting for Something . . .":
Theorizing Femme Narrative in *The Well of Loneliness*
CLARE HEMMINGS 179

The Well's Wounds

12. *The Well* of Shame
SALLY R. MUNT 199

13. *The Well of Loneliness* as War Novel
SUSAN KINGSLEY KENT 216

14. War Wounds: The Nation, Shell Shock,
and Psychoanalysis in *The Well of Loneliness*
JODIE MEDD 232

15. Of Trees and Polities, Wars and Wounds
TREVOR HOPE 255

On Location

16. "I Want to Cross Over into Camp Ground": Race
and Inversion in *The Well of Loneliness*
JEAN WALTON 277

17. "Something Primitive and Age-Old as Nature Herself":
Lesbian Sexuality and the Permission of the Exotic
SARAH E. CHINN 300

18. Once More unto the Breach: *The Well of Loneliness*
and the Spaces of Inversion
VICTORIA ROSNER 316

19. Great Cities: Radclyffe Hall at the Chicago School
JULIE ABRAHAM 336

20. *Well* Meaning: Pragmatism, Lesbianism,
and the U.S. Obscenity Trial
KIM EMERY 355

21. Writing by the Light of *The Well:* Radclyffe Hall
and the Lesbian Modernists
JOANNE WINNING 372

Afterword: It Was Good, Good, *Good*
TERRY CASTLE 394

Contributors 403
Suggested Readings 407
Index 411

Acknowledgments

The editors wish to thank those who gave permission for their work to be reprinted: Esther Newton and Teresa de Lauretis, the Crossing Press for Jane Rule's essay, Duke University Press for Judith Halberstam's essay, SUNY Press for Kim Emery's essay, and Columbia University Press for allowing the editors to revise their essays previously published. Our use of the sketch of Radclyffe Hall by Kathleen Shackleton as part of the cover design is courtesy of the National Portrait Gallery, London. We are grateful to Catherine E. Taylor who worked tremendously hard in scanning and word-processing the materials in parts 1 and 2, and to Marie Henry who helped with the index. We would also like to thank Susan Heath for her copyediting skills and Marlene Mussell for her assistance in proofreading. Finally, thanks to Nancy K. Miller and Carolyn Heilbrun as editors of this series. Their criticism has been foundational to the perspectives offered here.

The excerpt by Jane Rule originally appeared in *Lesbian Images* (Garden City, N.Y.: Doubleday, 1975). Esther Newton's article, first published in *Signs: Journal of Women in Culture and Society* 9, no. 4 (Summer 1984), was revised and republished in Martin Duberman, Martha Vicinus, and George Chauncey, eds., *Hidden from History: Reclaiming the Gay and Lesbian Past* (New York: New American Library, 1989), pp. 281–293. Teresa de Lauretis's

essay, "Perverse Desire: The Lure of the Mannish Lesbian," was published in
Australian Feminist Studies 13 (Autumn 1991): 15–26, and expanded in chap-
ter 4 of de Lauretis, *The Practice of Love: Lesbian Sexuality and Perverse
Desire* (Bloomington: Indiana University Press, 1994). Jay Prosser's " 'Some
Primitive Thing Conceived in a Turbulent Age of Transition': The Trans-
sexual Emerging from *The Well*" draws on chapter 4 of Prosser, *Second Skins:
The Body Narratives of Transsexuality* (New York: Columbia University
Press, 1998). Judith Halberstam's " 'A Writer of Misfits': 'John' Radclyffe Hall
and the Discourse of Inversion" appeared in different versions in
Halberstam, *Female Masculinity* (Durham, N.C.: Duke University Press,
1998). Laura Doan's " 'The Outcast of One Age Is the Hero of Another':
Radclyffe Hall, Edward Carpenter and the Intermediate Sex," and parts of
the introduction are drawn from Doan, *Fashioning Sapphism: The Origins of
a Modern English Lesbian Culture* (New York: Columbia University Press,
2001). Kim Emery's "*Well* Meaning: Pragmatism, Lesbianism, and the U.S.
Obscenity Trial" is published in an expanded version in chapter 3 of Emery,
*The Lesbian Index: Pragmatism and Lesbian Subjectivity in the Twentieth-
Century United States* (New York: SUNY Press, 2002).

Palatable Poison

Introduction: Critical Perspectives Past and Present

LAURA DOAN AND JAY PROSSER

On July 27, 1928, Radclyffe Hall's *The Well of Loneliness*, the first "long and very serious novel entirely upon the subject of sexual inversion," according to its author, appeared in bookshops and lending libraries throughout Britain.[1] Within weeks, however, the largely favorable response by sober reviewers was overshadowed by the journalist James Douglas's editorial in the *Sunday Express*, condemning the propagandistic aims of Hall's project and demanding the novel's suppression "without delay."[2] The home secretary, Sir William Joynson-Hicks, entirely agreed with Douglas's estimation and instructed the director of public prosecutions to initiate legal proceedings against the novel in accordance with the Obscene Publications Act of 1857 that "gave magistrates throughout the country statutory powers to order the destruction of 'any obscene publication held for sale or distribution on information laid before a court of summary jurisdiction.'"[3] In November the presiding magistrate, Sir Chartres Biron, argued that the "literary merit" he found in *The Well* only rendered it more dangerous: "The more palatable the poison the more insidious." At the appeal in December 1928 Biron's judgment was upheld and, consequently, the book was pronounced obscene and all copies seized by the police were ordered to be destroyed. Ironically, of course, the intense and sensational publicity surrounding the trial and the obscenity ban guaranteed *The Well of Loneliness*—the only one of Hall's eight published works to remain continuously in print—a place in literary history.

Palatable Poison is the first scholarly study to assemble a multiplicity of critical perspectives on this central and significant text. We include a wide range of materials—primary and secondary, classic and new—because we believe this innovative approach both reveals the unprecedented historical richness that surrounds *The Well* and, at the same time, demonstrates how the novel continues to unsettle and provoke. Generations of feminists, from Virginia Woolf and Rebecca West to the second wave of feminism (Lillian Faderman and Esther Newton) to the present (Terry Castle), may have dismissed or celebrated the novel on grounds literary or political, but they have never ignored it. Whether in pursuit of a female or lesbian literary tradition or in the construction of a lesbian subculture, sexuality, or identity, Hall's profoundly influential novel has held a secure place in the center of critical discourse. At the same time, however, our understanding of the novel's reception or influence has often been deeply entangled in myth: for instance, the view that Douglas's editorial was typical rather than exceptional is widely held, as is the sense that Hall's era was intensely homophobic. Thus, in our introduction, we begin our discussion of the novel's critical reception with an analysis of the initial response in 1928 ("The First Wave: 1928") and then move on to examine the novel's rediscovery by feminists in the late 1960s ("The Second Wave: 1968 to the Present"). In our last section, "The Third Wave: Perspectives Present," we present an overview of this volume's new readings which draw on recent theoretical frameworks.

The First Wave: 1928[4]

Radclyffe Hall approached the famous sexologist Havelock Ellis with a typescript of her new novel because she hoped his endorsement would, among other outcomes, lend the project legitimacy by declaring emphatically to potential readers everywhere that the novel was not simply a "salacious diversion."[5] Although Hall was thrilled with the original draft of the "Commentary" Ellis dutifully produced—technically, the first critical response to *The Well of Loneliness*—the statement in its final form is such an opaque and evasive endorsement of Hall's project that many uninformed readers were undoubtedly left wondering what the novel was about. This lack of specificity was the result of editorial tampering on the part of the novel's publisher, Jonathan Cape, whose intervention represents the first of several instances in *The Well*'s publication history where a professional opinion of the novel was deployed to serve multiple and sometimes contradictory purposes and agendas. In reworking certain key passages of Ellis's original, Cape took substantial liberties and effectively watered down the epistemological accuracy that is the hallmark of sexological methodology, a field obsessed with subtle variation and degree. What Ellis initially described as "various aspects of sexual inversion" was scaled back to "an aspect of sexual inversion" because Cape thought the phrasing could be construed to include male homosexuality, which at that time was a criminal offense.[6] Cape later expunged any reference to "inversion," a term he may have thought too bold or clinically precise, and replaced it with a phrase so vague as to be practically meaningless: "one particular aspect of sexual life." This change of phrase was accompanied by an equally oblique reference not to inverts or homosexuals but to "certain people." The final version, one that prefigures later reductive readings, thus achieved little more than an anodyne echo of the plea embodied in the novel itself: even if "certain people" are different, they nevertheless deserve understanding from a "hostile society."

An intelligent and savvy publisher, Cape appreciated the commercial value of a statement by a medical expert of Ellis's stature but intervened to ensure that the wording—innocuous and bland—would interest readers without causing the slightest offense. (Ellis himself later indicated privately to the lesbian writer Bryher that he found Hall's novel "a remarkable book by its frank recognition of inversion, but otherwise perfectly respectable and conventional. Not a word that anyone could object to."[7]) Ellis's participation had the desired effect: nearly half of the early reviews mention Ellis, although sometimes to protest that the novel, good in its own right, did not require his testimony. For example, a glowing piece in the *Morning Post*, the paper of choice for "the retired senior officer and his family," announced: "There can be nothing but respect and admiration for the author's handling of [the theme]. Mr. Havelock Ellis's brief commentary was not required to establish its challenge, which from the first page emerges with a frankness free of offense."[8] The "most important literary periodical," the

Times Literary Supplement (TLS), also objected to the jarring effect of a scientific preface and criticized Ellis's involvement.[9] While the unusual combination of the "scientific" and the "literary" struck some as inappropriate, unlike James Douglas these reviewers did not use the occasion to dismiss sexology as a "pseudo-scientific" and "terrible doctrine." The insertion of Ellis's affirmation of Hall's "faithful and uncompromising" negotiation of sexology, although an unwelcome distraction for the *TLS* and others, nevertheless alerted the literary establishment from page one that the long novel was, in certain respects, extraordinary.

Cape was fully aware that the subject of Hall's novel might be "called into question," as he put it, and he therefore proceeded with caution.[10] The large advertisements promoting *The Well* avoided its subject matter and instead noted prominently that Hall's last novel, *Adam's Breed* (1926), had received the Prix Femina Vie Heureuse-Bookman and the James Tait Black Memorial Prize (the only other winner of both awards had been E. M. Forster for his 1924 *A Passage to India*). The volume's physical appearance and high price worked in tandem to establish the project's credentials as serious and significant: the novel "was produced in a large format, in somber black binding with a plain wrapper, and priced at fifteen shillings, twice the average price for a new novel. . . . Review copies were sent only to the serious newspapers and weekly journals." Cape pitched the publicity, pricing, and reviews not to Hall's usual middlebrow following but to a more highbrow readership—a strategy that was, initially anyway, successful: between July 27 (the date of publication) and August 19 (the date of the Douglas editorial) the novel was reviewed in fourteen of the so-called quality newspapers and journals: "serious and authoritative critics . . . commended it both for its high-minded sincerity and for its literary quality."[11]

The Douglas editorial looms so large in most critical discussions of the novel's initial reception that the tenor of these early reviews has been eclipsed. True enough, some thought *The Well* "far less accomplished than her previous novels," but it is misleading to suggest that "in contemporary reviews of *The Well* and in private comment by her contemporaries, it was considered a pious and dreary book."[12] The novelist L. P. Hartley, for instance, discovered in *The Well* "passages of great force and beauty," while Leonard Woolf mentioned Hall's "very considerable gifts for novel writing."[13] The writer Ethel Mannin, who found the book "profoundly moving and beautiful, a delicate and lovely and sensitive piece of work," pointed out

that the novel "was selling . . . on the strength of the author's previous reputation and an almost *unanimously eulogistic press*."[14] The startling intervention of the *Sunday Express* has made it difficult to recuperate that short
period of time when both professional critics and the public were able to
judge the novel on its literary merits alone. As a result of the editorial, as
Margaret Lawrence lamented, Hall became "an example of the inability of
the public, even of the reading public, to hold more than one idea about
one writer. . . . [*The Well*] doomed her to be remembered in her own time
only as a student of sexual inversion. All the beauty and power of her prose
was, in general, lost."[15]

In the interregnum between *The Well*'s publication and the *Sunday
Express* editorial, some of the most prominent literary journals, including
the *Nation*, the *Saturday Review*, and the *TLS*, and many respected and
influential critics, such as Hartley, Woolf, and Arnold Bennett, assiduously
reviewed the novel, recognized the "danger, where a highly controversial
subject is being considered, that the essential qualities of a work may be
overlooked," and endeavored to assess the literary qualities in a fair and balanced manner; the novel's open discussion of lesbianism never interfered
with the task at hand.[16] An early commentator attributed this new sophistication in the handling of the subject of lesbianism to "an interesting development in fiction writing of late years . . . the large influx of young women,
many fresh from college . . . are apt to discuss phases of sexual life, and
some do not even hesitate to introduce a slight flavor of Lesbianism."[17]
When the *Glasgow Herald* expressed shock it was not, as we might expect,
with the subject but with Hall's uncharacteristic "lamentable inattention to
style."[18] All fourteen reviews prior to August 19 identified the novel's literary
strengths *and* weaknesses; some praised Hall's "beauty of style and delicate,
yet vivid, presentation of character and mood," while others found the narrative structure "formless" and "chaotic," or complained of Hall's "tendency
to preach."[19] Bennett thought that, although the novel was "disfigured by
loose writing and marred by loose construction, it nevertheless does hold
you. It is honest, convincing, and extremely courageous."[20] That the novel
attracted Bennett's attention was an impressive coup in the first place for
the author and publisher because Bennett had the "reputation as a maker of
'best sellers.'"[21]

Neither Bennett nor Woolf—representing, respectively, the literary middle and highbrow—had read any of Hall's previous work, even though her

last novel had won prestigious literary prizes.[22] Woolf seems to have been drawn to the book because of its "extremely interesting" topic, while Bennett admits his interest was piqued by the Ellis commentary.[23] The novel's success in enticing reviewers from such a broad spectrum of the literary establishment was quite unusual, for it constituted a crossing over of discrete literary boundaries or—put more pugnaciously—a transgressing of lines drawn in what Virginia Woolf described as the "Battle of the Brows."[24] As Q. D. Leavis observed in her sophisticated analysis of English literary culture: "A novel received with unqualified enthusiasm in a low-brow paper will be coolly treated by the middlebrow and contemptuously dismissed if mentioned at all by the highbrow Press; the kind of book that the middlebrow Press will admire wholeheartedly the highbrow reviewer will diagnose as pernicious; each has a following that forms a different level of public."[25] In the 1920s individual authors belonged to these distinctly separate, if not hostile, literary and interpretive communities and, like the distinctions of the class system, the boundaries were seldom breached; as critic Anthea Trodd explains, "the categorization of writing by heights of brow between the wars was not simply a media pastime; it was a means by which the literary world attempted to interpret the changes which had taken place in the expanding and fragmenting market."[26] Such categorization accounts for some of the mixed responses to Hall's novel, a point that has been often overlooked by feminist literary critics.

When Virginia Woolf famously declared, "No one has read [Hall's] book," she meant, of course, no one in her circle because, as sales figures indicate, before the ban *The Well*'s readership was immense; it included the prolific middlebrow writer and lesbian Naomi Jacob, who had the book on order and received it on the first day of publication: "I read it with deep interest, and found its sincerity very touching and fine."[27] When the initial print run (fifteen hundred copies) quickly sold out, Cape doubled that number for the second impression because, after Douglas's piece, orders for Hall's novel poured in. By the time Joynson-Hicks initiated proceedings, about five thousand copies "were in circulation, or available from shops and libraries."[28] Thus literary critic Gillian Whitlock is only partially correct when she speculates that Woolf's comment suggested "the novel lacked literary merit"; Woolf meant—more precisely—that the novel lacked merit from a highbrow modernist perspective.[29] Woolf's pronouncement that *The Well* was "lukewarm and neither one thing or the other" confirms her sense of it as thoroughly middlebrow, a phrase fully compliant with Woolf's own definition of the term: one "who ambles and saunters now on this side of the hedge, now on that, in pursuit of no single object, neither art itself nor life itself, but both mixed indistinguishably."[30] Of course, the positioning of individual writers within "brow culture" was—and still is—a highly subjective and slippery business, but we know that Woolf proudly claimed highbrow membership and revealed her animus toward middlebrow people, whom: "I confess, that I seldom regard with entire cordiality" (155). Rosenman perceptively accounts for Woolf's disapproval of *The Well* in terms of literary style ("she found it conventional, even old-fashioned"), but it is important to note that Woolf's uncordial comments (a "meritorious dull book" that was "pale, tepid, vapid") were directed as much at middlebrow literary culture as a whole as at *The Well* and its representation of lesbianism.[31]

Anticipating that *The Well*'s frank exploration of inversion was bound to attract attention, early reviewers warned their readers that the topic might not suit everyone's taste. Still, critics strongly urged readers to keep an open mind because the failure or inability to deal with this important and timely topic would constitute a loss. I. A. R. Wylie, herself a lesbian, novelist, and close friend of Hall's, divided potential readers into two groups: "those who insist that life as a whole is not a fit subject for nice-minded people to write or think about and those who believe that most of our troubles spring from our refusal to look ourselves honestly in the face."[32] With considerable boldness and panache in light of her own sexual identity, Wylie lavishly commended the novel to "those who care for truth and who believe that somehow or other 'we are all God's chil'un,'" and concluded with a statement impressive in terms of its prescience and accuracy: "the reward of [Hall's qualities of courage and honesty] is uncertain, and it will be interesting to watch the reception of this daring study. If it is received as it was written, it will be something of a landmark in the history of human development." Wylie well understood the dangers that lay in store for a book on such a topic, as did Richard King whose long review in the *Tatler*, which described the novel as "a work of considerable art," is the most sensitive to potential homophobia; in an audacious challenge to his society-conscious readers, King spoke of the "huge army of the narrow-minded" and asserted that "only the bigoted and the foolish seek to ignore an aspect of life which is as undeniable a fact as any concrete thing."[33] Like

Wylie, he broke readers into two camps: "You will either be interested by [the novel], or peradventure it will make you too furious and disgusted to do more than throw the book in the fire. We will leave it at that." This sympathetic review was the last to appear before Douglas abruptly shifted the critical framework from the narrow world of the literati to an entirely different group, some of whom had an entirely different agenda.

The most obvious and immediate result of the *Express*'s intervention was that all future critical discussion of the novel could not but engage with or refer to the controversy. For instance, before August 19 Hall's representation of the childhood of the protagonist, Stephen ("the first 150 pages") was regarded as "good," but after that crucial date, *Life and Letters* found that same "episode of the story . . . comparatively restrained and *noncontroversial*": the measuring-stick no longer related solely to the art of the novel but also to the manner in which the subject of lesbianism was negotiated.[34] Likewise, later that year the *British Journal of Inebriety* strenuously exhorted their (professional) readers not merely to "consider" the novel but also to "consider [it] *without prejudice.*"[35] The short review, noting incongruously that Hall was an award-winning author and "enthusiastic dog-breeder," thought it all the more regrettable and disturbing that her "remarkable" novel should become subject to government censorship, making "it increasingly difficult in the future for authors and publishers to deal with certain medico-sociological problems in works of fiction." Like other reviews produced *after* the Douglas editorial, the *British Journal of Inebriety* urges readers not to turn away from a book that is "without offense."

Another by-product of the *Express* attack was the tendency among reviewers to approach the text not as a new work of fiction by a popular writer but as a potentially titillating novel at the center of a growing controversy. After all, some readers may have reasoned, if a ban for obscene libel was in the offing, Hall's protagonist must be fast-living, hard-drinking, foul-mouthed, sexually promiscuous, or a combination of all of the above; to their disappointment, Stephen Gordon was an honorable upper-class Englishwoman who desired a quiet life with her female companion among the respectable county set. *The Well*, it seemed, was all too tasteful. As a result of the shift in inflated expectations arising from the hype, some critics who had imagined the narrative to be more shocking or graphic expressed surprise or dissatisfaction that it was only "a sadly ordinary novel."[36] In the October issue of *Life and Letters* the anonymous reviewer speculated that if one were to "rob Miss Radclyffe Hall of her challenging thesis . . . [*The Well*] would quite naturally slip back into the category to which it belongs; it would rank, that is to say, as a simple, pleasantly written love-story with an unhappy ending."[37] In a discussion notably flippant and irascible, newspaper critic W. R. Gordon observed that although Hall's protagonist may have had "a passion for a member of her own sex," the only discernible obscenity was the author's audacity in presenting Stephen—a woman with no "serious grievances against society"—as a figure of pity.[38]

Some earlier critics had thought Hall's plea irksome in certain respects, but when Douglas mentioned "martyrdom" in referring to the novel's primary objective ("a seductive and insidious piece of special pleading designed to display perverted decadence as a martyrdom inflicted upon these outcasts by a cruel society"), others followed suit. Thus Gordon found *The Well* objectionable because "it falsifies realities, and presents as a martyr a woman in the grip of a vice."[39] In a rare class-based critique, Gordon concluded that Stephen's suffering was no different from that of any other human being because "loneliness is the human lot," and indeed, as a member of the upper classes, Stephen was better off than many others: "There is no trace of persecution. She collected her dividends regularly. She lived as she pleased."

Finally, two post-Douglas reviews exhibited a new attentiveness to clothing and personal habits, indicating a heightened curiosity about the physical appearance of such women. A couple of early reviews mentioned Stephen's parents' desire for a son, Stephen's personal qualities ("athletic, clever, and scholarly"), or her aversion to men, but Stephen's manner of dress never came under discussion.[40] Suddenly, *Life and Letters*, which insisted on referring to the protagonist as "he," professed to find tedious the novel's sartorial detail: "We could have preferred a briefer account of the inessential part of the hero's life, the shirts, ties, underclothes he bought and the way he decorated his rooms."[41] Yet, as the reviewer fully recognized, the novel is no ordinary heterosexual love story and what in part signifies that difference is the preference of the "hero-heroine" for masculine clothing. In protesting too much, the reviewer reveals not boredom with Hall's "shirted and tailored" protagonist but fascination. The complex relationship between clothing and sexuality had become a source of unease, as can be seen in Gordon's observation about the way in which Stephen "liked wearing knickerbockers better than skirts, riding astride and screwing her hair well out of her eyes. . . . Exaggerating the importance of clothes in a thoroughly feminine fashion, she dresses herself in clothes of masculine character."[42] Hall's description of Stephen's wardrobe forces Gordon to scrutinize the importance of clothing in a new way by associating sartorial preferences with a particular (deviant) sexuality—in what Douglas had succinctly called a "display [of] perverted decadence."

The *Sunday Express* editor may have been energetic and clever, but did he engineer a genuine moral crusade or a cynical newspaper stunt? Biographer Sally Cline's juxtaposition of Hall's motives ("sincere and sensitive") with those of Douglas ("mercenary and malicious") lends credence to the characterization of the journalist as opportunistic.[43] Yet Douglas's interest in religion and morality—ironically, like Hall's—was passionate and long-standing. An exemplary "champion of the muscular Christian," a notion associated with late-Victorian culture, Douglas regularly used his column in the *Sunday Express* to rant against the "degeneracy and decadence" of modern life, in the hope of reinvigorating an "essentially . . . Protestant and Puritanical renaissance," which he defined as "a movement of the mind, the soul, and the heart."[44] Diana Souhami's unequivocal declaration that "James Douglas voiced his bigotry to sell his newspapers" may underestimate the depths of the editor's "moral delicacy"—it is more likely that Douglas's fervent sentiments happily dovetailed with the *Express*'s equally sincere desire to make money.[45] Douglas's masterful, if vicious, attacks on anything or anyone could not have been more advantageous for a newspaper intent on boosting sales during the middle of a sleepy August, the so-called "silly season."[46] The *Express* forced all other papers to scramble for their angle on the "story." With some "16 national newspapers, 21 Sundays and about 130 provincial papers" in operation after the First World War, "circulation wars were fuelled by more eye-catching layout, photographs, strip cartoons, crosswords, competitions and special offers for regular subscriptions. Newspapers set out to entertain in order to capture the largest market."[47] The war between the newspapers was noticeably intense in the latter part of 1928. As the *Tatler* observed: "The public always loves a fight and there is a lively public interest in the battle for public favor which is developing on all fronts between those two popular morning papers, 'The Daily Mail' and 'The Daily Express.'"[48] Lord Beaverbrook's *Sunday Express* was particularly notorious for its awesome range of ruthless tactics:

It regales its readers each week with a confection of spicy gossip and piquant pictures. If some poor creature is lying in jail under sentence of death in connection with an especially lurid and sensational murder every effort will be made to obtain from him a literary contribution to the *Sunday Express*. . . . Finally, to give a literary flavor to this luscious *compôte*, we find thrown in from time to time, an article in which a book is violently denounced as immoral, or a "love-story of the great" recalling in flamboyant fashion the romances or sexual tragedies of famous men and women of the past.[49]

Such well-planned gimmickry proved immensely successful: the *Daily Express* could be counted among the winners in the circulation race with a rise in the number of its readers from "half a million in 1910 . . . to almost two and a half million in 1939."[50]

"Unabashedly capitalistic," the *Express* group's launch of Douglas's call for a ban of *The Well*, like so many of their other "campaigns," was a brilliantly well-managed affair that started on August 18 when the *Daily Express*:

carefully aroused public expectations by printing a sharply edited resumé of Douglas's piece which omitted the name of the novel and its author. At the same time posters and bill-boards gave wide prominence to the impending thunderbolt. That Saturday night the *Evening Standard* obligingly kept the world on tenterhooks by reproducing the *Daily Express* "teaser" word for word. The result was that, come Sunday the 19th, other newspapers were leaping [on the story] with gusto.[51]

Beneath the headline "A Book That Should Be Suppressed" followed by Douglas's "prussic acid" line set in bold face, the *Daily Express* promised readers that the editorial on Sunday would undertake not a literary review or thoughtful discussion of an "astounding new novel" by "a well-known woman writer" but a "vigorous exposure."[52] The article alleged that the "utterly degrading" novel was "devoted to a particular hideous aspect of life as it exists among us today," a topic "decent people" would regard with "unspeakable horror." Who could resist such a tantalizing build-up?

That same day Douglas sent a copy of his editorial to Cape to give him fair warning of a possible controversy. On the following day the *Sunday*

Express, confidently anticipating their hype would stimulate curiosity, perversely provided up-to-date information about the book's availability, with brief statements from four leading sources of books for the middlebrow readership: W. H. Smith and Sons (bookseller and library), "an official" of Mudie's Library, the head librarian of Boots's Library, and Jonathan Cape, Ltd.[53] To maximize publicity for a news item of its own making, the *Sunday Express* strategically inserted a short front-page article under three bold and titillating headlines ("Novel That Should Be Banned," "Story of Perverted Lives," and "Nauseating"), intimating mysteriously that the novel in question dealt "with a subject taboo in decent circles." On the issue's tenth page was the Douglas column with an opening line that simulated an actual review, perhaps confusing some readers: "*The Well of Loneliness* (Jonathan Cape, 15s. net) by Miss Radclyffe Hall, is a novel." Adjacent to the piece was the finishing touch: what some regarded as an especially unflattering photograph of Hall, "monstrous-looking . . . with short hair and a bow tie."[54] Where Cape had undertaken every precaution to ensure the book was discreetly and tastefully published with a look, price, and expert testimony underlining the project's sincerity, seriousness, and "science," the *Express* called for the book's withdrawal with a lay-out trumpeting all the relevant information concerning the publisher, the cost, and its acquisition—the silencing of homosexual propaganda, it seems, was a noisy business.

One week later, on August 26, the *Sunday Express*, evidently pleased that the "story" had taken off, first denied that the attention they had given to the novel had resulted in an increase in sales of the offensive book and then distracted readers with a sampling from a few of the "hundreds of letters and telegrams" received "from all parts of the country" about "the obnoxious character of Miss Radclyffe Hall's new novel."[55] Of the nine letters printed, two chastised the newspaper for "stirring up the mud" and instigating a "slanderous attack." One correspondent wrote: "I feel it would be a grave injustice to the thousands whom you term 'moral derelicts' if your scathing criticism . . . were to go unchallenged. I am one of those individuals whom you so cruelly condemn, merely because you have no scientific knowledge." For this writer-invert, sexology was not coupled with the oppressors who condemn or stigmatize but was a powerful marker separating the ignorant from the informed. A second correspondent complained that the editor had gone too far: "This is the first time I have ever disagreed with Mr. James Douglas." This tolerant reader spoke of his willingness to "read an account of anything God allows to happen" and viewed the novel's subject as part of nature's diversity. All the remaining letters, of course, praised the paper for its bold moral stand against the "ever-growing menace" and commended the *Express* for its diligent efforts to safeguard innocent young people. The inclusion of the two dissenting voices suggests, however, that the selection of letters was designed to sustain the intensity of the controversy rather than simply to report public reaction to the "cause": the more urgent cause on behalf of an increase in newspaper sales was better served through the reproduction of opposing views.

If Douglas had really cared about his readers' innocence, other editorials argued, he would have brought the objectionable book to the attention of the Home Office quietly and without sensation. In this way, the *Yorkshire Post* conjectured, the *Express* would have circumvented the "storm of publicity" that only ensured the novel "an immediate 'succès de scandale.'"[56] The *Nation* surmised pragmatically that the *Express*'s primary motivation was the difficulty in obtaining "good copy . . . at this season" and found deeply disturbing the precedent set in the government's response to a newspaper editor's call for suppression of a "serious" book.[57] Any book, even one by "a writer of refinement and distinction," "weightily prefaced" by a medical authority, and "favorably reviewed," could now be attacked by an editor keen for a palpable hit or "a successful 'stunt.'" With the exception of one or two tabloids such as the *People* or *Sunday Chronicle*, both of which covered the controversy only briefly, the British press was not immensely hostile toward *The Well*—on the contrary, most major newspapers and journals were largely sympathetic either to Hall's predicament or to her right as an author to publish without legal hindrance.[58] Neither the topic of lesbian sexuality in general nor Hall's novel in particular, nor indeed the controversy over the banning of that novel generated the backlash against Hall or lesbians some critics have claimed; instead, most editors condemned the *Express*'s handling of Douglas's rhetoric of outrage, identified it as "stunt journalism," and exposed the hyperbole for what it was: flat and empty.[59]

The Second Wave: 1968 to the Present

The logic of palatable poison characterizes the second wave of *The Well*'s critical reception as much as it does the first. While critics read *The Well of*

Loneliness, they continue to express aversion to its subject and/or aesthetic mode of representation. Yet they find in its poison a pabulum sufficiently palatable that *The Well* is responsible for generating a wealth of criticism, indeed gives rise to some of the richest feminist thought to appear during this period. In Nancy K. Miller's formulation *The Well* is something of a "pre-text" for feminist criticism.[60] It precedes and gives cause to a layering of critical material on gender and sexuality, which are the preoccupations of commentary on *The Well* during this period. Read itself as a text, this critical commentary demonstrates the shifts in thinking about gender and sexuality and serves as an index to the changes in feminist thought from 1968 to the present day. Indeed, some might argue that the criticism on *The Well* makes for more interesting reading than the novel itself.

It is appropriate that 1968 inaugurates the second wave of *The Well's* critical reception. This was the year of student revolts and liberation movements, the year that Kate Millett filed *Sexual Politics* as her thesis, and the year that led the Gay Liberation Movement up to Stonewall.[61] 1968 also saw the publication of Vera Brittain's *Radclyffe Hall: A Case of Obscenity?*, one of only two books published before *Palatable Poison* that are devoted entirely to *The Well*. *Radclyffe Hall* combines Brittain's contemporaneous feminist critique of the novel with an account of and documents from the obscenity trial. In this double dimension it captures that transition from the first wave of *The Well of Loneliness's* reception, in which the novel was considered largely in terms of sexological subject, soon to be subsumed in notions of obscenity and the trial itself, to the second wave of reception, in which the novel has been considered in the light of the changing gender and sexual concerns of its readers' moment.

That *The Well* does not occupy the public stage to the same extent in the intervening years of the thirties, forties, fifties, and early sixties, can be explained both aesthetically and materially. First, on an aesthetic front, *The Well* did not chime with the literary tastes of modernism, a cultural movement that was, as hinted at by some of the earlier reviews, on the ascendant at the time of Hall's publication. The battles between modernism and realism that ensued did nothing to rehabilitate Hall's clumsy blend of realism and sentimental romanticism. Second, on a more material level, the novel was not easily available during this period. As Rebecca O'Rourke points out, after 1928 the novel could be obtained in English only in America and France.[62] While it was reprinted in Britain in the late forties, it was not published in paperback until the early fifties—a form of mass publication perhaps more than incidental to those liberation movements that were to arise in Britain and America in the sixties and seventies and in which *The Well* was to play such a figurative role. In the intervening years *The Well of Loneliness* was of course read. But as O'Rourke's *Reflecting on The Well of Loneliness* suggests, it was read mostly by private readers in England and America. O'Rourke's book, the other book besides Brittain's published on *The Well*, though appearing in 1989, is most useful for containing surveys of just these private readers in the forties, fifties, sixties, and seventies. Significantly, *The Well of Loneliness* seems removed in O'Rourke's book from the critical and cultural stage upon which it entered to a realm of private, identity, and sometimes medical identity discourse. In 1946, for instance, O'Rourke documents *The Well of Loneliness* as being cited in an English endocrinological text by a doctor who had read Hall's book as reflective of his own condition and would later go on to become the first transsexual.[63] *The Well of Loneliness* was read for identificatory, often conflicting identificatory, purposes.

These identities are made public and the novel reenters the public stage following the publication of Brittain's book simultaneously with the rise of the gay/lesbian and feminist movements of the early 1970s. With the combination of lesbianism and feminism, as well as the politicization of lesbians as feminists that constitutes lesbian feminism, the novel plays a prominent, but paradoxically negative, constructive role. In 1977 Lillian Faderman and Ann Williams give the novel a seminal lesbian place in their essay in the first issue of the lesbian feminist journal *Conditions*, yet they criticize the novel.[64] Faderman would go on to elaborate this criticism in her 1981 *Surpassing the Love of Men* in which she condemned the novel for not surpassing the love of men because it "morbidified" lesbianism by representing it as masculinity.[65] In 1979 Blanche Wiesen Cook would state the problem with *The Well* for lesbian feminism was that the novel was too representative of lesbianism, too much in the public eye as lesbian. In addition, Stephen's masculinity did not accord with the lesbian feminist ideal that, as Wiesen Cook, quoting Virginia Woolf, put it, "women alone stir my imagination": "Our only picture of lesbian love was the one presented by Radclyffe Hall, and that was joyless."[66] In 1982 Catharine Stimpson even found in the novel the lesbian's "narrative of damnation," the antithesis of that narrative of "enabling escape" the lesbian feminist sought.[67] Yet in this first stage of post-1968

reception *The Well of Loneliness* proved a paradoxically productive disestab-
lishing foundation for lesbian feminism, precisely a palatable poison. It was
the most famous representation of lesbianism that was its infamous misrepresentation, yet its misrepresentation helped give proof of the homophobic
and misogynist stigmatization of lesbianism from which the lesbian feminist
sought to emerge. The novel offered a journey into otherness, as Toni
McNaron wrote in 1982 of teaching the novel.[68] It failed to reconcile the lesbian hero with loyalty to the mother—a trope derived from a 1983 essay by
Inez Martinez that works similarly to suggest the novel's fraught and ultimately irreconcilable relationship to the lesbian feminist politics of this
moment.[69] In sum, in this first breaking of the second wave of reception,
The Well of Loneliness proved constitutive of the woman-centered ideals of
lesbian feminism in the early 1970s in its very default of them.

Jane Rule's 1975 writing on *The Well of Loneliness* captures this lesbian
feminist ambivalence exquisitely.[70] Rule adapts Del Martin and Phyllis
Lyon's famous designation of the novel as a "bible" for lesbianism in their
lesbian feminist classic *Lesbian/Woman* in order to cast the novel as a "bible
or a horror story for any lesbian who reads at all."[71] For Rule the novel
embodies the social stereotypes of lesbianism in its depiction of lesbianism
as masculinity and the failure of loving lesbian relations. Yet though Rule's
essay is representative in the sense of condemning the novel's stigmatization, it is also exceptional in that it works carefully to unpack this stigmatization; it is the first essay really to *read* Hall's novel, and it is for these reasons that we include it here. Rule's conclusion memorably sums up the
double-edged value of *The Well of Loneliness* for lesbian feminism: "*The
Well of Loneliness* is an important book because it does so carefully reveal
the honest misconceptions about women's nature and experience which
have limited and crippled so many people.... [T]he 'bible' [Radclyffe Hall]
offered is really no better for women than the Bible she would not reject."[72]

While Rule and Faderman in particular among lesbian feminist critics
note the historical restrictions placed on Hall's representation of lesbianism
by her moment of writing, no critics in this first stage are willing to find in
these limitations an excuse or justification for *The Well of Loneliness*'s
damning plot. This would require the intervention of the historian and the
sociologist/anthropologist who were at the vanguard of the next stage. In
1984 Esther Newton, working in tandem with historian Carroll Smith-
Rosenberg's research on the evolution of nineteenth-century romantic

female friendships into twentieth-century New Woman sexual relationships, argues that Hall represents an historically accurate, indeed, even historically necessary sexualization of lesbianism.[73] Writing at a moment in
which sexuality was apportioned wholly to the masculine, Newton argues,
Hall had no other choice but to appropriate masculinity as an instrument
to symbolize lesbian sexuality; masculinity was a sexualizing strategy. In
effect, Newton makes palatable the poison of lesbian masculinity with the
palliative of social history. Newton's essay is important for its historical
precedence, and it remains one of the most cited by subsequent critics on
The Well of Loneliness; it is for these reasons that we include it in this section. Around Newton there clustered in the mid-1980s a number of readings that likewise drew for their methodology on history to explain *The
Well*. Sonja Ruehl in 1982 and Jean Radford in 1986 enlist specifically
Foucauldian notions of history in order to read *The Well of Loneliness* as
reversing or exceeding the sexological discourse of its historical moment.[74]
For Ruehl the excess of this discourse lies in Hall's autographing of her sig-
nature (the invert superseded the expert); for Radford the excess is the
romantic Freudian subplot of *The Well of Loneliness*, one not imagined by
the sexologists. As well as overt commitment to historicism, what these two
essays have in common with Newton's is that their readings are informed as
much by their own historical moment of writing as the history conceived
in them. Newton's reading of Stephen's masculinity is manifestly indebted
to, and seeks to intervene in, the eighties debates around lesbian butchness
that followed the lesbian feminist stigmatization of masculinity. And Ruehl
and Radford's work similarly reflects the poststructuralization of feminist
studies that was taking place at the time they were writing. Their use of
Foucault, and indeed the effect of this use in the production of the lesbian
as a historically contingent figure, is a symptom of the importance of the
present moment of reading in the construction of the novel.

Once it was read and understood in its historical moment, *The Well of
Loneliness* could now be examined in terms of its literary history, in particular lesbian literary history. Stimpson's location of the novel as outside a
lesbian canon—Stimpson even inserted the pronoun "her" in referring to
Stephen into quotation marks so incredulous was she of Stephen's lesbian-
ism/womanhood—proved prescient however.[75] For in order to make sense
of the novel within the lesbian canon, critics had to perform often acrobatic
feats of reconfiguring gender as sexuality, of reconfiguring Stephen's mas-

culinity as lesbianism. In 1987 Gillian Whitlock finds the fact that "Everything Is Out of Place" in the novel's representation of gender actually places *The Well* at the vanguard of the lesbian canon.[76] Gertrude Stein, Virginia Woolf, Djuna Barnes, and Monique Wittig would join or follow Hall in questioning to what extent a lesbian was a woman. In 1989 Sandra Gilbert and Susan Gubar similarly read Hall's "struggl[e] in *The Well of Loneliness* with a sense of lesbianism as tragic transsexuality."[77] Lesbianism was not lesbianism per se then but a transsexualization symptomatic of the "no man's land of sex" that Gilbert and Gubar read as following the First World War in modernist writing, particularly in modernist lesbian writing. Indeed, the title of Gilbert and Gubar's tome on women's writing, "No Man's Land," and the subtitle of this volume in which the comments on *The Well* appear, "Sexchanges," indicate the foundational place of Hall's transgendered approach in Gilbert and Gubar's conception of modernist women's writing. For Terry Castle in 1990, *The Well of Loneliness* purportedly represents a "lesbian epic" or "lesbian Odyssey"; yet it is significant that in neither this essay nor in its 1993 reprinting in *The Apparitional Lesbian* does Castle fully read *The Well of Loneliness*.[78] Instead, she reads the clever experimental and less manifestly gendered plot of Sylvia Townsend Warner's *Summer Will Show* as archetypally lesbian. That *The Well of Loneliness* appears in all these essays "ghosted," to borrow Castle's trope, a troubling presence because of its absence of lesbianism, attests to the difficulty of configuring its masculinist vision of lesbian sexuality within a tradition of lesbian representation. If, as Whitlock alleges in her explanation of Hall's inverted representation, Hall used the old "bottles" of sexological gender stereotypes in order to ferment the new "wine" of lesbian sexuality, this dynamic, this reconfiguration of gender as sexuality—at least at this moment in feminist criticism—could only poison the wine.[79]

The discomfort that was felt at *The Well of Loneliness*'s displacement in a lesbian literary canon, to use Whitlock's metaphor, seemed to require a return in the 1990s to the trial, in order to rethink the novel's original discomfort in being charged with being an obscene text. What were the grounds for this obscenity, what was behind this discomfort? What in the novel prompted censorship? After all, other lesbian texts had been published at around the same time as *The Well of Loneliness*—most famously of course Virginia Woolf's *Orlando* in the very same year. Why was it that Hall's novel had attracted the censors when Woolf's had so artfully evaded them? What was it about Hall's style, or perhaps her lack of style, that courted the novel's fate? At this stage *The Well of Loneliness* criticism was taking place within the deconstructive, textually hyperconscious context of English departments of the early nineties, and in its attention to reading Hall's novel carefully and for its stylistic features, such criticism shows all the signs of the influence of this context. In reading Hall's novel stylistically, the consensus was that the novel is none too well written. In 1990 Jane Marcus proposes that *The Well of Loneliness*'s censorship trial forms the implicit subject of Woolf's *A Room of One's Own*, which was given as a lecture at the end of 1928 around the time of the trial.[80] Indeed, Marcus argues that Woolf's coding of lesbianism here and elsewhere in her work serves as a lesson to Hall on what should constitute a lesbian style, precisely in its allusions or ellipses of lesbianism. In 1994 two essays use other classically modernist texts as foils to criticize *The Well of Loneliness*'s clunky, overstated style. Adam Parkes juxtaposes Woolf's *Orlando* to Hall's *Well* to suggest that where "Hall points to the 'fact' of sexual identity," Woolf points to its fictionality.[81] *The Well of Loneliness* appears to be censored for being too literal, too prosaic in an era of literary play— and again, we must understand this as much the postsructuralist moment of the early nineties as the contemporaneous moment of Woolf and the modernist avant-garde. In a reading that similarly interweaves Djuna Barnes's *Nightwood* with *The Well of Loneliness*, Leigh Gilmore considers how both novels help to reveal how the obscenity law actually founded conceptions of modernism and sexuality, of literary and lesbian style.[82] As Parkes shows with *Orlando*, Gilmore writes that *Nightwood*'s modernist stylistic devices are what allowed its author to portray lesbianism and avoid the legal censorship that *The Well*'s lack of style with "its conventions of the bildungsroman [and] its links to the realist novel" brought upon itself.[83] Literary deviation conveyed, but escaped the stigma of, sexual deviance. Interestingly however, Gilmore acknowledges that it was the very banning of *The Well of Loneliness* that established it as a lesbian novel: "Hall's legacy for lesbian writing originates with the initial removal of *The Well of Loneliness* from the market."[84] Finally, in another example of these essays on censorship in *The Well of Loneliness*, Joan Scanlon in 1996 decides that Hall's novel contains the same degree of "bad language" and "bad prose" as a novel that was published and censored in the same year as *The Well*, D. H. Lawrence's *Lady Chatterley's Lover*.[85] Following her comparison of these two novels, Scanlon's conclusion is that bad language is bad prose, and it is fair to say that this belief is shared across this stage of the commentary on *The Well*. In these textually exacting times, the persistent implication is that if Hall had only been a better writer, she might have been a better modernist and certainly a better lesbian.

The 1990s material on modernism and obscenity repeats something of the reservations about *The Well of Loneliness* that we saw in the first moment of lesbian feminist criticism. It circles *The Well* uncomfortably, troubled by its outlaw status. If this is so, then the queer readings that followed the obscenity essays of the nineties echo something of the reversals and reclamations of the novel's outlaw status performed by mid-1980s historicists and Foucauldians. In an essay openly indebted to Newton, Teresa de Lauretis produces in 1991 the queerest, the most inverted reading of them all.[86] De Lauretis argues that what Stephen really wants, "the body she desires, not only in [the feminine other] but also autoerotically for herself . . . is a feminine, female body. Paradoxical as it may seem, the 'mythic mannish lesbian' (in Esther Newton's wonderful phrase) wishes to have a feminine body." De Lauretis explains this paradox through the substitution of the fetish. She reads *The Well of Loneliness* through psychoanalysis in order to make sense of lesbian desire. What begins as a historical "symbol" in Newton's essay returns in de Lauretis as a poststructuralist Lacanian "signifier." De Lauretis admittedly goes "against the grain of the novel" and embraces *The Well of Loneliness* for its "perverse desire." It is because of this going against the grain that her reading is seminally queer, and we include it here as such—even though de Lauretis would later unyoke the term "queer" from "theory," terms she was the first to conjoin.[87] The most recent essays on gender and sexuality have followed de Lauretis in their conception and embrace of Stephen's transgressive homosexuality, often configured as transgressive gendered desire. In 1991 Michèle Aina Barale uncovers the successive cover designs of *The Well of Loneliness* in order to show how queer desire has been policed by a heterosexual readership; the implication is that a queer desire is waiting to break out of *The Well* but has been repressed by these constraints.[88] In 1997 two essays read the novel in the light of queer performativity, that ironic staging of sexuality as gender that became the hallmark of the new queer identity in the 1990s. Line Pouchard uses Judith Butler's (the theorist who was the motor behind this move) conception of gender performativity and queer citationality in order to trace in the novel a (de)constructedness of gender and sexual categories.[89] And Loralee MacPike picks up the feminine thread of gender performativity in particular in order to find in Mary's story a narrative of inversion that queers the conventional fabric of masculine sexological inversion:[90] as feminine Mary's inversion is "necessarily absent" from a sexologically inverted narrative, both from the narrative of sexology and from the dominantly masculinist narrative of *The Well of Loneliness*, "Mary Llewellyn offers an excellent standpoint from which to begin deconstructing sexology's lesbian."[91] These readings are symptomatically queer in the sense that they work in the margins of *The Well of Loneliness* in order to skew its mainstream plot; the periphery becomes more important than the center, the way to queer the center. Through this route *The Well of Loneliness*'s very conventional, some would say heterosexualizing, plot comes to be configured as archetypally, parodically queer. We had come a long way from the lesbian feminist repudiation of the novel as slavishly reproductive of heterosexist norms.

The late nineties saw the novel open out with increasing swiftness and liberality onto issues not predominantly focused on gender or sexuality. In that same bumper year of *Well* criticism, 1997, Margot Gayle Backus reads the representation of Celticism in the novel in order to evaluate *The Well of Loneliness*'s disturbing manipulation of race and nation.[92] Her initial discussion of race is important, and many of the essays in our collection note the seminality of Backus's essay by citing it. Leslie J. Henson returns to voice the "articulate silence[s]" of femme subjectivity in the novel by finding them intricated with class.[93] And Ed Madden and Margaret Soenser Breen take a new and unusual approach in assessing the effect of the novel's "appropriation of Christian discourse."[94] For these critics, it is no longer sufficient to think the novel solely or even primarily in terms of gender and sexuality. Rather, as feminist and sexuality studies have opened out other areas of cultural and identity work, criticism on *The Well of Loneliness* has ramified from the roots of gender and sexuality other identity issues and social categories in the novel. It is with this ramification of feminist criticism into cultural studies that we come to the third wave of commentary, and the work of part 2 of our book begins.

The Third Wave: Perspectives Present

In the first section of the new essays in *Palatable Poison* we return to what most troubled the second wave about *The Well of Loneliness*. The novel's dependence on sexology has proven a constant stumbling block to reading the novel as a positive representation. The essays in our book follow recent recognitions about the need to reread nineteenth- and early twentieth-century sexology in all its complex components, far-reaching and sometimes surprising influences. "New Sexual Inversions" begins with the first set of focused debates on the significance of sexology in *The Well of Loneliness*. Unlike earlier essays on sexology, Newton's and Faderman's for instance, these essays do not simply assume the sexological sources of *The Well of Loneliness*, nor do they assume that the sexological invert is equivalent to the lesbian. Jay Prosser, for instance, begins by claiming *The Well of Loneliness* as a transsexual novel, the first in a transsexual canon. Reading the novel through sexology's transgendered paradigms, Prosser proposes his as the most literal reading of the sexological invert and thus of *The Well of Loneliness*. Judith Halberstam takes issue with such a transsexual reading and stretches out what she calls the "parsimony of science" to describe a new subject in the novel. Halberstam rejects the alternatives of lesbian or transsexual and instead reads the novel as one of female masculinity. That Halberstam's reading derives from Hall's life and letters as much as from the novel, whereas Prosser's derives exclusively from the novel itself, perhaps suggests something for the reasons for the differences between these two readings, as well as their charged overlap. Following Halberstam, Laura Doan stretches the limitedness of science even further in order to suggest that the sexology that we have taken for granted in *The Well of Loneliness* as that of Havelock Ellis and Richard von Krafft-Ebing has an additional, more oblique source. Doan introduces as Hall's "metaphysical seer" Edward Carpenter. She reads the novel next to his work in order to show that he is responsible for Hall's concept of the "intermediate sex." Doan's introduction of Carpenter as a new alternative source has the effect of enabling other subordinate and ostensibly normal characters in the novel to appear more intermediate (or what Doan calls, after Carpenter, "median"). Doan's reading of Mary and Martin as intermediates paves the way for Clare Hemmings's description of Mary's narrative as that of a bisexual femme. Like Doan, Hemmings seeks to set a limit on the reaches of Ellisonian sexology in *The Well of Loneliness* but with different goals. Her narrative of a bisexual femme opens up an unread middle ground between the heterosexual/homosexual opposition that has been assumed by much sexology, by Stephen's narrative, and indeed by most previous critical readings of the novel. Hemmings effectively uncovers an untold story in *The Well* that makes possible new readings of inverted subjects in sexology.

"*The Well*'s Wounds" explores the different levels of wounding in *The Well of Loneliness*. Counterbalancing Hemmings's attention to the femme narrative is Sally Munt's essay on the "maimed" protagonist in *The Well of Loneliness* as lesbian butch. Munt shows how the novel's "well of gender melancholy" and shame are the sources of the lesbian butch. Opening with an autobiographical excursion into the novel's themes, Munt's essay discovers the shame in *The Well* as produced through religious discourse. Reading shaming as a synonym for homosexuality in a post-Christian stigmatizing society, Munt asks an important question about homosexual identity in general: "Can there be a homosexual subject who is not formed from shame?" Susan Kingsley Kent's essay examines the more literal maiming in *The Well of Loneliness* to return the novel to its historical setting. Kent proposes that Stephen's wounded masculinity is a version of the injured masculinities that followed the First World War. In validating and heroizing damaged masculinity, these historical war wounds provided a template for Hall to describe Stephen's lesbian masculinity. The dependent relation of *The Well of Loneliness* on its war context effectively renders *The Well* a seminal war novel; Kent's essay adds another important tradition to those in which we have read *The Well*. Jodie Medd similarly considers wounds in the novel in the light of the war but focuses in particular on the psychological detritus of shell shock. Medd shows how Stephen's inversion emerges from the psychological trauma of shell-shocked victims; she argues, moreover, that shell shock's emergence as a diagnosis between the wars facilitated the introduction of and dissemination of psychoanalysis in England at the time of Hall's writing. In the network of these relations, Medd's essay suggests that *The Well of Loneliness* is more implicated in psychoanalysis as a historical discourse than we have up till now imagined. Following Medd's introduction of psychoanalysis into *The Well*'s scene, Trevor Hope uses psychoanalysis as his critical methodology in order to perform a virtuoso reading in which he finds in the wounds of the invert a reflection of the wounds of the nation. After the First World War the nation itself was in a wounded state and in need of "pruning" or "grafting"; the state of Stephen's body with its "afflicted member" mirrors the state of the body politic. The invert was nationalized and the nation simultaneously inverted. In describing this catachresis of the literary and the national, Hope reads the censoring of the trial as establishing the novel as a wound in the literary canon. Its censoring effectively made a cut—and made it a cut—in the English canon. If the first section of our contemporary readings takes its cue from sexology, this section of the book is more psychoanalytically informed. Yet it is important that this is a psychoanalysis inflected with concepts of history and nation, that sustains *The Well* in its historical moment, that uncovers, to use Medd's phrase, its "national symbolic."

The final section in part 2, "On Location," revisits the various locations in *The Well of Loneliness* in order to explore these concepts of place and nation more fully. The essays in this section are mostly spurred by recent developments in postcolonial, black and transatlantic, cartographic and spatial studies, as well as by new literary historicisms. Collectively they work to resituate *The Well of Loneliness*. Jean Walton hones in on one particularly underread scene: Stephen's exchange with two African American singers that takes place one evening in Paris. Uncovering new biographical material about Hall's encounter with two similar figures, Walton argues that Hall uses the black other to articulate Stephen's inversion. Sarah Chinn travels with the novel to Orotava, to the novel's scene of seduction: "And that night they were not divided." Chinn suggests that in Hall's vision, Tenerife provides the necessary backdrop for lesbian eroticization, its orientalism ensuring the novel's sexual orientation. The eroticization of the other leads the novel into surprising affiliations with other modernist representations that likewise idealized the primitive as a figure of the modern. Victoria Rosner treats location in *The Well of Loneliness* architecturally. Her essay on the "spaces of inversion" shows how Stephen's gendered subjectivity emerges through the rooms of the post-Victorian house, which were bifurcated by gender. Julie Abraham packs the novel off to North America in order to explore how *The Well of Loneliness* partakes in a particular conception of the city versus the country, one that was being developed by Robert Parks's Chicago school of sociology at the very time of the writing of *The Well of Loneliness*. From displaced country squire to cosmopolitan urban (and urbane) citizen, Stephen's trajectory renders her the ideal inhabitant of Parks's modern city. Kim Emery remains in the United States in order to consider the implications of the novel's obscenity trial, which had a very different outcome here. Emery contends that the novel's evasion of the censors in the United States symptomizes differing conceptions of lesbian identity on either side of the Atlantic. Her essay points toward ongoing possible differences in the transatlantic reception of *The Well*, with North American readers perhaps less attuned to the specific class and national differences that transect and trouble lesbian identity. Finally, Joanne Winning returns the novel to its history and considers it in the light of its modernist contexts. She argues that we have misplaced *The Well of Loneliness* by seeing it as antithetical to its modernist contemporaries. Winning reads the tropes of "Sapphic modernism" in the novel to bring it in from the "literary cold." By the hearth of good reading seems a fitting place with which to end these new critical essays on *The Well*.

As its final section dramatizes topographically, the readings in "Perspectives Present" seek to open the novel onto new vistas and perspectives. Yet what persists from the first and second waves of criticism to the third is the apprehension of *The Well of Loneliness* as a palatable poison. The oxymoron of a poison that can be palatable is most eloquently and certainly most humorously summed up by Terry Castle's afterword to this book. As Castle, in her conclusion to *Palatable Poison* suggests, *The Well of Loneliness* is a book that makes us cringe—and we read it because of that. From Perspectives Past to Perspectives Present the novel remains an infuriating but irresistible force.

Notes

1. Letter from Radclyffe Hall to Newman Flower, April 10, 1928; Correspondence—Publishers and Agents, vol. 4, Lovat Dickson Papers MG 30, D 237, National Archives of Canada, Ottawa. The American edition, published by Covici Friede, appeared in December 1928.

2. James Douglas, "A Book That Must Be Suppressed," *Sunday Express*, August 19, 1928, p. 38 in this volume. Unless noted otherwise, all references to Douglas appear in this editorial, pp. 36–38.

3. Vera Brittain, *Radclyffe Hall: A Case of Obscenity?* (London: Femina Books, 1968), p. 86.

4. A longer version of material in this section appears in another form in Laura Doan, *Fashioning Sapphism: The Origins of a Modern English Lesbian Culture* (New York: Columbia University Press, 2001).

5. Sally Cline, *Radclyffe Hall: A Woman Called John* (London: John Murray, 1997), p. 236.

6. Michael Baker, *Our Three Selves: The Life of Radclyffe Hall* (New York: William Morrow, 1985), p. 205.

7. Letter from Havelock Ellis to Bryher, September 18, 1928; GEN MSS 97, series 1, box 2, The Beinecke Rare Book and Manuscript Library, Yale University.

8. Robert Graves and Alan Hodge, *The Long Weekend: A Social History of Great Britain, 1918–1939* (1940; reprint, New York: Norton, 1963), p. 56, and *Morning Post*, August 10, 1928, p. 58 in this volume.

9. Graves and Hodge, *Long Weekend*, p. 55, and *TLS*, August 2, 1928, p. 51 in this volume.

10. Quoted by Michael S. Howard, *Jonathan Cape, Publisher* (London: Jonathan Cape, 1971), p. 103.

11. Arnold Dawson, *Daily Herald*, August 22, 1928, p. 7.

12. Joan Scanlon, "Bad Language vs. Bad Prose? Lady Chatterley and *The Well*," *Critical Quarterly* 38, no. 3 (1996): 5.

13. L. P. Hartley, *Saturday Review*, July 1928, p. 51 in this volume, and Leonard Woolf, *Nation & Athenaeum*, August 4, 1928, p. 54 in this volume.

14. Ethel Mannin, *Confessions and Impressions* (London: Jarrolds, 1930), p. 226. Emphasis ours.

15. Margaret Lawrence, *We Write As Women* (London: Michael Joseph, 1937), p. 260.

16. I. A. R. Wylie, *Sunday Times*, August 5, 1928, p. 56 in this volume.

17. Elsie M. Lang, *British Women in the Twentieth Century* (London: T. Werner Laurie, 1929), pp. 236–237.

18. *Glasgow Herald*, August 9, 1928, p. 57 in this volume.

19. *Morning Post*, August 10, 1928, p. 58 in this volume; Woolf, *Nation & Athenaeum*, August 4, 1928, p. 54 in this volume; and *Glasgow Herald*, p. 57 in this volume.

20. Arnold Bennett, *Evening Standard*, August 9, 1928, p. 56 this volume. Bennett's review of *The Well* also appeared on the same day in the *Liverpool Echo*, the *Glasgow Evening Citizen*, and the *Manchester Evening News*. Numerous reviews praised Hall for her courage in tackling such a delicate subject.

21. Quoted by Q. D. Leavis, *Fiction and the Reading Public* (London: Chatto and Windus, 1932), p. 281.

22. The terms "low-brow" and "high-brow" were imported from America by H. G. Wells. See Graves and Hodge, *Long Weekend,* p. 50.

23. Woolf, *Nation & Athenaeum*, August 4, 1928, p. 53 in this volume, and Bennett, *Evening Standard*, August 9, 1928, p. 56 in this volume.

24. Virginia Woolf's letter "To the Editor of the 'New Statesman'" was written in 1932 but never sent. It is reprinted in *The Death of the Moth and Other Essays* (Harmondsworth: Penguin Books, 1961), p. 152.

25. Leavis, *Fiction and the Reading Public,* pp. 20–21.

26. Anthea Trodd, *Women's Writing in English: Britain 1900–1945* (London and New York: Longman, 1998), p. 47.

27. Letter from Virginia Woolf to Vita Sackville-West, August 30, 1928, in Nigel Nicolson and Joanne Trautmann, eds., *The Letters of Virginia Woolf,* vol. 3, *1923–1928* (New York and London: Harcourt Brace Jovanovich, 1978), p. 520, and Naomi Jacob, *Me and the Swans* (London: William Kimber, 1963), pp. 120–121.

28. Howard, *Jonathan Cape, Publisher,* p. 106.

29. Gillian Whitlock, "'Everything Is Out of Place': Radclyffe Hall and the Lesbian Literary Tradition," *Feminist Studies* 13, no. 3 (Fall 1987): 581, n. 16. A highbrow, according to Woolf, "is the man or woman of thoroughbred intelligence who rides his mind at a gallop across country in pursuit of an idea," while the equally honorable lowbrow, is "a man or a woman of thoroughbred vitality who rides his body in pursuit of a living at a gallop across life." Although subject to a "mind/body" split, the interests of the "high" and "low" were not antithetical but complemented one another. See Woolf, *Death of the Moth,* pp. 152–153. Leonard Woolf characterized the highbrow as "genuinely attracted by elements in literature—which may conveniently be called aesthetic, and which are not primarily interesting or attracted to the great public." See *Hunting the Highbrow* (London: Hogarth, 1927), p. 20.

30. Letter from Virginia Woolf to Quentin Bell, November 1, 1928. See Woolf, *Letters,* 3:555, and Woolf, *Death of the Moth,* p. 155.

31. Ellen Bayuk Rosenman, "Sexual Identity and *A Room of One's Own*: 'Secret Economies' in Virginia Woolf's Feminist Discourse." *Signs* 14, no. 3 (Spring 1989): 642, and Virginia Woolf, *The Diary of Virginia Woolf,* vol. 3, *1925–1930,* ed. Olivier Bell (London: Penguin Books, 1980), pp. 193 and 207.

32. Wylie, *Sunday Times,* August 5, 1928, p. 55 in this volume.

33. Richard King, *Tatler,* August 15, 1928, p. 63 in this volume.

34. Woolf, *Nation & Athenaeum,* p. 54 in this volume and *Life and Letters,* p. 72 in this volume. Emphasis ours.

35. *British Journal of Inebriety,* p. 000 in this volume. Emphasis ours.

36. W. R. Gordon, *Daily News and Westminster Gazette,* August 23, 1928, p. 65 in this volume.

37. *Life and Letters,* pp. 71–72 in this volume.

38. Gordon, *Daily News and Westminster Gazette,* p. 66 in this volume.

39. Ibid., pp. 66–67 in this volume.

40. *Glasgow Herald,* August 9, 1928, p. 57 in this volume.

41. *Life and Letters,* p. 72 in this volume.

42. Gordon, *Daily News and Westminster Gazette*, p. 66 in this volume.

43. Cline, *Radclyffe Hall*, p. 243.

44. Beverley Nichols, *The Sweet and Twenties* (London: Weidenfeld & Nicolson, 1958), p. 106, and James Douglas, "Back to the Puritans," *Sunday Express*, November 4, 1928, p. 14.

45. Diana Souhami, *The Trials of Radclyffe Hall* (London: Weidenfeld & Nicolson, 1998), p. 183.

46. Connolly too observed that "in August, the reviewer's desert, [novels] loom up larger than they are." See *New Statesman*, August 25, 1928, p. 614.

47. Raymond Williams, *The Long Revolution* (Harmondsworth: Penguin, 1980), p. 233, and John Stevenson, *British Society 1914–1945* (Harmondsworth: Penguin, 1984), p. 405.

48. *Tatler*, November 28, 1928, p. 408.

49. Arnold Dawson, "The Literary Censorship Danger," *Clarion* no. 1861 (September 1928): 15.

50. Nicholas Rance, "British Newspapers in the Early Twentieth Century," in Clive Bloom, ed., *Literature and Culture in Modern Britain*, vol. 1, *1900–1929* (London and New York: Longman, 1993), p. 122.

51. Stephen Koss, *The Rise and Fall of the Political Press in Britain*, vol. 2, *The Twentieth Century* (London: Hamish Hamilton, 1984), p. 389, and Baker, *Our Three Selves*, pp. 223 and 224.

52. *Daily Express*, August 18, 1928, p. 1.

53. *Sunday Express*, August 19, 1928, p. 1.

54. Brittain, *Radclyffe Hall*, p. 52.

55. *Sunday Express*, August 26, 1928, p. 6.

56. *Yorkshire Post*, August 24, 1928, p. 8. As a result of the publicity the *Newcastle Daily Journal and North Star* reported the book "must have been pretty well sold out. Queues lined up for it at all the booksellers" (August 24, 1928, p. 8) and the *Manchester Daily Dispatch* noted that it "would be difficult, if not impossible, to buy a copy in the city at the moment." August 22, 1928, p. 4.

57. *Nation & Athenaeum*, September 1, 1928, p. 696.

58. See *People*, August 19, 1928, p. 2 and *Sunday Chronicle*, August 19, 1928, p. 1.

59. See, for example, *Evening Standard*, August 20, 1928, p. 6; *Manchester Daily Dispatch*, August 22, 1928, p. 4; *Newcastle Daily Journal and North Star*, August 24, 1928, p. 8; and *Daily Mirror*, November 20, 1928, p. 9.

60. Nancy K. Miller, "Feminist Literary Criticism," Graduate Seminar, City University of New York Graduate School, Spring 1992.

61. Kate Millett, *Sexual Politics* (New York: Simon & Schuster, 1969).

62. Rebecca O'Rourke, *Reflecting on The Well of Loneliness* (London: Routledge, 1989).

63. Michael Dillon, *Self: A Study in Endocrinology and Ethics* (London: Heinemann, 1946).

64. Lillian Faderman and Ann Williams, "Radclyffe Hall and the Lesbian Image," *Conditions* 1 (1977): 31–49.

65. Lillian Faderman, *Surpassing the Love of Men: Romantic Friendship and Love Between Women from the Renaissance to the Present* (London: The Women's Press, 1991), p. 323.

66. Blanche Wiesen Cook, "'Women Alone Stir My Imagination': Lesbianism and the Cultural Tradition," *Signs* 4, no. 4 (1979): 731.

67. Catharine Stimpson, "Zero Degree Deviancy: The Lesbian Novel in English," in *Where the Meanings Are: Feminism and Cultural Spaces* (New York: Routledge, 1990), p. 98.

68. Toni McNaron, "A Journey into Otherness: Teaching *The Well of Loneliness*," in Margaret Cruikshank, ed., *Lesbian Studies Present and Future* (New York: The Feminist Press, 1982), pp. 88–92.

69. Inez Martinez, "The Lesbian Hero Bound: Radclyffe Hall's Portraits of Sapphic Daughters and Their Mothers," in Stuart Kellog, ed., *Literary Visions of Homosexuality* (New York: Haworth, 1983), pp. 127–137.

70. Jane Rule, "Radclyffe Hall: 1886–1943," p. 77–78 in this volume.

71. Del Martin and Phyllis Lyon, *Lesbian/Woman* (San Francisco: Glide Publications, 1972), p. 22, and Rule, "Radclyffe Hall," p. 78 in this volume.

72. Rule, "Radclyffe Hall," p. 87 in this volume.

73. Esther Newton, "The Mythic Mannish Lesbian: Radclyffe Hall and the New Woman," pp. 89–108 in this volume. Carroll Smith-Rosenberg, "Discourses of Sexuality and Subjectivity: The New Woman, 1870–1932," in Martin Duberman, Martha Vicinus, and George Chauncey Jr., eds., *Hidden From History: Reclaiming the Gay and Lesbian Past* (New York: Penguin, 1990), pp. 264–280.

74. Sonja Ruehl, "Inverts and Experts: Radclyffe Hall and the Lesbian Identity," in Rosalind Brunt and Caroline Rowan, eds., *Feminism, Culture, and Politics* (London: Lawrence, 1982), pp. 15–36; Jean Radford, "An Inverted Romance: *The Well of Loneliness* and Sexual Ideology," in Radford, ed., *The Progress of Romance: The Politics of Popular Fiction* (London: Routledge, 1986), pp. 97–111.

75. Stimpson, "Zero Degree Deviancy," p. 100.

76. Whitlock, "'Everything Is Out of Place.'"

77. Sandra M. Gilbert and Susan Gubar, *Sexchanges*, vol. 2, *No Man's Land: The Place of the Woman Writer in the Twentieth Century* (New Haven: Yale University Press, 1989), p. 220.

78. Terry Castle, "Sylvia Townsend Warner and the Counterplot of Lesbian Fiction," *Textual Practice* 4 (1990): 235, n. 14; reprinted in *The Apparitional Lesbian: Female Homosexuality and Modern Culture* (New York: Columbia University Press, 1993).

79. Whitlock, "'Everything Is Out of Place,'" p. 573.

80. Jane Marcus, "Sapphistory: The Woolf and the Well," in Karla Jay and Joanne Glasgow, eds., *Lesbian Texts and Contexts: Radical Revisions* (New York: New York University Press, 1990), pp. 164–180.

81. Adam Parkes, "Lesbianism, History, and Censorship: *The Well of Loneliness* and the SUPPRESSED RANDINESS of Virginia Woolf's *Orlando*," *Twentieth Century Literature* 40, no. 4 (Winter 1994): 436.

82. Leigh Gilmore, "Obscenity, Modernity, Identity: Legalizing *The Well of Loneliness* and *Nightwood*," *Journal of the History of Sexuality* 4, no. 4 (1994): 603–624.

83. Ibid., p. 608.

84. Ibid., p. 614.

85. Joan Scanlon, "Bad Language vs. Bad Prose? Lady Chatterley and *The Well*," *Critical Quarterly* 38, no. 3 (1996): 3–13.

86. Teresa de Lauretis, "Perverse Desire: The Lure of the Mannish Lesbian," pp. 109–125 in this volume.

87. For de Lauretis's conjoining of the terms, see "Queer Theory: Lesbian and Gay Sexualities—An Introduction," in *Differences* 3, no. 2 (Summer 1991): iii–xviii. For her separation, see "Habit Changes," in *Differences* 6, nos 2 and 3 (Summer/Fall 1994): 296–311.

88. Michèle Aina Barale, "Below the Belt: (Un)Covering *The Well of Loneliness*," in Diana Fuss, ed., *Inside/Out: Lesbian Theories, Gay Theories* (New York: Routledge, 1991), pp. 235–258.

89. Line Pouchard, "Queer Desire in *The Well of Loneliness*," in Catherine Belsey and Jane Moore, eds., *The Feminist Reader: Essays in Gender and the Politics of Literary Criticism* (London: MacMillan, 1997), pp. 52–65.

90. Loralee MacPike, "Is Mary Llewellyn an Invert? The Modernist Supertext of *The Well of Loneliness*," in Elizabeth Jane Harrison and Shirley Peterson, eds., *Unmanning Modernism: Gendered Rereadings* (Knoxville: University of Tennessee Press, 1997), pp. 73–89.

91. Ibid., pp. 85 and 77.

92. Margot Gayle Backus, "Sexual Orientation in the (Post) Imperial Nation: Celticism and Inversion Theory in Radclyffe Hall's *The Well of Loneliness*," *Tulsa Studies in Women's Literature* 15, no. 2 (Fall 1996): 253–276.

93. Leslie J. Henson, "'Articulate Silence(s)': Femme Subjectivity and Class Relations in *The Well of Loneliness*," in Laura Harris and Elizabeth Crocker, eds., *Femme: Feminists, Lesbians, and Bad Girls* (New York: Routledge, 1997), pp. 61–67.

94. Ed Madden, "*The Well of Loneliness*, or The Gospel According to Radclyffe Hall," *Journal of Homosexuality* 33, nos. 3 /4 (1977): 163–186; Margaret Soenser Breen, "Narrative Inversion: The Biblical Heritage of *The Well of Loneliness* and Desert of the Heart," *Journal of Homosexuality* 33, nos. 4 /4 (1977): 187–206. Citation Madden, p. 165.

PART ONE

PERSPECTIVES PAST

The First Wave

1

Commentary

(1928)

HAVELOCK ELLIS

I have read *The Well of Loneliness* with great interest because—apart from its fine qualities as a novel by a writer of accomplished art—it possesses a notable psychological and sociological significance. So far as I know, it is the first English novel which presents, in a completely faithful and uncompromising form, one particular aspect of sexual life as it exists among us today. The relation of certain people—who, while different from their fellow human beings, are sometimes of the highest character and the finest aptitudes—to the often hostile society in which they move, presents difficult and still unsolved problems. The poignant situations which thus arise are here set forth so vividly, and yet with such complete absence of offence, that we must place Radclyffe Hall's book on a high level of distinction.

2

"A Book That Must Be Suppressed"
(August 19, 1928)

JAMES DOUGLAS

The Well of Loneliness (Jonathan Cape, 15s. net), by Miss Radclyffe Hall, is a novel. The publishers state that it "handles very skillfully a psychological problem which needs to be understood in view of its growing importance."

"In England hitherto," they admit, "the subject has not been treated frankly outside the region of scientific textbooks, but that its social consequences qualify a broader and more general treatment is likely to be the opinion of thoughtful and cultured people."

They declare that they "have been deeply impressed by this study; they have felt that such a book should not be lost to those who may be willing and able to understand and appreciate it. They believe that the author has treated the subject in such a way as to combine perfect frankness and sincerity with delicacy and deep psychological insight." . . . [Douglas then cites Ellis's "Commentary" in full.]

That is the defense and justification of what I regard as an intolerable outrage—the first outrage of the kind in the annals of English fiction.

The defense is wholly unconvincing. The justification absolutely fails.

In order to prevent the contamination and corruption of English fiction it is the duty of the critic to make it impossible for any other novelist to repeat this outrage. I say deliberately that this novel is not fit to be sold by any bookseller or to be borrowed from any library.

Its theme is utterly inadmissible in the novel, because the novel is read by people of all ages, by young women and young men as well as by older women and older men. Therefore, many things that are discussed in scientific textbooks cannot decently be discussed in a work of fiction offered to the general reader.

I am well aware that sexual inversion and perversion are horrors which exist among us today. They flaunt themselves in public places with increasing effrontery and more insolently provocative bravado. The decadent apostles of the most hideous and most loathsome vices no longer conceal their degeneracy and their degradation.

They seem to imagine that there is no limit to the patience of the English people. They appear to revel in their defiance of public opinion. They do not shun publicity. On the contrary, they seek it, and they take a delight in their flamboyant notoriety. The consequence is that this pestilence is devastating the younger generation. It is wrecking young lives. It is defiling young souls.

I have seen the plague stalking shamelessly through great social assemblies. I have heard it whispered about by young men and young women who do not and cannot grasp its unutterable putrefaction. Both aspects of it are thrust upon healthy and innocent minds. The contagion cannot be escaped. It pervades our social life.

Perhaps it is a blessing in disguise or a curse in disguise that this novel forces upon our society a disagreeable task which it has hitherto shirked, the task of cleansing itself from the leprosy of these lepers, and making the air clean and wholesome once more.

I agree with Mr. Havelock Ellis that this novel is "uncompromising." That is why criticism cannot compromise with it. The challenge is direct. It must be taken up courageously, and the fight must be fought to a finish. If our bookshops and our libraries are to be polluted by fiction dealing with this undiscussable subject, at least let us know where we are going.

I know that the battle has been lost in France and Germany, but it has not yet been lost in England, and I do not believe that it will be lost. The English people are slow to rise in their wrath and strike down the armies of evil, but when they are aroused they show no mercy and they give no quarter to those who exploit their tolerance and their indulgence.

It is no excuse to say that the novel possesses "fine qualities," or that its author is an "accomplished" artist. It is no defense to say that the author is sincere, or that she is frank, or that there is delicacy in her art.

The answer is that the adroitness and cleverness of the book intensifies its moral danger. It is a seductive and insidious piece of special pleading designed to display perverted decadence as a martyrdom inflicted upon these outcasts by a cruel society. It flings a veil of sentiment over their depravity. It even suggests that their self-made debasement is unavoidable, because they cannot save themselves.

This terrible doctrine may commend itself to certain schools of pseudo-scientific thought, but it cannot be reconciled with the Christian religion or with the Christian doctrine of free-will. Therefore, it must be fought to the bitter end by the Christian Churches. This is the radical difference between paganism and Christianity.

If Christianity does not destroy this doctrine, then this doctrine will destroy it, together with the civilization which it has built on the ruins of paganism. These moral derelicts are not cursed from their birth. Their downfall is caused by their own act and their own will. They are damned because they choose to be damned, not because they are doomed from the beginning.

It is meet and right to pity them, but we must also pity their victims. We must protect our children against their specious fallacies and sophistries. Therefore, we must banish their propaganda from our bookshops and our libraries.

I would rather give a healthy boy or a healthy girl a phial of prussic acid than this novel. Poison kills the body, but moral poison kills the soul.

What, then, is to be done? The book must at once be withdrawn. I hope the author and the publishers will realize that they have made a grave mistake, and will without delay do all in their power to repair it.

If they hesitate to do so, the book must be suppressed by process of law. . . .

Therefore, I appeal to the Home Secretary to set the law in motion. He should instruct the Director of Public Prosecutions to consider whether *The Well of Loneliness* is fit for circulation, and, if not, to take action to prevent its being further circulated.

Finally, let me warn our novelists and our men of letters that literature as well as morality is in peril. Fiction of this type is an injury to good literature. It makes the profession of literature fall into disrepute. Literature has not yet recovered from the harm done to it by the Oscar Wilde scandal. It should keep its house in order.

3

Judgment
(1928)

SIR CHARTRES BIRON,
CHIEF MAGISTRATE

THE MAGISTRATE: Before delivering my judgment in this case I thought it right to consider this book which is the subject of these proceedings in the light of the statements made by the learned Counsel for the Defense, for whose assistance in the matter I should like to say at once I am very much indebted.

First of all, one thing is clear which does not seem to have been clearly appreciated, that no question of censorship arises here at all. The only question here for me to decide is whether this book is an obscene libel according to the common law of this country because, although the proceedings under which this book has been seized are in the execution of a Statute, I have to be satisfied before I can order this book to be seized and to be destroyed (if I come to that conclusion) that at common law it is an obscene libel.

In the course of this case the issue has been very considerably simplified. It was contended at first by the Defense that this book nowhere in any way related to physical misconduct between these women; that was put forward and strongly urged by the Defense in this case on behalf of the publisher, Mr. Jonathan Cape: it was put forward in cross-examination, and, subsequently, Mr. Norman Birkett in his very interesting speech drew a subtle distinction between what he called "inverts" and what he called "perverts." As I understood his speech, "invert" is a term used to describe women who, born with certain masculine tendencies, are therefore or thereby born with an inclination in certain directions which make them averse to relationship with and intellectual sympathy with the male sex: that in consequence of that, which is an accident of birth for which they are not responsible, they are forced into intercourse (I use the word in its harmless sense) and into familiarity and companionship with their own sex, which might very easily be misunderstood by a censorious world; that, therefore, they should be deserving of sympathy, liable as they are to be misunderstood: and it is said that appeal to that sympathy is the purpose of this book. I confess, having read it, that I was amazed at that contention being put forward, and I was not surprised when, after the adjournment, Mr. Norman Birkett announced that he was not in a position to contend any further that this book did not relate to unnatural offences between women in every sense of those words. But he urged, and Mr. Melville also urged in a forcible speech, that there was nothing in this book which in any way outraged decency, that the subject was dealt with, I think he used the term somewhere in the course of his speech, with restraint, and I think he used the term "reverence"—that there was nothing in the book of any kind which would induce people to indulge in these horrible practices, that there was nothing in the book which could be said in any way to defend these unnatural practices or (he used the term) which was to their glorification. That of course very much simplifies the issue which I have to try.

Before I say more, I should like to say that there seems to have been a considerable misunderstanding about the meaning of the word "obscene." People very often do use words without any definite idea of what their meaning is, and it is suggested that this book cannot be described fairly as an obscene book because there are no gross words or filthy words in it; and that because it is, as it is said, well written therefore it is to be regarded as a work of literature, and, therefore, not properly a subject of these proceedings. First of all, in consulting a standard dictionary to find out what the real meaning of "obscene" is, I find it is defined as: "Offensive to chastity, delicacy or decency, or presenting to the mind something that decency, delicacy and purity forbids to be exposed; offensive to the moral sense because of a tendency to excite lustful passions." That is of peculiar interest, because when I look at what must guide me in arriving at a decision in this case, that is the test of an obscene book as laid down by that great Judge Chief Justice Cockburn in the leading case of *The Queen v. Hicklin*, Law Reports, 3 Queen's Bench Cases, page 360, he there says: "I think the test of obscenity is this, whether the tendency of the matter charged as obscenity is to deprave and corrupt those whose minds are open to such immoral influences, and into whose hands a publication of this sort may fall." It is interesting to find how the dictionary definition of "obscenity" so nearly is within the meaning of the exact words used in the legal test of what is or is not an obscene publication.

A considerable volume of evidence was tendered before me which, in my view, was quite inadmissible in law. It is not without some significance in this case that two witnesses who were available on this issue—those are the Defendants charged—have not been called into the box. I confess it would be a matter of some interest if they had been called to explain how it is that, although Mr. Jonathan Cape withdrew this book from circulation in deference to the opinion expressed by the Home Secretary, it should be subsequently found in his offices and seized—some in his possession and some in the possession of the Pegasus Press, in the latter case in considerable numbers. But upon that point both Mr. Jonathan Cape and the gentleman responsible for the Pegasus Press summoned before me have maintained a discreet silence. Before I pass from that I might say this at once: with regard to the point that this book is well written, and, therefore, should not be the subject of these proceedings, that is an entirely untenable proposition. I agree that this book has some literary merit, defamed, as I think everybody who has read it will admit, with certain deplorable lapses of taste; but the mere fact that a book is well written can be no answer to these proceedings, because otherwise we should be in this preposterous position, that because it is well written the most obscene book would be free from such proceedings. It is quite obvious to anybody of intelligence that the better an obscene book is written the greater the public to whom the book is likely to appeal. The more palatable the poison the more insidious.

To deal with what really now is the substantial question before me, which is Mr. Melville's contention, does this book as a whole defend unnatural practices between women, and, as he puts it, does it glorify them? That is the question to which I must direct my mind. In considering this question it is necessary to speak somewhat plainly. These unnatural offences between women which are the subject of this book involve acts which between men would be a criminal offence, and involve acts of the most horrible, unnatural and disgusting obscenity. That is a fact which no one could deny. Therefore, if I find in this book that those practices are defended or in any way held out to admiration, no reasonable person could say that the book which so does defend or uphold is not an obscene publication. There is one matter which I think should be cleared up, and that is that the mere fact that this book deals with unnatural offences between women would not in itself make it, in my view, an obscene libel. I can imagine a book written dealing with this subject presenting the whole matter as a tragedy, the tragedy being that there may be people so afflicted who try their best to fight against this horrible vice, find themselves impelled in that direction or unable to resist those tendencies, with the result of the moral and physical degradation which indulgence in those vices must necessarily involve; I can imagine a book dealing with the subject on those terms, presenting these women as the prisoners of circumstances which, however much they fight against them, they are unable to resist—I can imagine a book of that kind, whatever one's opinion may be as to whether it is or it is not desirable that these matters should form the subject of a novel for popular reading, having anything but an immoral influence; it might have a strong moral influence. But does that book do it? I am told here by Mr. Melville that the book is presented as a tragedy. It is true that in a sense that is so, but what is the tragedy of the book? It is not the tragedy which I have just indicated at all; it is not the tragedy of people fighting against horrible instincts and being unable to resist them; but, on the contrary, the tragedy as presented here is that people who indulge in these vices are not tolerated by decent people; they are not received in society and they are ostracized by decent people; and the whole note of the book is a passionate and almost hysterical plea for the toleration and recognition of these people who, in the view presented in this book, are people who ought to be tolerated and recognized, and their practices tolerated and recognized, in decent society. That is what is put forward in this book. It is a long book of some 500 pages dealing solely, or at any rate in the main, with unnatural offences. There is not a single word from beginning to end of this book which suggests that anyone with these horrible tendencies is in the least blameworthy or that they should in any way resist them. Everybody, all the characters in this book, who indulge in these horrible vices are presented to us as attractive people and put forward for our admiration; and those who object to these vices are sneered at in the book as prejudiced, foolish and cruel. Not merely that, but there is a much more serious matter, the actual physical acts of these women indulging in unnatural vices are described in the most alluring terms; their result is described as giving these women extraordinary rest, contentment and pleasure; and not merely that, but it is actually put forward that it improves their mental balance and capacity.

I will just deal, first of all, with the case which is known as the Angela case. For the purpose of this Inquiry I will call Stephen the heroine because she is in every sense the heroine of this book and is presented to all who read this book as a very fine character. As a girl when she is living at home with her mother she has an intrigue with a married woman whom she ultimately persuades to indulge in these practices with her. How does this describe it? Here is this girl indulging in these horrible practices and endeavoring to induce a married woman to share these horrible practices with her. How is it described in this book: "Her physical passion for Angela Crossby"—that is her desire to indulge in these filthy practices with her— "had aroused a strange response in her spirit, so that side by side with every hot impulse that led her at times beyond her own understanding, there would come an impulse not of the body; a fine selfless thing of great beauty and courage—she would gladly have given her body over to torment, have laid down her life if need be, for the sake of this woman whom she loved." That is the description of these practices. What happens? Without going into this in any great detail, this intrigue is ultimately discovered; it is discovered by the husband, who writes to the heroine's mother. Of course, there is no doubt about the relations between the parties; it is obvious from the contents of the book. The mother, having discovered this, objects to the daughter's conduct, and eventually says that it is quite impossible for her to live any longer with her in the house where she is, that although she may come to see her from time to time, she cannot have her under the same roof—not, I should have thought, an unreasonable conclusion under the circumstances, especially as there was no turning her daughter out of the house in the old style because she is represented all through this book as a woman of considerable wealth. What happens then? When this mother announces her intention, it says: "Then, suddenly, Stephen knew that unless she could, indeed, drop dead at the feet of this woman in whose womb she had quickened there was one thing which she dared not let pass unchallenged"—what is it that she dare not let to go unchallenged?—"and that was this terrible slur upon her love. And all that was in her rose up to refute it; to protect her love from such unbearable soiling. It was part of herself, and unless she could save it she could not save herself any more. She must stand or fall by the courage of that love to proclaim its right to toleration." "This terrible slur upon her love"—what does that mean? Then again, addressing her mother, "She held up her hand, commanding silence, commanding that slow, quiet voice to cease speaking, and she said: 'As my father loved you I loved'"—this practitioner of unnatural vice!—"'As a man loves a woman that was how I loved—protectively like my father. I wanted to give all I had in me to give.'" I am asked to say that this book is not a defense of these practices. What does it go on to say? What is the result of these horrible practices? "'It made me feel terribly strong . . . and gentle. It was good, good, good'"—repeated three times, the last "good" emphasized in order that one may make no mistake about what is meant in this book. There is another passage, "'I'm not ashamed of it, there's no shame in me. Good and—and fine it was, the best part of myself,'" and so forth. Afterwards in this book, while this incident goes on, she talks about when she has to leave the house, and she says: "All round her were gray and crumbling ruins, and under those ruins her love lay bleeding, shamefully wounded by Angela Crossby, shamefully soiled and defiled by her mother—a piteous, suffering defenseless thing, it lay bleeding under the ruins." "Shamefully wounded by Angela Crossby" is not without its importance because the shameful wounding inflicted by Angela Crossby is not the fact that there has been so much connection between them, but because she discovers Angela Crossby having an intrigue with a married man; and the shameful soiling of this love is the fact that her victim prefers to commit adultery with a man than with the heroine of this book. Then there is another passage concluding this incident of Angela. She writes to her mother in these terms: "You insulted what to me is natural and sacred." "What to me is sacred"? Natural and sacred! Then I am asked to say that this book is in no sense a defense of unnatural practices between women, or a glorification of them, or a praise of them, to put it perhaps not quite so strongly. "Natural" and "Sacred"! "Good" repeated three times.

Then we come to the incident which has been referred to as the Mary incident. The whole of this book, put on the most temperate basis, is a demand for the toleration and recognition of this type of woman, that is to say, that they should be received in ordinary society, that they are not to be made outcasts or pariahs or ostracized by decent people, which is the whole plea of the book. What do we find in the Mary incident? Here is this woman whom we are told decent people ought not to turn from their homes, having first seduced a married woman, who of course, I admit at once, is not described as a woman of any particular morality, but that was not present to the mind of Stephen when she seduced her and persuaded her reluctantly to indulge in these horrible practices. Then we come to the incident of Mary. This takes place at the Front where, according to the writer of this book, a number of women of position and admirable character, who were engaged in driving ambulances in the course of the war, were addicted to this vice.

MISS RADCLYFFE-HALL: [sic] I protest. I am that writer.

THE MAGISTRATE: I must ask people not to interrupt the Court.

MISS RADCLYFFE-HALL: [sic] I am the authoress of this book.

THE MAGISTRATE: If you cannot behave yourself in Court I shall have to have you removed.

MISS RADCLYFFE-HALL: [sic] It is a shame.

THE MAGISTRATE: When we deal with the Mary incident we have here a description of the heroine driving this car at the Front. There she is brought in contact with the girl Mary, who is a perfectly innocent girl, who comes out and is employed upon this duty. There she comes into contact with the heroine. The heroine, Stephen, in the course of this book debauches Mary, but before doing that she apparently has some qualms of conscience which are not directed apparently to the moral or physical effects of those acts on Mary, but to the effect it may have on her social life and her recognition by society after these acts have taken place. We are given a reflection by the heroine of this book in these terms, at page 350: "Men—they are selfish, arrogant, possessive. What could they do for Mary Llewellyn? What could a man give that she could not? A child? But she would give Mary such a love as would be complete in itself without children. Mary would have no room in her heart, in her life, for a child if she came to Stephen. All things they would be the one to the other." Then: "With the terrible bonds of her dual nature she could bind Mary fast"— that is, of course, indulge in obscene practices with her—"and the pain would be sweetness, so that the girl would cry out for that sweetness, hugging her chains always closer to her. The world would condemn but they"—that is Stephen and her victim—"would rejoice; glorious outcasts unashamed, triumphant." It is not surprising that, those being the meditations present to the mind of the heroine Stephen, she does debauch Mary.

Then they go to Orotava where they live together. Now it is put forward by the Defense as regards this book that there is nothing in this book which in any way is a defense of or appreciation of these practices. What is the description of these two people living in filthy sin at Orotava? "A strange, though to them a very natural thing it seemed, this new and ardent fulfillment; having something fine and urgent about it that lay almost beyond the range of their wills. Something primitive and age-old as Nature herself, did their love appear to Mary and Stephen." Then further on: "But beyond the bounds of this turbulent river would lie gentle and most placid harbors of refuge; harbors in which the body could repose with contentment, while the lips spoke slow, indolent words, and the eyes beheld a dim, golden haze that blinded the while it revealed all beauty. Then Stephen would stretch out her hand and touch Mary where she lay, happy only to feel her nearness." Then another passage: "And Stephen as she held the girl in her arms, would feel that indeed she was all things to Mary; father, mother, friend and lover, all things; and Mary all things to her—the child, the friend, the beloved, all things. But Mary, because she was perfect woman, would rest without thought, with exultation, without question; finding no need to question since for her there was now only one thing—Stephen." Then again she describes how they are "deeply and thankfully happy." I need not elaborate that. Only one other passage perhaps: "Thus their talk of the future would often drift into talk of love, that is always timeless. On their lips, as in their hearts, would be words such as countless other lovers had spoken, for love is the sweetest monotony that was ever conceived of by the Creator."

Then what are the effects of this book which is said to have been written on a note of tragedy? What are the results of these horrible practices—not that they were a tragedy in the people's lives, but, on the contrary, what are we told: "They no longer felt desolate, hungry outcasts; unloved and unwanted, despised of the world. They were lovers who walked in the vineyard of life, plucking the warm, sweet fruits of that vineyard. Love had lifted them up as on wings of fire, had made them courageous, invincible, enduring. Nothing could be lacking to those who loved—the very earth gave of her fullest bounty. The earth seemed to come alive in response to the touch of their healthful and eager bodies—nothing could be lacking to those who loved. And thus in a cloud of illusion and glory, sped the last enchanted days at Orotava." What are the results of these vices as described in this book, on Mary, an innocent girl who has been debauched: "Yet there was something quite new in her face, a sort of wise expression that Stephen had put there." There is another passage which concludes the Orotava incident: "And although they could not have put it into words, could not have explained it to themselves or to each other, they seemed at that moment to be looking beyond the turbulent flood of earthly passion; to be looking straight into the eyes of a love that was changed—a love made perfect, discarnate. But the moment passed and they drew together." In order that there may be no mistake what is meant by that passage there are four asterisks placed directly after it. There is another incident which one must not overlook in connection with this book, which is the next incident when Stephen, the heroine, is going to see her mother. From time to time the mother wants to see her on business matters, and so she writes and suggests she should come to see her. She does not invite her victim, Mary. What happens then? Stephen says with regard to that: "I don't allow her to be insulted"—and the mother is announced in the course of this book as a cruel, stupid, pitiless woman, who insults something wonderful and holy. Why?—because she will not allow Stephen to bring the girl she has debauched to live in the mother's house with her. I need not go into this book in all its details. On the point of the effect of these vices, which I am told this book does not defend, there is a description of a certain place in Paris, to which the heroine is introduced by a male character who is a sodomite and which is kept by a French woman named Valerie Seymour, who is presented to us as the leading depraved woman in Paris or the most perverted woman in Paris. There is an account of the people who frequent the place, all of whom are described, although they have this vice, in terms of considerable eulogy. There are a good many passages in regard to that incident. For instance, the views of the hostess, the depraved hostess, are given. It is true—one must be fair in this matter—that they are given as her views. It may be said that words were merely put into her mouth which might be used by a tradeswoman of that kind. But, on the other hand, she is written of with appreciation, and there is no protest or comment upon her views. Her views about this matter are these: "It was hard on the young"—that is apparently the fact that they were inverts—"she had thought so herself, but some came through all right, though a few might go under. Nature was trying to do her bit; inverts were being born in increasing numbers, and after a while their numbers would tell, even with the fools who still ignored Nature." That means the people who objected not merely to the vices, but the people who indulged in them. "They must just bide their time—recognition was coming. But meanwhile they should all cultivate more pride, should learn to be proud of their isolation." That deals with the effects of the vices. I only introduce that because it has an important bearing on the book, because at the end of the book there is this. There is a young man of the name of Martin who at one time had been attached to Stephen, and he falls in love with Mary; and then a considerable number of pages in this book are devoted to the struggle between Martin and Stephen for the possession of this girl. Martin is described as "struggling to discover some ray of hope in what seemed a well nigh hopeless situation. Night after night Stephen's masterful arms would enfold the warm smallness of Mary's body." Martin does his best to induce Mary to leave Stephen; but, however, as is pointed out I think by Stephen herself: "Although the days may be Martin's, the nights were Stephen's."

Before I conclude, there is another passage that I think I ought to mention, and that is the incident when the mother refuses to have Mary stop with her in her house with Stephen, and Stephen's answer to this is: "There is only one way to meet a situation like that, and that is to throw me into Mary's arms," or something to that effect. In this particular incident what happens is this, that Stephen eventually pretends to be tired of Mary, goes off to Valerie and persuades Valerie to pretend to be misconducting herself with her in order that this may throw her into the arms of Stephen. Such is almost the end of the book. It concludes with a very singular hysterical passage in which God is introduced. At the end the last sentence of the book is: "God" she gasped, "we believe; we have told You we believe. . . . We have not denied You, then rise up and defend us. Acknowledge us, oh God, before the whole world. Give us also the right to our existence." There are a good many other passages in which the name of the Deity is introduced in a way which is hardly appropriate. I do not know whether the word "reverence" is introduced in this discussion or whether it is necessary to introduce it, but I confess the way in which the Deity is introduced into this book seems to me singularly inappropriate and disgusting. There is a plea for existence at the end. That of course means a plea for existence in which the invert is to be recognized and tolerated, and not treated with condemnation, which they are at present, by all decent people.

This being the tenor of this book, I have no hesitation whatever in saying that it is an obscene libel, that it would tend to corrupt those into whose hands it should fall, and that the publication of this book is an offence against public decency, an obscene libel, and I shall order it to be destroyed.

[Biron then ruled on costs.]

BOW STREET POLICE COURT.
Friday, 16th November, 1928.

4

A Selection of Early Reviews

SATURDAY REVIEW, JULY 28, 1928

Miss Radclyffe Hall calls her book a novel, but it is also a tract and an apologia, and it is not always easy to disassociate the artist's intention from the propagandist's. "The Well of Loneliness" is a study of abnormal relationships between women; Miss Radclyffe Hall insists on this throughout with the greatest frankness, and those to whom such a subject is abhorrent would do well to leave the book alone. Many tender, romantic and innocent friendships would turn to loathing and self-loathing did they for an instant see themselves in the mirror which Miss Radclyffe Hall so unflinchingly holds up to this tormented province of the human passions. The story is conceived in a mood of tragedy. . . . One's instinct is to feel sorry for [Stephen]; but it is not enough for Miss Radclyffe Hall that one should feel sorry. She wants to justify her heroine and rehabilitate her in the eyes of the world. She demands justice as well as pity, and in her determination to put the case at its baldest she dots all the "i's" and introduces erotic and sentimental passages which would have been better left out; they would confer little honor on the passion of love, even if it had been more conveniently housed. But inflated and sentimental and diffuse as it sometimes is, one cannot deny the earnestness and sincerity which animate [the novel]. Miss Hall's . . . appeal is a powerful one, and it is supported by passages of great force and beauty.

L. P. Hartley

TIMES LITERARY SUPPLEMENT, AUGUST 2, 1928

Miss Radclyffe Hall's latest work, "The Well of Loneliness," is a novel, and we propose to treat it as such. We therefore rather regret that it should have been thought necessary to insert at the beginning a "commentary" by Mr. Havelock Ellis. . . . To the book as a work of art this testimony adds nothing; on the other hand, the documentary significance of a work of fiction seems to us small. The presence of this commentary, however, points to the criticism which, with all our admiration for much of the detail, we feel compelled to express—namely, that this long novel, sincere, courageous, high-minded, and often beautifully expressed as it is, fails as a work of art through divided purpose. It is meant as a thesis and a challenge as well as an artistic creation.

There is no ambiguity about the nature of the thesis. Stephen Gordon, the central figure, was meant by her parents to be a boy; and a boy she was born in all but the physical characteristics of sex. Her painful story, beginning in infancy and continuing to middle-age, is meant to express the bitter cry of the female invert, the man-woman, born through no fault of her own into a world which denies her a place in it and persecutes her kind by isolating them from all the happy and fine contacts of life, without regard for their highest mental qualities or for the invert's consciousness of loving no less nobly than any other human being. Stephen's life is one long tragedy, first of incomprehension, as one contact after another in childhood warns her that she is unlike other girls—and this part of the book, the childhood at Morton, passed under her loving but bewildered father's protection, shows all this writer's quality of evoking beauty and visualizing human scenes with an extraordinary clarity of outline—then of horrified repugnance when a man friend woos her, and of a romantic passion for the wife of a neighbor, ignobly betrayed and leading to an irreparable break with her home and her mother; thereafter of a long effort to forget herself in work, and finally of love realized with the girl called Mary Llewellyn, of the hideous exiled life in Paris to which such women are condemned, and of the last agony, when, by a desperate simulation of unfaithfulness, she drives Mary into the arms of the man who wishes to make her his wife—the very man-friend of her own early happiness. There is no relief; the stages of an abnormal person's life succeed one another inevitably, with a profusion of detail which, though adorned with a high and poetic literary talent, is excessive for the work of imagination. More and more, towards the end, one feels the artistic inspiration fade and the desire increase to probe to the bottom the pains of an abnormal growth upon the social body. The tone rises into that of a challenge, now angry, now pitiful, to the world and, as the heroine bows in her last agony, to the Creator. The final chapters, describing the unhappy, segregated, unreal life of Stephen, Mary and their congeners in Paris, are extremely painful, as they are intended to be. As such we must leave them to the interested reader, with all the discords unresolved; yet undoubtedly in this book the recognized talents of Miss Hall in themselves are as conspicuous as before, and against any feelings of repugnance at her uncompromising sincerity must be set respect for her intentions, frequent admiration for her treatment, and only regret that the statement of an insoluble problem so passionately presented itself as a theme.

NATION & ATHENAEUM, AUGUST 4, 1928

"The Well of Loneliness" . . . is a novel which will certainly cause a good deal of discussion. I have not read Miss Hall's two other books, though she is a serious novelist who has been crowned with two prizes for "Adam's Breed." Her present book invites consideration from two points of view: as a work of art and because of its subject. I will deal first with its subject. . . . The daughter of Sir Philip Gordon, of ancient family and the owner of Morton Hall, [Stephen] is born a Sapphic or Lesbian, a woman who falls in love with and is physically attracted, not by men, but by women. The cause of this perversion of the normal sexual feelings is represented in this book to be pre-natal. Sir Philip and his wife, Anna, were passionately desirous of a son and heir; they convinced themselves before the child's birth that it was going to be a boy. Stephen, the daughter, has the body of a woman, but the mind and instinct of a man. . . .

As a study of a psychology which is neither as uncommon nor as abnormal as many people imagine, the book is extremely interesting. It is written with understanding and frankness, with sympathy and feeling. The chief of those "unsolved problems," to which Mr. Havelock Ellis refers, is, of course, caused by the instinctive and barbarous attitude of society, and particularly British society, towards the abnormal. The county families feel instinctively that there is something not quite right about Sir Philip's daughter—and "something not quite right" means in plain English something morally wrong. When Stephen's relations with Angela Crossby, the wife of the Birmingham hardware manufacturer, are disclosed, Stephen's mother turns from her with horror and loathing. She is a moral pariah, and the scandal has to be hushed up, just as if she cheated at cards or forged a check. This moral attitude of the world and the reaction from it upon the mind of Stephen are well described in the book. Another problem, internal to the psychology of the invert (as Miss Hall rather strangely calls her heroine), is touched upon in the book, but is not dealt with so firmly or clearly. The reader is left in some doubt whether, in Miss Hall's view, the tragedy of Stephen's life is or is not partly due to a certain barrenness and sterility in her relationships, whether, in fact, her heroine is not condemned by fate—in other words by herself— as well as by society to drink of the well of loneliness.

Miss Hall's subject will be considered "unpleasant" by many people; as treated by her, it is far less unpleasant than many of the subjects of popular novels. But I must leave the subject for the novel. Miss Hall has written her book as a novel, and she is obviously a serious novelist who asks to be judged by high standards. According to those standards, the book is a failure, and why it fails is an interesting question. Up to a point it has great merits. Miss Hall is one of a large number of women writers who obviously have very considerable gifts for novel writing. She can construct a plot, tell a story, think of characters and make them sufficiently distinct and interesting, describe scenes vividly, set people talking. She has a much quicker, subtler, and, I think, more sincere, feeling for the psychology of her characters than have most male novelists of her caliber. And yet the book fails completely as a work of art. There are many reasons for this, but one of the chief reasons is that Miss Hall loses the whole in its parts, and is so intent on the stars that she forgets the heavens. Her book is formless and therefore chaotic. Its shape should have been given to it by the psychology of Stephen and by her tragic relation to society—that is clearly Miss Hall's intention. But the leaven of this central idea does not remain a creative principle for long in Miss Hall's mind or in the novel. The first 150 pages are good, for there the yeast is still working; but after the death of Sir Philip the novel becomes a catalogue, almost a ragbag. Incident is added to incident, and character to character, and one sees the relevance which Miss Hall intended each to have to the theme of the book. But their relevance is intellectual, not emotional, and therefore not artistic. They remain discrete patches which never join to form a pattern. Instead of the book gathering way as it goes, it loses it, and Miss Hall labors heavily in that terrible trough which is the middle of every long book. It is emotionally that the book loses way, and a sign of this is Miss Hall's use of language. At the beginning the language is alive; the style is not brilliant or beautiful, but it is quick and vivid, particularly in the descriptions of hunting. But as the book goes on, life and emotion die out of the language, and Miss Hall drops into journalese or the tell-tale novelist's cliches, when she wants to heighten the emotion. "They sat down close together. They were weary unto death. . . ." "Came a queer, halting voice. . . ." ". . . fared forth in the motor to visit divers villages. . . ." These are small points, but they show unmistakably a failure of the emotional impetus. It is the same emotional failure which is noticeable in Miss Hall's characters. Her characters are interesting, carefully constructed, and individualized. And yet disconcertingly they hardly seem to be persons. They appear to be the creations of the intellect and for the reader they have no emotional content. The consequence is that one does not feel the emotions appropriate to their tragedy or comedy.

Leonard Woolf

SUNDAY TIMES, AUGUST 5, 1928

The age-old quarrel between those who insist that life as a whole is not a fit subject for nice-minded people to write or think about and those who believe that most of our troubles spring from our refusal to look ourselves honestly in the face is certain to explode afresh over Radclyffe Hall's new novel. Even ten years ago the former party would have made her subject-matter impossible. But we have been moving fast. Our Conservatives have become Liberals and our Liberals Radicals. Psychoanalysis if it has done nothing else, has made us deal more gently with abnormality, since it has made us uncertain as to what the norm really is—whether it is, indeed more than a conventional mask covering our strangeness.

And of late the figure of the abnormal woman—the masculine woman—has been coming more and more clearly into the foreground. Not that she is a modern phenomenon. Almost certainly, like her male prototype, she has always existed, but not until late years has she been acknowledged openly. . . .

Now, Radclyffe Hall, sick no doubt of innuendo, has come right into the open. With courage and unquestionable sincerity she has made this mysterious phenomenon in nature her whole theme, and has treated the tragic history of the individual in a society which is for ever hostile to mysteries and minorities with compassion and understanding. There is no question, as Havelock Ellis points out in his introductory note, of the accuracy of her psychology, and the fact that Radclyffe Hall is an artist and a fine poet rids her novel, at least for those who care for truth and who believe that somehow or other "we are all God's chil'un," of any shadow of offense.

But there is always a danger, where a highly controversial subject is being considered, that the essential qualities of a work may be overlooked—indeed, that the artist may be lost in his theme. This, in the case of "The Well of Loneliness," would be more than usually unfortunate. For Radclyffe Hall writes with distinction, with a lively sense of characterization, and with a feeling for the background of her age which makes her work delightful reading. And, first and last, she has courage and honesty. But the reward of these qualities is uncertain, and it will be interesting to watch the reception of this daring study. If it is received as it was written, it will be something of a landmark in the history of human development.

I. A. R. Wylie

Evening Standard, August 9, 1928

In principle I am not favorable to literary godfathership: the sponsoring by famous names of books signed with less famous names. . . .

But there may be exceptions. It certainly would not have occurred to me to read Radclyffe Hall's "The Well of Loneliness" (Cape, 15s., a large and long novel) had I not been attracted by a line in the publisher's advertisement: "With a commentary by Havelock Ellis"—Havelock Ellis being a name which means much to me. I knew nothing of the author's previous work, nor of the subject of this new one.

I ought to have guessed its subject. It is Havelock Ellis, the essayist, to whom I am indebted for the enlargement of my outlook, but Havelock Ellis, in addition to being a very valuable philosophical essayist, counts among the greatest European authorities upon the vagaries or aberrations of nature in the matter of sexual characteristics.

"The Well of Loneliness" is the story of one of the victims of one of Nature's caprices. Havelock Ellis stands by it. He praises it for its fictional quality, its notable psychological and sociological significance, and its complete absence of offense. I cannot disagree with him.

Uncertain in touch at first, this novel is in the main fine. Disfigured by loose writing and marred by loose construction, it nevertheless does hold you. It is honest, convincing, and extremely courageous. What it amounts to is a cry for unprejudiced social recognition of the victims. The cry attains genuine tragic poignancy. The future may hide highly strange things, and therefore conservative prophecy is dangerous; nevertheless, I must say that I do not think the cry will be effectively heard.

Nature has no prejudices, but human nature is less broadminded, and human nature, with its deep instinct for the protection of society, can put up a powerful defense of its own limitations. "The Well of Loneliness" is not a novel for those who prefer not to see life steadily and see it whole.

Arnold Bennett

Glasgow Herald, August 9, 1928

[The novel's] . . . core is psychological, not sociological; its central situation arises directly from an abnormality in human nature, not from an ephemeral abnormality in society. Stephen Gordon is a girl born to a baronet and his wife, who both wholeheartedly longed for a boy. She is reared exactly as an heir to the estates and the title would have been reared. She is athletic, clever, and scholarly; she rides to hounds better than most men, and she startles her parents by her prowess in the gymnasium. In all but her physical attributes she is a man. Belonging, therefore, neither to the male nor to the female camp, she is regarded as she grows up with distaste and suspicion. She lives a rather solitary life, for girls shrink from her strange aversion to things that seem normal to them, while her one man friend horrifies her when he declares his love. She becomes a sort of white crow, hated and attacked by all because of her uncommonness, and her life is made a series of tragic misfortunes because she cannot understand the difference between herself and ordinary humanity. There is great power in the novel and considerable beauty; but it is marred by a tendency to preach and by a lamentable inattention to style. It is shocking to find a writer of Miss Hall's caliber capable of writing "No one of its own ilk" where she means species, or "such a homestead," or the even more heinous "Came the time, . . . Came the day."

Morning Post, August 10, 1928

The theme of this novel is one that—some will still think properly—has been hitherto reserved for treatment in the textbooks of medical science and psychology. It is the tragedy of the No-Man's-Land of sex, and the main implication of the story is the cruelty resulting from the refusal of society to recognize the problem of the abnormal. Miss Radclyffe Hall's chief character, the girl Stephen Gordon, in whom her parents had expected a boy, is represented as standing midway between the sexes. Unwilling respect for a conventional taboo overruled her father's finely perceptive affection, as it did later that of her gallant and estimable governess, Puddle; and subservience to its inquisition had lamentably disastrous consequences when her mother's eyes were opened. And in the later chapters this personal moral of Stephen's history broadens out into the wider one, that the sufferers from this abnormality are by a blind hostility herded together with all its malignant by-products.

Miss Radclyffe Hall's novel it will thus be seen, disarms criticism of fiction's incursion into the pathological field. The story is its own apology for its theme; and if that still leaves its wisdom debatable, there can be nothing but respect and admiration for the author's handling of it. Mr. Havelock Ellis's brief commentary was not required to establish its challenge, which from the first page emerges with a frankness free of offense and an increasingly passionate sincerity. It would be idle, then, to regard this as purely a work of fiction, the specific purpose of which may be an incidental consideration only.

Yet Miss Radclyffe Hall cannot escape the limitations and the obligations of her chosen literary form—the less so because of the authority of her fine and proficient gifts in it. The mode being the novel, her intention must, and can only, be justified by her selected imaginary case. Our response to her thesis depends on the emotional and intellectual appeal—the artistic validity—of Stephen's portrait. For that the author has taken a large canvas. Her novel runs to over 500 pages. Those describing Stephen's childhood and youth in her home at Morton Hall, with her tragic circumstance breaking on her dawning mind, display the author's powers of sensitive penetration and subtle expression. The vital incident of Martin, when the friend becomes the lover, is managed firmly, yet with a skillful reserve. Miss Radclyffe Hall's beauty of style and delicate, yet vivid, presentation of character and mood do not desert her in the later chapters with their harrowing Paris episodes.

TIME AND TIDE, AUGUST 10, 1928

. . . Miss Radclyffe Hall's important, sincere and very moving study demands consideration from two different standpoints. In the first place, it is presented as a novel, and is therefore open to criticism as a work of imagination, a creative effort which challenges comparison with other examples of fiction. In the second place it is a plea, passionate, yet admirably restrained and never offensive, for the extension of social toleration, compassion and recognition to the biologically abnormal woman, who, because she possesses the tastes and instincts of a man, is too often undeservedly treated as a moral pariah.

Many critics maintain that propaganda, of whatever kind, impairs a work of art. True as this aesthetic canon may be for the majority of such works, the fact remains that it is the problem which it discusses, rather than its rank in fiction, which lends to Miss Hall's book its undoubted significance. As a novel, written in language which is unfalteringly clear, sometimes beautiful and often irritatingly Biblical it is unduly long and overburdened with detail frequently irrelevant to the story's progress. Its shape is indefinite, and it leaves behind it a sense of lost links which might have fastened its various parts more connectedly together, though in spite of these shortcomings it never fails to hold the absorbed attention of the reader. I believe, however, that it was by her theme, rather than by the form in which that theme was embodied, that the author intended her book to stand or fall; hence it is by her success or failure in dealing with the problem that she has selected for treatment, that this particular example of her work must be judged.

It may be said at once that "The Well of Loneliness" can only strengthen the belief of all honest and courageous persons that there is no problem which is not better frankly stated than concealed. Persecution and disgusted ostracism have never solved any difficulty in the world, and they certainly do not make the position of the female invert less bitter to herself or less dangerous to others. Miss Hall's dignified challenge, presenting without sentimentality or compunction the dreadful poignancy of ineradicable emotions, in comparison with which the emotions of normal men and women seem so clear and uncomplicated, certainly convinces us that women of the type of Stephen Gordon, in so far as their abnormality is inherent and not merely the unnecessary cult of exotic erotics, deserve the fullest consideration and compassion from all who are fortunate enough to have escaped one of Nature's cruelest dispensations.

The book, however, raises and never satisfactorily answers another question—the question as to how far the characteristics of Stephen Gordon are physiological and how far they are psychological. Probably only an expert biologist could satisfactorily resolve such a difficulty. It certainly seems likely that a problem of this type must be intensified by that exaggeration of sex differences which has been peculiarly marked in certain ages of the world, and to which the English middle classes of the eighteenth and nineteenth centuries were particularly prone. Miss Hall appears to take for granted that this over-emphasis of sex-characteristics is part of the correct education of the normal human being; she therefore makes her "normal" women clinging and "feminine" to exasperation, and even describes the attitude towards love as "an end in itself" as being a necessary attribute of true womanhood. Many readers will know too many happy wives and mothers for whom it is not, to take on trust Miss Hall's selection of the qualities essential to one sex or the other.

This confusion between what is "male" or "female" and what is merely human in our complex makeup, persists throughout the book. We feel that, in describing the supposedly sinister predilections of the child Stephen Gordon, much ado is often made about nothing; so many of them appear to be the quite usual preferences of any vigorous young female who happens to possess more vitality and intelligence than her fellows. If one of the results of women's education in the eighteen-nineties really was to attach the ugly label "pervert" to a human being whose chief desire was for a wider expression of her humanity than contemporary convention permitted, then that education was an evil thing indeed. This is not to deny that the problem described by Miss Hall does exist in a grave and urgent form, and that her presentation of it deserves the serious attention of all students of social questions.

Vera Brittain

North Mail and Newcastle Chronicle, August 11, 1928

... I would ... hesitate to call "The Well of Loneliness" a novel. It is a plea, passionate, beautiful and sometimes a little shrill, not for toleration, but for recognition of what, although the phrase sounds offensive, can only be called abnormality.

Stephen Gordon was a boy in everything but the physical attributes of sex. As such, the love of men was abhorrent to her; the love of woman was not. That is the tragedy of the book, and a very real tragedy it is. There are many women like Stephen, just as there are many men who are the complement of her. It is easier for men—again, the injustice of sex—but for women such abnormality means social ostracism and a life altogether cut off and remote from the common life of the world. "The Well of Loneliness" . . . is a strange and powerful book, but much as I admire it, Miss Hall is less an artist in it than she was in "Adam's Breed." "The Well of Loneliness" was written by a propagandist on fire with the pity and righteousness of her crusade.

T.P.'s & Cassell's Weekly, August 11, 1928

It is a platitude to say that Miss Radclyffe Hall's new novel is an astonishing advance in plain speaking on any novel published in our recollection. The heroine, Stephen Gordon, is one whose parents had greatly longed for a boy, and she goes through life as something smitten by the hand of destiny, and no toleration or even mercy is extended to her or her kind by society. And all this time she is a woman of genius as well as of a profoundly emotional temperament, indulging or fighting against her own longings. The book strives to prove that those who, in their psychological nature, have to endure this living crucifixion can have a secret nobility, and compare in talent and good works with the rest of mankind. The lesson of this moving novel is here expressed by Stephen's lovable old governess: "Nothing's completely misplaced or wasted, I'm sure of that—and we're all part of Nature." No scenes could be more poignantly expressed than those in Paris, where some of those stricken people hold their counsels of despair. One cannot say what effect this book will have on the public attitude of silence or derision, but every reader will agree with Mr. Havelock Ellis in the preface, that "the poignant situations are set forth with a complete absence of offense." The whole thesis is that there is a particular nature from birth that is, in the inscrutable designs of God, set apart from the recognized divisions of mankind, and that the censures of society are therein unjust. Rarely does a novel maintain so consistently its note of emotion and indignation and tragedy and underlying despair. It says its message plainly, indignantly, always eloquently.

Con O'Leary

LIVERPOOL POST AND MERCURY, AUGUST 15, 1928

Ever since the war, when women displayed such unexpected ability in doing the work of men at the front, there has been a tendency to recognize and discuss in public and not merely in scientific textbooks—the painful problem of inversion, the existence of men and women who have inherited the constitution and psychology of the sex to which they do not rightly belong. The phenomenon has always existed, and the individual lives have been wrecked by the hostile attitude of society towards inverts of either sex. What other attitude on the part of society is possible? We may pity the invert from the bottom of our hearts, but we cannot lighten the burden which Nature—in an unnatural mood—has laid upon them.

It is to this poignant and still unsolved problem that Miss Radclyffe Hall directs our sympathy in her valiant and essentially fine-minded novel, "The Well of Loneliness." Plain speaking upon such a theme is not easy, but Miss Hall has succeeded in setting forth every aspect of her subject naturally and yet delicately, fully, but without offense. Her book is the first English novel to present artistically this particular mystery of sex. It is an essentially clean-minded book, yet it may easily antagonize certain normally- and perhaps selfishly-minded folk who are unwilling, or unable, to recognize the existence and the claims of the abnormal.

This study of an Amazonian soul is a fine effort to know, to experience, and to interpret the psychology of a woman in whom male power is abnormally developed. On Stephen Gordon this power seems naturally, rather than morbidly engendered. She is the only child of parents who deeply desired a son and heir, but here [sic] early training, though freer and more athletic than is usual with girls, was not calculated to extinguish her womanly characteristics. Stephen's abnormality is something quite beyond her own or other people's control, and is accompanied by fine intellectual and moral attributes. She becomes a distinguished writer, but her life is haunted by this puzzle of her dual sex and the inevitable outcome is a tragedy of frustration and self-abnegation.

Artistically the book suffers from the hopelessness of the problem it present [sic]. There is a complete inventory of the feelings, the anxieties, and the torments of the masculine woman, but no solution of her tragedy, and no hope for her future.

A. M. A.

TATLER, AUGUST 15, 1928

"The Well of Lonelines" . . . is a very difficult work to review. Should I praise it, then I can literally hear the huge army of the narrow-minded hinting that I am in sympathy with its publication. Should, on the other hand, I dismiss it as a novel written on a subject which is unmentionable, then I should condemn a work of considerable art; a story which is poignantly tragic to a degree; one of the few books I have ever read which illustrates the pitiful loneliness of sexual perversity as it is, apart from the pervert's psychological and biological significance. . . . In any case, only the bigoted and the foolish seek to ignore an aspect of life which is as undeniable a fact as any concrete thing. . . . There are few more inwardly tragic figures in the whole of the human world than those whose nature appears to the majority as unnatural. The world condemns this unnaturalness as if it were a willful thing. Alas! that everything which is natural to a man or woman belongs to Nature! Heaven help those, then, whose nature is not in accord with the majority! . . .

Sir Philip and Lady Anna Gordon had always longed for an heir. A son to inherit the lovely ancestral home among the Malvern Hills, of which they were so proud. Perhaps—who knows?—this intense longing for a boy may have had some psychological influence upon the character of their child while yet in her mother's womb. Unfortunately a girl was born to them. It is significant of their disappointment that they called this daughter Stephen, as if in protest against her sex. Except, however, that the girl was narrow-hipped and wide-shouldered there was nothing in this child to disclose anything abnormal. Only as she grew up her friends, especially her mother, were disquieted by the girl's dislike of all those interests and amusements which belong to a girl's life. She rode to hounds like a man; she loved reading and everything which belongs to a strenuous open-air life; she had no interest in clothes or boys, or any of those feminine frivolities which most girls enjoy. Her friends thought her queer and eccentric. . . . And so Stephen became a woman puzzled and distressed by those problems of her nature which she could not understand, though already she had begun to suffer the pitiful loneliness of those who are not as others are. . . .

The relation of this tragedy is remarkable for its truth and realism. The pining for love and affection which, cruelly enough, haunts the life of the pervert in direct ratio, it would appear, to the difficulty of its fulfillment, is disturbing in its verisimilitude. The wild generosity, the self-sacrifice, the humility by which poor wretched Stephen tried to gain and hold the love of those who returned, or pretended to return, her love, belongs entirely to those life-tragedies which few have dared to tell, so pitiful are they, so entirely without respite. And no one condemned her more when the truth was out than the woman who had given her birth, and, who knows, may all unconsciously have helped, to make her daughter what she was! Leaving the home she loved, the home which might have influenced her for good, or at least brought her peace, Stephen settled in Paris. Such as she can live out their lives there—a colony to themselves. . . . Stephen in Paris became no longer the complete "outlaw." And yet an outlaw she remained—she and her like. The normal world would not accept her for the woman she was in all that matters, in intelligence and dignity and kindness, because, in the really unimportant matter of sex-urge she was not as normal people are. . . . You must read the story. And yet you must *not* read it unless certain aspects of life do not terrify you. Most people will, I fancy, consider it a most unnecessary publication—and this is to put it mildly. They will see in the extraordinary truth and realism which makes the book in its way a little work of art, even in the acute appreciation of beauty and in the writer's pity for the class about whom she writes, an additional danger, perhaps an added insult. Well, these people must not read it. It is a story solely for the scientist, the psychologist, the earnest student of human nature. . . . Considered objectively, then, it is a very poignant plea for justice towards the unfortunate intermediate sex. Considered subjectively you will either be interested by it or peradventure it will make you too furious and disgusted to do more than throw the book in the fire. We will leave it at that.

Richard King

DAILY TELEGRAPH, AUGUST 17, 1928

This is a truly remarkable book. It is remarkable in the first place as a work of art finely conceived and finely written. Secondly, it is remarkable as dealing with an aspect of abnormal life seldom or never presented in English fiction—certainly never with such unreserved frankness.

As in all works of true art, subject and treatment are inseparably bound together in this book; it would be a mistake to compliment Miss Hall on her style, on her marvelously just selection of words, and on her burning sincerity, while at the same time condemning her choice of subject and accusing her of lacking restraint. Her book must be accepted as a whole, and so accepted it is likely to excite two directly opposite opinions, according as the reader admits or denies the subjects as legitimate material for art.

M. M.

DAILY NEWS AND WESTMINSTER GAZETTE, AUGUST 23, 1928

Miss Radclyffe Hall has contrived to write a sadly ordinary novel on a happily unusual theme. What she pleads for is the acceptance by society of the sexual pervert. These people, she maintains, are no worse than other citizens, mentally often above their level, and their abnormality only becomes a vice when they are driven by loneliness into the company of such really deplorable persons as drunkards and drug-takers.

Miss Radclyffe Hall does not state her case impartially as an artist. Instead, she sentimentalizes it. She is so bent on asserting the moral blamelessness of her heroine, that she has not paid nearly enough attention to the rest of life. She tells the story of a girl whose parents ardently desired a son, and, having chosen the name Stephen for the baby before it was born, bestowed it instead upon their daughter. Such undeviating persistence showed, we think, a rather unbeautiful and tram-like quality in these parents; but Miss Radclyffe Hall seems to find nothing wrong with them. They provide her with the first of her excuses for her heroine. Had Stephen been christened Mary, she would have us believe, her development might have been entirely different.

As it was, when Stephen began to grow up, she did not keep her hands clean without pressure. She wanted to fight with her fists when people teased her. She liked wearing knickerbockers better than skirts, riding astride and screwing her hair well out of her eyes. She took no interest in clothes, and showed no sign of what is called feminine vanity. All this Miss Radclyffe Hall takes to be a sign of Stephen's abnormality. To us it seems perfectly normal. Boys and girls are, in our experience, very much alike, in tastes, manners and habits.

Later, when Stephen was seventeen, she was gauche at garden parties, Miss Radclyffe Hall takes this as a serious portent, too, and also the fact that long skirts were a trouble to her, as to which of us old enough to have been afflicted by them, were they not? In all this Miss Radclyffe Hall appears to us to be particularizing from the general. Even her heroine's repugnance at being made love to for the first time by a man to whom she is deeply attached does not strike us as strange or unusual. Where Stephen's abnormality begins is where that repugnance persists; where, still more, she develops a passion for a member of her own sex; where, finally, exaggerating the importance of clothes in a thoroughly feminine fashion, she dresses herself in clothes of masculine character and lives in Paris as the lover of another woman. . . .

Miss Radclyffe Hall stresses the loneliness of her heroine, deprived of intimate bodily companionship. To this the simple reply is, that loneliness is the human lot.

Miss Radclyffe Hall is a singularly able counsel for the defense, though her prose is marred by recurring regular rhythms, the penalty of too much eloquence. She succeeds in making her heroine a potentially decent and comprehensible character. Even her case-making, however, cannot provide her heroine with any serious grievances against society. There is no trace of persecution. She collected her dividends regularly. She lived as she pleased. Lady Massey, it is true, did not invite her to stay in Cheshire, and there was no place save a disreputable cafe where she and her companion could dance publicly to a band. Those were her wrongs.

Well, there must have been a good many other people to whom Lady Massey did not tender invitations, and there are a thousand fairgrounds, schools and village fetes where women can and do dance with one another, failing masculine partners, and no two thoughts are given to the matter.

The chief objection to the sort of relationship which Miss Radclyffe Hall attempts to justify is that it poisons all those other innocent, cheerful affectionate relationships, and leaves no part of life secure from the wandering dragon of lust.

"The Well of Loneliness" is not an obscene or indecent book, nor is it the only recent novel into which the theme of perversion has been introduced. The objection to it is that it falsifies realities, and presents as a martyr a woman in the grip of a vice.

W. R. Gordon

COUNTRY LIFE, AUGUST 25, 1928

It must have required great courage to write "The Well of Loneliness." For the natural impulse of the normal human being is to recoil from the abnormal one, and the author's task has, therefore, been twofold; first, to persuade the reader past the initial distaste for her subject; second, to reveal that subject as one for compassion rather than condemnation. . . . Miss Radclyffe Hall treats her subject of the masculine woman with deep comprehension and great delicacy. She sets before us, in their pitiful human aspects, tragedies usually dealt with only in medical works, and she does it from the highest. . . . It need hardly be said that "The Well of Lonelines" is not a novel for every reader but the mature, the thoughtful, and the openminded will find in it much food for reflection, a window giving upon understanding, and a psychological study of profundity and pathos.

V. H. F.

NEW STATESMAN, AUGUST 25, 1928

"The Well of Lonelines" is a serious novel on the theme of homosexuality in women. It is a long, tedious and absolutely humorless book. There is a very simple literary rule in dealing with this kind of subject. What the author takes for granted, the reader will take for granted, what the author makes a fuss about the reader will fuss about too. . . . It is just this rule which Miss Hall has failed to keep. "The Well of Loneliness" is a melodramatic description of a subject which has nothing melodramatic about it. What literary interest it has, and it might have a great deal, is obscured by the constant stream of propaganda of every kind, and the author's perpetual insistence that the invert is a great tragic figure, branded with the mark of Cain, set apart from her kind as the victim of the injustice of God and the persecution of the world. The book is really a chronicle of the misfortunes of the invert, but since it assumes the invert to be born an invert and condemned beyond all hope of cure to remain one, it can hardly be said to point a moral of any kind. It is presumably a plea for greater tolerance, but the world is perfectly prepared to tolerate the invert, if the invert will only make concessions to the world. Most of us are resigned to the doctrine of homosexuals, that they alone possess all the greatest heroes and all the finer feelings, but it is surely preposterous that they should claim a right, not only to the mark of Cain, but to the martyr's crown. The tragedy of Stephen Gordon, the heroine of this book, is not really that of inversion but of genius; but if of genius, it is that of any sensitive, artistic, religious and uncompromising human being who refuses to adapt herself to the conditions of life. . . . The end is finely written and Stephen's eccentric childhood is admirably described. The whole middle of the book, however, is nothing but mechanical writing or desultory reporting broken only by Stephen's unhappy passion for Mary, and a few pleas for kindness to animals, halos for inverts, and a special paradise for trees. . . .

There is the typical post-war scene when a riotous party is brought to tears by a few Negro spirituals—but surely this has nothing to do with sexual inversion. All pleasure-seekers suffer from a maimed religious sense; appeal to that, and to the retrospective beauty of security and innocence, and no one of them can fail to be moved—but if this is the mark of Cain, then all humanity is branded. The most embarrassing parts are the sentimental animal passages. In particular the episode of the old hunter that Stephen insists on taking down in agony, all the way from London to Worcestershire, so that he may be shot outside his own loose-box, seems ridiculous in the extreme. No county family could be expected—quite apart from morals—to regard as normal such a crank as that.

"The Well of Loneliness" may be a brave book to have written, but let us hope it will pave the way for someone to write a better. Homosexuality is, after all, as rich in comedy as in tragedy, and it is time it was emancipated from the aura of distinguished damnation and religious martyrdom which surrounds its so fiercely aggressive apologists. Stephen Gordon is a Victorian character, an *âme damnée* once we are reconciled to her position, we are distressed by her lack of spirit, her failure to revenge herself on her tormentors. Sappho had never heard of the mark of Cain, she was also well able to look after herself, but never did she possess a disciple so conscious of her inferiority as Stephen Gordon, or so lacking—for 15s.!—in the rudiments of charm.

Cyril Connolly

PEOPLE, AUGUST 26, 1928

The story is that of a girl who, said the publishers in their description, "is born out of her own sphere."

That girl was born to parents who planned, hoped, and expected that their child would be a son. Their disappointment was great. The inference is that the parents' expectations had a disastrous effect upon the child, who began with a boy's instincts, a boy's thoughts, which later developed into the instincts and thoughts of a man.

So far, so good. The author has tried to explain just why this should come about. But explanation is no extenuation, and from then on Miss Hall seeks not only to explain her pervert "heroine," but also to justify her. She even comes near to giving her a halo.

From the moment when the "heroine" finds her friend in the arms of a lover, the horror of the book deepens and, in describing certain places and people in Paris, it goes even further beyond the limit of what is decent.

Especially do we revolt when we find her putting into the lips of her unfortunate character words, which one expects only from the lips of a man to the woman he loves.

TRUTH, AUGUST 29, 1928

. . . Had the Public Prosecutor failed today to secure a verdict, the evil would have been great in a society where so many of the old restraints upon sexual license are denounced and derided.

. . . I stake my reputation on the assertion that the book is neither obscene nor indecent. It would be less dangerous if it were so. However, so far as the public is concerned, the book has ceased to exist, and I think we might distribute our thanks between editor, publisher and Home Secretary without looking too closely into the share of praise earned by each.

What astonished me was that a great novelist like Mr. Arnold Bennett, and many, if not most, of the reviewers of serious newspapers should have praised the author and her work. That Miss Radclyffe Hall is a finished performer with her pen everybody who has read any of her novels will ungrudgingly admit. And "The Well of Loneliness" is a highly finished performance, for, without an indecent word or an obscene image, it pleads passionately, pathetically, artistically, and at great length, for the admission not only of our compassion, but to our respect, of the votaries of a sexual vice which for twenty centuries has been regarded by western races as an offense "not to be named among Christians." The ground on which these great critics base their praise of Miss Radclyffe Hall appears to be her courage in defending an abnormality which has been widely distributed among both sexes of nearly every race under the sun in varying degrees of intensity ever since the world began. Is that any reason for writing a novel about it? Is "The Well of Loneliness" a novel? It has neither plot nor incidents, except the attempts of a wealthy female "invert" to bend and tutor to her horrible will two normal young women. . . . In fact, the book is not a novel at all, but a clever and audacious piece of propaganda to secure the recognition by the serious world of female inversion or sensual passion between women.

That a large and increasing number of inverts in both sexes exists is an unfortunate fact; but what good can be done by writing so-called novels about it? . . . "The Well of Loneliness" has not been written to curse or cure sexual inversion. It has been written to prove that its practitioners are the inheritors of an unescapable taint, which is true, and that, therefore, they must not be shunned as lepers, but are entitled to a recognized place in the world, which is not true. . . . Is Miss Radclyffe Hall, or anybody else, prepared to put up a serious, emotional defense of homosexuality? It would, of course, be impossible; no publisher would print it. . . .

Much of the hysterical excitement, so powerfully portrayed in "The Well of Loneliness," comes out in the swarming of modern women, in the screaming adoration of certain actresses from the gallery and the pit. That is why such a book is peculiarly mischievous today; and I think the grave and reverend bench of critics might have discerned the danger.

A Truthful Tory

LANCET, SEPTEMBER 1, 1928

The fact that [Oscar Wilde's] "The Picture of Dorian Gray" is now available in cheap editions, while "The Well of Loneliness" has been withdrawn by Messrs. Jonathan Cape at the request of the Home Secretary, suggests that Miss Radcliffe [sic] Hall's book may at some future date be restored to circulation. It is not, of course, comparable in artistic merit with Wilde's work, nor even with Miss Radcliffe Hall's previous novel, but it is an honest attempt to portray the temptations, the emotional conflicts, and the social dilemmas of the homosexual woman. The author has considerable dramatic skill, though her emphasis is sometimes misplaced. The implication that the parents' desire to produce a son may alter the emotional affinities of the daughter born to them is difficult to accept; the origin of abnormal sex attractions cannot be so simply explained. The fallacy of the book lies in the failure to recognize that strong attachments between members of the same sex occur as a phase of normal development. Those who fail to outgrow this phase can be helped to divert their emotions into other channels. If their efforts are ineffectual their life must always be unhappy, for the race is bound to erect such barriers as will discourage the development of affinities dangerous to its existence. This duty is well recognized by Miss Radcliffe Hall. Her book, to which Mr. Havelock Ellis contributes a preface, is certainly not effective as a presentation of the case for social toleration of an abnormal habit of life, nor is there any evidence that the author holds a brief to this end.

LIFE AND LETTERS, OCTOBER, 1928

Rob Miss Radclyffe Hall of her challenging thesis, and her novel would quite naturally slip back into the category to which it belongs; it would rank, that is to say, as a simple, pleasantly written love-story with an unhappy ending. We should remark that the narrative was somewhat redundant, that we could have preferred a briefer account of the inessential part of the hero's life, the shirts, ties, underclothes he bought and the way he decorated his rooms. We should have noticed, on the other hand, that there was a kind of sincerity, an almost painful naivete about the telling which lent it an occasional charm. In fact, however, since the shirted and tailored hero is, so to speak, a hero-heroine, and the later and least successful chapters of the novel are concerned with the woes peculiar to her temperament, with the frequent plea that even female "inverts" self-styled deserve a share of sunshine, etc., "The Well of Loneliness" is likely to raise a different set of issues, foreign to aesthetics and outside the province of this report. It must be sufficient to add that the plea is put forward, half impersonally and half through the mouths of the protagonists, with the curious mixture of diffidence and defiance common to such discussions, the clash of "I can't help being what I am," and "I wouldn't change if I could"; and that, while the first episode of the story is related in a manner comparatively restrained and noncontroversial, the culmination is considerably overweighted, both by sentiment and by sectarian passion.

British Journal of Inebriety, 1928–9

Dr. Havelock Ellis in his sympathetic commendatory note rightly claims that this the first English novel of its kind possesses a notable psychological and sociological significance. It is an able piece of literary work, dealing with a class of exceptional human creatures who through no fault of their own are the subjects of a sex inversion. There is no doubt but that a large number of individuals who live and move and have their being in our community life are more or less homosexual. Medical advisers, educationists, legalists, members of religion, and others whose duties call them to understand and help all who stand in difficult situations, and are seeking to solve psycho-physiological problems relating to human conduct, will do well to consider without prejudice the poignant situation so vividly portrayed with real insight and without offense in Miss Radclyffe Hall's remarkable life-story of a female invert. Miss Radclyffe Hall is a woman of exceptional powers. She is a writer of distinction, having been awarded the "Femina-Vie Heureuse" prize of 1926 for her novel "Adam's Breed." She is also a member of the Council of the Society for Psychical Research, an experienced traveler, an enthusiastic dog-breeder, and takes an earnest interest in the drama. The withdrawal of her latest novel by her publisher at the suggestion of the Home Secretary, acting apparently on the advice of a well-known editor [James Douglas] of a popular daily newspaper, has given rise to considerable discussion. Certainly the suppression of Miss Radclyffe's serious psycho-pathological study without trial or authoritative judgment under an unjustifiable censorship strikes a blow at the liberty of scientific and medico-sociological literature, and will make it increasingly difficult in the future for authors and publishers to deal with certain medico-sociological problems in works of fiction.

❦

The Second Wave

5

"Radclyffe Hall"
(1975)

JANE RULE

I read Radclyffe Hall's *The Well of Loneliness* first when I was fiteen years old. I knew nothing about her real life and not very much about my own, but I was badly frightened. Like Stephen Gordon, the main female character in the book, I was six feet tall. I had broad shoulders and narrow hips, no bosom, and a deep voice. Though I had a feminine interest or two like needlework and collecting miniature animals, I had spent most of my childhood trying to horn in on my older brother's activities, whether it was touch football (when I split open my elbow, my mother sighed for the permanent damage to my feminine future, doomed at six to long-sleeved evening dresses) or fishing trips with my father (who indulgently defended my right to be the youngest and only female even though I was always car sick on the way and rarely caught anything but trees from which I had to be untangled). At twelve I was sent to a girls' school, grateful because I was already too tall, too active, and too bright to make anything but the most grotesque transition into heterosexual adolescence. Among girls I could still take pride in all those attributes my brother could carry into maturity without apology. I didn't want to be a boy, ever, but I was outraged that his height and intelligence were graces for him and gaucheries for me. Since I could not hide the one fault, I decided there was no point in hiding the other. In a girls' school to play basketball and argue the fine points of Latin grammar were not considered abnormal. But in *The Well of Loneliness*, I suddenly discovered that I was a freak, a genetic monster, a member of a third sex, who would eventually call myself by a masculine name (telephone operators were already addressing me as "sir"), wear a necktie, and live in the exile of some European ghetto. I don't remember how I came upon the book in the first place. I was not, in those days, a great reader. I do remember that it radically changed my understanding of my childhood and my perception of the more important friendships in my life at the time.

[. . .]

The Well of Loneliness by Radclyffe Hall, published in 1928, remains *the* lesbian novel, a title familiar to most readers of fiction, either a bible or a horror story for any lesbian who reads at all. There have been other books published since, better written, more accurate according to recent moral and psychological speculation, but none of them has seriously challenged the position of *The Well of Loneliness*. Often a book finds momentary identity only by negative comparison with that "noble, tragic tract about the love that cannot speak its name." Along with the teachings of the church and the moral translations of those teachings by psychologists, *The Well of Loneliness* has influenced millions of readers in their attitudes toward lesbians.

Radclyffe Hall's intention was to write a sympathetic and accurate book about inversion. She was already a novelist and poet of some reputation, and, if she had neither the craft nor the power of insight of her contemporary D. H. Lawrence, she shared his zeal for educating the public. Scientific books were not at that time generally available. Krafft-Ebing's famous *Psychopathia Sexualis* was directed at the medical profession, and details of case studies, like the title, were written in Latin lest the book fall into the wrong hands and corrupt the naive reader. Radclyffe Hall had read Krafft-Ebing, as well as the less well-known studies of Karl Heinrich Ulrichs, himself a homosexual trying to prove that inversion was as natural an orientation as left-handedness. She obviously read not only with a scholar's interest but with a desire to understand herself, a congenital invert in her own eyes whose sexual appetites were satisfied exclusively by women. *The Well of Loneliness* was, therefore, not only a novel intended to give insight into the experience of inverts but also to justify Radclyffe Hall's own life.

She must have been the more pressed to defend the innocence of her nature because she was a Catholic, apparently thoughtfully and deeply committed to most of the doctrines of the Church. She died, after a long struggle with cancer, serene in her belief that she would be only temporarily separated from Una, Lady Troubridge, the woman with whom she had lived for some years. She did not expect that reunion to take place in the appropriate circle of Dante's hell, for, if there was anyone responsible for her nature, it was God, who "in a thoughtless moment had created in His turn, those pitiful thousands who must stand forever outside His blessing."[1] Outside His blessing on earth, she must have rationalized. Or in some way she singled herself out, redeemed by the book she had written in which her last plea is "Acknowledge us, O God, before the whole world. Give us also the right to our existence" (last page). There is no final evidence for how she reconciled her sexual life with her faith. There is only the testimony of those closest to her that she had resolved the conflict for herself.

Emotionally and materially neglected in childhood by a father who deserted her and a mother who was by turns brutal and indifferent, Radclyffe Hall made a strength of her isolation, choosing to live only in her own terms, which were, once she was an adult, bizarre to most of her contemporaries. When she was of legal age and finally had control of the money her father and his family had provided for her, she enjoyed all the privilege and freedom of wealth. She loved riding and the hunt, though finally she gave up killing because she came to pity and identify with the fox. She liked fast cars, traveling, women, and before she settled into a serious relationship with Mabel Veronica Batten, twenty-some years her senior, with whom she lived until Mrs. Batten's death, Radclyffe Hall had probably loved more women than she had read books. Mrs. Batten, not only a great beauty but a very cultivated woman, dedicated herself to civilizing her young lover and encouraging her to write. By the time Una Troubridge met her, Radclyffe Hall was as tamed a creature as she would be, still interested in other passionate involvements but tempered by the self-discipline she had developed to become a writer. She had learned to take herself and her relationships seriously, not as the gentlewoman she was born to be but as the gentleman she had studied to become, through a conventional sowing of wild oats to the settled and convenient double standard of "marriage." Mabel Batten could not tolerate the love affair between Una Troubridge and Radclyffe Hall. In a row with her willful and much younger lover,

Mabel had a heart attack, which, a few weeks later, killed her. The guilt Radclyffe Hall felt led her into spiritualism for a time with the hope that she might contact Mabel and ask forgiveness for herself and Una. She dedicated all her books "To the three of us." Radclyffe Hall's involvement with other women would come to trouble Una, too, but she had either greater patience or a stronger heart and finally survived Radclyffe Hall.

She was known to everyone as John. She wore men's jackets and ties, had a short haircut, and in all manners was gallantly masculine. When she was criticized for calling such attention to herself, she explained that dress was simply an expression of nature, which she could not change, one of the honest ways she faced her inversion. This courage, or blatant exhibitionism according to those who did not approve, made it possible for Radclyffe Hall to contemplate writing *The Wellof Loneliness*. Though there were others of her contemporaries who might have written better books on the subject, Radclyffe Hall was the only one to risk the censure she and the book received.

The Well of Loneliness, with a sympathetic introduction by Havelock Ellis, was published in England and promptly tried for obscenity and banned. In the United States, after a similar decision in the lower courts, an appeal was successful, and the book was available not only there but in France and very soon in other countries as well. Illegal in England, it was nevertheless well known there, too, given so much publicity by the trial. Such important literary figures as Virginia Woolf and E. M. Forster had been willing to testify to its merit, and, while their statements were not admitted as evidence, their petitions and public support helped to give dignity as well as notoriety to the book. In private, they were not wholeheartedly enthusiastic. Virginia Woolf called it a meritorious, dull book. Her own *Orlando* had just been published and greeted as a delightful historical fantasy, a much more tasteful way of dealing with sexuality otherwise offensive. The sex change of Orlando, his/her appetite for both men and women, the dedication of the book to Vita Sackville-West, and the appearance of photographs of Vita Sackville-West in the book as representations of Orlando caused no scandal. Nor did the happy holiday Virginia Woolf and Vita Sackville-West took soon afterward alone together on the Continent. They were safely married women, who dressed and behaved like women, in public anyway. E. M. Forster, whose own homosexual novel, *Maurice*, had been written some years earlier but was not published until after his death in 1971, admitted to Virginia Woolf that he found lesbians disgusting. Though he had no interest in women himself, he did not like to think of them living independent of men. Radclyffe Hall could not have been a more offensive model to him.

The attitudes of these two important members of the Bloomsbury group, whose general liberality and lack of convention were well known, are indications of how brave or foolhardy an act writing *The Well of Loneliness* was. Sexuality was a subject of intense interest and speculation to the intellectuals of Bloomsbury, the concern of many letters, poems, and plays written for their own entertainment. But even Lytton Strachey, whose buggery was notorious, maintained relationships most important to him with men who would not have him and women in whom he was not sexually interested. He at one time proposed to Virginia Woolf and lived the last years of his life with the adoring Carrington, who was like a daughter to him. Gossip, bawdy jokes, and flights of inventive fantasy were Bloomsbury's way of dealing with bisexuality or inversion.

They were not prepared to deal publicly with sexual tastes nearly universally described as a sign of regression or degeneracy. Virginia and Leonard Woolf were the English publishers of Freud. If they were morally permissive, they were all of them psychologically ambivalent about themselves. They were Radclyffe Hall's brave allies (the Woolfs would have stood bail, not understanding at first that it was the book and not the author on trial), but they were not her friends, nor could they have been. She was too outlandish, too earnest, and too little gifted. There was nothing ambivalent about her at all.

Though Stephen Gordon, the main character in *The Well of Loneliness*, shares few of Radclyffe Hall's own experiences, she is Radclyffe Hall's idealized mirror. Both recognized from childhood their essential difference from other females. Both had early emotional ties with female servants. Both were fine horsewomen and successful writers. Neither had any erotic interest in men. Both affected the same masculine style and manners. But Radclyffe Hall gave Stephen basic securities she herself lacked, a father who loved and understood her, a childhood on a fine estate, good health, and a sound education. Stephen was also very tall, a mark of masculine power and beauty Radclyffe Hall probably envied, though it is said of her that she always gave the impression of being a good deal taller than she was. Of all the good fortunes they did not share, Stephen's opportunity to serve

England in the war was in Radclyffe Hall's eyes the greatest because she was a patriot and did not indulge in the political sophistication and skepticism of other more intelligent and subtle minds of her generation. Yet the one great blessing of Radclyffe Hall's own life, the faithful love of both Mabel Batten and Una Troubridge, she did not allow Stephen, who is required to give up the woman she loves to a man who can provide the protection and social acceptance Stephen can never offer. Stephen's final selfless gesture is undoubtedly calculated to strengthen reader sympathy, to allay moral doubts, and to deepen the tragedy of inversion. But for Radclyffe Hall herself, neither God nor man could interfere with her sexual life. She was not of a temperament for such a sacrifice.

A canny propagandist in plotting an unhappy ending, Radclyffe Hall also worked hard to provide a background of psychological information, intended to deepen understanding and acceptance for her main character. The books of both Karl Heinrich Ulrichs and Krafft-Ebing are in Mr. Gordon's library, and it is from them that he learns to understand and help his only and beloved child. Ulrichs not only argues that inversion is congenital and natural, but also that legal and social recognition should be given such sexual love, permission to marry granted to people of the same sex. Krafft-Ebing, taking issue with Ulrichs, grants that some inversion is congenital but insists that the cause is pathological rather than physiological, traceable in every case to inherited degeneracy. The family histories he offers are full of cases of insanity of one sort or another. Though he makes a strong plea for humane treatment of such people, since they cannot help their condition and cannot be cured of it (nor indeed do many of them even express a desire to be cured, one of the symptoms of their pathology being their view of themselves as natural), he is not so tolerant of acquired inversion, which is caused, he thinks, by excessive masturbation, isolation from the opposite sex, a conscious choice of vice. Sexual behavior of the conditioned invert is immoral. While Krafft-Ebing sees in this condition much more to blame, he also has a greater hope of cure. It is clear that, though Radclyffe Hall took a great deal of information from Krafft-Ebing, she is on Ulrichs' side of the argument.

Stephen must be established as a congenital invert to escape Krafft-Ebing's moral condemnation. There is no sign of insanity in Stephen's family history. The only causes of inversion are obviously physiological. Stephen is broad-shouldered, slim-hipped, unusually tall, with a striking resemblance to her father. That she is not unique is carefully underlined in the physical descriptions of a group of inverts she meets in Paris. "One had to look twice to discern that her ankles were too strong and too heavy for those of a female" (350). Or "one might have said a quite womanly woman, unless the trained ear had been rendered suspicious by her voice . . . a boy's voice on the verge of breaking" (351). Not trusting the reader to take this evidence alone, Radclyffe Hall makes general assertions about inverts, calling them "those who, through no fault of their own, have been set apart from the day of their birth" (389). Or she lets Stephen's tutor, a repressed invert herself, say to Stephen, "You're neither unnatural, nor abominable, nor mad; you're as much a part of what people call nature as anyone else; only you're unexplained as yet—you've not got your niche in creation" (154). Stephen is described as "like some primitive thing conceived in a turbulent age of transition" (52). Stephen's father wanted a son, then christened his female child Stephen, but these facts are offered not so much as suggestive of conditioning as some deep insight of his own into the real nature of his child.

Society's attitude toward the invert is presented by Stephen's mother, who is from the first offended and repelled by a child she does not understand. She objects to her husband's desire to raise Stephen as if she were a boy, but he, in what is presented as his real wisdom, overrules her. Stephen is allowed to ride horseback astride. She is encouraged in masculine virtues. Her father says, "And now I'm going to treat you like a boy, and a boy must always be brave. I'm not going to pretend as though you were a coward" (29). Later, when he feels her education is being neglected, he says, "You're brave and stronglimbed, but I want you to be wise" (61). In giving Stephen so unusually supportive a father, Radclyffe Hall is insisting that the accepted invert grows into a fine, moral person who can survive even the rejection of a mother. After her father's death, her mother discovers Stephen in an affair with a married woman in the neighborhood. "And this thing that you are is a sin against nature" (200). How accurately Radclyffe Hall anticipated the attitude of many of the critics when the book appeared, who would have liked to drive her into silence as Stephen is forced to leave her home, which has meant so much to her, able to take only her loyal and understanding tutor with her.

The husband of the woman Stephen so unwisely loved is given speeches like, "How's your freak getting on? . . . Good Lord, it's enough to make any man see red; that sort of thing wants putting down at birth, I'd like to institute state lethal chambers" (151). But his viciousness is seen as part of his general incapacity as a man.

Men, in *The Well of Loneliness*, are capable of the highest courage and insight. Stephen's father is "all kindness, all strength, all understanding" (42). Martin, the young man who befriends Stephen and then unfortunately falls in love with her, has "a man's life, good with the goodness of danger, a primitive, strong, imperative thing" (102). In him Stephen feels she has found a brother. "He spoke simply, as one man will speak to another, very simply, not trying to create an impression" (92). And Stephen has "longed for the companionship of men, for their friendship, their good will, their understanding" (96). When Stephen rejects Martin, she unwittingly rejects the tentative acceptance of the community which has developed during the period of their friendship. "He it was who had raised her status among them—he, the stranger, not even connected with their country. . . . Suddenly Stephen longed intensely to be welcomed and she wished in her heart that she could have married Martin" (108). Years later, when he appears again in Stephen's life and falls in love with Mary, the young woman Stephen herself loves and lives with, Stephen recognizes his superior power, as a man, to protect Mary. "I cannot protect you, Mary, the world has deprived me of my right to protect; I am utterly helpless, I can only love you" (303). Her father has taught her all the male virtues, "courage and truth and honor," and she rejects their vices, "Men—they were selfish, arrogant, possessive," perhaps as much because she has no social right to them as because she finds them morally repugnant (127; 300). Without those vices, she has no choice but to become a martyr to her love.

Though Stephen cannot claim social equality with men, in some ways she sees herself as superior to them, not only in rejecting their vices but in having the curious virtues of ambivalent sex. "She seemed to combine the strength of a man with the gentler and more subtle strength of a woman" (177). "Those whom nature has sacrificed to her own ends—her mysterious ends which sometimes lie hidden—are sometimes endowed with a vast will to loving, with an endless capacity for suffering also" (146). "But the intuition of those who stand midway between the two sexes is so ruthless, so poignant, so accurate, so deadly as to be in the nature of an added scourge" (83). Echoing Krafft-Ebing, Radclyffe Hall claims also for the congenital invert remarkable intelligence, great passion, and intense religious feeling.

Stephen was born on Christmas Eve. Radclyffe Hall followed *The Well of Loneliness* with a novel about a contemporary Christ with whom she felt it easy to identify after her own social crucifixion. During the writing of it, stigmata appeared on the palms of her own hands.

Neither she nor Stephen ever identifies with other women. Stephen's first love, Collins, the second maid, is a stupid, dishonest creature whom the child, Stephen, can forgive anything "since despising, she could still love her" (18). "I'd like to be hurt for you, Collins, the way that Jesus was for sinners" (21). Stephen's mother is loved by her father because she is restful, beautiful, passive. Stephen's own effort to make a relationship with her mother is protective and courtly. Stephen's tutor is made a sad example of. "She was what came from higher education—a lonely, unfulfilled middle-aged spinster" (111). When Stephen first falls seriously in love with a married woman, Angela is described as "idle, discontented, and bored and certainly not overburdened with virtue." She "listened, assuming an interest she was very far from feeling" (143). Mary, the lover for whom Stephen sacrifices her own happiness, "because she was perfect woman, would rest without thought, without exultation, without question, finding no need to question since for her there was now only one thing—Stephen" (314). "Mary, all woman, was less a match for life than if she had been as was Stephen" (423). Devoted to Stephen, subservient, with all wifely virtues, she cannot stand the social isolation of her life with Stephen, would have grown bitter at the judgments Stephen has the strength to rise above, for she has no work of her own as Stephen does, no identity of her own. She is simply a woman.

Occasionally Stephen does crave to be normal. "While despising these girls, she yet longed to be like them," but these are only moments of despair when she feels rejected in the company of men who have a preference for "killing ivy" (76; 77). Much more often, she longs to be a man, to take her natural and superior place among those of the sex she admires. Radclyffe Hall even asserts that Stephen "found her manhood," though always she knows that, trapped in a female body, she is a freak, and in the final contest between Stephen and Martin, even the dog can tell that Martin is the true man. Stephen has nothing left now but her work. "She must show that being the thing that she was, she could climb to success over all opposition," but she will go on being plagued by the doubt, "I shall never be a great writer because of my maimed and insufferable body" (202; 253; 217).

If Radclyffe Hall were alive today and writing *The Well of Loneliness*, how much of the detail would convince anyone that Stephen is congenitally different, except perhaps in her sexual tastes? On the sexual market, it is still better to be narrower-shouldered, broader-hipped, and shorter than Stephen, but those "defects" would not convince anyone that a woman is a born invert. And though intelligent women are still a threat to some men, no one would see in intelligence a signal for diagnosing inversion. As for the freedom of behavior Stephen craved, there isn't a woman today who doesn't prefer trousers and pockets for many activities, and only the Queen of England still occasionally appears in public riding sidesaddle. If few women have desired a masculine name in private, a great many have used male pseudonyms in order to win honor for their work in public.

Even in 1928 Vera Brittain commented in an otherwise generous review of the book.... [Here, Rule quotes approvingly and at length Brittain's criticism of the bifurcated sex roles in *The Well of Loneliness*; see this volume pp. 58–60.][2]

Obviously Radclyffe Hall so accepted that very teaching of her class and time she could not imagine a woman who wanted the privilege and power of men unless she was a freak.

Though *The Well of Loneliness* was viciously attacked for its sympathetic idealizing of the invert, giving it greater importance at the time than it deserved, its survival as the single authoritative novel on lesbian love depends on its misconceptions. It supports the view that men are naturally superior, that, given a choice, any woman would prefer a real man unless she herself is a congenital freak. Though inept and feminine men are criticized, though some are seen to abuse the power they have, their right to that power is never questioned. Stephen does not defy the social structure she was born into. Male domination is intolerable to her only when she can't assert it for herself. Women are inferior. Loving relationships must be between superior and inferior persons. Stephen's sexual rejection of Martin, though it is offered as conclusive proof of her irreversible inversion, is basically a rejection of being the inferior partner in a relationship. Her reaction is one of "repulsion—terror and repulsion ... a look of outrage" (98). In her relationship with Mary, Stephen is "all things to Mary; father, mother, friend and lover, all things, and Mary is all things to her— the child, the friend, the beloved, all things" (314). The repetition of "all things" is not persuasive enough to cover the inequality of the categories. When Stephen decides not to fight for Mary, she gives her to Martin much as one would give any other thing one owns. And though her altruism is sometimes associated with her female gender, it is more often likened to the virtues of Christ. It is courageous or foolhardy for a woman to behave like a man, but, since she accepts herself as a freak, since in fiction if not in life she is made to give up the ultimate prize, she is no political threat to anyone. The natural order of things is reasserted, and she is left on the outside, calling to God and to society for recognition.

[Donald] Cory, in *The Lesbian in American Society*, claims that "the lesbian stereotype is almost completely absent from any world of reality. Many people never meet her outside the pages of *The Well of Loneliness*."[3] If he means that, in the real world, there are few talented, successful, independently wealthy women who are free to lay claim to the world of masculine privilege in just the way Radclyffe Hall and her creation Stephen Gordon do, he is right, but, if he means there are no women who have taken on the style and manner of men, he is wrong. Admittedly, it isn't easy today to know what styles and manners are associated with one sex rather than the other, but it is still possible. Phyllis Lyon and Del Martin comment in *Lesbian/Woman* about *The Well of Loneliness* saying that it became "the Lesbian bible." "Unfortunately, to the uninitiated the book perpetuated the myth of the Lesbian as a pseudomale, and many young women, like Del, emulated the heroine, Stephen Gordon."[4] Others have read the book without so easy an identification, but, if they carefully avoid male role-playing, they are still left with the resentment of their political inferiority and their love of other women, with the fear that to the "discerning eye" any minor characteristic could identify them as freaks.

Radclyffe Hall was a courageous woman, and *The Well of Loneliness* is an important book because it does so carefully reveal the honest misconceptions about women's nature and experience which have limited and crippled so many people. Radclyffe Hall did think of herself as a freak, but emotionally and intellectually she was far more a "womanly woman" than many of her literary contemporaries. She worshiped the very institutions which oppressed her, the Church and the patriarchy, which have taught women there are only two choices, inferiority or perversion. Inside that framework, she made and tried to redefine the only proud choice she had. The "bible" she offered is really no better for women than the Bible she would not reject.

Notes

1. Radclyffe Hall, *The Well of Loneliness* (New York: Pocket Books, 1950), p. 188. Subsequent references to this novel will be noted parenthetically in the text.
2. Vera Brittain, *Radclyffe Hall, A Case of Obscenity* (London: A Femina Book, 1968), pp. 50–51.
3. Donald Cory, *The Lesbian in American Society* (New York: Macfadden-Bartell, 1965), p. 23.
4. Del Martin and Phyllis Lyon, *Lesbian/Woman* (San Francisco: Glide Publications, 1972), p. 22.

6

"The Mythic Mannish Lesbian:
Radclyffe Hall and the New Woman"
(1989)

ESTHER NEWTON

I hate games! I hate role-playing! It's so ludicrous that certain lesbians, who despise men, become the exact replicas of them!
> —*Anonymous interview in the* Gay Report, *ed. Karla Jay and Allan Young*

Thinking, acting, or looking like a man contradicts lesbian feminism's first principle: The lesbian is a "woman-identified woman."[1] What to do, then, with that figure referred to, in various times and circumstances, as the "mannish lesbian," the "true invert," the "bull dagger," or the "butch"? You see her in old photographs or paintings with legs solidly planted, wearing a top hat and a man's jacket, staring defiantly out of the frame, her hair slicked back or clipped over her ears; or you meet her on the street in t-shirt and boots, squiring a brassily elegant woman.

Out of sight, out of mind! "Butch and femme are gone," declares one lesbian author, with more hope than truth.[2] And what about those old photographs? Was the mannish lesbian a myth created by "the [male] pornographic mind"[3] or by male sexologists intent on labeling nineteenth-century feminists as deviant? Maybe the old photographs portray a few misguided souls—or perhaps those "premovement" women thought men's neckties were pretty and practical.

In the nineteenth century and before, individual women passed as men by dressing and acting like them for a variety of economic, sexual, and adventure-seeking reasons. Many of these women were from the working class.[4] Public, *partial* cross-dressing among bourgeois women was a late-nineteenth-century development. Earlier isolated instances of partial cross-dressing seem to have been associated with explicit feminism (e.g., French writer George Sand and American physician Mary Walker), although most nineteenth-century feminists wore traditional women's clothing. From the last years of the century, cross-dressing was increasingly associated with "sexual inversion" by the medical profession. Did the doctors invent or merely describe the mannish lesbian? Either way, what did this mythic figure signify, and to whom?

At the center of this problem is British author Radclyffe Hall (1880–1943).[5] Without question, the most infamous mannish lesbian, Stephen Gordon, protagonist of *The Well of Loneliness* (1928), was created not by a male pornographer, sexologist, legislator, or novelist, but by Hall, herself an "out" and tie-wearing lesbian. And *The Well*, at least until 1970, was *the* lesbian novel.[6] Why is it that *The Well* rather than all the other lesbian novels became famous?

Embarrassed by Radclyffe Hall but unable to wish her away, sometimes even hoping to reclaim her, our feminist scholars have lectured, excused, or patronized her.[7] Radclyffe Hall, they declare, was an unwitting dupe of the misogynist doctors' attack on feminist romantic friendships. Or, cursed with a pessimistic temperament and brainwashed by Catholicism, Hall parroted society's condemnation of lesbians. The "real" Radclyffe Hall lesbian novel, the argument frequently continues, the one that *ought* to have been famous, is her first, *The Unlit Lamp* (1924). Better yet, Virginia Woolf's *Orlando* (1928) *should* have been the definitive lesbian novel. Or Natalie Barney's work. Or anything but *The Well*.[8]

Heterosexual conservatives condemn *The Well* for defending the lesbian's right to exist. Lesbian feminists condemn it for presenting lesbians as different from women in general. But *The Well* has continued to have meaning to lesbians because it confronts the stigma of lesbianism—as most lesbians have had to live it. Maybe Natalie Barney, with her fortune and her cast-iron ego, or married Virginia Woolf, were able to transcend the patriarchy, but most lesbians have had to face being called, or at least feeling like, freaks. As the Bowery bum represents all that is most feared and despised about drunkenness, the mannish lesbian, of whom Stephen Gordon is the most famous prototype, has symbolized the stigma of lesbianism (just as the effeminate man is the stigma-bearer for gay men) and so continues to move a broad range of lesbians.[9] A second reason for *The Well*'s continuing impact, which I will explore briefly at the close of this essay, is that Stephen Gordon articulated a gender orientation with which an important minority of lesbians still actively identify, and toward which another minority is erotically attracted.

By "mannish lesbian" (a term I use because it, rather than the contemporary "butch," belongs to the time period in question) I mean a figure who is defined as lesbian because her behavior or dress (and usually both) manifest elements designated as exclusively masculine. From about 1900 on, this cross-gender figure became the public symbol of the new social/sexual category "lesbian." Some of our feminist historians deplore the emergence of the mannish lesbian, citing her association with the medical model of pathology. For them, the nineteenth century becomes a kind of lesbian Golden Age, replete with loving, innocent feminist couples.[10] From the perspective of Radclyffe Hall's generation, however, nineteenth-century models may have seemed more confining than liberating. I will argue that Hall and many other feminists like her embraced, sometimes with ambivalence, the image of the mannish lesbian and the discourse of the sexologists about inversion primarily because they desperately wanted to break out of the asexual model of romantic friendship. Two questions emerge from this statement of the problem. First, why did twentieth-century women whose primary social and intimate interest was other women wish their relationships to become explicitly sexual? Second, why did the figure of the mannish lesbian play the central role in this development?

The structure and ideology of the bourgeois woman's gender-segregated world in the nineteenth century have been convincingly described.[11] As British and American women gained access to higher education and the professions, they did so in all-female institutions and in relationships with one another that were intense, passionate, and committed. These romantic friendships characterized the first generation of "New Women"—such as Jane Addams, Charlotte Perkins Gilman, and Mary Wooley—who were born in the 1850s and 1860s, educated in the 1870s and 1880s, and flourished from the 1890s through the First World War. They sought personal and economic independence by rejecting their mothers' domestic roles. The goal of the battle to be autonomous was to stay single *and* to separate from the family sphere. They turned to romantic friendships as the alternative, and replicated the female world of love and commitment in the new institutional settings of colleges and settlement houses.

Whether or not these women touched each other's genitals or had orgasms together, two things seem clear: Their relationships were a quasi-legitimate alternative to heterosexual marriage, and the participants did not describe them in the acknowledged sexual language—medical, religious, or pornographic—of the nineteenth century. Letters between romantic friends exhibit no shame, in an era when lust was considered dirty and gross. On the contrary, the first generation had nothing to hide because their passionate outpourings were seen by others, and apparently by themselves, as pure and ennobling.

The bourgeois woman's sexuality proper was confined to its reproductive function; the uterus was its organ. But as for lust, "The major current in Victorian sexual ideology declared that women were passionless and asexual, the passive objects of male sexual desire."[12] Most bourgeois women and men believed that only males and déclassée women were sexual. Sex was seen as phallic, by which I mean that, conceptually, sex could only occur in the presence of an imperial and imperious penis. The low status of working women and women of color, as well as their participation in the public sphere, deprived them of the feminine purity that protected bourgeois women from males and from deriving sexual pleasure. But what "pure" women did with each other, no matter how good it felt, could not be conceived as sexual within the terms of the dominant nineteenth-century romantic paradigm. Insofar as first-generation feminists were called sexual deviants, it was because they used their minds at the expense of their reproductive organs.

The second generation of New Women were born in the 1870s and 1880s and came of age during the opening decades of the twentieth century. This was an extraordinarily distinguished group. Among them we count critics of the family and political radicals Margaret Sanger and Crystal Eastman; women drawn to new artistic fields, such as Berenice Abbot and Isadora Duncan; and lesbian writers such as Gertrude Stein, Willa Cather, Margaret Anderson, Natalie Barney, and Radclyffe Hall. For them, autonomy from family was, if not a given, emphatically a right. Hall's first novel, *The Unlit Lamp* (1924; hereafter called *The Lamp*), is a sympathetic analysis of the first generation from the perspective of the second. The novel portrays a devouring mother using the kinship claims of the female world to crush her daughter's legitimate bid for autonomy.[13]

Hall uses the family in *The Lamp* to symbolize society, the imposition of traditional gender divisions, and the subjugation of female fulfillment to traditional bourgeois norms. The family stands for bourgeois proprieties: proper dress, stifling garden parties, provincial gossip. Fearful of alternatives, uncreative and unimaginative, the mother seeks to bind her daughter to an equally banal and confining life. Conversely, Hall uses a masculinized body and a strong, active mind to symbolize women's rejection of traditional gender divisions and bourgeois values. Joan Ogden, the protagonist, wants to be a doctor. Her mind is swift, intelligent, her body large, strong, healthy. Although Hall does not strongly develop male body and clothing imagery in *The Lamp*, in a momentous confrontation near the novel's conclusion, masculine clothing is unambiguously used to symbolize assertiveness and modernity. Second-generation women are described as "not at all self-conscious in their tailor-made clothes, not ashamed of their cropped hair; women who did things well, important things . . . smart, neatly put together women, *looking like well bred young men*" (emphasis mine). When two such women see Joan, now faded and failed, they ridicule her old-fashioned appearance: "'Have you seen that funny old thing with the short gray hair?' . . . 'Wasn't she killing? Why moire ribbon instead of a proper necktie?' . . . 'I believe she's what they used to call a New Woman,' said the girl in breeches, with a low laugh. 'Honey, she's a forerunner, a kind of pioneer that's got left behind. I believe she's the beginning of things like me.'"[14]

There is no explicit discussion of sexuality. Joan tells a male suitor, "I've never been what you'd call in love with a man in my life" (p. 302), without a trace of embarrassment. Joan's passionate relationship with another woman is described in the traditional language of sentiment, never in a language of lust.

For many women of Radclyffe Hall's generation, sexuality—for itself and as a symbol of female autonomy—became a preoccupation. These women were, after all, the "sisters" of D. H. Lawrence and James Joyce. For male novelists, sexologists, and artists rebelling against Victorian values, sexual freedom became the cutting edge of modernism. Bourgeois women like Hall had a different relation to modernist sexual freedom, for in the Victorian terms of the first generation, they had no sexual identity to express. Women of the second generation who wished to join the modernist discourse and be twentieth-century adults had to radically reconceive themselves.

That most New Women of the first generation resented and feared such a development, I do not doubt. But many women of the second welcomed it, cautiously or with naive enthusiasm. (One has only to think of Virginia

Woolf's thrilled participation in Bloomsbury to see what I mean.) They wanted not simply male professions but access to the broader world of male opportunity. They drank, they smoked, they rejected traditional feminine clothing, lived as expatriates, and freely entered heterosexual liaisons, sometimes with such disastrous results as alcoholism, mental illness, and suicide. Modernism and the new sex ideas entailed serious contradictions for women,[15] who, no matter what their hopes, could not behave like men on equal terms; unwanted pregnancy and "bad" reputations were only two of the hazards from which men were exempt. Yet many women eagerly took up the challenge. This was what first-generation women had won for the second—the tenuous right to try out the new ideas such as psychoanalysis and sexual freedom and participate in the great social movements of the day.

It was in the first two decades of the twentieth century in Britain, with perhaps a ten-year lag in the United States, that, due to external attack and internal fission, the old feminist movement began to split along the heterosexual/homosexual divide that is ancestral to our own. If women were to develop a lustful sexuality, with whom and in what social context were they to express it? The male establishment, of course, wanted women to be lusty with men. A basic tenet of sexual modernism was that "normal" women had at least reactive heterosexual desire.[16] The sex reformers attacked Victorian gender segregation and promoted the new idea of companionate marriage in which both women's and men's heterosexual desires were to be satisfied.[17] Easier association with men quickly sexualized the middle-class woman, and by the 1920s the flapper style reflected the sexual ambience of working-class bars and dance halls. The flapper flirted with being "cheap" and "fast," words that had clear sexual reference.

But what of the women who did not become heterosexual, who remained stubbornly committed to intragender intimacy? A poignant example is furnished by Frances Wilder, an obscure second-generation feminist.[18] Wilder had inherited the orthodox first-generation views. In a 1912 letter to the radical *Freewoman*, she advocated self-restraint, denouncing the new morality for encouraging the "same degrading laxity in sex matters which is indulged in by most of the lower animals including man." She herself, aged twenty-seven, had "always practiced abstinence" with no adverse effects. But just three years later she was writing desperately to homosexual radical Edward Carpenter: "I have recently read with much interest your book entitled The Intermediate Sex & it has lately dawned on me that I myself belong to that class & I write to ask if there is any way of getting in touch with others of the same temperament" (p. 930). Wilder was aware of the price tag on the new ideas. "The world would say that a physical relationship between two of the same sex is an unspeakable crime," she admits, but gamely reasons, that, because of the "economic slavery" of women, "*normal sex*" is "*more* degrading."

The New Woman's social field was opening up, becoming more complex, and potentially lonelier. Thus, along with their desire to be modern, our bourgeois lesbian ancestors had another powerful reason to embrace change. Before they could find one another in the twentieth-century urban landscape, they had to become visible, at least to each other. They needed a new vocabulary built on the radical idea that women apart from men could have autonomous sexual feeling.

"I just concluded that I had . . . a dash of the masculine (I have been told more than once that I have a masculine mind . . .)," Frances Wilder had confessed to Carpenter in 1915, explaining her "strong desire to caress & fondle" a female friend.[19] Like most important historical developments, the symbolic fusion of gender reversal and homosexuality was overdetermined. God Himself had ordained gender hierarchy and heterosexuality at the Creation. The idea that men who had sex with other men were like women was not new. But in the second half of the nineteenth century, the emerging medical profession gave scientific sanction to tradition; homosexual behavior, the doctors agreed, was both symptom and cause of male effeminacy. The masculine female invert was perhaps an analogous afterthought. Yet the mannish lesbian proved a potent persona to both the second generation of New Women and their antifeminist enemies. Her image came to dominate the discourse about female homosexuality, particularly in England and America, for two reasons. First, because sexual desire was not considered inherent in women, the lesbian was endowed with a trapped male soul that phallicized her, giving her active lust. Second, gender reversal became a powerful symbol of feminist aspirations, positive for many female modernists, negative for males, both conservative and modernist.[20]

It was Richard von Krafft-Ebing who articulated the fusion of masculinity, feminist aspirations, and lesbianism that became, and largely remains, an article of faith in Anglo-American culture.[21] Krafft-Ebing categorized lesbians into four increasingly deviant and masculine types.[22] The first category of lesbians included women who "did not betray their anomaly by external appearance or by mental [masculine] sexual characteristics." They were, however, responsive to the approaches of women who appeared or acted more masculine. The second classification included women with a "strong preference for male garments." By the third stage "inversion" was "fully developed, the woman [assuming] a definitely masculine role." The fourth state represented "the extreme grade of degenerative homosexuality. The woman of this type," Krafft-Ebing explained, "possesses of the feminine qualities only the genital organs; thought, sentiment, action, even external appearance are those of the man."[23] Not only was the most degenerate lesbian the most masculine, but any gender-crossing or aspiration to male privilege was probably a symptom of lesbianism. In these pathological souls, "The consciousness of being a woman and thus to be deprived of the gay college life, or to be barred out from the military career, produces painful reflections."[24] In fact, lesbianism is a congenital form of lust caused by and manifested in gender reversal, as Krafft-Ebing makes clear in discussing one "case": "Even in her earliest childhood she preferred playing at soldiers and other boys' games; she was bold and tom-boyish and tried even to excel her little companions of the other sex . . . [After puberty] her dreams were of a lascivious nature, only about females, with herself in the role of the man . . . She was quite conscious of her pathological conditions. Masculine features, deep voice, manly gait, without beard, small breasts; cropped her hair short and made the impression of a man in woman's clothes."[25] Krafft-Ebing was so convinced of his thesis that the woman's most feminine feature—"without beard"—is lined up with the masculine traits as if they all prove the same point.

Havelock Ellis simplified Krafft-Ebing's four-part typology,[26] but retained an ascending scale of inversion, beginning with women involved in "passionate friendships" in which "no congenital inversion is usually involved" and ending with the "actively inverted woman." Ellis's discussion of the former was devastating; it turned the value that first-generation feminists had placed on passionate friendships upside down. A "sexual enthusiast,"[27] he saw these "rudimentary sexual relationships" as more symptomatic of female sexual ignorance and repression than of spiritual values. At the same time, his inclusion of such friendships in a discussion of inversion inevitably marked them with the stigma of "abnormality."

When Ellis got to the hard-core inverts, he was confounded by his contradictory beliefs. He wanted to construct the lesbian couple on the heterosexual model, as a "man" and a woman invert. But his antifeminism and reluctance to see active lust in women committed him to fusing inversion and masculinity. What to do with the feminine invert? His solution was an awkward compromise:

> A class of women to be first mentioned . . . is formed by the women to whom the actively inverted woman is most attracted. These women differ in the first place from the normal or average woman in that they are not repelled or disgusted by lover-like advances from persons of their own sex. . . . Their faces may be plain or ill-made but not seldom they possess good figures, a point which is apt to carry more weight with the inverted woman than beauty of face . . . they are of strongly affectionate nature . . . and *they are always womanly* [emphasis mine]. One may perhaps say that they are the pick of the women whom the average man would pass by. No doubt this is often the reason why they are open to homosexual advances, but I do not think it is the sole reason. So far as they may be said to constitute a class they seem to possess a genuine, though not precisely sexual, preference for women over men.[28]

This extraordinary mix of fantasy, conjecture, and insight clashes with Ellis's insistence that "the chief characteristic of the sexually inverted woman is a certain degree of masculinity."[29] No mention is made of "congenital" factors in regard to this "womanly" invert, and like most examples that do not fit pet paradigms, she is dropped. Gender reversal is not always homosexual, Ellis contends, exempting certain "mannish women" who wear men's clothes out of pragmatic motives, but the "actively inverted woman" always has "a more or less distinct trace of masculinity" as "part of an organic instinct."[30] Because of her firm muscles, athletic ability, dislike of feminine occupations, and predilection for male garments "because the wearer feels more at home in them," the sexually inverted woman, people feel, "ought to have been a man."[31]

Thus the true invert was a being between categories, neither man nor woman, a "third sex" or "trapped soul." Krafft-Ebing, Ellis, and Freud all associated this figure with female lust and with feminist revolt against traditional roles, toward which they were at best ambivalent, at worst horrified.[32] But some second-generation feminists, such as Frances Wilder, Gertrude Stein, and Vita Sackville-West, identified with important aspects of the "third sex" persona. None did so as unconditionally and—this must be said—as bravely as Radclyffe Hall did by making the despised mannish lesbian the hero of *The Well of Loneliness*, which she defended publicly against the British government. Hall's creation, Stephen Gordon, is a double symbol, standing for the New Woman's painful position between traditional political and social categories and for the lesbian struggle to define and assert an identity.

Even newborn, Stephen's body achieves a biologically impossible masculinity: "Narrow-hipped and wide shouldered" (p. 13).[33] She grows and her body becomes "splendid," "supple," "quick"; she can "fence like a man"; she discovers "her body for a thing to be cherished . . . since its strength could rejoice her" (p. 58). But as she matures, her delight degenerates into angst. She is denied male privilege, of course, in spite of her masculine body. But her physical self is also fleshly symbol of the femininity Stephen categorically rejects. Her body is not and cannot be male; yet it is not traditionally female. Between genders and thus illegitimate, it represents Every New Woman, stifled after World War I by a changed political climate and reinforced gender stereotypes. But Hall also uses a body between genders to symbolize the "inverted" sexuality Stephen can neither disavow nor satisfy. Finding herself "no match" for a male rival, the adolescent Stephen begins to hate herself. In one of Hall's most moving passages Stephen expresses this hatred as alienation from her body:

> That night she stared at herself in the glass; and even as she did so, she hated her body with its muscular shoulders, its small compact breasts, and its slender flanks of an athlete. All her life she must drag this body of hers like a monstrous fetter imposed on her spirit. This strangely ardent yet sterile body. . . . She longed to maim it, for it made her feel cruel . . . her eyes filled with tears and her hate turned to pity. She began to grieve over it, touching her breasts with pitiful fingers . . . (p. 187)

Stephen's difference, her overt sexuality, is also represented by cross-dressing. But if male writers used cross-dressing to symbolize and castigate a world upside down, while Virginia Woolf and other female modernists used it to express "gleeful skepticism" toward gender categories,[34] Stephen's cross-dressing asserts a series of agonizing estrangements. She is alienated from her mother, as the New Woman often was, and as the lesbian was, increasingly, from heterosexual women. Unlike Orlando, Stephen is trapped in history; she cannot declare gender an irrelevant game. She, like many young women then and now, alternately rebels against her mother's vision of womanhood and blames herself for failing to live up to it. Preferring suits from her father's tailor, she sometimes gives in to her mother's demand that she wear "delicate dresses," which she puts on "all wrong." Her mother confirms Stephen's sense of freakishness: "It's my face," Stephen announces, "something's wrong with my face." "Nonsense!" her mother replies, "turning away quickly to hide her expression" (p. 73). Cross-dressing for Hall is not a masquerade. It stands for the New Woman's rebellion against the male order and, at the same time, for the lesbian's desperate struggle to be and express her true self.

Hall, like the sexologists, uses cross-dressing and gender reversal to symbolize lesbian sexuality. Unlike the sexologists, however, Hall makes Stephen the subject and takes her point of view against a hostile world. Though men resent Stephen's "unconscious presumption," Hall defends Stephen's claim to what is, in her fictional universe, the ultimate male privilege: the enjoyment of women's erotic love. The mythic mannish lesbian proposes to usurp the son's place in the oedipal triangle.[35]

Hall had begun to describe what I take to be a central component of lesbian orientation, mother/daughter eroticism,[36] several years earlier in *The Unlit Lamp*, where presumably the nonsexual framework of the novel as a whole had made it safe.[37] I write "eroticism" because sexual desire is distinct from either "identification" or "bonding." A woman can be close to her mother ("bond," "identify") in many ways and yet eroticize only men. Conversely, one can hate one's mother and have little in common with her, as did Radclyffe Hall, and yet desire her fiercely in the image of other women. In my view, feminist psychology has not yet solved the riddle of sexual orientation.

As bold as Hall was, she could not treat mother/daughter eroticism directly in *The Well*; instead, she turned it inside out. Stephen is strangely uncomfortable with all women, especially her mother. For her part, Stephen's mother gives her daughter only a quick good-night peck on the forehead "so that the girl should not wake and kiss back" (p. 83).

Instead, the oedipal drama is played out with the maid standing in for the mother. At seven, Stephen's intense eroticism is awakened by Collins (who, as working-class sex object, never gets a first name), in an episode infused with sexual meaning. Collins is "florid, full-lipped and full-bosomed" (p. 16), which might remind informed readers of Ellis's dictum that the good figure counts more with the "congenital invert" than does a pretty face. Thinking of Collins makes Stephen "go hot down her spine," and when Collins kisser her on impulse, Stephen is dumbfounded by something "vast, that the mind of seven years found no name for" (p. 18). This "vast" thing makes Stephen say that "I must be a boy, 'cause I feel exactly like one" (p. 20). In case the 1928 reader hasn't gotten the message, Hall shows Stephen's father reading sexologist Karl Heinrich Ulrichs and making notes in the margins. Later Stephen reads Krafft-Ebing in her dead father's library and recognizes herself as "flawed in the making."

A high price to pay for claiming a sexual identity, yes. But of those who condemn Hall for assuming the sexologists' model of lesbianism I ask, Just how was Hall to make the woman-loving New Woman a sexual being? Despite Hall's use of words like "lover" and "passion" and her references to "inversion," her lawyer actually defended *The Well* against state censorship by trying to convince the court that "the relationship between women described in the book represented a normal friendship." Hall "attacked him furiously for taking this line, which appeared to her to undermine the strength of the convictions with which she had defended the case. His plea seemed to her . . . 'the unkindest cut of all' and at their luncheon together she was unable to restrain 'tears of heartbroken anguish.'"[38]

How could the New Woman lay claim to her full sexuality? For bourgeois women, there was no developed female sexual discourse; there were only male discourses—pornographic, literary, and medical—about female sexuality. To become avowedly sexual, the New Woman had to enter the male world, either as a heterosexual on male terms (like Emma Goldman and eventually the flapper) or as a lesbian in male body drag (the mannish lesbian ... al invert). Feminine women like Alice B. Toklas and Hall's ... ridge could become *recognizable* lesbians by association ... line partners.

Ideas, metaphors, and symbols can be used for either radical or conservative purposes.[39] By endowing a biological female with a masculine self, Hall both questions the inevitability of traditional gender categories *and* assents to it. The mannish lesbian should not exist if gender is natural. Yet Hall makes her the hero—not the villain or clown—of her novel. Stephen survives social condemnation and even argues her own case. But she sacrifices her legitimacy as a woman and as an aristocrat. The interpersonal cost is high, too: Stephen loses her mother and her lover, Mary. *The Well* explores the self-hatred and doubt inherent in defining oneself as a "sexual deviant." For in doing so, the lesbian accepts an invidious distinction between herself and heterosexual women.

Heterosexual men have used this distinction to condemn lesbians and intimidate straight women. The fear and antagonism between us has certainly weakened the modern feminist movement. And that is why lesbian feminists (abetted by some straight feminists) are fanatical about redefining lesbianism as "woman-identification," a model that, not incidentally, puts heterosexual feminists at a disadvantage.[40] Hall's vision of lesbianism as sexual difference and as masculinity is inimical to lesbian feminist ideology.

Like Hall, I see lesbianism as sexual difference. But her equation of lesbianism with masculinity needs not condemnation, but expansion. To begin with, we need to accept that whatever their ideological purposes, Hall and the sexologists were describing something real. Some people, then and now, experience "gender dysphoria," a strong feeling that one's assigned gender as a man or a woman does not agree with one's sense of self.[41] This is not precisely the same thing as wanting power and male privilege—a well-paid job, abortion on demand, athletic prowess—even though the masculine woman continues to be a symbol of feminist aspirations to the majority outside the movement. Masculinity and femininity are like two dialects of the same language. Though we all understand both, most of us "speak" only one.[42] Many lesbians, like Stephen Gordon, are biological females who grow up thinking in and "speaking" the "wrong" gender dialect.

Obviously, the more narrow and rigid gender categories are, the more easily one can feel "out of role." And if there were no more gender categories, gender dysphoria would disappear (as would feminism). However, feminist critiques of traditional gender categories do not yet resolve gender dysphoria if only because we have made so little impact on child-rearing practices; it appears that individual gender identity is established in early childhood. Although gender dysphoria exists in some simple societies,[43] it may be amplified by the same socio-historical processes—radical changes

in the economy, in family structure and function, and in socialization—
that have given rise to feminism. Why should we as feminists deplore or
deny the existence of masculine women or effeminate men? Are we not
against assigning specific psychological or behavioral traits to a particular
biology? And should we not support those among us, butches and queens,
who still bear the brunt of homophobia?

Hall's association of lesbianism and masculinity needs to be challenged,
not because it doesn't exist, but because it is not the only possibility. Gender
identity and sexual orientation are, in fact, two related but separate systems;
witness the profusion of gender variations (which are deeply embedded in
race, class, and ethnic experience) to be found today in the lesbian community. Many lesbians *are* masculine; most have composite styles; many are
emphatically feminine. Stephen Gordon's success eclipsed more esoteric,
continental, or feminine images of the lesbian, such as Renée Vivien's *decadent*, Colette's bisexual, or Natalie Barney's *Amazone*. The notion of a feminine lesbian contradicted the congenital theory that many homosexuals in
Hall's era espoused to counter demands that they undergo punishing "ther-
apies." Though Stephen's lovers in *The Well* are feminine and though Mary,
in effect, seduces Stephen, Hall calls her "normal," that is, heterosexual.
Even Havelock Ellis gave the "womanly" lesbian more dignity and definition. As a character, Mary is forgettable and inconsistent, weakening the
novel and saddling Hall with an implausible ending in which Stephen
"nobly" turns Mary over to a man. In real life, Hall's lover Una Troubridge
did not go back to heterosexuality even when Hall, late in her life, took a
second lover.

Despite knowing Una, Natalie Barney and others like them, Hall was
unable to publicly articulate—perhaps to believe in—the persona of a *real*
lesbian who did not feel somehow male. If sexual desire is masculine, and if
the feminine woman only wants to attract men, then the womanly lesbian
cannot logically exist. Mary's real story has yet to be told.[44]

Notes

1. Two key texts are Radicalesbians, "The Woman Identified Woman," reprinted in
Radical Feminism, ed. Anne Koedt, Ellen Levine, and Anita Rapone (New York:
Quadrangle, 1973), pp. 240–245; and Adriene Rich, "Compulsory Heterosexuality and

Lesbian Existence," *Signs: Journal of Women in Culture and Society* 5, no. 4 (Summer 1980): 631–660. The best analysis of how these ideas have evolved and of their negative consequences for the feminist movement is Alice Echols, "The New Feminism of Yin and Yang," in Ann Snitow, Christine Stansell, and Sharon Thompson, eds., *Powers of Desire* (New York: Monthly Review Press, 1983), pp. 439–459.

2. Sasha Gregory Lewis, *Sunday's Women* (Boston: Beacon Press, 1979), p. 42.

3. Andrea Dworkin, *Pornography and Silence: Culture's Revenge Against Nature* (New York: Harper & Row, 1981), p. 219.

4. On passing women, see San Francisco Lesbian and Gay History Project, "She Even Chewed Tobacco": Passing Women in Nineteenth-Century America (1983), slide-tape distributed by Women Make Movies, 225 Lafayette Street, New York, N.Y. 10012; Jonathan Katz, *Gay American History: Lesbians and Gay Men in the U.S.A.* (New York: Thomas Y. Crowell, 1976), pp. 209–280.

5. Since I wrote this essay, a useful biography of Radclyffe Hall has appeared, *Our Three Selves: The Life of Radclyffe Hall* by Michael Baker (New York: William Morrow, 1985), along with a biography of Hall's lover, *Una Troubridge: The Friend of Radclyffe Hall* by Richard Ormrod (New York: Carrol & Graf, 1985). Although these works contain fascinating material I had not seen before, they did not impel me to modify the ideas expressed here. See my review, ". . . Sick to Death of Ambiguities," in *The Women's Review of Books*, January 1986.

6. "Most of us lesbians in the 1950s grew up knowing nothing about lesbianism except Stephen Gordon's swagger," admits Blanche Wiesen Cook, herself a critic of Hall; see Cook's "'Women Alone Stir My Imagination': Lesbianism and the Cultural Tradition," *Signs* 4, no. 4 (Summer 1979): 719–720. Despite Stephen Gordon's aristocratic trappings, her appeal transcended geographic and class barriers. We know that the *The Well* was read early on by American lesbians of all classes (personal communication with Liz Kennedy from the Buffalo Oral History Project [1982]; and see Vern Bullough and Bonnie Bullough, "Lesbianism in the 1920s and 1930s: A Newfound Study," *Signs* 2, no. 4 [Summer 1977]: 895–904, esp. 897). *The Well* has been translated into numerous languages. According to Una Troubridge, in the 1960s it was still steadily selling over a hundred thousand copies a year in America alone; Troubridge was still receiving letters of appreciation addressed to Hall almost twenty years after Hall's death (Una Troubridge, *The Life and Death of Radclyffe Hall* [London: Hammond, Hammond & Co., 1961]). Even today, it sells as much as or more than any other lesbian novel, in straight and women's bookstores (personal communication with Amber Hollibaugh [1983], who has worked at Modern Times Bookstore [San Francisco], Djuna Books, and Womanbooks [New York City]).

7. Hall deserves censure for her possible fascist sympathies, but this is not the focus of feminist attacks on her. In any case, such sympathies developed after she wrote *The Well*; see Troubridge, pp. 118–124.

8. For the anti-*Well* approach, see Cook; Lillian Faderman and Ann Williams, "Radclyffe Hall and the Lesbian Image," *Conditions* 1, no. 1 (April 1977): 31–41; Catharine R. Stimpson, "Zero Degree Deviancy: The Lesbian Novel in English," in Elizabeth Abel, ed., *Writing and Sexual Difference* (Chicago: University of Chicago Press, 1982), pp. 243–260; Lillian Faderman, *Surpassing the Love of Men* (New York: William Morrow & Co., 1981), pp. 322–323; Vivian Gornick, "The Whole Radclyffe Hall: A Pioneer Left Behind," *Village Voice* (June 10–16, 1981). Only Inez Martinez, whose approach is quite different from mine, defends Hall: see "The Lesbian Hero Bound: Radclyffe Hall's Portrait of Sapphic Daughters and Their Mothers," *Journal of Homosexuality* 8, nos. 3/4 (Spring/Summer 1983): 127–137.

9. Many lesbians' connection to the mannish lesbian was and is painful. The relation of any stigmatized group to the figure that functions as its symbol and stereotype is necessarily ambiguous. Even before lesbian feminism, many lesbians hastened to assure themselves and others that they were not "like that." Lesbians who could pass for straight (because they were married or appeared feminine) often shunned their butch sisters. I have dealt with these concepts at length in *Mother Camp: Female Impersonators in America* (Chicago: University of Chicago Press, 1979).

10. See esp. Faderman, *Surpassing the Love of Men*. The pro-romantic friendship, anti-Radclyffe Hall line of thought has recently led to its logical absurdity in the encyclopedic *Women of the Left Bank* (Austin: University of Texas Press, 1986). Shari Benstock arguing, correctly, that Natalie Barney's vision of lesbianism was different from Hall's, concludes that Barney and Vivien were almost a different species from Hall and a long list of other women who formed a "later generation, one that had been liberated to dress, talk, smoke, and act like men" (p. 307). Unfortunately for this hypothesis, Barney and Vivien were only four and two years older than Hall; Una Troubridge, supposedly one of the mannish ones, hardly ever dressed or acted like a man, despite Romaine Brooks's famous portrait. Benstock continues, "Barney was democratic enough to encourage the participation of both types of women [in her salon], just as she invited men . . ." (p. 307). Since Barney had affairs with many of the mannish women Benstock mentions, I wonder how "democratic" her motives were.

11. See Carroll Smith-Rosenberg, "The Female World of Love and Ritual," *Signs* 1, no. 1 (Autumn 1975): 1–30; and Faderman, *Surpassing the Love of Men*. On the con-

tradictions within the romantic friendship system, see Martha Vicinus, "'One Life to Stand Beside Me': Emotional Conflicts of First-Generation College Women in England," *Feminist Studies* 8, no. 3 (Fall 1982): 602–628.

12. George Chauncey Jr., "From Sexual Inversion to Homosexuality: Medicine and the Changing Conceptualization of Female Deviance," *Salmagundi*, nos. 58/59 (Fall 1982/Winter 1983), pp. 114–145, esp. 117. Chauncey argues that even if some doctors began to assert a female sexual subjectivity in the last third of the nineteenth century, this remained a minority opinion until the twentieth, see p. 118 fn. 6. He has reached the same conclusion I have regarding the "necessary" masculinity of the early lesbian persona.

13. For a related approach, see Carolyn Burke, "Gertrude Stein, the Cone Sisters, and the Puzzle of Female Friendship," in Abel, ed., *Writing and Sexual Difference*, pp. 221–242. Gertrude Stein shared the second generation's frustrations with "daughters spending a lifetime in freeing themselves from family fixations" (p. 223).

14. *The Unlit Lamp* (New York: Dial Press, 1981), p. 284.

15. Among many examples, the heterosexual misery of Jean Rhys's heroines; Emma Goldman's love problems as documented in Alice Wexler's recent biography *Emma Goldman in America* (Boston: Beacon Press, 1984); the female suffering documented by Ellen Kay Trimberger among Greenwich Village sex radical women, "Feminism, Men, and Modern Love: Greenwich Village, 1900–1925," in *Powers of Desire*.

16. See Paul Robinson, *The Modernization of Sex* (New York: Harper & Row, 1976), pp. 2, 3, and chap. 1.

17. Christina Simmons, "Companionate Marriage and the Lesbian Threat," *Frontiers* 4, no. 3 (Fall 1979): 54–59.

18. Ruth F. Claus, "Confronting Homosexuality: A Letter from Frances Wilder," *Signs* 2, no. 4 (Summer 1977): 928–933.

19. Ibid., p. 931.

20. Sandra Gilbert has developed this idea in the context of modernist literature in "Costumes of the Mind: Transvestism as Metaphor in Modern Literature," in Abel, ed., *Writing and Sexual Difference*, pp. 193–220.

21. Chauncey argues that medical opinion began to shift from an exclusive focus on "inversion" as gender reversal to "homosexuality" as deviant sexual orientation in the 1930s. The change has had only limited effect on popular ideology.

22. I am most indebted here to Carroll Smith-Rosenberg, who developed the prototype of this section on the sexologists. See "The New Woman as Androgyne" in *Disorderly Conduct*.

23. Richard von Krafft-Ebing, *Psychopathia Sexualis*, trans. Franklin S. Klaf (1886; New York: Bell Publishing Co., 1965), pp. 262–264.

24. Ibid., p. 264.

25. Ibid., pp. 278–279.

26. Havelock Ellis, "Sexual Inversion in Women," *Alienist and Neurologist* 16 (1895): 141–158.

27. See Robinson, *Modernization of Sex*, for a balanced appraisal of Ellis's radicalism in sexual issues vs. his misogyny.

28. Ellis, "Sexual Inversion," pp. 147–148.

29. Ibid., p. 152.

30. Ibid., p. 148.

31. Ibid., p. 153.

32. Freud's analysis was by far the most sophisticated. He rejected the trapped-soul paradigm and distinguished between "choice of object" and "sexual characteristics and sexual attitude of the subject." However, his insights were distorted by his antifeminism and his acceptance of a biological base for gender. See esp. "The Psychogenesis of a Case of Homosexuality in a Woman," in Philip Rieff, ed., *Freud: Sexuality and the Psychology of Love* (New York: Collier Books, 1963), pp. 133–159.

33. All page numbers cited in the text are from Radclyffe Hall, *The Well of Loneliness* (New York: Pocket Books, 1950).

34. Gilbert, "Costumes," p. 206.

35. My use of Freud's concepts indicates my conviction that it does begin to explain sexual desire, at least as it operates in our culture. Hall rejected or ignored Freud, presumably because of the implication, which so many drew from his work, that homosexuality could be "cured" (see Faderman and Williams "Radclyffe Hall," p. 41 n. 11).

36. Ruth-Jean Eisenbud asserts that "primary lesbian choice" occurs at about age three, resulting from the little girl's "precocious eroticism" directed toward a mother who is excluding her ("Early and Later Determinates of Lesbian Choice," *Psychoanalytic Review* 69, no. 1 [Spring 1982]: 85–109, esp. 99); Martinez, "Lesbian Hero Bound," whose theme is the mother/daughter relationship in Hall's two novels, ignores the concept of mother/daughter eroticism, rejecting any relevance of the psychoanalytic model.

37. See especially the extraordinary passage beginning, "The mother and daughter found very little to say to each other," p. 75.

38. Vera Brittain, *Radclyffe Hall: A Case of Obscenity?* (New York: A. S. Barnes, 1969), p. 92.

39. The sexologists' discourse, itself hostile to women, "also made possible the formation of a 'reverse' discourse: homosexuality began to speak in its own behalf, to demand that its legitimacy or 'naturality' be acknowledged, often in the same vocabulary, using the same categories by which it was medically disqualified" (Michel Foucault, *The History of Sexuality*, vol. 1, *An Introduction* [New York: Vintage Books, 1980], p. 102).

40. Superficially, cultural feminism reunites lesbians and straight women under the banner of "female values." As Echols points out, hostility still surfaces "as it did at the 1979 Women Against Pornography conference where a lesbian separatist called Susan Brownmiller a 'cocksucker.' Brownmiller retaliated by pointing out that her critic 'even dresses like a man'" (Echols, "New Feminism," p. 41).

41. Sexologists often use the concept of "gender dysphoria syndrome" synonymously with "transsexualism" to describe the "pathology" of people who apply for gender reassignment surgery. Of course the effort to describe and treat transsexualism medically has been awkward since gender is a cultural construct, not a biological entity. My broader use of "gender dysphoria" is in agreement with some sexologists who limit the word "transsexual" to people who actually have had surgery to alter their bodies. Gender dysphoria, then, refers to a variety of difficulties in establishing conventional (the doctors say "adequate" or "normal") gender identification; intense pain and conflict over masculinity and femininity is not limited to people who request reassignment surgery. See Jon K. Meyer and John Hoopes, "The Gender Dysphoria Syndromes," *Plastic and Reconstructive Surgery* 54 (October 1974): 447. Female-to-male transsexuals appear to share many similarities with lesbian butches. The most impressive difference is the rejection or acceptance of homosexual identity. Compare *The Well* to the lives described in Ira B. Pauly, "Adult Manifestations of Female Transsexualism," in Richard Green and John Money, eds., *Transsexualism and Sex Reassignment* (Baltimore: Johns Hopkins University Press, 1969), pp. 59–87. Gender dysphoria could very fruitfully be compared with anorexia nervosa, a more socially acceptable and increasingly common female body-image problem. As feminists, we need a much more sophisticated vocabulary to talk about gender. Sexologists are often appallingly conservative, but they also deal with and try to explain important data. See e.g., John Money and Anke A. Ehrhardt, *Man & Woman, Boy & Girl* (Baltimore: Johns Hopkins University Press, 1972). For a radical scholarly approach, see Suzanne J. Kessler and Wendy McKenna, *Gender: An Ethnomethodological Approach* (University of Chicago Press, 1985). One of the best recent pieces on gender reversal is Pat Califia, "Gender-Bending: Playing with Roles and Reversals," *Advocate* (September 15, 1983).

42. See Money and Ehrhardt, *Man & Woman*, pp. 18–20.

43. There is a long and complicated debate within anthropology about this. See Harriet Whitehead, "The Bow and the Burden Strap: A New Look at Institutionalized Homosexuality in Native North America," in Sherry B. Ortner and Harriet Whitehead, eds., *Sexual Meanings: The Cultural Construction of Gender and Sexuality* (Cambridge: Cambridge University Press, 1981), pp. 80–115; Walter Williams, *The Spirit and the Flesh* (Boston: Beacon Press, 1986); several articles in Evelyn Blackwood, ed., *Anthropology and Sexual Behavior*(New York: The Haworth Press, 1985); and Paula Gunn Allen's essay "Lesbians in American Indian Cultures," in Martin Duberman, Martha Vicinus, and George Chauncey Jr., eds., *Hidden from History: Reclaiming the Gay and Lesbian Past* (New York: Penguin, 1989).

44. Two impressive beginnings are Joan Nestle, "Butch-Fem Relationships," and Amber Hollibaugh and Cherríe Moraga, "What We're Rollin' Around in Bed With," both in *Heresies12* 3, no. 4 (1981): 21–24, 58–62. The latter has been reprinted in Snitow, Stansell, and Thompson, eds., *Powers of Desire*, pp. 394–405.

7

"Perverse Desire: The Lure of the Mannish Lesbian"
(1991)

TERESA DE LAURETIS

Lesbian scholarship has not had much use for psychoanalysis. Developing in the political and intellectual context of feminism over the past two decades, in the Eurowestern "First World," lesbian critical writing has typically rejected Freud as the enemy of women and consequently avoided consideration of Freudian and neo-Freudian theories of sexuality. Certainly, the feminist mistrust of psychoanalysis as both a male-controlled clinical practice and a popularized social discourse on the "inferiority" of women has excellent, and historically proven, practical reasons. Nevertheless, some feminists have persistently argued that there are also very good theoretical reasons for reading and rereading Freud himself. All the more so for lesbians, I suggest, whose self-definition, self-representation, and political as well as personal identity are not only grounded in the sphere of the sexual, but actually constituted in relation to our sexual difference from socially dominant, institutionalized, heterosexual forms.[1]

One direction of my current work, of which this paper presents a small but pivotal fragment, is to reread Freud's writings against the grain of the dominant interpretations that construct a positive, "normal," heterosexual and reproductive sexuality, and to look instead for what I would call Freud's negative theory of perversion. For it seems to me that, in his work from the *Three Essays on the Theory of Sexuality* (1905) on, the very notions of a normal sexuality, a normal psychosexual development, a normal sexual act are inseparable—and indeed derive—from the detailed consideration of their aberrant, deviant or perverse manifestations and components. And we may recall, furthermore, that the whole of Freud's theory of the human psyche, the sexual instincts and their vicissitudes, owes its foundations and development to psychoanalysis, his clinical study of the psychoneuroses; that is to say, those cases in which the mental apparatus and instinctual drives reveal themselves in their processes and mechanisms, which are "normally" hidden or unremarkable otherwise. The normal, in this respect, is only conceivable by approximation, more in the order of a projection than an actual state of being.

What is the advantage of such a project to a lesbian theorist? For one thing, in the perspective of a theory of perversion, lesbian sexuality would no longer have to be explained by Freud's own concept of the masculinity complex, which not only recasts homosexuality in the mold of normative heterosexuality, thus precluding all conceptualization of a female sexuality autonomous from men; but it also fails to account for the non-masculine lesbian, that particular figure that since the nineteenth century has consistently baffled both sexologists and psychoanalysts, and that Havelock Ellis named "the womanly woman," the feminine invert.[2] Secondly, if perversion is understood with Freud as a deviation of the sexual drive (*Trieb*) from the path leading to the reproductive object, that is to say, if perversion is merely another path taken by the drive in its cathexis or choice of object, rather than a pathology (although, like every other aspect of sexuality it may involve pathogenic elements), then a theory of perversion would serve to articulate a model of perverse desire, where perverse means not pathological but rather non-heterosexual or non-normatively heterosexual.[3]

In one of the rare attempts to look at lesbianism in a feminist and psychoanalytic perspective, a recent article by Diane Hamer suggests that lesbianism, for some women, may be "a psychic repudiation of the category "woman," and sees a direct correspondence between feminism as "a political movement based on a refusal to accept the social 'truth' of men's superiority over women" and lesbianism as "a psychic refusal of the 'truth' of women's castration." In this context, she remarks, "it is interesting to note that Freud referred to both his homosexual women patients as 'feminists.'"[4] Even more interesting, to me, is to see a lesbian theorist decisively and explicitly reappropriate, in feminist perspective, this most contended of Freud's notions, the masculinity complex in women. For, once taken, this step—a very important one, in my opinion, without which our theorizing may just keep on playing in the pre-Oedipal sandbox—Hamer has left behind years of debates on Freud's sexism and feminist outrage, and volumes on Freud's historical limitations and feminist exculpation (debates and volumes, I may add, to which I have myself contributed in some measure). But when she then attempts to define lesbian desire, in Lacanian terms, she runs aground of the corollary to the masculinity complex, namely, the castration complex. This latter, she states, we must refuse:

> Classically, lesbians are thought to pretend possession of the phallus . . . and are thus aligned, albeit fraudulently, on the side of masculinity. In this rather simplistic account lesbian desire becomes near impossible; desire cannot exist *between lesbians*, since they are both on the same side of desire, or, if a lesbian does experience desire, it is bound to be towards a feminine subject who could only desire her back as though she were a man. However, as I have suggested, lesbianism is less a claim to phallic possession (although it may be this too) than it is a refusal of the meanings attached to castration. As such it is a refusal of any easy or straightforward allocation of masculine and feminine positions around the phallus. Instead it suggests a much more fluid and flexible relationship to the positions around which desire is organized. (p. 147)

The problem with this solution—the "refusal of the meanings attached to castration"—is that it begs the question: in the Lacanian framework, symbolic castration is the condition of desire and what constitutes the paternal phallus as the "allocator" of positions in desire. In other words, castration and the phallus as signifier of desire go hand in hand, one cannot stir without the other. Thus, to reject the notion of castration (to refuse to rethink its terms) is to find ourselves without symbolic means to signify desire.

In this paper, I will up Hamer's defiant gesture and, just as she reappropriates the masculinity complex, I want to reappropriate castration and the phallus for lesbian subjectivity, but in the perspective of Freud's negative theory of perversion. I will propose a *model of perverse desire* based on the one perversion the Freud insisted was not open to women—fetishism.

I take as my starting point a classic text of lesbianism, the classic novel of female sexual inversion, Radclyffe Hall's *The Well of Loneliness*, which, from its obscenity trial in London in 1928 to well into the 1970s, has been the most popular representation of lesbianism in fiction.[5] Thus, it needs no other introduction, except a word of warning: my reading of a crucial passage in the text—crucial because it inscribes a certain fantasy of the female body that works against the grain of the novel's explicit message—is likely to appear far-fetched. This is so, I suggest, because my reading also works against the heterosexual coding of sexual difference (masculinity and femininity) which the novel itself employs and in which it demands to be read.

The Scene at the Mirror

The passage I selected occurs during Stephen's love affair with Angela Crosby, at the height of her unappeased passion and jealousy for the woman who, Stephen correctly suspects, is having an affair with Roger, her most loathed rival. The only things in which Stephen is superior to Roger are social status and, even more relevant to Angela, wealth: Stephen is an independently rich woman at age 21 and some day will be even richer. Though bothered by this "unworthy" thought, Stephen nevertheless seeks to use her money and status to advantage; to impress Angela, she buys her expensive presents and orders herself "a rakish red car" as well as several tailor-made suits, gloves, scarves, heavy silk stockings, toilet water and carnation-scented soap. "Nor could she resist," remarks the narrator, "the lure of pyjamas made of white crêpe de Chine [which] led to a man's dressing-gown of brocade—an amazingly ornate garment" (p. 186). And yet, "on her way back in the train to Malvern, she gazed out of the window with renewed desolation. Money could not buy the one thing that she needed in life; it could not buy Angela's love." Then comes the following short section (book II, chapter 24, section 6):

> That night she stared at herself in the glass; and even as she did so she hated her body with its muscular shoulders, its small compact breasts, and its slender flanks of an athlete. All her life she must drag this body of hers like a monstrous fetter imposed on her spirit. This strangely ardent yet sterile body that must worship yet never be worshipped in return by the creature of its adoration. She longed to maim it, for it made her feel cruel; it was so white, so strong and so self-sufficient; yet withal so poor and unhappy a

thing that her eyes filled with tears and her hate turned to pity. She began to grieve over it, touching her breasts with pitiful fingers, stroking her shoulders, letting her hands slip along her straight thighs—Oh, poor and most desolate body!

Then, she, for whom Puddle was actually praying at that moment, must now pray also, but blindly; finding few words that seemed worthy of prayer, few words that seemed to encompass her meaning—for she did not know the meaning of herself. But she loved, and loving groped for the God who had fashioned her, even unto this bitter loving. (pp. 186–187)

The typographical division that separates the last sentence of the first paragraph, describing the movement of Stephen's hands and fingers on her own body, from the second and last sentence of the second paragraph cannot disguise the intensely erotic significance of the scene. At face value, the paragraph division corresponds to the ideological division between body and mind, or "spirit," announced in the first paragraph ("all her life she must drag this body of hers like a monstrous fetter imposed on her spirit"), so that the physical, sexual character of Stephen's unappeased love and thwarted narcissistic desire is displaced onto an order of language which excludes her—the prayer to a distant, disembodied God by one who can pray to him because she also has no body, i.e., Puddle, Stephen's tutor and companion, and her desexualized double. While in the first paragraph Stephen "stares" at her own body in the mirror, in the second she is blind, groping—a sudden reversal of the terms of vision which recalls the "nothing to see" of the female sex in psychoanalysis and, in a rhetorical sleight-of-hand, forecloses its view, its sensual perception, denying its very existence.

But a few words belie the (overt) sublimation and the (covert) negation of the sexual that the second paragraph would accomplish: "Then," the first word in it, temporally links the movement of the hands in the preceding paragraph to the final words of the second, "even unto this bitter loving," where the shifter "this" relocates the act of loving in a present moment that can only refer to the culmination or conclusion of the scene interrupted by the paragraph break, the scene of Stephen in front of the mirror "touching her breasts with pitiful fingers, stroking her shoulders, letting her hands slip along her straight thighs [and, if we might fantasize along with the text, watching in the mirror her own hands move downward on her body] . . . even unto this bitter loving." No wonder the next paragraph must rush in to deny both her and us the vision of such an intolerable act.

The message of the novel is clear: Stephen's groping blind and wordless toward an Other who should provide the meaning, but does not, only leads her back to the real of her body, to a "bitter" need which cannot accede to symbolization and so must remain, in Lady Gordon's words, "this *unspeakable* outrage that you call love" (p. 200, emphasis added). As the passage anticipates, the narrative resolution can only be cast in terms of renunciation and salvation, in an order of language that occludes the body in favor of spirit and, with regard to women specifically, forecloses the possibility of any autonomous and non-reproductive female sexuality. Stephen's "sacrifice" of her love for Mary—and, more gruesome still, of Mary's love for her—which concludes Radclyffe Hall's "parable of damnation" (in Catharine Stimpson's words) will ironically reaffirm not just the repression, but indeed the foreclosure or repudiation of lesbianism as such; that is to say, the novel cannot conceive of an autonomous female homosexuality and thus can only confirm Stephen's view of herself as a "freak," a "mistake" of nature, a masculine woman.[6]

The passage, however, contains another, ambiguous message. The scene represents a fantasy of bodily dispossession, the fantasy of an unlovely/unlovable body—a body not feminine or maternal, not narcissistically cherished, fruitful or productive, nor, on the other hand, barren (as the term goes) or abject, but simply imperfect, faulty and faulted, dispossessed, inadequate to bear and signify desire. Because it is not feminine, this body is inadequate as the object of desire, to be desired by the other, and thus inadequate to signify the female subject's desire in its feminine mode; however, because it is masculine but not male, it is also inadequate to signify or bear the subject's desire in the masculine mode. Stephen's body is not feminine, on the stereotypical Victorian model of femininity that is her mother Anna. It is "ardent and sterile," and its taut muscular strength, whiteness and phallic self-sufficiency make Stephen wish to "maim" it, to mark it with a physical, indexical sign of her symbolic castration, her captivity in gender and her semiotic dispossession ("she did not know the meaning of herself") by the Other, the God who made her "a freak of a creature." For she can "worship" the female body in another but "never be worshipped in return." If she hates her naked body, it is because that body is masculine, "so strong and so self-sufficient," so phallic. The body she desires, not only in Angela but also autoerotically for herself, the body she can make love to, is a feminine, female body. Paradoxical as it may seem, the "mythic mannish lesbian" (in Esther Newton's wonderful phrase) wishes to have a feminine body, the kind of female body she desires in Angela and later in Mary—a femme's body. How to explain such a paradox?

The Fantasy of Castration

I want to argue that this fantasy of bodily dispossession is subtended by an original fantasy of castration, in the sense elaborated by Laplanche and Pontalis, with the paternal phallus symbolically present and visible in the muscular, athletic body of Stephen who "dares" to look so like her father.[7] It is that paternal phallus, inscribed in her very body, which imposes the taboo that renders the female body (the mother's, other women's, and her own) for ever inaccessible to Stephen, and thus signifies her castration. But before I discuss in what ways, and in what sense, the notion of castration may be reformulated in relation to lesbian subjectivity, I want to point out how the paradox in the passage cited above contradicts, or at least complicates, the more immediate reading of Stephen's masculinity complex. For on the one hand, Stephen's sense of herself depends on a strong masculine identification; yet, on the other hand, it is precisely her masculine, phallic body which bears the mark of castration and frustrates her narcissistic desire in the scene at the mirror. So, in this case, it is not possible simply to equate the phallic with the masculine and castration with the feminine body, as psychoanalysis would have it. And hence the question, What does castration mean in relation to lesbian subjectivity and desire?

The difficulty of the psychoanalytic notion of castration for feminist theory is too well known to be rehearsed once again. To sum it up in one sentence, the problem lies in the definition of female sexuality as *complementary* to the physiological, psychic, and social needs of the male, and yet as a *deficiency* vis-à-vis his sexual organ and its symbolic representative, the phallus—a definition which results in the exclusion of women not from sexuality (for, on the contrary, women are the very locus of the sexual), but rather from the field of desire. There is another paradox in this theory, for the very effectiveness of symbolic castration consists precisely in allowing access to desire, the phallus representing at once the mark of difference and lack, the threat of castration, and the signifier of desire. But access to desire through symbolic castration, the theory states, is only for the male. The female's relation to symbolic castration does not allow her entry into the field of desire as subject, but only as object.

This is so, Freudians and Lacanians join forces in saying, because women lack the physical property that signifies desire: not having a penis (the bodily representative and support of the libido, the physical referent which in sexuality, in fantasy, becomes the signifier, or more properly the sign-vehicle , the bearer, of desire), females are effectively castrated, symbolically, in the sense that they lack—they do not have and will never have—the paternal phallus, the means of symbolic access to the first object of desire that is the mother's body. It is the potential for losing the penis, the *threat* of castration, that subjects the male to the law of the father and structures the male's relation to the paternal phallus as one of insufficiency; and it is that potential for loss which gives the penis its potential to attain the value or the stature of the paternal phallus. Having nothing to lose, the theory goes, women cannot desire; having no phallic capital to invest or speculate on, as men do, women cannot be investors in the marketplace of desire but are instead commodities that circulate in it.[8]

Feminist theorists, following Lacan, have sought to disengage the notion of castration from its reference to the penis by making it purely a condition of signification, of the entry into language, and thus the means of access to desire. Silverman, for example, states: "One of the crucial features of Lacan's redefinition of castration has been to shift it away from this obligatory anatomical referent [the penis] to the lack induced by language."[9] Yet the semiotic bond between the signification of the phallus and the "real" penis remains finally indissoluble: "No one has the phallus but the phallus is the male sign, the man's assignment. . . . The man's masculinity, his male world, is the assertion of the phallus to support his having it."[10]

In all such arguments, however, nearly everyone fails to note that the Lacanian framing of the question in terms of having or being the phallus is set in the perspective of normative heterosexuality (which both analysis and theory seek to reproduce in the subject), with the sexual difference of man and woman clearly mapped out and the act of copulation firmly in place.[11] But what if, I ask, we were to reframe the question of the phallus and the fantasy of castration in the perspective provided by Freud's negative theory of perversion?

With regard to the passage from *The Well of Loneliness* (but it could be shown of other lesbian texts as well), let me emphasize that, if it does inscribe a fantasy of castration, it also, and very effectively, speaks desire, and thus is fully in the symbolic, in signification. Yet the desire it speaks is not masculine, not simply phallic. But, if the phallus is both the mark of castration and the signifier of desire, then the question is: What manner of desire is this? What acts as the phallus in this lesbian fantasy? I will propose that it is not the paternal phallus, or a phallic symbol, but something of the nature of a fetish, something which signifies at once the absence of the object of desire (the female body) and the subject's wish for it.

A Model of Perverse Desire

In the clinical view of fetishism, the perversion is related to the subject's disavowal of the mother's castration, which occurs by a splitting of the ego as a defense from the threat of castration. Disavowal implies a contradiction, a double or split belief: on the one hand, the recognition that the mother does not have a penis as the father does; and yet, on the other hand, the refusal to acknowledge the absence of the penis in the mother. As a result of this disavowal, the subject's desire is metonymically displaced, diverted onto another object, part of the body, clothing, etc., which acts as "substitute" (Freud says) for the missing maternal penis. In this way, Freud writes, to the child who is to become a fetishist "the woman has got a penis, in spite of everything, but this penis is no longer the same as it was before. Something else *has* taken its place, has been appointed its substitute, as it were, and now inherits the interest which was formerly directed to its predecessor."[12] In this diversion consists, for Freud, the *perversion* of the sexual instinct, which is thus diverted or displaced from its legitimate object and reproductive aim. But since the whole process, the disavowal [*Verleugnung*] and the displacement [*Verschiebung*], is motivated by the subject's fear of his own possible castration, what it brings into evidence is the fundamental role in fetishism of the paternal phallus (that which is missing in the mother). And this is why, Freud states, fetishism does not apply to women: they have nothing to lose, they have no penis, and thus disavowal would not defend their ego from an already accomplished "castration."

However, argues an interesting essay by Leo Bersani and Ulysse Dutoit, Freud placed too much emphasis on the paternal phallus. "The fetishist can see the woman as she is, without a penis, because he loves her with a penis somewhere else," they say:

> The crucial point—which makes the fetishistic object different from the phallic symbol—is that the success of the fetish depends on its being seen as authentically different from the missing penis. With a phallic symbol, we may not be consciously aware of what it stands for, but it attracts us because, consciously or unconsciously, we perceive it *as* the phallus. In fetishism, however, the refusal to see the fetish as a penis-substitute may not be simply an effect of repression. The fetishist has displaced the missing penis from the woman's genitals to, say, her underclothing, but we suggest that if he doesn't care about the underclothing resembling a penis it is because: (1) he knows that it is not a penis; (2) he doesn't want it to be only a penis; and (3) he also knows that *nothing* can replace the lack to which in fact he has resigned himself.[13]

Thus, to the fetishist, the fetish does much more than *re-place* the penis, "since it signifies something which was never anywhere": it "derange[s] his *system of desiring*," even as far as "deconstructing and mobilizing the self." Unlike a phallic symbol, which stands for the perceived penis, the fetish is a "fantasy-phallus," "an inappropriate object precariously attached to a desiring fantasy, unsupported by any perceptual memory." Fetishism, they conclude, outlines a model of desire dependent on "an ambiguous negation of the real. . . . This negation creates an interval between the new object of desire and an unidentifiable first object, and as such it may be the model for all substitutive formations in which the first term of the equation is lost, or unlocatable, and in any case ultimately unimportant." And they suggest that "the process which *may* result in pathological fetishism can also have a permanent psychic validity of a formal nature" (p. 71, emphasis added).

I will follow up their argument and propose that if (and admittedly it's a big if, but not a speculation alien to or unprecedented in psychoanalytic theory[14])—if the psychic process of disavowal that detaches desire from the paternal phallus in the fetishist can *also* occur in other subjects, and have enduring effects or formal validity as a psychic process, then this "formal

model of desire's mobility," which I prefer to call *perverse desire*, is emi-
nently applicable to lesbian sexuality.

The Fetish as Fantasy-Phallus

Consider the following three statements from their essay cited above, with
the word lesbian in lieu of the word fetishist: 1) the lesbian can see the
woman as she is, without a penis, because she loves her with a penis somewhere else; 2) the lesbian also knows that nothing can replace the lack to
which in fact she has resigned herself; 3) lesbian desire is sustained and signified by a fetish, a fantasy-phallus, an inappropriate object precariously
attached to a desiring fantasy, unsupported by any perceptual memory. In
other words, what the lesbian desires in a woman and in herself ("the penis
somewhere else") is indeed not a penis but the whole or perhaps a part of
the female body, or something metonymically related to it, such as physical,
intellectual or emotional attributes, stance, attitude, appearance, self-pre-
sentation, and hence the importance of performance, clothing, costume,
etc. She knows full well she is not a man, she doesn't have the paternal phallus, but that does not necessarily mean she has no means to signify desire:
the fantasy-phallus is at once what signifies her desire and what she desires
in a woman. As Joan Nestle put it,

> For me, the erotic essence of the butch-femme relationship was the external
> difference of women's textures and the bond of knowledgeable caring. I
> loved my lover for how she stood as well as for what she did. Dress was a
> part of it: the erotic signal of her hair at the nape of her neck, touching the
> shirt collar; how she held a cigarette; the symbolic pinky ring flashing as she
> waved her hand. I know this sounds superficial, but all these gestures were a
> style of self-presentation that made erotic competence a political statement
> in the 1950s. . . . Deeper than the sexual positioning was the overwhelming
> love I felt for [her] courage, the bravery of [her] erotic independence.[15]

The object and the signifier of desire are not anatomical entities, such as
the female body or womb and the penis respectively; they are fantasy entities, objects or signs that have somehow become "attached to a desiring fantasy" and for that very reason may be "inappropriate" (to signify those

anatomical entities) and precarious, not fixed or the same for every subject, and even unstable in one subject. But if there is no privileged, founding object of desire, if "the objects of our desires are always substitutes for the objects of our desires" (as Bersani and Dutoit put it), nevertheless desire itself, with its movement between subject and object, between the self and an other, is founded on difference and dependent on "the sign which describes both the object and its absence" (Laplanche and Pontalis).

This is why a notion of castration and a notion of phallus as signifier of desire are necessary to signify lesbian desire and subjectivity, although they must be redefined in reference to the female body, and not the penis. It is not just that fantasies of castration have a central place in lesbian texts, subjectivity and desire. It is also that what I have called the fetish or fantasy-phallus, in contradistinction to the paternal penis-phallus, serves as the bearer, the signifier, of difference and desire. Without it, the lesbian lovers would be merely two women in the same bed. The lesbian fetish, in other words, is any object, any "inappropriate object precariously attached to a desiring fantasy," any sign whatsoever, that marks the difference and the desire between the lovers—for instance, again in Nestle's words, "the erotic signal of her hair at the nape of her neck, touching the shirt collar," or "big-hipped, wide-assed women's bodies."

The Wound and the Scar

Returning, then, to the text I started from, it may now be possible to see its fantasy of bodily dispossession as related to a somewhat different notion of castration. Let me recall for you the passage in *The Well of Loneliness* where, in describing Stephen's purchase of clothes intended to impress Angela—and they are, as we know, masculine-cut or mannish clothes—the narrator tells us: "Nor could she resist the lure of pyjamas made of crêpe de Chine [which] led to a man's dressing gown of brocade—an amazingly ornate garment." Now, we can be almost sure that Angela would never see those pyjamas and dressing gown. And yet Stephen *could not resist* their *lure*. Just as she hates her masculine body naked, so does she respond to the lure of masculine clothes; and we may remember, as well, the intensity with which both Stephen Gordon and her author Radclyffe Hall yearned to cut their hair quite short, against all the contemporary appearance codes. What I am driving at, is that masculine clothes, the insistence on riding astride, and all the other accoutrements and signs of masculinity, up to the war scar on her face, are Stephen's fetish, her fantasy-phallus. This does explain the paradox of the scene at the mirror, in which she hates her *naked* body and wants to "maim" it (to inscribe it with the mark of castration) precisely because it is masculine, "ardent and sterile . . . so strong and so self-sufficient," so phallic, whereas the body she desires and wants to make love to, another's or her own, is a feminine, female body.

Consider, if you will, this scene at the mirror as the textual reenactment of the Lacanian mirror stage which, according to Laplanche and Pontalis, constitutes the matrix or first outline of the ego.

> The establishment of the ego can be conceived of as the formation of a psychical unit paralleling the constitution of the bodily schema. One may further suppose that this unification is precipitated by the subject's acquisition of an image of himself founded on the model furnished by the other person—this image being the ego itself. Narcissism then appears as the amorous captivation of the subject by this image. Jacques Lacan has related this first moment in the ego's formation to that fundamentally narcissistic experience which he calls the *mirror stage.*[16]

What Stephen sees in the mirror (the image which establishes the ego) is the image of a phallic body, which the narrator has taken pains to tell us was so from a very young age, a body Stephen's mother found "repulsive." This image which Stephen sees in the mirror does not accomplish "the amorous captivation of the subject" or offer her a "fundamentally narcissistic experience," but on the contrary inflicts a narcissistic wound, for that phallic body, and thus the ego, cannot be narcissistically loved.[17]

The fantasy of castration here, is explicitly associated with a failure of narcissism, the lack or threatened loss of a *female* body, from which would derive in consequence the defense of disavowal, the splitting of the ego, the ambiguous negation of the real. What is formed in the process of disavowal, then, is not a phallic symbol, a penis-substitute (indeed Stephen hates her masculine body), but a fetish—something that would cover over or disguise the narcissistic wound, and yet leave a scar, a trace of its enduring threat. Thus Stephen's fetish, the signifier of her desire, is the sign of both an absence and a presence; the denied and wished-for female body is both displaced and represented in the fetish, the visible signifiers and accoutrements of masculinity, or what Esther Newton has called a "male body drag." That is the lure of the mannish lesbian—a lure for her and for her lover. The fetish of masculinity is what lures and signifies her desire, and what in her lures her lover, what her lover desires in her. Unlike the masculinity complex, the lesbian fetish of masculinity does not refuse castration but disavows it; the threat it holds at bay is not the loss of the penis in women but the loss of the female body itself, and the prohibition of access to it.

To conclude, in this lesbian text, the subject's body is inscribed in a fantasy of castration, which speaks a failure of narcissism. I cannot love myself, says the subject of the fantasy, I need another woman to love me (Anna Gordon was repulsed by her daughter) and to love me sexually, bodily (the sexual emphasis is remarked by the masturbation scene barely disguised in the passage). This lover must be a woman, not a man, and not a faulty woman, dispossessed of her body (such as I am) but a woman-woman, a woman embodied and self-possessed, as I would want to be and as I can only become by her love.

> But in fact we were always like this,
> rootless, dismembered: knowing it makes the difference.
> Birth stripped our birthright from us,
> tore us from a woman, from women, from ourselves
> so early on
> and the whole chorus throbbing at our ears
> like midges, told us nothing, nothing
> of origins, nothing we needed
> to know, nothing that could re-member us.
> Only: that it is unnatural,
> the homesickness for a woman, for ourselves,
> for that acute joy at the shadow her head and arms
> cast on a wall, her heavy or slender
> thighs on which we lay, flesh against flesh,
> eyes steady on the face of love; smell of her milk, her sweat,
> terror of her disappearance, all fused in this hunger
> for the element they have called most dangerous, to be
> lifted breathtaken on her breast, to rock within her

—even if beaten back, stranded again, to apprehend
in a sudden brine-clear thought
trembling like the tiny, orbed, endangered
egg-sac of a new world:
This is what she was to me, and this
is how I can love myself—
as only a woman can love me.

(Adrienne Rich, from *"Transcendental Etude")*[18]

Nevertheless, the fantasy of dispossession is so strong in the text that Stephen ends up still dispossessed, in spite of having had (and given up) a woman lover. If the sense of belonging to "one's own kind," the political presence of a community—the "thousands" and "millions" like her for whom Stephen writes and implores God at the close of the novel, mirroring the author's purpose in writing it and predicting its enormous success and impact on its readers—can soothe the pain and provide what Radclyffe Hall calls "that steel-bright courage . . . forged in the furnace of affliction," nevertheless the narcissistic wound remains, unhealed under the scar that both acknowledges and denies it. The wound and the scar, castration and the fetish, constitute an original fantasy that is repeated, reenacted in different scenarios, in lesbian writing and in lesbian eros.

Notes

1. A shorter version of this paper was presented at the 1990 MLA convention in Chicago.

2. Havelock Ellis, "Sexual Inversion in Women," *Alienist and Neurologist,* vol. 16 (1895), pp. 141–158. A similar view of female homosexuality is expressed in Ernest Jones, "The Early Development of Female Sexuality," *International Journal of Psycho-Analysis* 8 (1927): 459–472, and later repeated by Jacques Lacan, "Guiding Remarks for a Congress on Feminine Sexuality," in Juliet Mitchell and Jacqueline Rose, eds., *Feminine Sexuality* (New York: Norton, 1983), pp. 96–97.

3. This reconceptualization of perversion is made possible by Freud's notion of the sexual drive as independent of its object. See Arnold Davidson, "How To Do the History of Psychoanalysis: A Reading of Freud's *Three Essays on the Theory of*

Sexuality," in Françoise Meltzer, ed., *The Trial(s) of Psychoanalysis* (Chicago: University of Chicago Press, 1987–1988), pp. 39–64.

4. Diane Hamer, "Significant Others: Lesbianism and Psychoanalytic Theory," *Feminist Review*, no. 34 (Spring 1990): 143–145.

5. Radclyffe Hall, *The Well of Loneliness* (New York: Avon Books, 1981). See Esther Newton, "The Mythic Mannish Lesbian: Radclyffe Hall and the New Woman," *Signs* 9, no. 4 (Summer 1984): 557–575, and Catharine R. Stimpson, "Zero Degree Deviancy: The Lesbian Novel in English," in Elizabeth Abel, ed., *Writing and Sexual Difference* (Chicago: University of Chicago Presso, 1982), pp. 243–260. Rebecca O'Rourke, *Reflecting on THE WELL OF LONELINESS* (London: Routledge, 1989), contains an interesting, if partial, study of the novel's reception.

6. The distinction between repression (*Verdrangung*) and repudiation or foreclosure (*Verwerfung*) is that, while the repressed contents are accessible to consciousness and to be worked over, for example in analysis, what is repudiated or foreclosed is permanently repressed, for ever lost to memory.

7. J. Laplanche and J.-B. Pontalis, "Fantasy and the Origins of Sexuality," in Victor Burgin et al., eds., *Formations of Fantasy* (London: Methuen, 1986), pp. 5–34.

8. See Luce Irigaray's critique in "Commodities Among Themselves," in *This Sex Which Is Not One*, trans. Catherine Porter (Ithaca, N.Y.: Cornell University Press, 1985).

9. Kaja Silverman, "Fassbinder and Lacan," *Camera Obscura* 19 (1989): 79.

10. Stephen Heath, "Joan Riviere and the Masquerade," in *Formations of Fantasy*, p. 55.

11. As Lacan himself puts it, "The phallus is the privileged signifier of that mark where the share of the logos is wedded to the advent of desire. One might say that this signifier is chosen as what stands out as most easily seized upon in the real of sexual copulation, and also as the most symbolic in the literal (typographical) sense of the term, since it is the equivalent in that relation of the (logical) copula. One might also say that by virtue of its turgidity, it is the image of the vital flow as it is transmitted in generation" (*Feminine Sexuality*, p. 82).

12. Sigmund Freud, "Fetishism," in *The Standard Edition of the Complete Psychological Works of Sigmund Freud*, trans. and ed. James Strachey (Hogarth Press) London, 1953–1974, vol. 21, pp. 155–156.

13. Leo Bersani and Ulysse Dutoit, *The Forms of Violence: Narrative in Assyrian Art and Modern Culture* (New York: Schocken Books, 1985), pp. 68–69.

14. Juliet Mitchell also extrapolates from disavowal and fetishism a more general, formal model of the constitution of the subject in her "Introduction I" to Lacan,

Feminine Sexuality, p. 25.

15. Joan Nestle, *A Restricted Country* (Ithaca, N.Y.: Firebrand Books, 1987), pp. 104–105.

16. Laplanche and Pontalis, "Narcissism," in *The Language of Psychoanalysis* (New York: Norton, 1973), p. 256.

17. "A second theoretical characteristic of the castration complex is its impact upon narcissism: the phallus is an essential component of the child's self-image, so any threat to the phallus is a radical danger to this image; this explains the efficacity of the threat, which derives from the conjunction of two factors, namely, the primacy of the phallus and the narcissistic wound" (Laplanche and Pontalis, *The Language of Psychoanalysis*, p. 57).

18. Adrienne Rich, *The Dream of a Common Language: Poems 1974–1977* (New York: Norton, 1978), pp. 75–76.

PART TWO

PERSPECTIVES PRESENT

§

New Sexual Inversions

8

"Some Primitive Thing Conceived in a Turbulent Age of Transition": The Transsexual Emerging from *The Well*

JAY PROSSER

"Do you think I could be a man, supposing I thought very hard—or prayed, Father?"

—The Well of Loneliness, *Radclyffe Hall*

The Well of Loneliness has proven the most famous representation of lesbianism that yet provides the most infamous *mis*representation of lesbianism. Lesbian criticism has been characterized by the repeated attempt but persistent failure to make sense of Stephen's masculinity and the heterosexual conclusion of the novel. Does this failure to fit Stephen within the framework of lesbian not suggest another subject in the novel, one that is not lesbian but heterosexual and male, or constituted by the desire to be heterosexual and male? In fact Stephen is not lesbian but an invert, and nowhere does this most famous lesbian novel name its subject lesbian or homosexual. The category of invert in the critical reception of sexology, which not incidentally has been dominated by lesbian and gay criticism, has wrongly been reduced to homosexual. The invert is seen as figure for homosexual, and the transgendered paradigms that are definitive of inversion are consequently overridden, rendered figurative. George Chauncey writes that given the nineteenth-century construction of desire as masculine "a complete inversion or reversal of a woman's sexual character was required for her to act as a lesbian; she had literally to become man-like in her sexual desire."[1] And Foucault, in a phrase that has become a touchstone, fixes inversion in *The History of Sexuality* as the marker of homosexuality, the moment of its invention when homosexuality becomes a subject or "a species."[2] This same symptomization or figuration has been followed through in application to *The Well*. Stephen's masculinity has been reduced to a figure, a confounding and irresolvable one, at best an anachronism of lesbianism. Sandra Gilbert and Susan Gubar believe that Hall, writing "with a sense of lesbianism as tragic transsexuality," uses "sexchanges" as a "metaphor" for gender anomie following the First World War.[3] And Esther Newton in the most sympathetic rendition of Stephen's transgender because at least it treats her transgendered feelings as real nevertheless argues similarly that Hall "uses cross-dressing and gender reversal to symbolize lesbian sexuality," that Stephen is a "lesbian in male body drag."[4] Ironically Stephen's transgender gets greater validation in lesbian feminist criticism because at least in rejecting the novel as lesbian this criticism recognizes a qualitative difference between, and the irreducibility of, transgender and homosexuality in *The Well* Catharine Stimpson for instance holds Stephen's femaleness at a suspicious distance with her quotation marks around the feminine pronoun, "her."[5]

It is the contention of this essay that *The Well* and the category of inversion are in fact key to the emergence of the transsexual—to the interlinked literal and literary construction of the transsexual. The case histories of sexological inversion upon which Hall's novel relied so heavily for its material produced the transsexual narrative that has become the very symptom of transsexuality. This narrative, and the precedent of the subject telling his or her transgendered story before the clinician in order to access the gateway of clinical treatment, allowed the literal bodily reconstruction of the transsexual. The bodily transition of the transsexual emerged as and remains dependent on the narrative transitions of the subject's story.[6] *The Well*'s sexological moment of sexual inversion, and the novel itself, are key to the emergence of this new subject—unread in *The Well*. And once the transsexual in *The Well* is read and diagnosed, this subject and this context provide a much better fit for this novel than lesbian.

The Well is thoroughly enmeshed in the sexological discourse of inversion. Key sexologist of inversion Havelock Ellis vouched in what became its preface for the novel's "notable psychological and sociological significance" ("it is the first English novel which presents, in a completely faithful and uncompromising form, one particular aspect of sexual life as it exists among us today").[7] While Ellis's note was not written as a preface, Hall's eager request for his support and the attachment of his note to the novel have the effect of authorizing her text as a sexological narrative.[8] And within the novel two explicit citations of sexology at key moments are crucial in diagnosing the subject. In the first instance Sir Philip Gordon, Stephen's father, uses a copy of Karl Heinrich Ulrichs, the first thinker of sexual inversion, to decode a portrait of Stephen with her mother, "that indefinable quality in Stephen that made her look wrong in the clothes she was wearing as though she and they had no right to each other."[9] In the second, following her father, Stephen finds the key to her own identity. Emphasizing this moment as one of unlocking the truth, Hall writes that Stephen unlocks her father's

> special book case. . . . As she slipped the key into the lock and turned it, the action seemed curiously automatic. . . . Then she noticed that on a shelf near the bottom was a row of books standing behind the others; the next moment she had one of these in her hand and was looking at the name of the author: Krafft-Ebing—she had never heard of that author before. All the same she opened the battered old book, then she looked more closely, for there on its margins were notes in her father's small, scholarly hand and she saw that her own name appeared in those notes. (207)

Locating Stephen in a sexological textbook with the annotations of the father, who in the absence of a sexologist in the novel is the diagnostician, the one who "knows" Stephen's condition, this complex referencing builds Stephen's narrative into the framework of sexology. With the sexologist's preface to the narrative and the sexological citations in Stephen's story, the intertextual layering between sexological text and novel makes clear that Stephen's story depends on sexological case histories and that Stephen's narrative could in turn be read *as* a sexological case history of inversion. In these sexological authorizations *The Well* is thoroughly embedded in and interchangeable with sexological narrative.

In the reception of sexology the devaluation of gender inversion as homosexuality has derived from and amounted to a failure to distinguish narratives. The notion that inversion was really homosexuality, that the gender-inverted paradigms of sexual inversion are really same-sex desire, has discounted the subjects' autobiographical speech and credited the sexologist with authoring a master narrative. While we must take the discursive framework into account (we wouldn't have inversion or indeed transsexuality as a diagnosis without it—in both cases medicalizations of narrative), we must note first the internal sense of difference that compelled subjects to seek a clinician, and second that in the case histories of inversion the sexologist played as much the role of editor as doctor, indeed was an oral historian before he was a diagnostician (the autobiographical narrative was his means of diagnosis). He collected and collated the subjects' autobiographies. There was moreover an increasing tendency as the diagnosis of inversion became more fine-tuned from Krafft-Ebbing to Havelock Ellis for the sexologist to render these subjects' autobiographies in their own words, most often prefacing them or interlinking them with diagnostic commentary. This is most obvious in Ellis himself who was especially conscious of what it meant to be the discursive channel for such stories and the problems of truth and authenticity this method raised. Ellis questions the notion that narrative is inauthentic and unreliable because it is embedded in a sexological framework, discursive. Though "there is no doubt that inverts have frequently been stimulated to set down the narrative of their own experiences through reading those written by others . . . the stimulation has, as often as not, lain in the fact that their own experiences have seemed different, not that they have seemed identical."[10] In other words he credits the difference of the subject's story, precisely the distinguishing power of autobiographical narrative. In the contemporary reception of sexology in conjunction with the poststructuralist suspicion toward narrative—particularly autobiographical narrative, which has become indistinguishable from fiction—the subject's speech in the sexological case history, its difference, has been devalued; it has not been recognized by Foucault and his acolytes who have underestimated the subject's speech in order to emphasize construction. Such autobiographies in their very difference produce certain patterns, certain kinds of distinguishing tropes, and indeed a different *genre* of transgendered narrative emerges even when (especially when) told in the subjects' own words. This genre or different kind of story remains remarkably consistent even up to that of today's transsexuals and its narrative patterns share much with Stephen in *The Well*. In the most extreme cases of inversion, which I suggest are transsexual, these patterns can be noted as a sense of not fitting in in sex, of wrong embodiment, of a split between sex and gender; and a compulsion to live as much as possible according to the opposite sex—to transition *anyway*.

There is also in many cases, a crucial distinction between homosexual and transsexual narratives, a rejection of same-sex relations as same sex. In the case of Ellis's D, for example, she sees her body not her gender as a mistake—"Ever since I can remember anything at all, I could never think of myself as a girl. . . . I regarded the conformation of my body as a mysterious accident"—and, feeling a "hiatus . . . between my bodily structure and my feelings," puts it down to being trapped in the wrong body: "I thought that the ultimate explanation might be that there were men's minds in women's bodies."[11] Or Krafft-Ebing's Countess Sarolta V/Count Sandor V, who with his aristocratic upbringing, the father who raises her as a boy, with a love of riding and fencing, seems of all sexological case histories closest to Stephen's plot; while loving women indeed profusely—frequenting brothels, marrying twice *and* having affairs—he himself remained profoundly untouchable, used a sexual prosthesis ("a stocking stuffed with oakum as a priapus"), and is clearly sex dysphoric in rejecting sexual stimulation and feeling revulsion at his own menstruation and living all his life as a man.[12] In these most inverted narratives given the extent of cross-gendered identification it is questionable to what extent any sexual activity can be termed "homosexual" or same sex. What emerges is a split between bodily feeling and body, gender, and sex that cannot be compensated by love for the other. While some inverted subjects certainly were homosexual—for the typology of inversion bought these subjects together—in the most inverted cases, that is in the condition in its essence, homosexual love is not predominant but rather a profound gender dysphoria. It seems that rather than inversion being a symptom or construction of homosexuality as it has been read, homosexuality was on the contrary one symptom of transgender. Cross-gender was structured into the very definition of inversion in its origins. Thus Ulrichs described his own male inversion as a case of "a womanly soul in a man's body": "*Sunt mihi barba maris, artus, corpusque virile/His inclusa quidem: sed sum maneoque puella.*"[13] [I have a manly beard, limbs and a masculine body; these indeed trap me; but I am and remain a woman.] And Krafft-Ebing's antipathic or inverted sexual instinct mapped out and measured after Ulrichs's typology for the first time in a medicalized framework a *psychopathia sexualis*: transgender, not homosexuality. We should not be surprised then, though again it has been overlooked in the reading of sexology, that it is under the category of inversion that we find the earliest instances of subjects already attempting actual sex change: for example, a woman who had undergone a bilateral mastectomy in 1922[14] and another female who had undergone some form of genital masculinization as early as 1882.[15] Sexual inversion *was* gender inversion.

Decoding herself according to a sexological case history Stephen is aware of herself as a qualitatively different subject. She is the most "pronounced" (356) in her inversion among inverts in the novel—all of whom are marked by some form of gender inversion; she is quite different from Valérie Seymour who has successful lesbian relationships and can't understand Stephen's moroseness, her sense of embodied tragedy and of a different plot. Stephen is also quite set apart from Hall's other novelistic protagonists, for instance Joan Ogden,[16] though she comes closest to Miss Ogilvy in the short story "Miss Ogilvy Finds Herself," who discovers herself to be a reincarnated man.[17] What marks Stephen as distinct is above all her narrative, the gender-inverted body narrative of the transsexual. This narrative is installed in Stephen from the beginning; at work in the unfolding of Stephen's plot is the syntax of the transsexual narrative, which is in type reconstructive both literally and literarily, a desire for surgical reconstruction in body and a retrospective narrative, a constant looking back that will allow this surgery, a nostalgic attempt to get back what should have been—that is the original felt gender belied by the body. This "should have been" is repeated like a mantra in the novel. The narrative voice as much as Stephen and others articulates what should have been. Stephen's naming as a boy is the one moment in the novel that daringly puts into practice what should have been, the one moment in the real of the plot that refuses to accept the real of her sex. Lady Anna is described as "great with the child who should have been her son" (93). And Stephen herself grows up envying "a man's life, the life that should have been hers" (100)—wanting to fight in the war, wear men's clothes, marry, and so forth. The narrative is driven forward by this "should have been," its direction compelled by this conditional perfect of the modal auxiliary, by the desire to return to reconstruct a past that failed. Reconstruction of the transsexual's body and his/her narrative is above all nostalgic: a pain for home (*nostos* + *algos*), a longing for the home of gender in the sexed body.

This desire to go home, this should have been, is manifested in Stephen's sexed body. It is the female sexed body that is *unheimlich* in Stephen, setting up a disruption in coherent gendered syntax between sex and gender, the transsexual's split between sex and gender that is the schematic identifier of the transsexual's narrative; they do not agree. Stephen is a perfect copy of a man in her gender, but because of her female sex this manliness becomes pastiche. She grows up in her body "dar[ing] to resemble" (203) her father yet crucially failing to reproduce him: she is a "caricature of Sir Philip; a blemished, unworthy, maimed reproduction" (11). She is too strong, tall, narrow-hipped, broad-shouldered, large-handed, cleft-chinned, big-jawed for a woman, a man visibly in a woman's body. Her transgendering is thus embodied. This accords in sexology with its most extreme forms of inversion where the gender inversion is embodied almost as sex inversion. Thus for Krafft-Ebing, his fourth type of invert or antipathic sexual instinct, what he called the "complete cases" of inversion, are manifestly cross-sexed, in which "the physical form is correspondingly altered."[18] And Ellis also notes symptoms of embodied inversion from hirsuitism to "genuine approximations to the masculine type."[19] The reason for this embodiment is that often glandular theories of inversion are at work, one belief being that sexual inversion had a somatic cause and manifested itself in the body; Ellis for instance documents a number of what we would call hormonal theories of inversion not so different from some theories of transsexuality today. And Stephen's gender inversion is also embodied in the sense that her transgendering is deeply felt, so that even when not visible in the body her feeling is as a man, and this is of course much more important for motivating the transsexual desire for reconstruction. The narrative thus drives toward the revelation of a body that is maimed or lacking. The novel accretes images of bodily lack for Stephen, suggesting that something—something material—is missing. A phantom morphology haunts Stephen in the text, a body that is completely male, which when overlaid on her real female body renders this incomplete. Stephen suffers "some great sense of loss, some great sense of incompleteness" (101); she is "defrauded" (12, 163); her body is "maimed" (104), "maimed and insufferable" (217), "sorely afflicted" (217); and she suffers from "bodily dejection" (140), is a "genius . . . in the chains of the flesh, a fine spirit subject to physical bondage" (217). This is a body narrative that shows Stephen as a female-to-male transsexual, not woman or lesbian, undergoing progressive realization of her wrong embodiment. The narrative does not ease up on or allow accommodation to her body through desire but shows a worsening of its uninhabitability as the discrepancy between her gender identification as male and her sex as female becomes more obvious.

This progression can most economically be documented in three scenes, one each from childhood, adolescence, and young adulthood, turning points in all gender careers and as much so in Stephen's narrative. The first scene, of Stephen as a child, shows her realizing for the first time through crossdressing the discrepancy between her gender identification and her sex. At first her felt body image is consistent with her projected/reflected image. She dresses as Nelson and is told that she that she "look[s] exactly like a boy" (16). In response she says that she is one: "Yes, of course I'm a boy. . . . I must be a boy, 'cause I feel exactly like one" (16). Ontology equals feeling. However, Stephen discovers that feeling like does not constitute being, and she uncovers the split between her gender identification and her biological sex. She finds that dressing up as Nelson is "only pretending or playing" (38) and "*being* a girl spoilt everything—even Nelson" (33, emphasis mine). In other words, on her discovery of the sexed real performing boyness not only doesn't compensate for not being a boy, it brings into relief that not being in the body—the discrepancy between feeling and sexed ontology. Thus in the second scene Stephen turns on her body. Now an adolescent not fitting in as a girl, she vents her anger at her femaleness, her ineluctable location as a woman. Her mother has sought to feminize her with a dress, and Stephen is now more conscious of the discrepancy between feminine placement and gendered feeling. Stephen realizes the "inimical feelings" between dress and model: "'It's my face,' she announced, 'something's wrong with my face'" (71), at first blaming her flesh, her face serving here to metonymize her *unheimlich* body. However a shift occurs as she turns on the dress itself—realizing that it is not what makes her masculine that needs changing but what makes her feminine, what is feminine about her. That the dress like the face serves as metonymy or rather metaphor of her (since femininity is not *really part* of her) is clear from the slippage from dress to self in the first sentence:

> She wrenched off the dress and hurled it from her, longing intensely to rend it, to hurt it, longing to hurt herself in the process, yet filled all the while with that sense of injustice. But this mood changed abruptly to one of self pity; she wanted to sit down and weep over Stephen; on a sudden impulse she wanted to pray over Stephen as though she were someone apart, yet terribly personal in her trouble. Going over to the dress she smoothed it out slowly; it seemed to have acquired an enormous importance; it seemed to

have acquired the importance of prayer, the poor, crumpled thing lying crushed and dejected. (71–72)

The language of violence—rend, hurt—and the slippage between the dress and herself suggest that more is invested in the dress than simply clothing—that something of her female body is invested. And the shift in mood, from injustice to self-pity, from wrenching off the dress to feeling sorry for it and treating it smoothly, dramatizes the terrible split in Stephen between gender and sex—a split that is in and defines the transsexual subject, that, as this scene suggests, can be traumatic, and that a transsexual narrative would seek to reconcile.

The third scene makes this split schematic in a mirror scene and this is most symptomatic of a transsexual narrative, in which mirror scenes proliferate as motifs because they dramatize the difference between the image reflected and the body image projected; this scene is remarkably congruent with contemporary transsexual narratives. That it is also one of the most quoted passages in the book (see Newton, de Lauretis, and Halberstam in this volume) also makes evident that it is very revealing of the body narrative of this book. The scene appears at a crucial point in the narrative, when Stephen realizes she is being rejected by her lover Angela Crossby for the "real" man Roger Antrim, replaced by this rival whose "right to be perfectly natural" she has always envied (44). This is Stephen's first real relationship and Angela has already confirmed Stephen's worst fears that the reason for her replacement is her inadequacy as a man, that she is *not* a man: "If you were a man—[Angela] stopped abruptly, and burst into uncontrollable weeping" (177). It is soon after this that Stephen returns home to enact the mirror scene and the mirror's reflection serves to bring home her not being male in body.

That night she stared at herself in the glass; and even as she did so she hated her body with its muscular shoulders, its small compact breasts, and its slender flanks of an athlete. All her life she must drag this body of hers like a monstrous fetter imposed on her spirit. This strangely ardent yet sterile body that must worship and yet never be worshiped in return by the creature of its adoration. She longed to maim it, for it made her feel cruel; it was so white, so strong, and so self-sufficient; yet withal so poor and unhappy a thing that her eyes filled with tears and her hatred turned to pity. She began to grieve over it, touching her breasts with pitiful fingers, stroking her shoulders, letting her hands slip along her straight thighs—Oh, poor and most desolate body! (187–188)

Read in the unfolding plot of the transsexual's body narrative, and a progressive realization of the traumatic discrepancy between sex and gender, the mirror scene heightens in its cathexes, in the split between body and self, in the change in mood, the symptoms of the earlier scenes. It is the most embodied and yet also strangely disembodied scene in the novel. Because the scene enacts the same shift from anger and the desire to maim/rend to pity and a strange stepping outside of the body, we are now clear that the earlier dress is a substitution for the body. What makes this body uninhabitable is its femaleness. The body is visibly transgendered—"its muscular shoulders . . . and its slender flanks of an athlete . . . so strong, and so self sufficient"—as Stephen has sought to make it more so with her swinging of dumbbells and riding. Yet it is still a discernibly female body with its "compact breasts." *Pace* de Lauretis who explicitly "works against the grain" of the novel and thus must issue "a word of warning,"[20] it is this very transgendered ambivalence that Stephen hates; it is masculine yet fails adequately to be male; its femaleness, which renders it *unheimlich*, is evident. The thrice repetition of the "yet" in this short passage underscores syntactically precisely this ambivalence, the shifting irreconcilable splits between Stephen's transgendered desires and her intractable body that we saw in earlier scenes, between her sex and her gender. And if the sense of corporeal imprisonment suggests the transsexual's plight of being "trapped in the wrong body," the desire to maim this body precisely because it is already experienced as maimed, castrated, incomplete suggests the transsexual's desire to rectify this entrapment with surgical reconstruction, to take the knife to rend the flesh.

That Stephen does not of course transition in the novel I would suggest has less to do with its early moment than because of the discrepancy between the subject and her author. As we have seen, some inverts did transition. Though she called herself an invert, it would seem that Radclyffe Hall herself was not the most inverted type, differing most from her protagonist in having long and successful relationships with two women. Stephen infamously does not have successful relationships and, as recognized by generations of lesbian critics, the novel shows lesbian relations repeatedly and irredeemably doomed; it is "a narrative of damnation" as Stimpson says.[21] As in the most inverted of sexological case histories her lovers, the bodies of others, notably fail to compensate for this lack in Stephen's body and Stephen is always trumped by the "real" man, shown as lacking, maimed next to his completion. First Stephen loses Collins the housemaid to the footman; then she loses Angela to Roger Antrim, and finally, as the novel ends, Stephen herself pushes Mary to Martin Hallam, a triple triangulation that leaves Stephen uncoupled, always the odd one out. While Stephen notably attempts to compensate for "natural" sexed differences in her relationships with those of class, this attempt to mark herself out as different and dominant also proves insufficient next to the norm of embodied heterosexuality. This is surely what it is at work in her repeatedly selecting a lover of lower class than herself. And it is in this feature that the novel veers clearly from any affiliation with a lesbian butch narrative, because it shows the body of the lover failing to compensate for the "wound" of the butch. Hall herself was probably, as Halberstam convincingly argues, more in this category of lesbian or transgendered butch since she did have successful queer relationships. Why she chose to represent a different (transsexual) invert in her novel suggests something about the borders of these subjects in her own unconscious; as Gayle Rubin has argued, the borders between stone butch and transsexual are of course crossable[22]—and where else but inversion in this shared history is this more the case?

However, while Hall doesn't transition Stephen's plot on to transition in *The Well of Loneliness*, there is one moment of bodily healing in the novel displaced appropriately enough from the real of the plot to a dream to the unconscious of this text. That it is the sole dream in the novel, a phantasmagoric narrative embedded in this otherwise realistic novel, also makes it especially prominent. Yet it is only now with the increasing attention to body narratives of diverse subjects that it is receiving critical attention.[23] The dream figures the fantastic possibilities of reconfigured flesh. The dream occurs during Stephen's childhood love for Collins, sparked by the "housemaid's knee" episode in which Collins's knee has swollen with fluid as a result of polishing floors on her hands and knees. In her childhood fantasy Stephen desires this swelling to be transferred from Collins to herself so that she can undergo the "'orrible operation" (17) that Collins fears. It is in the midst of her prayers for this fleshly transference (prayers that prefigure later prayers Stephen will make over her body) that Stephen slips into a dream:

> "Please, Jesus, give me a housemaid's knee instead of Collins—do, *do*, Lord Jesus. Please Jesus, I would like to bear all Collins' pain the way You did. . . . I would like to wash Collins in my blood, Lord Jesus—and I would like very much to be a Saviour to Collins—I love her, and I want to be hurt like You were. . . . Please give me a knee that's all full of water."
>
> This petition she repeated until she fell asleep to dream that in some queer way she was Jesus and that Collins was kneeling and kissing her hand, because she, Stephen, had managed to cure her by cutting her knee with a bone paper-knife and grafting it on to her own. The dream was a mixture of rapture and discomfort and it stayed quite a long time with Stephen. (18)

The identificatory shifts in the dream originate in a prior real moment in which Collins exposes her "afflicted member" (17) to the young anxious Stephen. These shifts allow Stephen to take on or *as* herself both the afflicted body of the other and the healing of this body via fleshly substitution. Within this fantasy of healing via substitution, Stephen uncovers her own "afflicted member"—the maimed and defrauded body evident in the Nelson, dress, and mirror scenes—and this becomes the unconscious focus of the dream. This chain of substitution (Stephen = Jesus = Collins) is suggested in the syntactic confusion in the passage. Subjects and objects are ambiguous; pronouns quickly lose their referents and properties are left unspecified. It is clear that Collins is kneeling and Stephen is curing. Yet whose knee is being cut and what part of the body is receiving the grafted swelling (her own what?) are left wonderfully obscure. Does not this ambiguity allow the dream to stand, in its context of inversion and the transgendering of inversion, as a transsexual narrative of flesh grafted from one part of the body to heal the female-to-male transsexual's own "afflicted member"? The donor site here is the body of the other, and Stephen effectively rescues herself from her own defrauded maleness through her beloved's body, compensating for her lack with the other's donation. Cutting through the flesh with a bone paper-knife, *The Well*'s reassignment dream omits the as yet unrealized details of surgical intervention, passing over the surgery by placing it in the past tense ("*had* managed to cure her"). Yet the dream of transferable flesh resonates powerfully as a reassignment dream in the context of the novel's inverted narrative and its inverted moment. In the absence of real healing of Stephen's body in the plot of The Well, the dream unconsciously takes Stephen's transgendered narrative to its logical somatic conclusion and fantastically prefigures the healing possibilities of the surgical grafting of the flesh.

While Stephen's transition takes place only in fantasy and she does not escape from the "no man's land of sex" (77), in reality the first transsexual to undergo full technological transition and become the first full female-to-male transsexual did so in 1946.[24] In this momentous transition The Well played a crucial pivotal role. For Michael Dillon the key text that he turns to to illustrate his explanation of transsexuality and the text with which he identifies is The Well of Loneliness and Stephen's story: "Some years ago Radclyffe Hall published a novel entitled The Well of Loneliness. It was a penetrating title and the story was concerned with this subject, the life of a girl of this type and her difficulties at the attitude of others towards her."[25] "This type" turns out to be a "masculine homosexual," a term Dillon uses to refer to both Stephen and himself. Writing in the absence of inverted categories, when homosexuality and psychology were on the ascendant, Dillon must use a typology of homosexuality to write this first treatise on transsexuality; critics of sexology agree that it was psychoanalysis that led to the replacement of sexology. But while for the lesbian and gay context in which sexology has been received this replacement is seen as progressive, for both Dillon and Hall the turns away from the body and material sex that accompanied psychoanalysis were a setback. Hall takes care in The Well to mock psychoanalysis, in one brief reference to Sándor Ferenczi, showing that she knows it and doesn't need it: Brockett refers to Stephen developing complexes and says she better take to reading Ferenczi. For Dillon, like Hall eschewing the turn to psychoanalysis and the passing of sexology, the solution is to perform a quasi-sexological typology in which feminine and masculine homosexuals come to stand for the most inverted, i.e. transsexual, as distinguished against effeminate and mannish homosexuals who, more performative in their gender with less desire to cross to be feminine and masculine, are homosexual.

That the feminine and masculine homosexuals are not really homosexuals is evident from the typography of quotation marks around homosexuals that Dillon uses to hold the term at a distance; these are gendered subjects not sexual. What distinguishes feminine and masculine homosexuals from effeminate and mannish homosexuals, transsexual from homosexual, is above all a narrative that seeks to reconstruct. Dillon finds in feminine and masculine a clearly different retroactive narrative, one that is marked from the beginning and expresses retrodiction.

> The pretty curly-headed boy with pink complexion . . . objects to fights, to mud and dirt and to sports, and . . . prefers his sister's doll. . . . The girl, on the other hand, lean and wiry, scorns dolls and girl's games, likes to play Indians and soldiers, and is ever ready for some risky adventure or a fight. . . . Invariably the cry is "I have always felt as if I were a girl," or alternatively from the girl comes the cry: "I always felt as if I were a man." In these instances the body may approximate in essentials to one sex, male or female, but the personality is wholly peculiar to the opposite one.[26]

With the symptom of the body expressed in this narrative the solution must be somatic reconstruction according to Dillon: "Surely, where the mind cannot be made to fit the body, the body should be made to fit, approximately, at any rate to the mind."[27] This argument would be taken up to become the engine of transsexual research.

It is at the end of the forties that the transsexual would be diagnosed in the first transsexual sexological texts and the medical technology would be harnessed to such arguments to allow the transsexual, as a transsexual, to transition in body as well as narrative. That primitive thing, as Hall calls Stephen, will be named and medical treatment justified; as Puddle explains, "you're unexplained as yet—you've not got your niche in creation" (153). And in the fifties and sixties the sexologists who worked with transsexuals, what we might call the second wave of sexology, would, as they undertook this task, go back to the first wave of sexologists and their case histories of inversion in order to understand this cross-gendered as distinct from homosexual condition. Far from being anachronistic then, Stephen in this turbulent age of transition is prefigurative, primitive only in the sense of being a forerunner. It is not surprising that within this sexological material and by the subjects of it, *The Well* is read literally and quite comfortably over and over again as a transsexual narrative.

Notes

1. George Chauncey, "From Sexual Inversion to Homosexuality: Medicine and the Changing Conceptualization of Female Deviance," *Salmagundi* 58/69 (1982/1983): 118.

2. Michel Foucault, *The History of Sexuality*, vol. 1, *An Introduction*, trans. Robert Hurley (New York: Vintage, 1990), p. 43. For new contexts for sexology see Lucy Bland and Laura Doan (eds.), *Sexology in Culture: Labelling Bodies and Desires* (Cambridge: Polity Press, 1998), in which my essay "Transsexuals and the Transsexologists: Inversion and the Emergence of Transsexual Subjectivity" (116–132) maps out the nonhomosexual, transgendered patterns of sexual inversion.

3. Sandra M. Gilbert and Susan Gubar, *Sexchanges*, vol. 2, *No Man's Land: The Place of the Woman Writer in the Twentieth Century* (New Haven: Yale University Press, 1989), p. 220.

4. Esther Newton, "The Mythic Mannish Lesbian: Radclyffe Hall and the New Woman," pp. 99 and 100 in this volume.

5. Catharine Stimpson, *Where the Meanings Are: Feminism and Cultural Spaces* (New York: Routledge, 1984), p. 100.

6. This essay draws on material from my book *Second Skins: The Body Narratives of Transsexuality* (New York: Columbia University Press, 1998) where I analyze the transsexual narrative in more depth.

7. Havelock Ellis, Commentary, p. 35 in this volume.

8. Michael Baker, *Our Three Selves: The Life of Radclyffe Hall* (New York: William Morrow, 1985), pp. 205–206. Laura Doan's research elucidates that Hall probably intended Ellis's note as book copy.

9. Radclyffe Hall, *The Well of Loneliness* (1928; reprint, London: Virago, 1982), p. 23. All further references from this text.

10. Havelock Ellis, *Studies in the Psychology of Sex*, vol. 2, *Sexual Inversion* (New York: Random, 1936), p. 90.

11. Ellis, *Sexual Inversion*, pp. 235, 234, 241.

12. Richard von Krafft-Ebing, *Psychopathia Sexualis: With Especial Reference to the Antipathic Sexual Instinct*, trans. from the 10th German edition by F. J. Rebman (London: Rebman Ltd., 1901), p. 425.

13. Hubert Kennedy, *Ulrichs: The Life and Work of Karl Heinrich Ulrichs, Pioneer of the Modern Gay Movement* (Boston: Alyson, 1988), p. 56.

14. Leslie Lothstein, *Female-to-Male Transsexualism: Historical, Clinical, and*

Theoretical Issues (Boston: Routledge, 1983), p. 59.

15. Vern Bullough and Bonnie Bullough, *Cross-Dressing, Sex, and Gender* (Philadelphia: Pennsylvania University Press, 1993), p. 255.

16. Radclyffe Hall, *The Unlit Lamp* (London: Virago, 1981).

17. Radclyffe Hall, "Miss Ogilvy Finds Herself," in Sandra Gilbert and Susan Gubar, eds., *The Norton Anthology of Literature by Women* (New York: Norton, 1996), pp. 1395–1407.

18. Krafft-Ebing, *Psychopathia Sexualis*, p. 188.

19. Ellis, *Sexual Inversion*, p. 255.

20. Teresa de Lauretis, "Perverse Desire: The Lure of the Mannish Lesbian," p. 112 in this volume.

21. Stimpson, *Where the Meanings Are*, p. 45.

22. Gayle Rubin, "Of Catamites and Kings: Reflections on Butch, Gender, and Boundaries," in Joan Nestle, ed., *The Persistent Desire: A Femme-Butch Reader* (Boston: Alyson, 1992), pp. 466–482.

23. See also Trevor Hope's reading of this dream in this volume, p. 259.

24. Liz Hodgkinson, *Michael Née Laura* (London: Columbus, 1989).

25. Michael Dillon, *Self: A Study in Endocrinology and Ethics* (London: Heinemann, 1946), p. 51.

26. Ibid., pp. 50–51.

27. Ibid., p. 53.

9

"A Writer of Misfits": "John" Radclyffe Hall
and the Discourse of Inversion

JUDITH HALBERSTAM

And it may be that being myself a "misfit," for as you know beloved, I am a born invert, it may be that I am a writer of "misfits" in one form or another—I think I understand them—their joys & sorrows, indeed I know I do, and all the misfits of this world are lonely, being conscious that they differ from the rank and file.
—John Radclyffe Hall, letter to Evguenia Souline, October 24, 1934[1]

Introduction

At the beginning of the twentieth century, as Michel Foucault has argued, the discourse of sexuality became a medical discourse and sexual acts were transformed through complex discursive practices into stable notions of identity.[2] By the early teens and the 1920s, communities of inverts and their "wives" had developed into visible and elaborate subcultures and, with the publication in 1928 of Radclyffe Hall's novel of inversion, *The Well of Loneliness,* the topic of inversion became highly publicized. Hall's complex understanding of her own sexual subjectivity has been handed down to modern readers in the form of her novels, her letters, and recollections of her life made by her partner Una Troubridge and many other literary luminaries. The recent publication of Hall's letters allows for new insights about the psychic mechanisms of inversion and the romantic relations between inverts and their lovers. By historically contextualizing here the life of Radclyffe Hall—or John as she insisted upon being called—I want to call attention to the multiple and contradictory models of female masculinity produced by not only John but also her many inverted friends and contemporaries.

Inversion as a theory of homosexuality folded gender variance and sexual preference into one economical package and attempted to explain all deviant behavior in terms of a firm and almost intuitive belief in a binary system of sexual stratification in which the stability of the terms "male" and "female" depended upon the stability of the homosexual-heterosexual binary. When, some fifty years later, lesbian feminists came to reject inversion as an explanation for same-sex sexuality, they also rejected female masculinity as the overriding category of lesbian identification, putting in her place the woman-identified woman who is most often gender androgynous. In order to reconstitute the history of female masculinity, we actually have to accept that the invert may not be a synonym for "lesbian" but that the concept of inversion both produced and described a category of biological women who felt at odds with their anatomy. The literature on inversion and the medical category of "invert" in many ways collapsed all of the different distinctions between masculine women, distinctions that we can read back into our understanding of sexual variance and gender deviance by examining just a few different kinds of female masculinity from the 1920s. The most elaborate of all the depictions of early twentieth century female masculinity, of course, came from John Radclyffe Hall.

In an odd and even fantastical short story called "Miss Ogilvy Finds Herself," written in 1926 and published in 1934, John Radclyffe Hall tells the story of a "sexually inverted woman" who had served in the army during the Great War and then had been cast aside after the war ended. Both this short story and The Well of Loneliness explore the supposedly melancholic existence of women who feel themselves to be men. In and around Hall herself were dozens of masculine women, many living under male names, some cross-dressing and passing, some switching back and forth between male and female drag, some serving in the army, some in the Women's Auxiliary Police Force, some living with other masculine women, some settling down with more feminine "wives," some even settling into odd threesomes. Most of these women were aristocratic or middle-class or had inherited wealth; many were artists. In the past, their stories have been read into and out of the story of sexual inversion and their specificities have been lost in what we might call the parsimony of science. Medical experts, in other words, tried to force multiple expressions of sexual and gender deviance into a very narrow range of categories and they tried to explain a huge array of physicalities in relation to the binary system of sexual difference that they were absolutely committed to bolstering and preserving. Closer examination of the lives of even a few inverts restores some of the complexity of early twentieth-century sexual identifications to the historical record. While it is by no means satisfactory to study only the lives of rich and even aristocratic inverts, it is much harder to trace the patterns of identification of lower-class women. Given the many stories of passing women infiltrating the military and other male-dominated spaces at this time, we can assume that working-class women took other routes to masculinity.[3]

"Miss Ogilvy Finds Herself" was both a trial run for *The Well of Loneliness* and a sort of tribute to Hall's good friend Toupie Lowther. Hall and her partner, Una Troubridge, had met Toupie in 1920 and Hall was quite taken with Toupie's military career and her generally gallant demeanor. Toupie Lowther was an overtly masculine aristocratic woman who had flourished during the war when she ran a women's ambulance unit. Hall's biographer Michael Baker cites a "probably apocryphal" story about Toupie Lowther that tells of her arrest at the "Franco-Italian frontier for cross-dressing as a man." On the way home, the story has it, Lowther was arrested again "for masquerading as a woman"! (125). After the war Lowther, perhaps surprisingly, did not disappear into oblivion and ignominious death; in fact, she received a Croix de Guerre for her service and enjoyed considerable notoriety as a war hero.[4] A newspaper article from 1919 describes Lowther as "one of the first women in England to have ridden a motorcycle," and it celebrates her as "sportswoman who could hold her own at anything that required skill and brains."[5] Lowther was also a first-class tennis player and a champion fencer. According to Una Troubridge's diaries, John and Toupie went car shopping together and would spend time together working on their vehicles. Una and John came to call Toupie "Brother," and they referred to Toupie using male pronouns. The First World War obviously gave some masculine women the opportunity to live out the kinds of active lives that in peacetime they could only fantasize about. Although Lowther's ambulance unit was constantly hampered by conventional notions of female activity, they also did see active combat and many of these women were applauded for the first time in their lives for behaving more like men than women. The newspaper stories celebrating Lowther's heroics praise her for precisely those activities that may earlier in the century have been opposed to notions of true womanhood. Furthermore, the public celebration of Lowther suggests that the masculine woman, at least briefly in the postwar years, was not always reduced to being a misfit or a figure of abject loneliness.

Toupie and Miss Ogilvy, as well as Hall's more famous hero, Stephen Gordon, seem much more closely related to what we now call a "transsexual" identity than they do to lesbianism. Indeed, the history of homosexuality and transsexuality was a shared history at the beginning of the twentieth century and only separated in the 1940s when surgery and hormonal treatments were available to and demanded by some cross-identifying subjects. Because masculine identified lesbians and transsexuals seem to share an investment in the narratives of inversion, there has been some dispute about the place of *The Well of Loneliness* in histories of gender variance: in other words, is this a lesbian novel or a transgender novel? I think there is no way to decide such a dispute since lesbian and transsexual were not separate categories in the 1920s and the word "invert" covered a wide range of cross-identifications. It is very possible to read *The Well*, as I do here, as an early narrative of female masculinity, and by doing so, I do not claim the novel for a "lesbian" history; rather, I attempt to place it squarely within its proper historical context as a novel of inversion. Inversion and masculinity and same sex desire meant many different things to many different women in the 1920s in Europe. Even if we just compare Hall's fictional characters Miss Ogilvy and Stephen Gordon, it is clear that Miss Ogilvy quite distinctly desires to be a man while Stephen Gordon desires masculinity and female companionship. Similarly, there are clear differences and even rivalries between masculine women who note differences between themselves that others may not pick up on. Hall, for example, seemed to envy Lowther her heroism and her mechanical aptitudes. Clearly, the differences between and among inverts, as well as the similarities between them contributed to the strengthening of the sense of sexuality as an identity. These differences also provide different trajectories for the experience of female masculinity. Some women may have seriously wanted to change their sex, others, we must conclude, were less intent upon the notion of a sex change and more interested in sexual tolerance for masculine women.

Masculine identification with social impunity required money and social status. As independently wealthy people with high social standing and money to travel, Una Troubridge and John Radclyffe Hall lived the good life. What is more, they lived among a large community of other couples and other "inverts," all of whom were managing to find their place and leave their marks. In *Our Three Selves*, Michael Baker remarks upon Una and John's community and he gives details from a reading of Una's diaries of some of the other masculine women, such as Toupie Lowther, and their lovers who populated John and Una's life. John and Una knew the masculine artist Romaine Brooks, the salon diva Natalie Barney; they were friends with the cross-dressing Vita Sackville-West and many other less public "sexual deviants." Among their personal friends were a strange ménage à trois made up of Edy Craig (the actress Ellen Terry's daughter), the writer Christopher St. John (real name Christabel Marshall), and the painter Clare Atwood who was known as Tony. Chris and Tony both wore men's clothing and, obviously, took men's names. They also knew the policewomen Mary Allen and Margaret Damer Dawson, both of whom were masculine women who rarely appeared in public without their mannish police uniforms.[6]

Critics have disagreed profoundly on the meaning of Hall's own masculinity. Esther Newton reads Hall's masculinity as part of her sexual personae and as an expression of a true self.[7] Terry Castle, in a book on the otherwise obscured relationship between Noel Coward and Radclyffe Hall, reads Hall's masculinity as, at least in part, an imitation of Coward's look. She writes: "Was Hall—whose studious cultivation of the same "slick and satiny" masculine look throughout the '20's made her famous—one of Coward's many imitators?"[8] Of course, Castle is not suggesting that Hall simply copied Coward's style, but she is arguing for the importance of "vibrant cross-gender relationships" within the history of homosexuals (12). Calling them "kindred spirits," Castle reads Coward and Hall through and alongside each others' work and biography. While this is an admirable project in some respects, with regard to the question of Hall's masculinity and indeed Coward's femininity, Castle links female masculinity to the imitation of queer maleness and male femininity to the imitation of queer femaleness and thereby renders cross-gender expressions as wholly derivative.

Another commentator also remains an unbeliever on the topic of Hall's masculinity. Joanne Glasgow has produced an edited volume of some of Hall's obsessive love letters in the last decade of Hall's life to Evguenia Souline. The volume, *Dear John*, is an amazing addition to the record of Hall's life and to the history of inversion in general. Glasgow provides an introduction to the letters and, as well as establishing the history of Hall's relationship with Souline, she also attempts to situate Hall's thoughts on inversion. Stephen Gordon, Glasgow proposes, is clearly not an autobiographical protagonist or "John's last word on the nature of inversion."[9] As Glasgow understands John's views on inversion from her letters, it lies in "the profound difference in her erotic desires" rather than an inverted expression of masculinity. Glasgow writes:

> As the letters reveal, it is precisely this difference in erotic desires that defines the invert in John's view—not "mannishness," certainly not dress or personal style or mannerisms or activities. She believed that sexual orientation was not determined by how one acts, but rather by whom one desires, an object-relations theory of inversion. Thus, she believed that most people were probably bisexual, Souline among them. The congenital invert, like herself, was one who never had any erotic attraction to a member of the "opposite" sex. (10)

This summary of John's notions of inversion is helpful but a bit confusing. While John may well have thought that congenital inversion expressed itself in the desire for same-sex relations, she also fairly clearly stated that this expression was channeled through an essential masculinity. It was both masculinity and the desire for more feminine women that defined inversion for John. Furthermore, John's masculine aspirations are clearly stated in the letters. At numerous points in these letters to Souline, John compares herself to a man or a husband and states various desires to father Souline's children and to marry Souline. In 1934 John writes to Souline, "had I been a man I would have given you a child—as it is I am angry that I cannot do so" (97). At a later point she describes herself as "jealous as a school boy" (107). In a humorous note to Souline in 1935, John tells her lover: "I think its a good thing for a woman to be able to cook, even if she has no need to do so"; to make it clear that "a woman" in this context refers not to herself and only to Souline, John adds: "Don't laugh. I am laughing a little myself—as I write this I feel that I am thinking like an early Victorian man: 'A woman's place is in the nursery and kitchen.' No—but there's something homey about the thought of you frying ham & eggs!" (135).

Glasgow also refutes the notion that John wanted to be a man at all. She notes that in relation to the triangular relations between John, Una, and Souline, many commentators "have read John as the 'husband' in this triangle" (12). Hall's biographer Baker in particular argues that John played the role of the unfaithful husband with a wife and mistress. Glasgow responds: "I believe that Baker is simply wrong, primarily because he believes John wanted to be and tried to 'be' a man, which the letters show to be patent nonsense. John was a lesbian—not the same thing at all" (12). Glasgow may be quite right that John did not in any simple way want to be a man and she is also right to resist simply reading this complex love triangle on the model of patriarchal marriage; however, there is certainly something of the husband in John and something very mannish and not so mythic about her masculinity. Glasgow, I believe, wants to protect John's letters from a very literal reading that would find them to be a melancholic rendition of failed heterosexuality. Rather than deny all masculinity to John, however, I think the letters must be read as expressions of a complex female masculinity, one that neither copies male homosexuality nor male heterosexuality but that carves out its own gender expression. As we shall see in The Well of Loneliness, John linked her masculinity or manhood to, not simply men's clothing but to a sartorial aesthetic that actively opposed the notion of a "true sex" by equating gender and costume.

A Writer of Misfits: The Well of Loneliness (1928)

If Oscar Wilde's "The Picture of Dorian Gray" allows us to access what Eve Sedgwick has named "the epistemology of the closet,"[10] The Well of Loneliness charts a rather different sexual topography. Not the closet but the wardrobe, we might say, constitutes the epistemological terrain of The Well of Loneliness; for Stephen Gordon in no way lives her life as an open secret—in fact, she represents the unmistakable visibility of female sexual perversion when it appears in male clothing.[11] Stephen positively wears her sexuality and accordingly the novel dwells in luxurious detail upon her fetish for men's clothing and the ways in which she covets and wears it. A sartorial semiotic provides this novel with its system of knowing and unknowing, concealment and disclosure, and the trace of secrecy in this text involves not secret desires but the secret female body—Stephen's body—which of necessity remains covered. In my reading of this novel, I want to focus on the relations between the invert and her male costume and argue for the importance of recognizing an elaborate construction of gender, sexuality, and self that takes place through a dressing that is not exactly cross-dressing and that positions itself against an aesthetic of nakedness. The object of this reading is first, to question the coherence of the category of "masculine invert"; second, to examine the very specific contours of Stephen Gordon's desire and embodiment and measure it against contemporary notions of lesbianism and transsexualism; and third, to posit a gender identity that constitutes itself through clothing not simply fetishistically but in such a way as to equate nakedness with binary sexual and gender codes and the clothed self with the construction of gender itself.[12]

The Well of Loneliness operates through a number of different semiotic systems that relate sexuality to nature in various ways. One such trope is inversion and the novel deploys inversion as a narrative strategy as well as a description of Stephen Gordon's condition. For example, Stephen finds domesticity repulsive and she prefers the outdoors, the hunt, nature to the domestic hearth. Similarly in relation to her beloved home, Morton, she identifies with the house itself not the domesticity it encloses; however, she experiences Morton as a spirit "that would always remain somewhere deep down within her" (35). After she is forced to leave Morton, she carries its memory within her so that inversion now becomes a kind of mourning technique by which Stephen incorporates the places and the people she loses. Also, Stephen's relation to and rebellion from her mother is represented as a kind of inversion. When her mother is pregnant with Stephen, she assumes along with her husband that the child will be a boy; thus she carries within her own body an image of inversion, of the boy in the woman. Pregnancy, of course, is the kind of productive inversion that contrasts with the sterility of homosexual inversion. It is also interesting that Stephen's inversion is a secret to her but not to the reader for a large part of the early narrative, and we witness her first love for the housemaid Collins with an understanding that she is denied. While this seems to conform to the structure of the closet whereby knowledge and ignorance both produce queer identity, in actuality the novel suggests that Stephen is never closeted but only ignorant. There is no double structure of revelation and secrecy that the subject plies but only a system of deception in which everyone else keeps the crucial information from Stephen herself. When Stephen finally sees the housemaid kissing the footman, she responds violently to the revelation of what has been kept hidden from her alone: that is, her difference. Stephen describes the scene of heterosexual love as "catastrophic" because sexuality has been revealed to her as an act that excludes her.[13] Sir Philip,

Stephen's father, reads books about inversion and he knows what Stephen does not know about herself. In other words, the secret is a secret only to Stephen because her physical form, which she does not examine closely early on, gives her away to everyone else who sees her. The problem of self-knowledge in this novel is presented as much more difficult than the recognition of difference by others.

Since self-knowledge is the secret kept by society from the invert, it is not surprising that the climactic scene in *The Well of Loneliness* takes place in front of a mirror. Building up to this climactic scene, Stephen visits her mirror image several times along the way to self-knowledge. At the age of seventeen, Stephen attempts to manage her queerness by dressing in ways that felt appropriate: "Sometimes Stephen would appear in a thick woolen jersey, or a suit of rough tweeds" (73). Meanwhile her mother would insist that she try to wear "soft and very expensive dresses." Stephen observes her image in a mirror as this war of clothes rages on and she notes: "*Am* I queer looking or not?" (73). The omniscient narrator answers the question for her by confirming that Stephen's efforts to dress in the way her mother approved produced results that were "always far from becoming." The narrator observes: "it was open warfare, the inevitable clash of two opposing natures who sought to express themselves in apparel, since clothes after all are a form of self-expression" (73). Clothing, indeed, becomes the means by which Stephen covers her queerness and finds a comfortable gender expression. Clothing is her way of making her masculinity both real and potent, convincing and natural; without her male clothes, she is either awkward (in women's clothes) or inadequate next to the "real" embodied masculinity of a man. While Stephen's inherent masculinity does work sometimes to undermine the social conventions that allow Roger Antrim, her childhood nemesis, "his right to be perfectly natural" (47), more often it places her in competition with men in a battle that she is doomed to lose.

In a scene that has been much discussed by lesbian critics, Stephen Gordon examines her female body in the mirror and "longed to maim it for it made her feel cruel" (187). The scene, the apex of what looks like Stephen's self-hatred, has been understood by critics to represent the tragic meaning of the invert: lost in "the no-man's land of sex," the invert must constantly negotiate between her male spirit and her female body, her status as female and her masculine bearing. Esther Newton sees the scene as an expression of Stephen's "alienation from her body" (570), an alienation that she covers with men's clothing. As Newton astutely notes: "Cross-dressing for Hall is not a masquerade" (570). The mirror scene, indeed, is preceded by a short chapter detailing Stephen's shopping spree in which she buys among other things "pajamas made of white crêpe de Chine," a man's dressing gown that she describes as "an amazingly ornate garment," gloves, and an umbrella.[14] In the next section Hall describes Stephen's confrontation with a self she claims not to understand:

> That night she stared at herself in the glass; and even as she did so she hated her body with its muscular shoulders, its small compact breasts, and its slender flanks of an athlete. All her life she must drag this body of hers like a monstrous fetter imposed on her spirit. This strangely ardent yet sterile body that must worship yet never be worshiped in return by the creature of its adoration. She longed to maim it; for it made her feel cruel; it was so white so strong and so self-sufficient; yet withal so poor and unhappy a thing that her eyes filled with tears and hate turned to pity. She began to grieve over it, touching her breasts with pitiful fingers, stroking her shoulders, letting her hands slip along her straight thighs—Oh poor and most desolate body! (187)

This is an immensely complicated passage expressing as it does strange combinations of self-hate, self-pity, and awe. Stephen expresses her feelings about her body as essentially contradictory. On the one hand the body is a female "fetter" to her masculine "spirit." On the other hand, it is quite masculine in its muscularity, "compact breasts," and "slender flanks." It makes her feel like maiming it and yet it is already maimed by her sense of its incompleteness. It is "so strong" and "so self-sufficient" and yet it makes her feel pity for its strength and its sterility. Stephen furthermore feels that her body is doomed to a lifetime of worshiping without being worshiped. What are we to make of these complex contradictions, this wild swerving between self-admiration and self-hatred?

This particular version of female masculinity comes to be named "stone butch" within a lesbian vernacular in the 1950s and as such it represented a privileged and ideal version of butch gender and sexuality among butch-fem communities.[15] What is noticeable about Hall's representation of stone butchness in 1928 is that it tends to be read as a sign of self-hatred and shame by contemporary critics; if we read it alongside John's letters to

Souline, however, we can understand the dynamic between the lover and the beloved within a complex matrix of emotional economics.

Teresa de Lauretis has argued that the dynamics of this scene in *The Well of Loneliness* must be located in a "fantasy of dispossession" in which Stephen mourns her lack of femininity and must seek for this femininity constantly in other women's bodies.[16] Thus, her desire for women is always a melancholic attempt to make up for her masculinity that is not male and her femaleness that is not feminine. I want to vigorously resist such a reading because I believe it confirms the most conservative attempts to shore up the essential and historical relations between masculinity and men and it condemns masculine women once more to the pathos of male mimicry. It is not surprising that de Lauretis is committed to this reading because her book in general is an attempt to fashion a theory of lesbian desire out of Freud's "negative theory of sexuality—sexuality as perversion" (1). De Lauretis asserts that lesbian theory in general has avoided psychoanalytic readings of desire and that this avoidance has allowed Freud's assertion of the lesbian "masculinity complex" to remain undisputed and therefore potent.[17] The masculinity complex, she suggests, "has consistently precluded the conceptualization of female sexuality autonomous from the male" (xiii) and has simultaneously failed to offer any explanations for the "non-masculine lesbian" or "feminine invert." Obviously, then, de Lauretis's mission becomes the retooling of a psychoanalytic theory of lesbian desire that resists the centrality of the masculine woman and begins with the feminine lesbian; the lesbian, in other words, whose sexuality is more likely to function autonomously from men. De Lauretis's sense that the masculine woman has been wrongly installed at the center of theories of perverse female desire also leads to a version of homophobia or butchphobia that forces her to constantly read the masculine woman into a narrative of cultural conservativism (masculine women are like men and therefore not radical in any way), and she discounts over and over the masculine woman's account of her desire and her gender in favor of a model of false consciousness in which the masculine woman really wants to be feminine but because she cannot be she must hate herself and women in general.

When de Lauretis comes to the mirror scene in which Stephen confronts her "sad" body, she uses this confrontation to emblematize her theory of the fantasy of dispossession that dooms the invert to loneliness and unbelonging. De Lauretis comments that because Stephen's body is not

[margin, handwritten] Seen in her lovers— both overtly ffm. But is this her preferring the "man's" ideal woman?

feminine, it cannot receive desire from an other; however, "because it is masculine but not male, it is also inadequate to bear the subject's desire in the masculine mode" (212). One question arises here: why? Why is the masculine female body "inadequate to bearing the subject's desire in the masculine mode"? Male masculinity all too often depends upon the functionality of the penis and its ability to literally be phallic; the masculine woman, on the other hand, is not limited to the unpredictable movements of phallic desire, she can "bear the subject's desire in a masculine mode" through an artificial phallus, in her fingers, through tribadism, and so on.

John's letters to Souline give specific evidence for the idea that neither the masculine woman nor her beloved find the masculine female body "inadequate to bearing the subject's desire in the masculine mode." John references taking her lover's virginity as a sign of the functionality of female masculinity: John claims, in her letters, to have deflowered her lover Souline and this fact becomes very important in their relationship because it allows John to think of herself as the person who introduced Souline to her own passion: on June 7, 1935, John wrote to Souline: "And I thought of how virginal & innocent you were, how ignorant of physical passion—you the most passionate of all women. Oh, Soulina it is a wonderful thing that has come to me through you, for I was your first lover. Through me you are no longer a child."[18] Obviously, in her own life, John did not experience her masculinity as lack.

Finally, de Lauretis argues that this mirror scene registers that for Stephen, "the body she desires not only in Angela but also autoerotically for herself, the body she can make love to and mourns for, is a feminine, female body" (213). Nowhere, of course, does the narrative even hint at such a notion of the inadequacy of Stephen's masculinity. In fact, John provides a detailed description of Stephen taking Mary's virginity: "Like a barrier of fire her [Mary's] passion for [Stephen] flared up to forbid her the love of the man; for as great as the mystery of virginity itself, is sometimes the power of the one who destroyed it, and that power still remained these days with Stephen" (431). In The Well of Loneliness it is social disapproval that causes Stephen finally to "give away" her lover to a man and resign herself to loneliness. The novel never allows us to think that Stephen really wants to be feminine; she certainly expresses the desire to be a man but not the desire to be a womanly woman. Furthermore, for Stephen the martyr (as her name suggests) the acts of worshiping her beloved and sacrificing for her beloved are pleasurable activities; certainly, sacrifice and worship and desire are contradictory activities for Stephen, but contradiction is the name she gives to what she calls "this bitter loving" (187).

Worshiping and loving the beloved fall into an economic system of exchange for John Radclyffe Hall. Giving is not simply sacrificing, although the notion of sacrifice lends a little nobility to the form of love-making that John describes in relation to Stephen Gordon. In her letters to Souline, again, John gives great insights into the dynamics of giving and receiving that motivated the relations between the invert lover and her bisexual beloved. John is writing to Souline to try to explain the difference between "inverts" and "bisexuals"; she begins the letter as she begins many others: "My beloved."[19] John wants Souline to see inversion as "natural" and explains that "nothing in natures scheme is ever waisted [sic]." In other words, everything in nature has its place and its purpose and inverts and bisexuals both occur as part of some natural principle. While bisexuals far outnumber inverts by John's reckoning, this fact does not render the invert as "morbid" or "lonely"; as long as love is unselfish, she opines, love is natural. Unselfish desire, within John's theory of inversion, involves complex systems of giving and receiving between the invert and her lover. John writes: "If I am the 'giver' then take what I give—love and deep, deep friendship, and take it without misgiving. If I am the 'Master' then obey me in this: don't worry yourself ill by doubts and fears" (52). But the role of master can also slip into the role of slave and John tells Souline a short time after this last letter: "I'm not going to have you anyone's slave. If your anyone's slave your going to be mine, only I'd hate to have you my slave— I prefer to have that the other way round" (53). Later still John tells Souline: "I give because I love, please accept because you love" (158). John financially supported Souline throughout their involvement and then left money for her after her death. The emotional economics of the drama between beloved and the lover were also backed therefore by a financial arrangement, and throughout John positioned herself as the one who gives, as a generous lover and as a giving partner within a give-and-take arrangement. This in no way makes Souline selfish and John selfless or John noble and Souline base, nor does it guarantee even that Souline could feel secure in her role as the other woman. What it does signify, however, is an elaborate system of desire in which mutuality was not a principle and in which giving on the part of the lover does not signify her own depletion or her beloved's inadequacy or her own morbidity and her beloved's desperation.

Rather than consent then in any way, shape, or form to the idea of a "fantasy of dispossession," it makes more sense to read Stephen Gordon's mirror scene in *The Well of Loneliness* in relation to a fantasy of transformation and an economic model of desire based upon exchange value. As I have mentioned earlier, the category of invert predicts the category of transsexual as it emerges in the 1940s and 1950s. However, while the modern invention of the transsexual turns upon the medical capability to produce sex reassignment, the invention of the invert rests upon the impossibility of the sex change. Since one cannot change sex in the 1920s, the fantasy of a male body becomes the basis for a transformation of the female body into a masculine one. For Stephen, this transformation occurs through the act of dressing. Stephen's coming to consciousness about her female masculinity is accompanied by a greater and greater need for masculine clothing. While early on in her life, as we have seen, Stephen attempts to make feminine clothing fit her body, as she achieves adulthood she realizes that she is not in thrall to her female body. Stephen literally redresses the wrongs of her embodiment by taking on male clothing, meticulously tailored and fashioned to fit her masculine spirit. What she confronts then in this crucial mirror scene is not the frustrated desire for femininity or her hatred of her body but her disidentification with the naked body. Stephen's repudiation of nakedness or the biological body as the ground for sexual identity suggests a modern notion of sexual identity as not organically emanating from the flesh but as a complex act of self-creation in which the dressed body not the undressed body represents one's desire.

While some critics have obscured crucial differences between atypical women from different times, others suffer from an inadequate sense of the historical specificity of certain modes of self-understanding. The scene that I have analyzed here from *The Well of Loneliness* makes much more sense when we recall the complex ideas about clothing and masquerade that circulated between masculine women in the early twentieth century. In fact, it is perhaps only the contemporary reader who understands this mirror scene as a dreadful representation of self-hatred. In Hall's circle there were many women who felt that their masculine clothing represented their identities. The newly formed Women Police Service was filled with women who seemed to want to join up in order to wear the handsome uniforms.[20] One of the first women in the force, the extremely masculine Mary Allen (who later took the name Robert) "seems never to have taken her uniform off, even wearing it for traveling."[21] Michael Baker, reading from Una Troubridge's diaries, comments that Robert "was never happier than when wearing her uniform and highly polished boots."[22] Una and John became quite friendly with Robert and her lover, Miss Tagart, and they sympathized with Robert who felt that an earlier incarnation of the Women Police Service, the Women Police Volunteers, had been disbanded because "all they wanted were fluffy policewomen."[23] One does not want to gloss over the fact that the police force and the army are conservative institutions dedicated to the often violent preservation of law and order, yet the presence of mannish women in the ranks of these governing bodies does not always and everywhere signify politically conservative aims. Masculine women in the 1920s sought widely for political and social equality and for contexts in which their masculinity could flourish and prosper. They chose uniforms and homosocial environments, they chose occupations where they could drive cars and trucks and motorbikes, and they formed a formidable force of cross-identifying women who wore their gender and sexualities literally on their sleeves.

Among these women was John Radclyffe Hall and so we should not be surprised to find a climactic scene in her classic novel on inversion in which a woman rejects the naked image of herself. The invert rejected the female body but did not always give up on femaleness; instead she fashioned it into a masculinity she could live with. John understood herself as "a writer of misfits," but her writing very often worked toward finding complex ways of finding a fit. When modern lesbian critics, historians, and theorists try to read an idealized history of lesbian identification into and out of the bodies and lives of masculine women, a great violence is done to the meaning of those lives in the name of a politically pure lesbianism. As long as masculinity is annexed in our society to power and violence and oppression, we will find some masculine women whose gender expression becomes partially wedded to the worst aspects of a culturally mandated masculinity. However, as the complicated lives of some masculine women show, there are also ways for women to pioneer forms of masculinity that change the meaning of modern gender and sexual identity.

Notes

1. Joanne Glasgow, ed., *Your John: The Love Letters of Radclyffe Hall* (New York: New York University Press, 1997), p. 78.

2. Michel Foucault, *The History of Sexuality*, vol. 1, *An Introduction*, trans. Robert Hurley (New York: Vintage, 1980).

3. For information on gender-variant working-class women during this period see The San Francisco Lesbian and Gay History project, "She Even Chewed Tobacco": A Pictorial History of Passing Women in America" in Martin Duberman, Martha Vicinus and George Chauncey Jr., eds., *Hidden From History: Reclaiming the Gay and Lesbian Past* (New York: Penguin, 1989), pp. 183–194. See also, Jonathan Katz, *Gay American History: Lesbians and Gay Men in the USA—A Documentary Anthology* (New York: Cromwell, 1973).

4. Michael Baker, *Our Three Selves: The Life of Radclyffe Hall* (New York: William Morrow, 1985), pp. 125–126.

5. "Englishwomen with the French Army," *The London Times* (August 5, 1919), n.p. This article was included in a file on Toupie Lowther's ambulance corps held at the London Imperial War Museum in the "Women in War Special Collection."

6. Emily Hamer, *Britannia's Glory: A History of Twentieth-Century Lesbians* (London: Cassell, 1996), pp. 40–53.

7. Esther Newton, "The Mythic Mannish Lesbian: Radclyffe Hall and the New Woman," p. 89–108 in this volume.

8. Terry Castle, *Noël Coward and Radclyffe Hall: Kindred Spirits* (New York: Columbia University Press, 1996), p. 31.

9. Glasgow, "Introduction," *Your John*, p. 9.

10. Eve Sedgwick, *The Epistemology of the Closet* (Berkeley and Los Angeles: University of California Press, 1990).

11. Marjorie Garber has commented upon the overlap of sartorial and erotic style in the cross-dressing of some women in the 1920s. However, Garber's account of transvestism relies too much on the transvestite as a "third" term between male and female and she makes transvestism the repository for all sexual and gender variance. See *Vested Interests: Cross-Dressing and Cultural Anxiety* (New York: Routledge, 1992), pp. 153–155.

12. Histories of modern dress that trace the evolution of gender through the vicissitudes of fashion tend to neglect the history of the cross-dressing woman. Anne Hollander, for example, sees female cross-dressing at the end of the nineteenth

century as a sad imitation of male costume but not as part of any kind of developing aesthetic. Hollander writes: "But women who adopted male clothes or heavily masculinized clothes could not strike the right note that way: they might look serious but they couldn't be taken seriously if they looked somehow falsified or too wilfully unappetizing." The oddly conservative resonance of this observation is made emphatic in her last sentence: "Perversely negative effects may startle but they always fail to persuade" (123) *Sex and Suits; The Evolution of Modern Dress* (New York: Kodansha, 1995).

13. Radclyffe Hall, *The Well of Loneliness* (1928; reprint, New York: Anchor Books, 1990). p. 28. All further references from this text.

14. Hall's letters to Souline also mention her obsessive and even erotic relation to clothes. There are many accounts of clothes shopping and her outfits are sometimes described in loving detail: "I have ordered a new over-coat, same as the shabby faun one but dark blue this time, it should be very smart. I have ordered two flannel suits, a grey and a blue. And a pair of faun coloured trowsers (sic) for St. Maxime" (April 5, 1935, p. 114).

15. Elizabeth Lapovsky Kennedy and Madeline Davis, *Boots of Leather, Slippers of Gold: The History of a Lesbian Community* (New York: Routledge, 1993).

16. Teresa de Lauretis, "The Lure of the Mannish Lesbian: The Fantasy of Castration and the Signification of Desire" in *The Practice of Love: Lesbian Sexuality and Perverse Desire* (Bloomington: Indiana University Press, 1994), p. 203.

17. Sigmund Freud, "The Psychogenesis of a Case of Homosexuality in a Woman" (1920) in Philip Rieff, ed., *Sexuality and the Psychology of Love* (New York: Collier Books, 1963), pp. 133–159.

18. Glasgow, ed. *Your John*, pp. 129–130.

19. Ibid., (August 19, 1934), p. 52.

20. Laura Doan has written about the historical significance of the emergence of the Women Police Service. She claims that this group was attacked mercilessly by the commissioner of the Metropolitan Police because he was concerned about the predominance of masculine women in their ranks. See Laura Doan, *Fashioning Sapphism: The Origins of a Modern English Lesbian Culture* (New York: Columbia University Press, 2001).

21. Joan Lock, *The British Policewoman: Her Story* (London: Robert Hale, 1979), p. 150. Lock reports this fact, however, as evidence of Allen's "silliness."

22. Baker, *Our Three Selves*, p. 267.

23. Ibid.

10

"The Outcast of One Age Is the Hero of Another": Radclyffe Hall, Edward Carpenter and the Intermediate Sex

LAURA DOAN

On July 19, 1928, Radclyffe Hall wrote to Havelock Ellis concerning his brief statement on *The Well of Loneliness*: "I was so overjoyed and proud at winning your good opinion for my book that I should have liked to walk up and down Piccadilly with it on a sandwich board.... [There is] nothing I prize so highly or consider so vitally important for my book as your friendship and approval."[1] Why would a successful novelist—the only Englishwoman to win two of the most prestigious literary prizes in a single year—invest so much capital in the approval of a man famed more for his knowledge of human sexuality than for his literary expertise?[2] If Hall was the avid student of Ellis's theories on sexual inversion some critics claim, perhaps his endorsement of her study of female inverts represented yet another "prize" for a job well done. Alternatively, such a gushing tribute to the "greatest living authority on the tragical problem of sexual inversion" might be read as the response of a dutiful daughter toward a powerful father figure.[3] A more cynical reading of Hall's overreaction would be to suggest that, savvy in the ways of publicity, she fully appreciated how Ellis's willingness to provide a statement constituted a significant coup. The great sexologist's name conjoined with her new novel—often characterized by critics of *The Well* as virtually a fictional version of his theories—might pay handsome dividends in the literary marketplace. Indeed, novelist Arnold Bennett confessed that he "knew nothing of the author's previous work" and that if he had "not been attracted by a line in the publisher's advertisement: 'With a commentary by Havelock Ellis,'" he might have overlooked the novel entirely.[4] As Hall and her publisher had anticipated, Ellis's participation seemed sufficient to ensure the novel would be noticed and taken seriously. A final possibility for Hall's response, however, and one congruent with the argument I propose in this essay, was that Hall felt considerable relief upon reading Ellis's sign-off on her project, for she—and Ellis too, one suspects—undoubtedly realized that her handling of sexual science was, at best, haphazard and, at worst, wildly eclectic.

Hall paid a high price for the sexologist's "good opinion," if critic Adam Parkes is correct in his assessment of the stakes: "Granting priority to Ellis's commentary, Hall effectively asked him to authorize her novel so that it could be seen to perform his theory of female inversion. The 'sincerity' exuded by the novel would simply reflect the degree to which Hall succeeded in mimicking Ellis's voice."[5] Those who overstate the sexologist's influence on the novelist regard Ellis's commentary as only the tip of the iceberg. Beneath the glaringly obtrusive imprimatur lies a theoretical foundation slavishly faithful to the wise master because, this critical perspective argues, Hall effectually relinquished authorial control "so that ultimately Ellis's word would count for more than her own" (441). Sandra Gilbert and Susan Gubar also contend that Hall advanced a theory of the origins of inversion essentially lifted from the pages of Ellis's *Sexual Inversion*: the protagonist, Stephen Gordon, is "a congenitally masculine girl born to a father who confirmed her inversion by treating her as the son he wanted."[6] Such a "myth of origins," these critics confidently assert, "accords with the etiology of homosexuality Havelock Ellis had developed and therefore explains his defense of the novel in the famous court case brought against it." Leaving aside the historical inaccuracy (Ellis refused to help Hall with her court case[7]), this reading interestingly draws our attention to the way in which Hall in fact pulls away from the congenitalist position advocated by medical men such as Ellis, thus inadvertently revealing that she was far from "mimicking Ellis's voice." That this particular critical view persists even in this present volume attests to the power of the assumption that Ellis's theories were paramount for Hall.[8]

That *The Well* both conformed to and deviated from Ellis's congenitalist view was first discerned as early as 1928 in the medical journal *Lancet*,

which praises Hall's "considerable dramatic skill," but finds her "emphasis . . . sometimes misplaced": "The implication that the parents' desire to
produce a son may alter the emotional affinities of the daughter born to
them is difficult to accept; the origin of abnormal sex attractions cannot be
so simply explained."[9] To suggest that Sir Philip's intense desire for a son,
compounded by his unorthodox form of child rearing (from naming his
daughter Stephen to treating her like a boy), contributes to Stephen's inversion, is to subscribe to a "nurture over nature" etiology antithetical to the
congenitalists, whose major proponent was, of course, Ellis. As Alison
Hennegan, in her astute introduction to *The Well*, notes:

> For much of the book Hall seems to be allowing two different theories of
> sexuality to run in tandem. Explicitly she argues that sexual orientation is
> inborn. Yet often explanations based on environment and psychology seem
> to hover in the background, especially in her account of Stephen's child-
> hood and adolescence.[10]

Hennegan's recognition of the way in which Hall replicates the disjunc-
tions and ruptures within the early theorizing of homosexuality is an
insight shared by a handful of others. Sonja Ruehl, for instance, observes
that Hall both keenly accepted "the parameters set up by Ellis" and veered
off in multiple directions, so that her novel "is not simply an exemplifica-
tion of Ellis's views in literary form."[11] Gillian Whitlock too proposes:
"rather than merely reproducing Ellis's theories, Hall transformed them
into a quite different discourse that generates quite different effects."[12]
Finally, Jean Radford, in perhaps the most thorough investigation of Ellis's
theory of inversion, claims that "the co-existence of contradictory discourses about homosexuality" constitutes a "'reverse' discourse."[13]
Drawing on the formulations of Foucault, Radford argues: "the object of
the medical category 'homosexual' adopts terms like 'inversion' transfor-
matively in order 'to demand legitimacy.'" As all these critics concur, Hall's
handling of the topic of inversion is more encyclopedic than systematic
and, as a result, she exposed her curious and sympathetic middle-class
readers to a wide spectrum of explanations. The only consistency in the
novel, as Bonnie Kime Scott concisely explains, is its "inconsistent view of
lesbianism."[14] One vital ingredient is, however, missing from most previous accounts of Hall's sexological "stew," whether in the biographies or in

the critical literature. Scholars have rarely associated directly or extensively the considerable influence on Hall's novel of the radical thinker Edward Carpenter (1844–1929), a homosexual, socialist, and ardent supporter of feminism, who argued that the "intermediate sex" (that is, "bearers of the sexual characteristics of one sex and many of the emotional characteristics of the other") would play a key evolutionary role.[15]

Although not, technically speaking, a "sexologist," a term normally reserved for professionals in the field of sexology with training or expertise in science or medicine, Carpenter's theories—"informed by the most advanced ideas on sex"[16]—permeate and, at times, even displace all others in this novel. Oddly enough, however, few have noticed. While Ellis's "Commentary," frequently reprinted in the opening pages of *The Well*, continually serves as a highly visible and constant reminder of how his theories of inversion helped shape Hall's treatment of the subject, our understanding of Carpenter's influence remains rather more obscure. By the early 1920s Carpenter's once huge reputation had gone into eclipse—and knowledge of his work has since largely vanished. Still, critical neglect of Carpenter is surprising since, as historian Lucy Bland observes, his "writings on homosexuality . . . were at least as influential as those of Ellis," and his numerous writings on a variety of subjects, including sex psychology and human relationships, were widely available and avidly discussed.[17] Of all the published material on homosexuality circulating in the early twentieth century, Carpenter's essays were by far the more accessible to a nonspecialist reader, a fact that the medical establishment held against him. In a vicious and disparaging review of Carpenter's *The Intermediate Sex* (1908), the *British Medical Journal* complained that the volume's affordability called into question its scientific value and warned: "serious people in England might be spared the waste of time consumed in reading a lowpriced book of no scientific or literary merit advocating the culture of unnatural and criminal practices."[18] Despite such hostility from the professionals, Carpenter's work sold extremely well; the volume containing his essay on "The Homogenic Attachment" (the term "homogenic" is synonymous with "homosexual") enjoyed "phenomenal" sales and was reprinted three times in 1915 alone.[19] In 1915 and 1916 nearly ten of Carpenter's books were in circulation, along with important new assessments of his oeuvre.[20] With figures such as E. M. Forster, D. H. Lawrence, and Siegfried Sassoon, among others, acknowledging Carpenter's tremendous influence, it seems unlikely that his work did *not* have an impact on Hall since his "*mass appeal* . . . was very large over a period of twenty or thirty years."[21]

Just as Ellis's crisp and "scientific" conceptualization of inversion was undeniably central for Hall, so too were Carpenter's powerful models of intermediate types, as well as his appealingly vague utopian evolutionary theories, useful and provocative for a novelist with an ambitious political agenda. In this essay's first section I argue that in an episode in *The Well* often seen as *the* crucial moment in Stephen's self-discovery—when she stumbles upon sexological treatises in her father's library—Hall actually replicates three distinct and opposing positions on female inversion (as degeneration, as sin, and as advantage). Of these competing positions, however, the final pronouncements on the subject resonate with pure Carpenter. Next I explore how several of the novel's characters (namely, Stephen, her old friend Martin Hallam, and Stephen's lover Mary Llewellyn) conform to Carpenter's typology of the intermediate sex. Carpenter's radical proposal that the homosexual constitution and sensibility signaled a new evolutionary stage allows Hall to imagine a new role for female intermediates, particularly with regard to Stephen who is singularly poised to play a special part in the salvation of her people. As Hall writes: "had nature been *less daring* with [Stephen], she might well have become very much what [her neighbors] were—a breeder of children, an upholder of home."[22] Most audaciously perhaps, I conclude that from a Carpenteresque perspective, *The Well of Loneliness* may be seen to end on a hopeful note as the narrative resolution, a vivid depiction of Stephen's transition from "outcast" to "hero," calls on all "intermediate types" to fulfill their biological destiny in the evolutionary development of a new society.[23]

"You May Write with a Curious Double Insight—Write Both Men and Women": The Intermediate Advantage

Stephen Gordon's first sustained encounter with the writings on sex psychology occurs when she extracts a "battered old" copy of Richard von Krafft-Ebing's unnamed but undoubtedly *Psychopathia Sexualis* from her father's secret cache in the library at Morton (204). Hall's selection of this text for Stephen is most peculiar, but so too is the fact that Ellis apparently did not find this scene in any way objectionable. As anyone thoroughly versed in *Sexual Inversion* would know, Ellis clearly and sharply refutes Krafft-Ebing's early views that homosexuality signaled degeneration (a reversal of the evolutionary process) as well as his formulations of a typology of inversion: "The early attempts of Krafft-Ebing and others at elaborate classification are no longer acceptable. Even the most elementary groupings become doubtful when we have definitely to fit our cases into them."[24] Ellis recognized Krafft-Ebing's unique contribution to the etiology of sexual perversions, but argued that he should best be remembered "as a clinician, rather than as a psychologist" (70). Ellis's serious reservations about both Krafft-Ebing's theories and his "rather fine-spun classification" system suggests that *Psychopathia Sexualis* would hardly have been Ellis's first choice as a useful introduction for the novice-invert. Scientifically dubious, the handbook "for lawyers and doctors discussing sexual crimes in court" could prove more damaging than illuminating for inverts unable to subject its findings to thoughtful critique.[25]

Not unexpectedly, after prolonged scrutiny of the work, Stephen becomes obsessively preoccupied with the notion of inversion as bodily or psychical affliction. However, her initial internalization of Krafft-Ebing's equivalence of inversion with degeneracy slips quickly into the biblical discourse of sin: inverts, she agonizes, "have no right to love, no right to compassion because they're maimed, hideously maimed and ugly—God's cruel; He let us get flawed in the making" (204). To be inverted, Stephen concludes after a cursory reading of Krafft-Ebing, is to be maimed. Yet this troubling equation is at odds with the conclusions of the major sexologists, as Carpenter notes:

> Formerly it was assumed as a matter of course, that the type [the inverted or "intermediate sex"] was merely a result of disease and degeneration; but now with the examination of the actual facts it appears that, on the contrary, many are fine, healthy specimens of their sex, muscular and well-developed in body, of powerful brain, high standard of conduct, and with nothing abnormal or morbid of any kind observable in their physical structure or constitution.[26]

Ironically, Hall's characterization of Stephen in body and mind is more congruent with this 1908 description of the intermediate type by Carpenter than with Krafft-Ebing's study of 1886, with its outmoded emphasis on degeneration and pathology. Stephen, in addition to moral and class supe-riority, possesses a "splendid young body," "splendid physique," extraordi-nary intelligence, and, of course, the "intuition of those who stand midway between the sexes"—a phrase found in Carpenter's *The Intermediate Sex*, in which he referred to those "who stand midway between the extremes of the two sexes."[27] Hall thus scrupulously ascribes to her protagonist the same qualities Carpenter outlines: a well-developed body, powerful brain, and high standard of conduct. If Stephen had first opened volumes by Carpenter or Ellis, she might have been thrilled with self-recognition and proclaimed the naturalness of her inversion as well as her perfect right to love, but instead she dwells on the work of a psychiatrist whose work was incompatible with most contemporaneous sexology; the question, then, is: why?

Hall represents Stephen's education in sexual science as a kind of pil-grim's progress (from the outmoded pronouncements of early sexological theory toward a more positive self-understanding): no sooner has Stephen's exposure to the likes of Krafft-Ebing resulted in a dramatic bout of breast beating than she is interrupted by her tutor Miss Puddleton (Puddle), who neutralizes the damaging linkage of homosexuality with morbidity. The more experienced and well-read Puddle arrives on the scene at just the right moment to correct Stephen's flawed reading, and together the women form an incipient interpretive community, with the older instructing the younger in the ways sexological systems of knowledge must be subjected to negotiation. In this way Hall disrupts Stephen's orgy of self-pity with the assurances of a fellow intermediate, whose voice echoes the mysticism of Carpenter and supersedes Krafft-Ebing: "we're all part of nature" (205). Puddle's Oxford education has apparently included *The Intermediate Sex*, since she tells her pupil, "Because you are what you are, you may actually find that you've got an *advantage*. You may write with a curious double insight—write both men and women from a personal knowledge" (empha-sis mine). Carpenter's very term for homosexuals, the "intermediate sex," highlights this advantage of a (superior) vantage point between the two sexes: intermediate types possess an "extraordinary gift" in their "double point of view, both of the man and of the woman," and their "double nature" enables them to open "the secrets of the two sexes."[28] Puddle's minisermon—a swift riposte to Krafft-Ebing's negative discourse of "taint" and "morbidity"—sensibly iterates the more positive and idealistic approach to homosexuality advanced by Carpenter, although the lingering effects of Stephen's initial encounter with the discourse of sexual abnormality never dissipate completely.

"Her Barren Womb Became Fruitful": The Intermediate and Moral Evolutionism

Carpenter dismissed Darwin's notion of evolutionary development because of its emphasis on external factors and opted instead for what historian Jeffrey Weeks terms "moral evolutionism": "a concept of internal growth, of spiritual development towards a higher form of consciousness.... There was in man, even under the toils of civilization, the growth of a higher awareness, of love and comradeship. In this Carpenter saw the hope for a better society which would transcend 'civilization.'"[29] Carpenter was also the most influential and resolute advocate in England of the superiority of the "intermediate type": he stood "almost alone ... in publicly asserting the possibly higher moral possibilities of homosexuality" (76). Even if this belief was not widely accepted among the educated elite by the late 1920s, it was at least well known; this can be seen, for instance, in writer Cyril Connolly's review of *The Well of Loneliness*: "Most of us are resigned to the doctrine of homosexuals, that they alone possess all the greatest heroes and all the finer feelings."[30] In Carpenter's parlance, intermediates were a "respectable and valuable class," with an "extraordinary gift for, and experience in, affairs of the heart ... it is not difficult to see that these people have a special work to do as reconcilers and interpreters of the two sexes to each other."[31] Within this "intermediate race," Carpenter identified two broad types, conceptualized not as a wide spectrum but as a rigid binary: first, what for the sake of convenience might be termed class A, "the extreme and exaggerated types of the race," and second, class B, "the more normal and perfect types."[32] Stephen falls into class A—those more flamboyant intermediates who, as Carpenter and Hall both suggest, attract attention in public spaces: Stephen is frequently stared at wherever she goes.[33] The extreme female intermediate, Carpenter contends, is easily recognizable in her "strong passions, masculine manners and movements," eccentric "attire," and "muscular" figure (30; 31). Carpenter thought the extreme types useful "from a scientific point of view as marking tendencies and limits of development in certain directions," but "it would be a serious mistake to look upon them as representative cases of the whole phases of human evolution" (32). Hall, however, thought otherwise, as we shall see.

On the other side of Carpenter's binary is class B: "the more normal type," as exemplified by the characters of Martin and Mary. Martin, with his "strong, young body" yet so "sensitive" and "restrained," embodies Carpenter's description of "the more normal type of the Uranian man" who:

> while possessing thoroughly masculine powers of mind and body, combines with them the tenderer and more emotional soul-nature of the woman.... Such men ... are often muscular and well-built ... but emotionally they are extremely complex, tender, sensitive, pitiful and loving.[34]

Stephen is drawn to Martin's sensitivity and intense responsiveness to beauty and declares to him: "we're like brothers" (95). Her interaction with this "queer, sensitive fellow" becomes inextricably bound up with her keen longing "for the companionship of men, for their friendship, their good-will, their toleration" (94; 96). The sexual frisson of this relationship is not that of man and woman; rather, it is a love immensely superior to the love of ordinary men and women. Tinged with the homoeroticism of comrade-love in the mode of Carpenter, who in turn was inspired by Walt Whitman, Stephen "felt so contented, so natural with [Martin]; but that was because they had been like two men, companions" (100). Martin, who discovers in Stephen "the perfect companion," addresses Stephen "as one man will speak to another"—Stephen in turn asks "thoughtful questions ... such as one man will ask of another" (94; 92; 93). For a short time in the narrative Hall explores the potential for such a relationship between a class A female intermediate (Stephen) and a class B male intermediate (Martin); however, on a day in early spring, the fecundity of new buds and blossoms arouses another side of Martin, who turns away from what Carpenter termed the homogenic attachment between men: "Martin looked into his heart and saw Stephen—saw her suddenly there as a woman" (97). Stephen's response of "outrage" and horror over Martin's advances stems less from her realization that Martin recognizes her "as a woman" than from the fact that he is attracted to her as a fellow "normal" intermediate (98).

Mary too clearly falls somewhere within the range of Carpenter's notion of a class B, "more normal" type in "her frankness" and in her "great longing to be independent" (429; 285); as Carpenter writes: "the frank, free nature of the [intermediate] female, her masculine independence and strength [is] wedded to thoroughly feminine grace of form and manner."[35] The boyish Mary, sexually attracted to the manly Stephen, also has a capacity for attraction to the rare intermediate type of man.[36] In a complicated passage Hall writes: "In her very *normality* lay her danger. Mary, all woman, was less of a match for life than if she had been as was Stephen" (423, emphasis mine). Esther Newton argues that in calling Mary "normal" Hall means "heterosexual," but if we turn instead to the language of Carpenter that so pervades this novel, we see that Hall's Mary fits Carpenter's typology rather well: "To come now to the more normal and perfect specimens of the homogenic *woman*," Carpenter writes, "we find a type in which the body is thoroughly feminine and gracious."[37] Mary, feminine without being one of "those purely feminine women," as Hall refers to them, is the quintessential female intermediate occupying the "median" of the human spectrum: Carpenter "felt that there were many signs of an evolution of a new human type which would be *median* in character, neither excessively male nor excessively female."[38] Through Mary, Hall advocates an active and significant role for the "normal" intermediate female in the propagation of the new humanity and, consequently, subjects Carpenter's evolutionary theory to modification. According to critic Beverly Thiele, Carpenter believed that "the real alliance to be forged was between homosexual men and heterosexual women who most closely approximated the type of sexuality which a free society needed and which evolution favored."[39] Hall, on the other hand, proposes an alternative configuration between male and female "normal" intermediates at an unspecified moment in the future, beyond the boundaries of the narrative; this belief explains the seemingly abrupt transformation of Martin from a man who is indisputably "different somehow" to a "thoroughly normal" man (96; 417).

In a dream-vision near the end of the narrative, Hall writes: "suddenly Martin appeared to Stephen as a creature endowed with incalculable bounty. . . . In a kind of dream she perceived these things. In a dream she now moved and had her being" (430). Such unusually poetic language in an otherwise quite conventional realist novel sets this strange passage apart, especially because Hall has already informed her reader that dreaming holds the "only truth" (331). By foreshadowing how an "extreme" *female* intermediate might engender the new race, this passage intriguingly plays both off and against the metaphysical discourse of Carpenter, whose "work placed increased emphasis on individual emancipation through spontaneity and mystical experience."[40] In engineering the union between Mary and Martin, Stephen becomes the progenitive facilitator, thus marking an exchange of barrenness for fruitfulness (Stephen's "barren womb became fruitful").[41] The rhythmic repetition in the subsequent series of (Blakean) phrases in which Stephen terminates her relationship with Mary simulates the painful contractions of a birthing process with a difference ("with each fresh blow . . . with every fibre . . . with every memory . . . with every passion . . . with every instinct" [431]). In severing the cord that binds the extreme to the normal intermediate, and in launching Mary toward Martin's "incalculable bounty," Stephen surpasses the "ordinary love" to assume the more heroic and awesome task of enabler.[42] In this respect, Stephen fulfills the special purpose that Puddle had prophesied for her early in the narrative: "You're neither unnatural, nor abominable, nor mad; you're as much a part of what people call nature as anyone else; only you're unexplained as yet—you've not got your niche in creation. But some day that will come" (154). That "some day" arrives *not* in what is commonly regarded as a disappointingly conventional heterosexual plot, and *not* in the manner of Carpenter who did not, as does Hall, foresee the potential in pairing normal female and male intermediate types. Instead, it arrives in Hall's appropriation of Carpenter's utopian evolutionary theory, whereby the "extreme" intermediate type is cast in the most important role of all.

"Her Own Voice in Which Those Millions Had Entered": The Outcast as Hero

Influenced by Rousseau, Hegel, and Marx, Carpenter's utopian theory of evolution saw in the primitive stage, which offers an appealing unity of man and nature ("the natural life of the people was in a kind of unconscious way artistic and beautiful. . . . Nature and man lived friendly together"), only the first step to what Carpenter termed the "third state," that is, "where every object . . . is united to every other object . . . by infinite threads of relation."[43] Martin embodies both the positive and negative aspects of the *primitive* stage in that he is wholly interconnected with nature ("this young man loved trees with a primitive instinct, with a strange and inexplicable devotion"), yet he finds social interaction and interpersonal relations exceedingly difficult ("Had you asked Martin . . . to explain why it was that he accepted [Stephen] . . . he would surely have been unable to tell you").[44] Mary and Stephen, on the other hand, fall into what Carpenter described as the "strange condition of illusion which belongs to the second stage," among the "exiles from the Eden-garden."[45] In Hall's appropriation of Carpenter's schema, humans progress from the primitive (where Martin resides) to the modern industrial age (occupied by Mary and Stephen) to the third and final destiny of the universe (the union of Martin and Mary through Stephen). Hall's first tactic—to advocate an active and significant role for the "normal" female in the propagation of the new humanity—is, as I have argued, a slight modification of Carpenter's utopian evolutionary theory. However, in the designation of the extreme homogenic female as the facilitator in the progression to what Carpenter calls a "third state of consciousness," Hall makes a complete ideological break with Carpenter. Stephen's rise is at Martin's expense: the virility or "bounty" of the "normal" intermediate male is, if not a backward slide in Hall's evolutionary schema, less central. This is because Stephen's productivity is two-fold: she is the force underlying the reproduction of the new humanity while, as a writer, she possesses what Carpenter describes as a "special function in social and heroic work, and in the generation—not of bodily children—but of those children of the mind, the philosophical conceptions and ideals which transform our lives and those of society."[46] Stephen thus stands apart from—and above—normal intermediates as a new kind of savior who demands on behalf of the entire race "the right to our existence!" (437).

The Well of Loneliness signals a daring new direction in twentieth-century lesbian literary representation because in Hall's protagonist Stephen, we find not a tragic or pathetic invert-victim debilitated by self-loathing, frogmarched into heterosexual marriage, or doomed to a lonely outcast existence, but an exceptional woman in possession of an array of rare and extraordinary gifts: high intellect, artistic sensitivity, and the fabulous vantage point of those lucky few who stand between the sexes. Carpenter is everywhere in evidence in Stephen's spiritual mission and in every aspect of her being as an exemplary "extreme" of the "intermediate sex," a phrase firmly rejected by Ellis as it "merely crystallized into a metaphor the superficial appearances."[47] Ellis's theories enabled Hall to claim a biological, congenital basis for inversion, but Carpenter's emphatic insistence on the unique advantage of all intermediates and the superiority of some—hardly scientific and hardly endorsed by Ellis—provided an irresistible justification for their social existence and their special place in evolutionary development. True to form in this most eclectic of narratives, Stephen hasn't *achieved* the greatness Carpenter reserves for intermediates (superior sensibilities and temperaments); such Carpenteresque qualities of her nature are inborn or, as Ellis argued, the result of a quirk of nature and therefore ineradicable. No wonder Hall experienced considerable relief when Ellis, the great sexologist, testified that Hall's project was: "the first English novel which presents, in a completely faithful and uncompromising form, one particular aspect of sexual life as it exists among us today."[48] In reality, Hall had freely plundered, contradictions and all, anything deemed useful to her project, from notions wholly incompatible with sexual science (hearsay or myths) to notions culled from Ellis and other theorists, including Ulrichs, Krafft-Ebing—and the metaphysical seer, Edward Carpenter.

Notes

1. Letter from Radclyffe Hall to Havelock Ellis, July 19, 1928. Havelock Ellis Papers, ADD70539, British Library. Some of the material presented in this essay appears in a different form in the chapter, "Lesbian Writers and Sexual Science: A Passage to Modernity?" in my *Fashioning Sapphism: The Origins of a Modern English Lesbian Culture* (New York: Columbia University Press, 2001).

2. Hall's novel *Adam's Breed* won the Femina Vie Heureuse Prize as well as the James Tait Black Prize. The only other author to have received both in a single year was E. M. Forster. See Sally Cline, *Radclyffe Hall: A Woman Called John* (London: John Murray, 1997), p. 2.

3. Michael Baker, *Our Three Selves: The Life of Radclyffe Hall* (New York: Morrow, 1985), p. 203.

4. Arnold Bennett, *Evening Standard*, August 9, 1928, p. 56 in this volume.

5. Adam Parkes, "Lesbianism, History, and Censorship: *The Well of Loneliness* and the SUPPRESSED RANDINESS of Virginia Woolf's *Orlando*," *Twentieth Century Literature* 40, no. 4 (Winter 1994): 441.

6. Sandra M. Gilbert and Susan Gubar, *No Man's Land: The Place of the Woman Writer in the Twentieth Century*, vol. 2, *Sexchanges* (New Haven: Yale University Press, 1989), p. 354.

7. Ellis excused himself from the court proceedings by telling Hall that he did not perform well in the witness box and also, as the author of a book (*Sexual Inversion*) "judicially condemned," he was "tarred with the same brush." Quoted by Cline, *Radclyffe Hall*, p. 256.

8. See, for instance, Line Pouchard's characterization of Hall's characters as "textbook examples illustrating the categories of 'inversion,'" in "Queer Desire in *The Well of Loneliness*," in Catherine Belsey and Jane Moore, eds., *The Feminist Reader: Essays in Gender and the Politics of Literary Criticism* (1989; reprint, Malden, Mass.: Blackwell, 1997), p. 54.

9. *Lancet* 2 (September 1, 1928), p. 71 in this volume. This explains the reviewer's assessment that the novel, "to which Mr. Havelock Ellis contributes a preface, is certainly not effective as a presentation of the case for social toleration of an abnormal habit of life."

10. Alison Hennegan, "Introduction," in Radclyffe Hall, *The Well of Loneliness* (1928; reprint, London: Virago, 1982), pp. xiv–xv.

11. Sonja Ruehl, "Inverts and Experts: Radclyffe Hall and the Lesbian Identity," in Rosalind Brunt and Caroline Rowan, eds., *Feminism, Culture, and Politics* (London: Lawrence and Wishart, 1982), p. 20.

12. Gillian Whitlock, "'Everything Is Out of Place': Radclyffe Hall and the Lesbian Literary Tradition," *Feminist Studies* 13, no. 3 (Fall 1987): 560.

13. Jean Radford, "An Inverted Romance: *The Well of Loneliness* and Sexual Ideology," in Radford, ed., *The Progress of Romance: The Politics of Popular Fiction* (London: Routledge, 1986), p. 106.

14. Bonnie Kime Scott, *Refiguring Modernism: The Women of 1928*, vol. 1 (Bloomington: Indiana University Press, 1995), p. 249. For a careful investigation of the semantic history of "sexual inversion" vis-à-vis categories of gender and sexuality, see Jay Prosser's chapter on *The Well of Loneliness* in his book *Second Skins: The Body Narratives of Transsexuality* (New York: Columbia University Press, 1998).

15. Jeffrey Weeks, *Coming Out: Homosexual Politics in Britain from the Nineteenth Century to the Present* (1977; reprint, London: Quartet Books, 1990), p. 75. For more on Edward Carpenter's theories, see also pp. 68–83. Carpenter's notion of the "intermediate sex" developed from the work of Karl Heinrich Ulrichs, whose preferred term "Urning" or "Uranian" referred to "people born . . . on the dividing line between the sexes—that while belonging distinctly to one sex as far as their bodies are concerned they may be said to belong *mentally* and *emotionally* to the other." See Edward Carpenter, *The Intermediate Sex: A Study of Some Transitional Types of Men and Women* (1908; reprint, London: George Allen and Unwin, 1916), p. 19. Hall included Carpenter's name among several others mentioned by Ellis in her

"Notes from 'Sexual Inversion.'" Since Una Troubridge kept careful note of books she read it would seem that Carpenter's name would appear in her diaries, but it does not. This may be due to the fact that during the years when Carpenter's work was most influential, Troubridge seems to have destroyed the diaries (none exist between 1914 and 1917, the period covering the courtship and first sexual experience between Hall and Troubridge). I am grateful to Joanne Glasgow for informing me that Hall's handwritten list includes Carpenter. See Radclyffe Hall/Lady Una Troubridge Collection. Box 12, Folder 5, Harry Ransom Humanities Research Center, the University of Texas at Austin. Cline's biographical study is one of the few to include a brief mention of Carpenter, but does not trace his influence on the novel. See Cline, *Radclyffe Hall*, pp. 227–228.

16. Carpenter was well informed on the work of Ellis, as well as other major sexologists, including Otto Weininger and Magnus Hirschfeld. See Jeffrey Weeks, *Sex, Politics, and Society: The Regulation of Sexuality Since 1800*, 2d ed. (London and New York: Longman, 1989), p. 172.

17. Lucy Bland, *Banishing the Beast: English Feminism and Sexual Morality* (London: Penguin Books), p. 263.

18. *British Medical Journal*, June 29, 1909. Newspaper cutting, NC623, Sheffield Archives, Sheffield (hereafter referred to as Carpenter Collection.)

19. The volume was *Love's Coming-of-Age: A Series of Papers on the Relation of the Sexes*, which first appeared in 1896. Keith Nield, "Edward Carpenter: The Uses of Utopia," in Tony Brown, ed., *Edward Carpenter and Late Victorian Radicalism* (London: Frank Cass, 1990), p. 20.

20. Nield, "Edward Carpenter," p. 20.

21. Ibid., pp. 26–27. In 1911 one admirer, L. D. Abbott, called him "the greatest man of Modern England" who "whether as mystic or scientist, prophet or poet, critic or appreciator, religionist or idol-breaker, scholar or workman, disciple or teacher, health-giver to the body or light-giver to the soul, is always masterly and always easily great." See L. D. Abbott, *The Free Comrade*, June, 1911, C per 37, Carpenter Collection.

22. Radclyffe Hall, *The Well of Loneliness* (1928; reprint, New York: Anchor Books, 1990), p. 108. Emphasis mine. All further citations from this edition will be cited by page number in the text.

23. Edward Carpenter, *Civilization: Its Cause and Cure, and Other Essays* (1889; reprint, London: George Allen, 1912), p. 100.

24. Havelock Ellis, *Studies in the Psychology of Sex*, vol. 2, *Sexual Inversion* (1897; reprint, 3d ed., Philadelphia: F. A. Davis, 1921), p. 82.

25. Harry Oosterhuis, "Richard von Krafft-Ebing's 'Step-Children of Nature': Psychiatry and the Making of Homosexual Identity," in Vernon A. Rosario, ed., *Science and Homosexualities* (New York: Routledge, 1997), p. 70. Oosterhuis notes that by 1901 Krafft-Ebing's views had shifted remarkably so that he no longer believed homosexuality was "incompatible with mental health or even with intellectual superiority. It was not a pathological phenomenon, but a biological and psychological condition that had to be accepted as a more or less deplorable but natural fate" (p. 79). Oosterhuis traces these important shifts in Krafft-Ebing's thought to his last writings for Hirschfeld's *Jahr für sexuelle Zwischenstufen*, namely an article entitled "Neue Studien auf dem Gebiete der Homosexualität."

26. Carpenter, *Intermediate Sex*, p. 23.

27. Hall, *Well of Loneliness*, pp. 82, 301, and 83; and Carpenter, *Intermediate Sex*, p. 41.

28. Carpenter, *Intermediate Sex*, pp. 14 and 38.

29. Weeks, *Coming Out*, p. 72.

30. *New Statesman*, August 25, 1928, p. 68 in this volume.

31. Edward Carpenter, *Homogenic Love, and Its Place in a Free Society* (Manchester: Labor Press, 1894), p. 51; Carpenter, *Intermediate Sex*, p. 14.

32. Carpenter, *Intermediate Sex*, p. 29. By 1914 Carpenter significantly modified this typology: "As we have seen that the varieties of human type, intermediate and other, are very numerous, almost endless, so we shall do well to keep in mind that the varieties of love and sex-relation between individuals of these types are almost endless, and cannot be dispatched in sweeping generalizations." See Carpenter, *Intermediate Types Among Primitive Folk: A Study in Social Evolution* (London: George Allen, 1914), p. 164. Unlike Carpenter and Ellis, Hall remains committed to classificatory systems: "Why, the grades were so numerous and so fine that they often defied the most careful observation. The timbre of a voice, the build of an ankle, the texture of a hand, a movement, a gesture" (pp. 352–353).

33. Another example of an "extreme" is Jonathan Brockett, who observes that Stephen shuns others of her "own ilk" (that is, other "extremes") and feels "far more at ease" with the "so-called normal" intermediates. See Hall, *Well of Loneliness*, pp. 346 and 416.

34. Hall, *Well of Loneliness*, pp. 101 and 98; Carpenter, *Intermediate Sex*, pp. 32–33. Loralee MacPike similarly argues that because Martin "seems to be attracted to inverts and to inverts alone . . . [he] is excludable from the ranks of 'ordinary men.'" See "Is Mary Llewellyn an Invert? The Modernist Supertext of *The Well of Loneliness*," in Elizabeth Jane Harrison and Shirley Peterson, eds., *Unmanning Modernism: Gendered Re-Readings* (Knoxville: University of Tennessee Press, 1997), pp. 87–88n.

35. Hall, *Well of Loneliness*, pp. 429 and 285; Carpenter, *Intermediate Sex*, pp. 37–38.

36. MacPike likewise observes that Mary does not conform to Ellis's conceptualization of the "pseudohomosexual": Mary "is someone new . . . [she] is a member of a group . . . [of] lesbians who for social reasons create heterosexual (or heterosexual-appearing) unions while retaining a primary attraction to, and often an emotional commitment to, women. Mary's conflicting history suggests that she is one of them, but this does not mean she is not a true invert. . . . Martin's attraction to Mary is in fact an indication that *she* is a true invert." See "Is Mary Llewellyn an Invert?" pp. 85 and 87n.

37. Esther Newton, "The Mythic Mannish Lesbian: Radclyffe Hall and the New Woman," p. 102 in this volume; Carpenter, *Intermediate Sex*, pp. 35–36.

38. Hall, *Well of Loneliness*, p. 271 and Weeks, *Coming Out*, p. 75.

39. Beverly Thiele, "Coming-of-Age: Edward Carpenter on Sex and Reproduction," in Brown, ed., *Edward Carpenter*, p. 110.

40. Weeks, *Coming Out*, p. 73.

41. Hall, *Well of Loneliness*, p. 437. Angela Ingram perceptively observes: "at the end of the novel Stephen becomes a mother . . . of the whole homosexual race." See "Un/Reproductions: Estates of Banishment in English Fiction After the Great War," in Mary Lynn Broe and Angela Ingram, eds., *Women's Writing in Exile* (Chapel Hill: University of North Carolina Press, 1989), p. 333.

42. Hall, *Well of Loneliness*, p. 430 and Carpenter, *Intermediate Sex*, p. 70.

43. Edward Carpenter, *Angels' Wings: A Series of Essays on Art and Its Relation to Life* (London: Swan Sonnenschein, 1898), pp. 6–7 and *Art of Creation: Essays on the Self and Its Powers* (London: George Allen, 1904), p. 60.

44. Hall, *Well of Loneliness*, pp. 92 and 93. Christopher E. Shaw explains that Carpenter saw "primitive harmony" as "deficient in its lack of human self-awareness." See Shaw, "Identified with the One: Edward Carpenter, Henry Salt, and the Ethnical Socialist Philosophy of Science," in Brown, ed., *Edward Carpenter*, p. 35.

45. Carpenter, *Art of Creation*, p. 61. Stephen and Mary are both described as "exiles. Stephen turned the word over in her mind—exiles; it sounded unwanted, lonely." Hall, *Well of Loneliness*, p. 336.

46. Carpenter, *Intermediate Sex*, p. 70.

47. Sheila Rowbotham and Jeffrey Weeks, eds., *Socialism and the New Life: The Personal and Sexual Politics of Edward Carpenter and Havelock Ellis* (London: Pluto Press, 1977), p. 159.

48. Havelock Ellis, "Commentary," p. 35 in this volume.

11

"All My Life I've Been Waiting for Something . . .":[1] Theorizing Femme Narrative in *The Well of Loneliness*

CLARE HEMMINGS

Introduction: Critically Femme

I am one of the few people I know who does not find *The Well of Loneliness* a dull, labored, or even absurd read. Like many contributors to this collection no doubt, I devoured the story of Stephen and her tragic loves in my teens, casting aside the text in disgust at the end, but returning again and again to the pages where feminine women exert their magic over the masculine protagonist. Rereading *The Well* now, I can still scarcely believe Stephen's stupidity in pushing Mary away; I still experience unsophisticated satisfaction at the notorious conclusion to chapter 38, "and that night they were not divided."[2]

Despite the extensive body of critical material concerned with *The Well*,[3] very few writers have seriously considered the role femininity plays in the novel, either through attention to feminine characters such as Mary Llewellyn or Angela Crossby or through the theorization of feminine location or narrative in *The Well*.[4] Even the defenders of *The Well* in lesbian literary criticism remain apologetic for what they perceive to be Mary's stereotyped failings. Thus Esther Newton gestures toward the potential importance of Mary, in her acknowledgment that "Mary's real story has yet to be told," yet she herself offers no suggestions of what such a project might entail.[5] And while both Lisa Walker and Joan Nestle acknowledge that it is sexological discourse that requires the feminine invert to retreat from her "bewildered but innocent" perversion to the safety of heterosexuality, both writers continue to understand Mary's "betrayal" of Stephen as an individual failure of will.[6] While Nestle astutely observes that Hall uses Mary's abandonment as a mechanism to elicit sympathy for her tragic heroine, "thus enabling the author to make a plea for greater understanding of the deviant's plight," she continues to long for a more positive role model, contrasting Lady Una Troubridge, "this steadfast femme woman" and Hall's life partner with Mary, whom she finds lacking.[7] Like Nestle, Walker rather apologetically argues that both Mary and Angela Crossby lack "the strength, or finally the desire, to stay 'in the life.'"[8]

One central reason for this critical embarrassment in relation to Mary and Angela is that both women, sympathetic and manipulative respectively, fit the model of the sexological invert *and* her contemporary cousin the "traitorous femme," who remains untrustworthy because she may leave you for a man. Whatever difficulties Stephen Gordon may hold for the lesbian historiographer, her desire for women is never in doubt. What I have called elsewhere "the spectre of straightness"[9] lingers over the contemporary femme, marking her as a close cousin of the bisexual woman— "Mary . . . becomes the precursor to the negative image of the bisexual woman who leaves her woman lover for a man."[10] This threatened collapse of feminine inversion into bisexuality forces the discursive creation of an absolute difference between lesbian femmes (who remain "in the life") and pretend (bisexual) femmes (who cannot or will not). Mary Llewellyn, then, becomes consigned to the latter category, a fate that at least partly explains lesbian literary critics' reluctance to reclaim Mary for a lesbian imaginary. Despite being a pivotal character in *The Well*, then, Mary becomes a contemporary femme's repudiated other that cannot be claimed, her place as the lover of the masculine woman overshadowed by Una Troubridge, who can provide the continuity of self-perception the lesbian femme needs if she is to challenge the centrality in the lesbian imaginary of the masculine woman.

In the rest of this essay I want to begin to rectify the critical imbalance in queer and feminist readings of *The Well* by foregrounding femininity as fundamental to the narrative structure and progression of the novel. I will argue that reading *The Well* in terms of femme narrative is important, not only as a challenge to the contemporary lesbian gaze that can only see itself in Stephen Gordon but also as a way of rethinking the novel as a whole. My approach to sexual and gendered narrative in *The Well* draws on the seminal work of Laura Mulvey,[11] read here alongside Judith Roof's discussion of lesbian narrative.[12] While Mulvey's work is much criticized for its oversimplification of gendered dynamics, her observations that "the determining male gaze projects its fantasy on to the female figure," and "women are simultaneously looked at and displayed . . . so that they can be said to connote *to-be-looked-at-ness*,"[13] are useful when they are understood to describe the *ideal* mechanisms of heterosexual narrative. That the female figure is relentlessly placed within (hetero)sexual narrative as the passive, feminine object of the active male gaze is precisely why lesbian narrative, in which woman is neither passive, nor mere object of this gaze, is so difficult to delineate. Roof's explanation for the heterosexuality of narrative is that "narrative and sexuality join at the oedipal."[14] Freud's "riddle of the nature of femininity" can only be solved by men, since it is assumed to be men who take femininity as their object.[15] Sexual narrative, then, is driven by a heterosexual male imperative to overcome a (feminine) "riddle," or obstacle, in order to achieve selfhood/climax and thus close the narrative.

In linking the above understandings of (hetero)sexual narrative to femininity in *The Well*, I am interested, first, in the ways in which this landmark lesbian novel enacts a similar narrative progression. Remembering Vera Brittain's regret at Hall's portrayal of "her 'normal' women . . . [as] . . . clinging and 'feminine' to exasperation,"[16] I want to explore the extent to which femininity in *The Well* is simply a foil for the masculine resolution of narrative, an object to be "surpassed" in order for true (heroic and/or tragic) masculinity to be attained. Certainly, Mary Llewellyn's position as infantilized object and means for Stephen to reach her own understanding of the true nature of the deviant's plight seems to mirror a conventional narrative structure. Marilyn Farwell underscores the narrative implications of Mary's passivity when she argues that "Mary is the passive figure with whom we are structurally comfortable and who in the end can become a 'real woman' and go with a 'real man.'"[17] One might also consider the role of feminine characters such as Stephen's first lover, Angela; and Stephen's mother, Anna. In the first case, Angela, as object of Stephen's affection, serves to bring Stephen to an awareness of her own, now undeniable, sexuality. The ill-

fated affair also precipitates Stephen's necessary departure from Morton—
necessary in the sense of the distance from her home proving fundamental
to Stephen's "heroic" travels in search of herself. In leaving Morton, Stephen
also narratively enacts the oedipal break from the mother that is necessary
for her to form adult attachments and become an adult masculine subject.

But what of the marked difference from heterosexual oedipal plots that
is so central to narrative meaning in *The Well*? If Stephen, as a masculine
woman, can be its protagonist, thereby disturbing any residual biological
base to Freud's oedipal drama, can Mary also become a subject? This question brings me to my second intention in tracing feminine narrative in *The
Well*—to show that Mary can and does return the masculine gaze, and in
doing so refuses her position as mere object or foil for masculine narrative.
I argue that these "refusals" not only offer us an alternative sexual and gendered narrative in the novel, but also expose the tensions within oedipal
narrative formations and effects.

Reading Femme Subjects

I begin my femme reading by highlighting some of the internal faultlines in
Havelock Ellis's rendering of the feminine invert[18] that resurface as "tactics"
in *The Well*. The feminine invert poses a problem for sexology, since her
desire for masculine women cannot be understood as the result of a gendered inversion and therefore attributable to a fault of nature, as can the
masculine woman's perverse desire. If the properly gendered feminine
invert desires masculinity, why is her desire not restricted to men?

Havelock Ellis circumvents this indescribability of the feminine invert in
three ways: rendering her passive (object, not subject, of desire); suggesting
she is innocent of her perversion (unworldly and therefore unknowing);
and insisting that she is most open to being "cured" of her perversion.[19]
Providing a heterosexual endpoint for the feminine invert's narrative allows
for a clinical resignification of her desire for the masculine woman as
"error," as something that she never really meant to do. In this way, Ellis
deflects the lack of gender base for the feminine invert's sexual perversion,
locating it in her very feminine ignorance of the world and its ways. But
instead of resolving the problem the feminine invert poses, Ellis raises the
possibility that *all* heterosexuality-bound women have the capacity to com-

mit the same narrative "error," their passive feminine passivity and innocence allowing them to mistake the masculine woman's attention for "the
real thing." Remarkably enough, Ellis manages to position femininity itself
as susceptible to seduction by *any* masculine gaze. The feminine woman is
thus located as the potential object of both a heterosexual and a homosexual gaze; while her femininity is conferred upon her through the masculine
gaze, one cannot tell, just by looking, which gaze she will return.

And if the feminine woman refuses to be "cured"? Ellis can do nothing
other than attribute a marked lack of femininity (though less marked than
in the masculine invert's case) to such a woman, reproducing the closed
ontological circle in which, for women, masculinity can only belong to
perversion and femininity to heterosexuality. Thus, in his discussion of
"the women to whom the actively inverted woman is most attracted," Ellis
describes them as "the pick of the women whom the average man would
pass by,"[20] adding that it is their "coldness, rather than lack of charm" that
precipitates this indifference from men.[21] This curious construction serves
several purposes. First, it repositions the feminine invert as unworthy of a
heterosexual male gaze, rather than as refusing it herself. Second, while she
is not quite attractive enough (that is, feminine enough) to hold the attention of the truly masculine (that is, male) gaze, the untrained eye of the
masculine woman (or, presumably, the less than average man) may be
more easily seduced. Ellis's turn of phrase places scare quotes around feminine and masculine inverts, relegating both to the realms of *inauthentic-
ity*—the former because of her lack of real feminine charms; the latter
because of her inability to tell the difference.

Once again, however, Ellis's formulation extends beyond the bounds of
his description. In the process of calling the gender of his inverts into question, Ellis necessarily also casts doubt over the masculinity of the heterosexual male in whose arms the feminine invert's cure is to be realized, since an
ordinary man would have passed such a woman by. Such a man is necessary for the feminine invert's return to heterosexuality, to fulfill the narrative quest for closure, yet his desire for her simultaneously unmans him.
The question remains as to whether she returns his gaze because it is different from, or similar to that of the masculine woman.

If we think for a moment of Martin Hallam, the man to whom Mary
runs at the end of the novel, we can see this ambivalence in action. Martin's
status as ideal heterosexual male is cast in doubt in a number of ways

throughout *The Well*. First, there is his perhaps too gentle love of trees, and his curious isolation. In terms of desire, Martin has already proved his judgment to be flawed, through his declaration of love for Stephen earlier in the novel. Additionally, when Martin reappears in the novel he suffers from a very particular war wound—a bullet to the head that "affected the optic nerve rather badly" (416). The very gaze required to structurally seduce the feminine invert away from the masculine woman is damaged.

That phrase—"the pick of the women whom the average man would *pass by*" (my italics)—suggests yet another subversion of its unstable basis. The feminine invert may indeed not so much be passed *over*, here, as provide the means for a man to enact his own passing, his own entry into a narrative that offers few options. In this vein, I cannot resist the temptation to suggest that Martin Hallam's desire for Stephen was not for her as a mistaken feminine object but her as a masculine subject, his like rather than his un-like. It is perhaps only in reading his desire as always already heterosexual that Martin's declaration to Stephen seems jarring.

In addition, one might simply reverse the heterosexist grammar of Ellis's text, as the contemporary "foremothers of femme" so movingly have done. Nestle writes inspiringly on the subject of femmes who are not so much "passed by" in terms of the heterosexual male gaze but who actively refuse that gaze,[22] seeking out alternative spaces, such as the lesbian bars and beaches in 1950s Eastern United States.[23] And contemporary butch writer Sally Munt lines the lesbian streets of Brighton in 1990s Southern England[24] with femmes who position themselves as part of a frank exchange of female glances.

In terms of femme narrative, then, the contradictions are evident. On the one hand, the femme is the object of the gaze, visible in gendered but not initially in sexual terms; not masculine, yet not truly feminine either. On the other hand, the femme is a thorn in the side of a heterosexual/homosexual opposition because she is central to the confirmation of gendered and sexualized gaze, yet her refusal of the gaze throws the sexuality of both the masculine subject and feminine object into question. Her refusal or return of the masculine gaze is the pivot upon which dominant gendered sexual narratives rely. Contrary to Mulvey's assertion of a static relationship of the gendered gaze then, I want to argue that the repeated consignment of the feminine to the status of object belies its power to undo the prioritization of the masculine on which narratives of desire rely.

The femme's return of the (traditionally, butch) gaze is considered less a disruption of sexual plots and more its cornerstone in a lesbian cultural context. In *Heroic Desire: Lesbian Identity and Cultural Space*,[25] Munt's heroic butch's desire is confirmed not through the masculine gaze alone but through a complicated exchange of gazes *between* women:

> Brighton introduced me to the dyke stare. It made me feel I was worth staring at, and I learned to dress for the occasion. Brighton constructed my lesbian identity, one that was given to me by the glance of others, exchanged by the looks I gave them, passing—or not passing—in the street. (31)

Munt pays homage to this tradition of the exchange of queer gendered gazes by reinventing her masculine lesbian subject as the lesbian flâneur, thereby overtly expressing the ambivalence that typifies a perverse narrative. For the lesbian, both the subject and object slip in and out of sight, alternately visible and invisible amid the urban landscape.[26] Seductive though the figure of the lesbian flâneur is, however, I am not convinced that she is as useful for imagining the trajectory and gaze of the femme as she is for the butch.[27]

While Munt acknowledges the exchange of gazes that results in lesbian desire, in her narrative it is nevertheless the masculine woman who initially possesses the gaze, and who wishes to have it returned. Thus Munt's lesbian flâneur quite explicitly "swagger[s] down the street in her *butch drag*, casting her roving eye left and right." (43, emphasis mine) As with conventional narratives, the femme does not enter the frame until gazed upon; Mary Llewellyn does not enter *The Well* for several hundred pages. She may become a subject of narrative through her ability to return or refuse the gaze, but the feminine woman's refusal of the masculine protagonist's gaze often marks her disappearance as subject of the narrative.[28] So, Mary's unspoken unhappiness in Paris, which veils her from Stephen, also signals a marked increase in her being spoken for or about. In certain contexts, such as the positioning of Teresa in Leslie Feinberg's *Stone Butch Blues*,[29] and, of course, with Mary's "betrayal" of Stephen at the end of *The Well*, the femme's withdrawal of the gaze may in fact mark her exit from the text altogether.

I want to suggest instead that the femme be considered, not flâneur, but *passante*—the one marked by passing. Recalling my reading of Ellis, the femme both passes by and is passed by. Where Munt's butch "lesbian flâneur signifies a mobilized sexuality *in control,* not out of control" (43), the femme is "uncontrollable": as the one who passes by, she is watched; but she also returns the flâneur's gaze, perhaps fleetingly, and then disappears from view. She enters the narrative as object, confuses gendered and sexual narrative in her possession of the gaze, and is forced from the narrative in order that gendered, sexual, and narrative order may be restored. Reading the femme as passante allows us to track her temporary control over narrative, without the expectation that she will become the protagonist. And, importantly, the figure of the passante recalls Ellis's unexpected opening up of nonheterosexual readings of gendered narrative—allowing us to read the end of *The Well* from within the possibilities offered by "passing" rather than from the masculine perspective that banishes Mary from the dominant narrative.

Framing Femme Narrative

Stephen Gordon's lover Mary Llewellyn enters the narrative of *The Well* only when she crosses the masculine hero's direct line of vision. The first time Mary is mentioned, it is characteristically as unnamed object of Stephen's gaze: "Stephen stared down at the girl who lay curled up at her feet" (280); when she is subsequently named, she is "the immature figure . . . Mary Llewellyn." Faithful to Havelock Ellis (who wrote the commentary to the 1928 text), Hall renders Mary innocent, unworldly, without prior gendered or sexual knowledge. And again in faith with Ellis, such innocence is what enables Mary both to respond to Stephen and to "return" to heterosexuality at the end of the novel.

Initially the text seeks to convince the reader that Stephen and Mary propel each other's narratives to the same extent. Thus the narrator inquires: "Why should this girl have crossed Stephen's path, or indeed Stephen hers, if it came to that matter?" (286). Yet, although this introduction suggests parity of representation, Mary and Stephen's paths are traced through the novel in dramatically different ways. At the point in the text where Mary appears (almost two-thirds of the way through the novel), the reader already knows the intricacies of Stephen's past, the significant events and relationships that have brought her to this point. In addition, the closeness that develops between Stephen and Mary is not demonstrated simply by Stephen's concern for Mary's safety. Their relationship is cemented by Mary's desire for Stephen to talk to her about her past, and Stephen's desire to do so, in minute detail:

> Mary would want to be told about Morton, she was never tired of hearing about Morton. She would make Stephen get out the photographs of her father, of her mother whom Mary thought lovely, of Puddle, and above all of Raftery. Then Stephen must tell of her life in London, and afterwards of the new house in Paris; must talk of her own career and ambitions. (288)

The shift in the above passage from Mary's desire—"Mary would want . . . she would make Stephen"—to Stephen's reciprocal urgency in meeting that desire—"Stephen must tell . . . must talk"—suggests that, for Stephen, the repetition of her story is a necessity rather than simply an indulgent fulfillment of Mary's repeated requests.

It is not that Mary's past is entirely absent, however. Immediately following the suggestion that the two women's narratives are intertwined, for example, we hear that, "An orphan from the days of her earliest childhood, Mary had lived with a married cousin in the wilds of Wales; an unwanted member of a none too prosperous household. She had little education beyond that obtained from a small private school in a neighbouring village" (286). But in contrast to the active grammar of Stephen's storytelling, Mary's past is told through layered negatives. She is without parents, unwanted, little educated, whereas Stephen's history is brimming with events and people. Stephen's past also has a positive resonance in the present, in the form of photographs brought and letters sent from home— "and these she would want to read to Mary" (292). By contrast, Mary has no mementos, and what little we do hear of her story is told impersonally, as if in a deadpan voice.

In addition to its different register, marking Stephen's narrative as more active, more urgent, Mary's past also serves a very particular function. Aside from the obvious differences between the two women in financial and class terms, Mary's history is significant in *The Well* only insofar as it prepares her for her relationship with Stephen. She has no other ties to complicate the narrative; her past took place *somewhere else*, the unknowable (to the English protagonist) "wilds of Wales"; and, in contrast to Stephen's scholarly knowledge and acute self-awareness, Mary is presented as uneducated, a blank sheet. In particular, she "knew nothing of life or of men and women; and even less did she know of herself, of her ardent, courageous, impulsive nature" (287). This description of Mary's ignorance again mirrors Ellis's view that feminine inverts are "seduced" by the masculine gaze whose perversion they are unaware of. It is through association with Stephen that Mary will learn of both life and "men and women," and through that association that she will come to know her own strength of character.

Interestingly, when Mary does speak of or for herself it is not to go over her past but to further articulate her relationship to Stephen and to anticipate their future together. Thus the evening of Stephen's decoration with the Croix de Guerre, Mary begs: "Let me come with you—don't send me away, I want to be near you. . . . I can't explain . . . but I only want to be near you, Stephen. Stephen—say you won't send me away. . . ." (295).

In case one were to misinterpret this outpouring as a simple girlish desire not to be rejected, Mary states her position more clearly still: "All my life I've been waiting for something. . . . I've been waiting for you, and it's seemed such a dreadful long time, Stephen." The positioning of Mary as passive complement to Stephen's active masculinity seems complete. The one moment when we think we are to hear about Mary's history, and maybe even her dreams—"And now she began to talk in her turn. She could type fairly well, was a very good speller" (300)—is undercut by Mary using this opportunity to further highlight the benefits of Stephen keeping her close: "She would type Stephen's books, take care of her papers, answer her letters, look after the house, even beard the lugubrious Pauline in her kitchen." In effect, when Mary articulates her own desires here, it is to further enrich Stephen's narrative, adding her wish for Stephen to succeed as a writer to Stephen's own ambitions.

In *The Well*, then, Mary is seemingly visible to herself, to others in the text, and to her reader only because of her juxtaposition, her relationship to the visible masculine subject, Stephen, whose narrative she supports. Her past is vague and underdelineated, is rather carelessly passed by, while her future is secured to Stephen's. Mary's life in Paris, in which her days merge into one in the service of Stephen's career needs, similarly underlines the fact that the novel's momentum requires that Mary's place in Stephen's life be temporary. She belongs to a feminine space, not a heroic masculine one. Once she is pushed from Stephen's sphere at the end of the novel, and into the arms of the waiting Martin Hallam, her future remains again undetermined, except in structural terms as a "return" to heterosexuality. What "counts" in narrative terms, and what is necessary for closure, is that the masculine protagonist has overcome the (feminine) obstacles impeding his heroic progress to subjecthood. The fact that Stephen's progress is marked by "loss" (of his mother and lover) is of course precisely in line with the oedipal trajectory. As the archetypal passante, Mary is only intelligible for the time she is controlled by the protagonist's masculine gaze, her imagined past and future given meaning only through that relationship.

Femme Persistence

As I suggested in part 1 of this essay, femme narrative is also marked by its refusal to accede to dominant discursive limitation. In Mary's case, simply ending the novel with her rather ambiguous departure cannot account for her enduring desire for Stephen. Nor is there any evidence that Mary does actually return Martin Hallam's gaze, despite the lasting legacy of Mary's "betrayal." In this section, I want to examine the ways in which the masculine narrative of *The Well* that would consign Mary to a passive heterosexuality is shot through by Mary's refusal of that narrative, both in terms of her active desire for Stephen and in terms of the possibilities opened up by positioning Mary as passante, as "out of control" of the masculine gaze at the end of the novel.

In response to Lisa Walker's claim that Mary lacks "the strength, or finally the desire, to stay 'in the life,'"[30] I would argue that, on the contrary, it is Mary's *active desire* for Stephen, and her admirable persistence in pursuit of that desire, that marks the emergence of Mary as a femme subject of her own narrative. First, although as readers we are encouraged to see Mary as unworldly, innocent, and unknowing, her desire for and devotion to Stephen challenge Ellis's theorization of the feminine invert as passively accepting the advances of any masculine subject. Mary seems absolutely certain that it is Stephen she desires. In matters of sex, it is Mary who proves impatient with Stephen's "other-worldly" reticence, as well as with Stephen's wish not to "corrupt" the one she loves.

In the same scene where she begs Stephen not to send her away and identifies her as "the one" she has been waiting for all her life, Mary demonstrates a feminine desire that cuts through the prevailing masculine narrative. She strokes "the new Croix de Guerre" (a sign of the bravery that marks Stephen's masculinity throughout the book) and catches "hold of Stephen's sleeve" (295), literalizing her entreaty. Shortly after this, at what will become their home in Rue Jacob, Stephen is tense in their isolated intimacy, while Mary is again forthright. The speech in which Mary imagines her future helping Stephen with her writing, and that confirms femininity as object of masculine narrative, is framed by two direct and knowing expressions of desire on Mary's part. Just prior to their musings, Mary lays her hand on Stephen's knee, "but Stephen appeared not to notice that hand, for she just let it lie there and went on talking" (299). This is neither simply a friendly gesture nor an unconscious one on Mary's part—Mary is "very conscious of the unnoticed hand." While Stephen's gestures are erratic—"she suddenly laid her hand over Mary's" (300)—Mary is persistent in her advances, later in the same scene asking Stephen to kiss her directly: "Stephen . . . won't you kiss me good night? It's our first night together here in your home. Stephen, do you know that you've never kissed me?" (301). Again, Stephen is reticent:

> "Do you want me to kiss you?"
> "More than anything else in the world" . . . .
> She kissed the girl quietly on her cheek. (301–302)

Mary is not innocent of the kiss she is asking for; the tension in the passage derives from the fact that we know Mary cannot be satisfied with the merest peck on the cheek that she receives.

Once in Orotava at the Villa del Ciprés, Mary continues to seduce Stephen, while the latter continues to act nervously and inconsistently, clasping Mary to her one moment, pushing her away with a patronizing word the next.

> But Mary Llewellyn was no coward and no weakling, and one night, at long last, pride came to her rescue. She said: "I want to speak to you, Stephen."
> "Not now, it's so late—tomorrow morning."
> "No, now." And she followed Stephen into her bedroom. (315)

Mary threatens to leave Stephen, to go back to that place we can scarcely imagine—her home in Wales—rather than suffer the indignity of what she imagines to be unrequited love. This particular threat of the passante (to leave the control of the masculine gaze) provokes a crisis in Stephen's narrative, forcing her to relinquish, if temporarily, her narrative control:

> Stephen stared at her, white and aghast. Then all in a moment the restraint of years was shattered as though by some mighty convulsion. She remembered nothing, was conscious of nothing except that the creature she loved was going. (315)

As well as rupturing the hitherto unbroken narrative of Stephen's past ("she remembered nothing") Mary's expression of desire, her agency, produces the equality of the gaze through which the passante comes into her own: "They stood there lost to all sense of time . . . to all things save each other." But as Teresa de Lauretis sagely notes, that sense of timelessness in love arising from "a marriage of true minds"[31] is bound to give way to a narrative struggle for dominance. While de Lauretis ironically points out "how rarely [this marriage] lasts beyond the first few chapters,"[32] harmony between competing gendered narratives barely lasts beyond a few lines in *The Well*. In an attempt to reinstate control, Stephen breaks their embrace, forcing Mary to "stand . . . and listen" (316) to the masculine invert's narrative once more. Once again, it is Mary's conscious decision to return her soon-to-be lover's gaze in this renewed moment of crisis—"But Mary turned on her with very bright eyes"—that wrests narrative control (in which Mary figures only as object to be protected) from Stephen. The result of this narrative "tussle" is the infamous first night of passion—"and that night they were not divided." This narrative tussle is only temporarily resolved, however. Aside from the occasional moment of "timeless joy," the two narratives—masculine and feminine—do not coexist happily in the novel. The dominance of Stephen's masculine narrative silences Mary, while Mary's assertion of feminine desire results in the disruption of masculine linearity. Put bluntly, for the masculine narrative to predominate, Mary's story must be silenced.

To return to the progression of the novel as a whole, one might argue that Mary's desire at the beginning of their relationship nevertheless gives way to the world-weariness that convinces Stephen to return her to the heterosexual life that Mary believes will make her happy. But it is highly significant that Mary's desire for a "normal life" nearly always reaches us second-hand, witnessed through Stephen's and, later, Martin Hallam's (damaged) eyes. Any dissatisfaction that Mary expresses herself concerns her relationship with Stephen—her regret that Stephen works such long hours, or her confusion over Stephen's reluctance to embrace her as her lover. The final, critical scene between Stephen and Mary, through which lesbian posterity has judged Mary so harshly, can also be revisited in terms of Mary's desire. It is not by arguing for the benefits of a heterosexual "return" that Stephen "cures" Mary of her perversion, but by cruelly rejecting her as a lover through her masquerade of infidelity with Valérie Seymour. It is not Mary's gaze that is turned away from the masculine woman here, but Stephen who insists that she no longer desires *her*. Mary's rage and disbelief is the response of a lover spurned:

> Stephen, I can't believe this thing—Valérie! Is that why you always repulse me . . . why you never want to come near me these days? Stephen, answer me; are you her lover? Say something, for Christ's sake! Don't stand there dumb. (445)

There is no relief here, no thought for her "impending cure." There is no sense here that Mary's desire for Stephen is ambivalent and therefore easy to redirect to its proper male object.

At the end of *The Well* it is Stephen who pushes Mary away, forces her beyond the range of her gaze. Appropriately enough for my reading of femme narrative through the figure of the passante, the last words we hear from Mary are, "I'm going" (445). This final utterance can be read in two ways, mirroring the dual function of the passante for my reading of femme narrative in *The Well*. First, Mary could be seen to be performing the banishment of the feminine from the masculine narrative once the bounds of narrative convention are broken. Stephen's refusal of Mary's desire in this scene is a refusal to acknowledge Mary as subject of her own destiny, as effectively a subject of her own narrative. The narrative "tussle" in Oratova that I have already described, then, is resolved here in favor of the masculine gaze that reinstates control of the narrative—even if that means a tragic rather than comedic closure to the narrative. The second reading of Mary's final declaration, "I'm going," reflects rather better the active nature of the statement—Mary chooses to depart in preference to being banished. Here Mary (the passante) eludes Stephen's (the flâneur's) gaze, deliberately moving beyond the reaches of Stephen's narrative, and therefore sexual, control.

The instant Mary has left, the masculine narrative moves relentlessly toward its grim and faintly surreal conclusion. The tension that has been present in the last third of the book (between masculine and feminine narrative) has been eliminated, and the result is that the novel, like its protagonist, seems stripped of life. Going one step further than simply narrating Mary's departure for her, Stephen, even before Mary leaves, begins to refer to her in nongendered terms ("it"), or in the third person ("the girl"). The devastating loss that Stephen quite clearly already feels is expressed by confusion and disbelief at her (seemingly instant) lack of control over Mary's future: "Going? But where could it go? Somewhere out of the mist, somewhere into the light?" (445).

This lack of knowledge concerning Mary's flight—where could she go?—is resolved through the production of the scene in which Mary stumbles across a waiting Martin Hallam. What Stephen sees from the window is "the girl" finding solace in Martin's arms—"They were side by side, he was gripping her arm. . . . They were gone" (445). A reading of this scene in terms of masculine narrative is the familiar one: Mary runs from Stephen to Martin and in doing so moves from a perverse space to a heterosexual space.[33] Depending on one's position, this movement is seen either as a suitable resolution of the heterosexual plot or as a failure of lesbian narrative; Mary's "return" itself is never questioned. But this resolution of the story is again shot through with problems that a femme narrative reading illuminates. First, as I argued earlier, Martin's manliness is itself compromised within the dominant narrative—the average man would, if we remember, pass a woman like Mary by. Second, if we consider Mary's "return" as desirable, both for Stephen (to justify her martyrdom) and in order to effect narrative closure at the end of the novel, we can see how other possible readings of its ending are obscured. If we return to the scene between Mary and Martin that Stephen interprets, we see certain ambiguities bubble to the surface. Stephen gives us her interpretation as truth—"He questioned her, yes, that was it, he questioned" (445)—but what she actually sees is the following: Mary rushing away and stumbling; Martin Hallam's hands on her shoulders; her movement away while Martin looks back in Stephen's direction and then rushes to catch up with Mary; and finally their departure, Martin gripping Mary's arm. In *The Well* Mary's future with Martin

Hallam is presumed by Stephen but not mapped for the reader other than through her vision. But as Stephen's rather desperate overreading of this scene and Mary's own parting statement, "I'm going" suggest, Mary has already passed out of Stephen's narrative control. As the passante in a masculine narrative, Mary's future is as opaque as her past.

Against the existing critical readings of *The Well* that read with Stephen and consign Mary to a certain heterosexual future, I want to insist that there is no evidence for her presumed heterosexuality outside a masculine viewpoint. Against a closed reading of *The Well*, I want to suggest that reading *Mary's story* undoes the inexorability of the dominant narrative. We have no way of knowing which way Mary went. And if she exceeds the "plot-space"[34] assigned her by the masculine narrative structure, then we also remain ignorant of the nature of her desire. If I am correct in my reading of feminine narrative in *The Well*, Mary can no longer be dismissed as reflective of the role of the feminine in hetero(sexual) narrative. Instead, as Cixous has done with Medusa,[35] and Jean Rhys with Bertha,[36] we must seek out Mary's possible futures in other texts, rather than accepting masculine closure:

> The future must no longer be determined by the past. I do not deny that the effects of the past are still with us. But I refuse to strengthen them by repeating them, to confer upon them an irremovability the equivalent of destiny, to confuse the biological and the cultural. Anticipation is imperative.[37]

Notes

1. Radclyffe Hall, *The Well of Loneliness* (1928; reprint, London: Virago, 1992), p. 285.
2. Hall, *The Well*, p. 316. All further references to *The Well* will be by page number in the text.
3. This criticism is engaged with or included elsewhere in this volume, so there is no need for me to rehearse it here.
4. Leslie Henson's recent article on *The Well* does foreground Mary's position in the text but focuses primarily on the gendered power imbalance produced through class/economic differences in Stephen and Mary's relationship, rather than on femininity itself. Leslie Henson, "'Articulate Silence(s)': Femme Subjectivity and Class Relations in *The Well of Loneliness*" in L. Harris and L. Crocker, eds., *Femme:*

Feminists, Lesbians, and Bad Girls (New York: Routledge), pp. 61–67.

5. Esther Newton, "The Mythic Mannish Lesbian: Radclyffe Hall and the New Woman," p. 102 in this volume.

6. Joan Nestle, "The Femme Question," in J. Nestle, ed., *The Persistent Desire: A Femme-Butch Reader* (Boston: Alyson, 1992), pp. 138–146; Lisa Walker, "How to Recognize a Lesbian: The Cultural Politics of Looking Like What You Are," *Signs: Journal of Women in Culture and Society* 18, no. 4 (Summer 1993): 866–891.

7. Nestle, "The Femme Question," p. 144.

8. Walker, "How to Recognize a Lesbian," p. 881.

9. Clare Hemmings, "Waiting for No Man: Bisexual Femme Subjectivity and Cultural Repudiation," in S. R. Munt, ed., *Butch/Femme: Inside Lesbian Gender* (London: Cassell, 1998), pp. 90–100.

10. Frann Michel, "Do Bats Eat Cats? Reading What Bisexuality Does," in D. Hall and M. Pramaggiore, eds., *RePresenting Bisexuality: Subjects and Cultures of Fluid Desire* (New York and London: New York University Press, 1996), p. 60.

11. Laura Mulvey, ed., "Visual Pleasure and Narrative Cinema," in *The Sexual Subject: A* Screen *Reader in Sexuality* (New York: Routledge, 1992), pp. 22–34.

12. Judith Roof, *Come As You Are: Sexuality and Narrative* (New York: Columbia University Press, 1996).

13. Mulvey, "Visual Pleasure and Narrative Cinema," p. 27.

14. Roof, *Come As You Are*, p. xxiii.

15. Teresa de Lauretis, "Desire in Narrative," *Alice Doesn't: Feminism, Semiotics, Cinema* (Bloomington: Indiana University Press), p. 111.

16. Vera Brittain, *Time and Tide*, August 10, 1928, p. 60 in this volume.

17. Marilyn Farwell, "Heterosexual Plots and Lesbian Subtext: Toward a Theory of Lesbian Narrative Space," in K. Jay and J. Glasgow, eds., *Lesbian Texts and Contexts: Radical Revisions* (New York: New York University Press, 1990), p. 97.

18. Havelock Ellis, "Sexual Inversion in Women," *Studies in the Psychology of Sex*, Vol. 2, *Sexual Inversion* (1901; reprint, Philadelphia: F. A. Davis Company, 1918).

19. Ibid.

20. Ibid., p. 222.

21. Ibid.

22. Joan Nestle, *A Restricted Country* (Ithaca, N.Y.: Firebrand Books, 1987); Nestle, ed., *The Persistent Desire*; Munt, ed., *Butch/Femme*.

23. Joan Nestle, "Restriction and Reclamation: Lesbian Bars and Beaches of the 1950s," in G. B. Ingram, A-M. Boutillette, and Y. Retter, eds., *Queers In Space: Communities, Public Places, Sites of Resistance* (Seattle: Bay Press, 1997), pp. 61–68.

24. Sally Munt, "The Lesbian *Flâneur,*" in D. Bell and G. Valentine, ed., *Mapping Desire: Geographies of Sexualities* (London: Routledge, 1995), pp. 114–125.

25. Sally Munt, *Heroic Desire: Lesbian Identity and Cultural Space* (London: Cassell, 1998). Subsequent references to *Heroic Desire* will be by page number in the text.

26. My thanks to Elizabeth Wilson for drawing my attention to the flâneur's invisibility.

27. I elaborate this theoretical positioning of the femme in more depth an earlier essay: Clare Hemmings, "Out of Sight, Out of Mind: Theorising Femme Narrative," *Sexualities* 2, no. 4 (November 1999): 451–464.

28. De Lauretis, "Desire in Narrative," pp. 109–111.

29. Leslie Feinberg, *Stone Butch Blues* (Boston: Alyson, 1993).

30. Walker, "How to Recognize a Lesbian," p. 881.

31. De Lauretis, "Desire in Narrative," p. 108.

32. Ibid.

33. Farwell, "Heterosexual Plots and Lesbian Subtext," pp. 93–94.

34. Jurij M. Lotman, "The Origin of Plot in the Light of Typology," p. 167, cited in de Lauretis, "Desire in Narrative," p. 118.

35. Hélène Cixous, "The Laugh of the Medusa," in E. Marks and I. De Courtivron, ed., *New French Feminisms* (Amherst: The University of Massachusetts Press, 1980), pp. 245–264.

36. Jean Rhys, *The Wide Sargasso Sea* (London: Penguin, 1998).

37. Cixous, "The Laugh of the Medusa," p. 245.

§

The Well's Wounds

12

The Well of Shame

SALLY R. MUNT

In my teenage years I went rather spectacularly off the rails and, flying in the face of my socialist family, became an Evangelical Christian. My nights were spent in the tremors of biblical exposition and prayer; in a state of stunning abjection I would exhort God to release me from the dirty flesh into a state of transcendent enlightenment. Shame had marred my childhood significantly, slipping into my own subconscious like a snake. The situational shame of having divorced parents—rare in the 1960s—had dispersed into a more permeated, and permanent state. My enabling escape at the time stubbornly became God, whose mythical omnipotence seemed to lift me out of a nexus of compounded mortification. In late adolescence I became a career Christian; gaining a place at theological college, I intended to transform my discomposure through the ideals of ministry. The Church promised, through the sacrament of cleansing and renewal, to turn my self-hatred into a gift. It gave me a space of potential transformation, a romantic parable of love triumphing over iniquity.

Ring any bells?

Meantime, as a young adult living in a rural religious community in Dorset, England, I was falling in love with women and finding ways to worship Him and, surreptitiously, her. But, a year later, came my own traumatic expulsion: I was thrown out and was rescued by lesbian feminism. I needed another religion, one that offered a more corporeal set of beliefs. Being a lesbian, rather than a Christian, was in fact to exist in a rather similar frame; both invoked rules, aspirations, and bounded identities, and both were marked by an ambivalence toward shame in its potential for convergence. Around this same time, in 1981, Catharine Stimpson identified two types of lesbian novel, the "dying fall" and the "enabling escape," illustrating the former with a critical treatise on *The Well of Loneliness* (1928).[1] Stimpson famously described *The Well* as a narrative of damnation, but religion had given me a conditional sense of belonging and security that temporarily relieved my personal abasement. Rereading *The Well* in 1999, it is impossible not to be struck by the novel's religiosity. Hall was known to be a committed Catholic, and Joanne Glasgow has explained this apparently irregular connection:

> the erasure of lesbian existence and the phallocentric ontology of sex that Catholicism presents actually provided . . . the necessary space and lack of intrusion or control that allowed Hall to find her place in a radically alien universe. She did not have to fight a church or a God to be a lesbian.[2]

Hall deploys the figure of Stephen to great messianic effect in the novel. She reads inversion *through* the lens of Christian martyrdom and agency. The two are not exclusive: to exist in the communion of saints, we are impelled to die to self, to be "born again" as a new, shining creature, laundered by Christ. Held deep within the promise of cleansing is the reinvention of a self in which pain and degradation are eliminated, implying an unspoiled signifying space in which to conceive a new beginning, a new belonging. The parallel between religious conversion and contemporary lesbian identity politics is too tempting: thus, nostalgically, I set out to explore a number of thematic conjunctions between shame, subjection, loss, and belonging in that "bible" of lesbianism, *The Well of Loneliness*.[3]

Shame and Subjection

In the Authorized King James Version of the Holy Bible (the edition familiar to Hall), the Fall of Adam is described in chapter 3 of the book of

Genesis. Remember that Genesis 2:25 ends with the creation of Eve from Adam's rib: "And they were both naked, the man and his wife, and were not ashamed." They are on probation; God has warned them not to disobey Him and eat the fruit of the forbidden tree, so the serpent tries to tempt Eve: "For God doth know that in the day ye eat thereof, then your eyes shall be opened, and ye shall be as gods, knowing good and evil" (Gen. 3:5). So of course they eat it, "And the eyes of them both were opened, and they knew that they were naked" (Gen. 3:7); they clothe themselves and try and hide. In theological terms, the Fall is densely symbolic; the consequences for disobeying are that humankind will experience first, spiritual death, as sin separates from us from God, and second, physical death, which is the punishment for this original, mortal sin. The original traumatic separation, the expulsion from Eden, ensues. We need to notice that this is the foremost shame narrative of Western culture, one that has a number of elements: sexual desire disrupts the bond of spiritual connection; the ensuing rejection by God instigates Man's individuation; Man's self-consciousness occurs because of separation. This is the vacillation of subjection and individuation, and it is locked into the dynamics of shame, an affect that pulls toward and against its source. What we see in the creation myth is that the origin of human experience, individuation, and desire resides in a locus of shame, and it is out of that shame, separation, and loss that sexual differentiation occurs.

Now, let us compare the story of Stephen Gordon, the hero of *The Well of Loneliness* with this creation myth. Stephen's ancestral home is the country seat of the Gordons of Morton Hall. Morton is Eden, and to it comes Lady Anna, "the archetype of the very perfect woman," to marry Sir Philip, "a dreamer and a lover."[4] The novel starts by establishing this ideal gender conformity, expressed in the courtly heterosexuality of an echoed creation story. But the dream is corrupted by shame's antithesis, pride:

> It never seemed to cross his mind for a moment that Anna might very well give him a daughter; he saw her only as a mother of sons, nor could her warnings disturb him. He christened the unborn infant Stephen. (9)

Stephen is born on Christmas Eve, "a narrow-hipped, wide-shouldered little tadpole of a baby" who yells with outrage, without ceasing, in the face of all those predetermining desires. Stephen remains "cock of the roost" (11), as no other child is forthcoming. It is Lady Anna's discomfort with Stephen that mars Stephen's childhood. Hall describes with cutting detail the estrangement—"that queer antagonism" between them:

> But her eyes would look cold. . . . The hand would be making an effort to fondle, and Stephen would be conscious of that effort. Then looking up at the calm, lovely face, Stephen would be filled with a sudden contrition, with a sudden deep sense of her own shortcomings; she would long to blurt all this out to her mother, yet would stand there tongue-tied, saying nothing at all. (12)

It would seem to Anna that "Stephen were in some way a caricature of Sir Philip; a blemished, unworthy, maimed reproduction" (13).

Stephen's sexual development is painstakingly described through a series of religious epiphanies. The first test on this pilgrim's progress is the "florid, full-lipped and full-bosomed" (15) maid, Collins. Stephen strokes Collins's sleeve, and:

> Collins picked up the hand and stared at it. "Oh, my!" she exclaimed, "what very dirty nails!" Whereupon their owner flushed painfully crimson and dashed upstairs to repair them. (15)

Stephen's desire is inflamed by this shame scenario—hands, of course, are powerful signifiers of lesbian desire. She indulges in heroic delusions of herself as William Tell, Nelson, and more pertinently dreams "that in some queer way she was Jesus" (21). In an orgy of prayer, she beseeches, "I'd like to be awfully hurt for you, Collins, the way Jesus was hurt for sinners" (20), and she begs, "I would like to wash Collins in my blood" (21). This may read to us now as so much s/m schlock-fiction, but it is a juvenile foreshadowing of Hall's brazen, blasphemous, future figuration of Stephen as Christ.

Collins is dismissed, and Anna and Stephen try to achieve rapprochement. Walking through the woods one day, with Stephen clinging to Anna with "anxious fingers," this curiously sexual scene occurs:

> The scents of the meadows would move those two strangely—the queer, pungent smell from the hearts of dog-daisies; the buttercup smell, faintly green like the grass; and then meadow-sweet that grew close by the hedges.

Sometimes Stephen must tug at her mother's sleeve sharply—intolerable to bear that thick fragrance alone!

One day she had said: "Stand still or you'll hurt it—it's all round us— it's a white smell, it reminds me of you!" And then she had flushed, and had glanced up quickly, rather frightened in case she should find Anna laughing. (33)

The scene clearly articulates Stephen's sexualized dissmell/disgust.[5] Indeed the color white, and unpleasant smells, recur in the novel to connote sexual disgust (this is repeated ad nauseam in the descriptions of Brockett's queenly white hands). In this scene, Stephen recognizes the sexual potency of Anna as something disgusting and dangerous to her, which later she will recast as all femininity. As in Genesis, knowledge of sexual difference emerges here from sexual shame, and Stephen begins to experience consciousness of herself as a thing apart (from femininity).

There are several instances where Stephen gazes at her mother, and Anna responds by shaming her, averting her own gaze. Charles Darwin, in *The Expression of Emotion in Man and Animals* (1872) described how shame is the most social and reflective of emotions, as it is always concerned with the viewing of the self, both from the point of view of the other and as a kind of internal theatre. Blushing is a key indicator of that shame—Silvan Tomkins has suggested how shame is peculiarly written on the body, specifically the face:

The shame response is an act which reduces facial communication. . . . By dropping his eyes, his eyelids, his head, and sometimes the whole upper part of his body, the individual calls a halt to looking at another person, particularly the other person's face, and to the other person's looking at him, particularly at his face.[6]

Tomkins memorably states how "shame strikes deepest into the heart of man," describing it, significantly, as a "sickness of the *soul*,"[7] alluding to its spiritual potency. Shame is personified as a weapon that cleaves asunder, that renders and splits the self from itself and all others:

Why are shame and pride such central motives? How can loss of face be more intolerable than loss of life? How can hanging the head in shame so mortify the spirit? In contrast to all other affects, shame is an experience of the self by the self. At that moment when the self feels ashamed, it is felt as a sickness within the self. Shame is the most reflexive of affects in that the phenomenological distinction between the subject and object is lost. Why is shame so close to the experienced self? It is because the self lives in the face, and within the face the self burns brightest in the eyes. Shame turns the attention of the self and others away from other objects to this most visible residence of the self, increases its visibility, and thereby generates the torment of self-consciousness.[8]

Critically, this self-consciousness is an act of lonely individuation, perhaps of existential isolation, cast adrift from all relational options. No wonder then, that "the soul" yearns for God, made manifest through Christ on the Cross, as an escape from that very material life of pain, grief, and mourning. God can become the one and only perfect mirror, a utopian projection of wholeness.

Stephen is transubstantiating into this very imago, into the crucified Christ, the compensatory, transitional figure who brings us to God by banishing sin. Next in Stephen's Stations of the Cross is tea with Roger, the child who is later to humiliate her sexually with Angela *Cross*by. Stephen is already internalizing the paranoidal sensibility of someone who is by now living in a state of shame: "She would think that the children were whispering about her, whispering and laughing for no apparent reason" (49). Roger is incredibly cruel, exposing Stephen's momentary masculinity on the hunting field as a foolish sham—"What about a fat leg on each side of her horse like a monkey on a stick, and everybody laughing!" (55). Roger has the real (erect, not flaccid) penis, and Stephen knows this is the source of her envy. Hall returns Stephen to her father, the one with the honorable phallus, who imputes to Stephen the idealized masculinity she is to pursue through the rest of the novel. Existing in this wilderness of gender indeterminacy, this "no-man's-land of sex" (89), Stephen is wandering through Eden, wearing the mantle of shame: "I'm lost, where am I? Where am I? I'm nothing—yes I am, I'm Stephen—but that's being nothing" (79). She searches for herself:

> Staring at her own reflection in the glass, Stephen would feel just a little uneasy: "Am I queer looking or not?" she would wonder. . . . Came a day

when Stephen was suddenly outspoken: "It's my face," she announced, "something's wrong with my face."

"Nonsense!" exclaimed Anna, and her cheeks flushed a little, as though the girl's words had been an offence, then she turned away quickly to hide her expression. (82–83)

Shame's contagion ensures Stephen's spiritual torment.

Stephen's first adult affair is with the shallow, nouveau riche Angela Crossby. Stephen, "a little grotesque in her pitiful passion" (172), is reduced to begging for "schoolgirlish," "crude," and "sterile" kisses. Angela's crushing question, "Could you marry me, Stephen?" (172), is delivered to inflict the keenest sexual humiliation. Ralph Crossby reinforces it by regularly enquiring of his wife, "How's your freak getting on?" (174), and remarking "that sort of thing wants putting down at birth" (175). This episode contains unremitting passages on Stephen's shame, including the introjection of wounding, imputing that, as her father prophesied, she is maimed by God. Stephen is relentless:

> With head bowed by her mortification of spirit, Stephen rode once more to The Grange. And from time to time as she rode she flushed deeply because of the shame of what she was doing. (180)

Her perception is not all it could be, however. Traveling to Bond Street she buys Angela a precious pearl (symbol of clitoral love), "Angela's colouring demanded whiteness" (191), in *The Well* the color of sexual dissmell. Stephen ignores the portents:

> People stared at the masculine-looking girl who seemed so intent upon feminine adornments. And someone, a man, laughed and nudged his companion: "Look at that! What is it?"
> "My God! What indeed?" (191)

That Stephen is displaced as Angela's lover by Roger is somewhat of a narrative inevitability. This phase of the novel is the most arduous and agonizing for the reader, as Stephen sinks into total abasement and solitude. On finding the two together sneaking out of The Grange at dawn, Stephen "laughed and she laughed like a creature demented—laughed and laughed until she must gasp for breath and spit blood from her tongue" (227). She returns to Morton and writes a letter pleading to Angela "I'm some awful mistake—God's mistake" (229). The letter has an important narrative function, which is that it allows Stephen to be totally repudiated by her mother:

> And this thing that you are is a *sin against creation*. Above all is this thing a *sin against the father* who bred you, the father whom you dare to resemble. You dare to look like your father, and *your face is a living insult* to his memory. . . . I can only thank God that your father died before he was asked to endure *this great shame*. As for you, I would rather see you dead at my feet than standing before me with this thing upon you—this unspeakable outrage that you call love." (233–234, emphasis mine)

It appears that Stephen is lost, she is an abomination, a depraved, corrupted unnatural grotesque, an animal. The shaming of Stephen is intensified by religious condemnation; with the whole weight of purgatorial suffering behind it, Stephen is cast into spiritual and psychological annihilation. She is expulsed from Eden. She is severed.

Hall has layered Stephen's shame like a thick shroud that should have silenced and even suffocated the bravest apologist. It is lesbian folklore that Radclyffe Hall's life with Una Troubridge was a happy one. Perhaps we tell ourselves this in order to mitigate the pain of her fictional protagonist, to reassure that no one could experience such abuse, *and survive*. To me, this passage is the most powerful of the book. My identification with Stephen's shame is strong and convincing. This scenario is a distillation of common experiences of homophobic rejection, even today. In Silvan Tomkins's typology of the "total affect-shame bind,"[9] and in Helen Block Lewis's description of the "feedback loops" of shame,[10] Stephen is in a state of near-ontological shame—shame is her being and hence also her nonbeing. Hall's oppressive layering of shame has the effect of finally reducing Stephen to nothing. From here, she can only disconnect, in order to survive. Her psychological environment is toxic, and she is displaying the symptoms of those shame binds. Her only chance is an enforced renunciation of the love object; she must leave behind both the bad mother (Anna) and the good mother (Morton), mourn, and then become the fantasy parent herself.

Shame and the Self

Alfred Douglas, Oscar Wilde's lover, wrote a poem "In Praise of Shame" in which he eulogized "Of all sweet passions Shame is loveliest."[11] Published in 1894, the poem was read at the time for its references to the Oscar Wilde trials, as shame, in common nineteenth-century parlance, was understood as a synonym for homosexuality. Although *The Well* can be read nihilistically as a ritual of self-sacrifice, it is also possible to detect in the novel a discursive reinscription of shame. Shame, as we know from its pervasive presence in sadomasochism, is a script that can be rewritten.[12] In a sense, it is possible to *enjoy* shame; perversely, it is also possible to be shamelessly shameful, to be put into the psychic location of shame and languish there. In part this may be because shame is a pungently intransigent affect, one that requires reexperiencing in order to relinquish it. There are clues to this in Hall's text: the sheer quantity of references to shame imply not just an invocation but also an attempt to batter the reader with Hall's intention to commute shame into selfhood. In the episode with Collins and her prosaic "housemaid's knee," there is enough affection in Hall's description to suggest that Stephen's fervent masochistic tendencies are to be viewed with amusement. But it is the adult Stephen who makes the agenda unmistakably clear; in the book's pivotal drawing-room scene, Stephen confronts Anna:

> She held up her hand [in benediction or malediction?], commanding silence; commanding that slow, quiet voice to cease speaking, and she said: "As my father loved you, I loved. As a man loves a woman, that was how I loved—protectively, like my father. I wanted to give all I had in me to give. It made me feel terribly strong . . . and gentle. It was good, good, *good*. . . . I don't know what I am; no one's ever told me that I'm different and yet I know that I'm different—that's why, I suppose, you've felt as you have done. And for that I forgive you, though whatever it is, it was you and my father who made this body—but what I will never forgive is your daring to try and make me ashamed of my love. I'm not ashamed of it, there's no shame in me." (234–235)

This is the moment of individuation for Stephen, for her to loose the shackles of the shame bind. This is also a moment of semiotic vulnerability, for in her state of indecipherability, she does not know who or what she is. In that instant though—and this is shame's potential—she is a floating sign, disattached; she is all possibility. This is related to the radical uncertainty of shame, which has a double effect—to sever the connection between self and other and to annihilate the individuated self. This means, therefore, that unshame (that is, pride), is an act of connection with another, something that *The Well* now seeks to demonstrate.

Book 3 ensues, in which Stephen, like any sensible invert in this position, goes off to become a writer, to *write* the self, in a kind of Barthesian utopic impulse. Book 4 brings war and, of course, Mary. By this time Stephen has acquired her conspicuous scar, the "mark of Cain." I have discussed elsewhere, through rereading Judith Butler and Teresa de Lauretis, how this scar can be interpreted as the lesbian fetish, that which always stands for the lost object of the female body.[13] This loss is tempting to relate to the oft melancholic, wounded quality of lesbian love. Being wounded is pandemic to literary butches, whether the wound is caused by (1) being a "Woman," (2) being "castrated," (3) losing the Mother, or (4) homophobia is unascertainable, but in this purview injury appears to be The Lesbian, or at any rate The Butch Condition.[14] Scars, of course, are also signs of *pride*. They are the morphology of bravery, of privileged membership. Stephen's scar is her "war wound" in more ways than one; it is the visible transmutation of her shame into pride—which, like shame, is always conferred by others. We read that the "little French doctor" assures her that "Mademoiselle will carry an honourable scar as a mark of her courage" (338), and shortly after Mary makes her move:

> "All my life I've been waiting for something."
>
> "What was it, my dear?" Stephen asked her gently.
>
> And Mary answered: "I've been waiting for you, and it's seemed such a dreadful long time, Stephen."
>
> The barely healed wound across Stephen's cheek flushed darkly. (339)

Stephen then goes through her own dark night of the soul, pacing with anxious responsibility over the corruption of her "child," Mary. She reenters shame: "Then Stephen must tell her the cruel truth, she must say: 'I am one of those whom God marked on the forehead. Like Cain I am marked and blemished. If you come to me, Mary, the world will abhor you, will persecute you, will call you unclean'" (347). The sexual tension between them is finally addressed by Mary, who cries for Stephen, and explains: "Do you think I'm crying because of what you've told me? I'm crying because of your dear, scarred face . . . the misery on it. . . . Can't you understand that all that I am belongs to you, Stephen?" (361).

The few lines end with the most famous phrase in lesbian literature: "and that night they were not divided." Crucially, it is Mary who transmutes Stephen's shame, thus reforming the bonds of shame as love. As E. M. Forster put it, "only connect."

Shame, Separation, and Gender Melancholy

Mary, the mother of Christ, gives birth to Stephen. Mary is the good love object who enables Stephen to determine her selfhood. Conversely, Stephen aspires to be the ideal parent to Mary. At first, she gazes with the unflinching "eyes of a mother" (376), but Stephen's mothering begins to misfire. She fails to read her child properly, infantilizing Mary ("Go and have your luncheon, there's a good child" [392]), rather than provoking her agency. Interestingly, Hall explains this in the language of shame behavior—"*blinded* by love . . . she erred towards Mary" (395). Shame is a very specular affect; shame is caused not just by gaze aversion but also by misrecognition. The gradual attrition of their intimacy is stimulated by Stephen's steady interpolation back into her psychic environment of shame, upon which she unwittingly puns when she claims "real life must be *faced* once again" (390). The social rejection of the couple by Lady Massey provokes this lament: "She seemed to be striving to obliterate, not only herself, but the whole hostile world through some strange and agonised merging with Mary" (430).

Obliteration is not unlike the shame allusion, "losing face"; in the code of the book, this "merging" is a sexual encounter in which shame has now entered as *unheimlich*—the strange, the uncanny. Their union is now a loss of self, an unhoming. Stephen begins to exist in the place of shame; she sinks into the Parisian bars populated with that "miserable army" of foreigners who are "covered by shame" (450). To their like Stephen exhibits a violent antipathy and revulsion:

> He bent forward, this youth, until his face was almost on a level with Stephen's—a grey, drug-marred face with a mouth that trembled incessantly.
>
> "Ma soeur," he whispered.

For a moment she wanted to strike that face with her naked fist, to obliterate it. (451)

Suicide, poverty and death are the endings promised for those inverts without the cultural capital of class. Stephen's inculcation into this new familial bond results in her returning to shame-humiliation and contempt-disgust. There is also ambivalence though, a prevarication symptomatic of the push-pull dynamic of shame. Shame is ambivalent because it is founded upon the interruption of love, where the self is dependent upon the acceptance of the other yet the inception of identity is predicated upon separation from the other, even the renunciation of the other. Shame is a kind of imperative to the emergent self. It is only once Stephen has allowed herself identification with *others like her* that she is able to gain herself an identity as "invert." She has reformed the bond, through shame, and commuted shame into love (with all its attendant aggression).

> Stephen Gordon was dead; she had died last night. . . . No, assuredly this was not Stephen Gordon. (507–508)

Stephen dies to Mary, and is resurrected as Stephen the martyr, the messiah. This Mary, unlike in the scenes of the pietà in Catholic iconography, does not hold the dying Christ in her arms. The Stephen/Christ analogy echoes with Anna's annihilating curse "I would rather see you dead"; this is a perverse meshing of the childish fantasy "I wish I were dead, then they'd be sorry!" Righteous epiphany returns though, the loss of Mary enabling Stephen to extend into her calling as a pious intercessor. Remembering that sin separates us from God, an inverted heavenly host cries out from the shadows for spiritual restitution. Sin, in *The Well*, is located in the bars of Sodom, but only in the sense that those "sinned against" have fallen into despair. Stephen incarnates their voices, she becomes shame's witness: "Acknowledge us, oh God, before the whole world. Give us also the right to our existence!" (510).

It is extreme loneliness that compels us to seek God, who is so much a projection of our own needs. Perhaps, for the shamed soul, He becomes the only safe repository for those angry, crushing, inexorable emotions that we dare not impose on another. The hope of that transcendence is itself shaming, for at the same time as we are reaching, we are also falling.

Shame is contagious; we are ashamed of our shame, and when those around us catch it, they flush and blush in awkward sympathy. Vacillating, they turn. In this (melancholic) state of loss, such is the desire to be homed, to salve the *unheimlich*, that we reach a state of self-knowledge of our differentiation. To be within the law, the ordering/signifying system, to have a place, we must be put into place, by shame. Shame, in this schemata, functions as a kind of originary myth, as Francis Broucek has described it, a "keystone effect"[15]. Isn't this process rather similar to Judith Butler's project in *Bodies That Matter*, which describes how:

> The term "queer" has operated as one linguistic practice whose purpose has been the shaming of the subject it names or, rather, the producing of a subject *through* that shaming interpellation. "Queer" derives its force precisely through the repeated invocation by which it has become linked to accusation, pathologization, insult. This is an invocation by which a social bond among homophobic communities is formed through time.[16]

And surely, some homo*sexual* communities too. I am well enough versed in Butlerisms not to suggest that this is the end of the story, that "the magic of the name" suddenly imputes legitimacy and restores agency, but there is an "I" and a "we" emerging here, from the double-valenced interstices of shame. Shame, then, has a contradictory latency. On the one hand it can reinforce conformity, and on the other it can liberate new grammars of gender that emerge in pride, shame's corollary. Dizzying isn't it? Performing and citing shame carries the same implicit risk that identity summons, always open to that critical reinscription, of discursive thievery. Returning to *The Well*, it would seem irrefutable that this text has constituted readers and reading communities in shame and through shame, and in its own significant way has "made" new inverts/butches/lesbians/queers of us all. *The Well* figures highly in coming-out stories.[17] As a narrative of sexual evolvement it continues to resonate with plastic identifications for diverse predilections. Which sexual community "owns" *The Well* is a redundant question, reflecting the kind of competitive behavior that is compulsive to marginal, shame-based identities.

In Butler's *The Psychic Life of Power* she describes this paradoxical dynamic within the production of subjectivity:

power that at first appears as external, pressed upon the subject, pressing the subject into subordination, assumes a psychic form that constitutes the subject's self-identity.

The form this power takes is relentlessly marked by a figure of turning, a turning back upon oneself or even a turning *on* oneself . . . the turn appears to function as a tropological inauguration of the subject, a founding moment whose ontological status remains permanently uncertain.[18]

She comments upon the psychoanalytic tenet that "no subject emerges without a passionate attachment to those on whom he or she is fundamentally dependent,"[19] an attachment that cannot be clearly "seen," that has to be at least in part denied, for the subject to form properly. How evocative is this turning, this volte-face, of the dynamics of shame: shame is not just laid upon the subject, delivered by a gaze that is then deflected ("cutting"[20]), it sets in motion a double turn, it activates its recipient to turn also, to turn away from the source of shame and in doing so to be *lost from view*, thus to inaugurate a condition of possibility. Needfully, we must remain modest about the extent of this possibility; Butler cautions:

Painful, dynamic, and promising, this dynamic between the already-there and the yet-to-come is a cross-roads that rejoins every step by which it is traversed, a reiterated ambivalence at the heart of agency.[21]

That inchoate figure turning at the cross-roads, turning away from us, winding into itself, twisting against itself, doubling back, is a tormented one. Because its desires always outrun their fulfillment, it is also ashamed. Yet we are reminded that shame is predicated on the yearning for reconnection, for love, and that those in the most chronic state of shame will be amongst the most deeply loving, because they will not relinquish hope of restitution.[22] The logic of *The Well of Loneliness* is precisely this: to show the reader that in order to transcend shame, we have first to enter it and know its deleterious effects. We can then explore its capacity for mutation.

Can there be a homosexual subject who is *not* formed from shame? In any personal trajectory, the growing consciousness of same-sex desire must, in a Western context, give rise to feelings of difference and exclusion. An identity may be imposed, or it may be wished for, but there is ultimately no choice, if one wants to live out erotic attachment to one's own gender, over experiencing some form of ascribed exclusion/prohibition. Coming out into the modern lesbian and gay movement we have celebrated a rubric of pride. The presence of shame has been repressed in the discourse of homosexual rights in an unhelpful way. Cognizant of our outlaw status we have imposed a heterodoxical sense of pride as a strategic deployment against the pathological homo, but its counterpoint of shame is no less (or more) real. I don't want to reinscribe a "cultural probity" of homosexual shame here, reinventing the iconography of victimization and playing into the hands of homophobia. Pride remains strategically essential, but shame and its effects are powerful historical players and cannot be subsumed. Shame itself is often repressed because to acknowledge shame is to (unwillingly) invoke shame; we need therefore to examine modalities of shame-avoidance more scrupulously. Remembering that shame is an embodied emotion that primarily resides in the face, centered on the composition of the gaze, it is as though acknowledging the injurious effects of shame can free us to grasp the transformative moment and *look them right back in the eye.* Thus "turning" is not so much "to be turned" as the more agentic *to* turn, to rotate the axis of determination/signification in such a way as to deviate the terms. To inaugurate blasphemy.

The Well of Loneliness is a refractory polemic, its theological audacity is remarkably scandalous; the novel manages to shift the Church's biblical interpretation of homosexuality as a sin "against nature" (in Paul's Epistle to the Romans, 1:6–7) to an interpretation of inversion as itself a God-given, natural state. It is an audacious legitimation, one that contributed significantly to the twentieth-century rhetoric of homosexual rights.

Notes

I am indebted to Sarah Chinn, and the editors of this volume, Laura Doan and Jay Prosser, for their kind input on earlier drafts.

1. Catharine Stimpson, "Zero Degree Deviancy: The Lesbian Novel in English," *Critical Inquiry* 8, no. 2 (1981):363–379; reprinted as "The Lesbian Novel in English" in Stimpson, *Where the Meanings Are: Feminism and Cultural Spaces* (London and New York: Methuen, 1988), pp. 97–110.

2. Joanne Glasgow, "What's a Nice Lesbian Like You Doing in the Church of Torquemada? Radclyffe Hall and Other Catholic Converts," in Karla Jay and Joanne Glasgow, eds., *Lesbian Texts and Contexts: Radical Revisions* (New York: New York University Press, 1990), pp. 241–254, 252.

3. Jane Rule, *Lesbian Images*, p. 78 in this volume.

4. Radclyffe Hall, *The Well of Loneliness* (1928; reprint, London: Corgi/Jonathan Cape, 1968), pp. 8, 9. All parenthetical page citations are to this edition.

5. In Silvan Tomkins's work, dissmell and disgust are "drive auxiliary responses" that have evolved to protect humans from ingesting harmful foods; they often manifest as contempt and are associated, like shame, with rejection. He argues that when shame shifts the self into hopeless despair, then contempt emerges as a defense. These feelings are often projected onto parents, so much so that one eventually renounces one's own love object and longs to become one's own fantasy parent. Silvan Tomkins, "SHAME-HUMILIATION AND CONTEMPT-DISGUST," in Eve Kosofsky Sedgwick and Adam Frank, eds., *Shame and Its Sisters: A Silvan Tomkins Reader* (Durham and London: Duke University Press, 1995), pp. 133–178.

6. Ibid., p.134.

7. Ibid., p.133.

8. Ibid., p.136.

9. Ibid., p.163.

10. In Helen Block Lewis, *Shame and Guilt in Neurosis* (New York: International Universities Press, 1971).

11. Lord Alfred Douglas, "In Praise of Shame," December 1894. See further Ed Cohen, *Talk on the Wild Side* (London: Routledge, 1994).

12. See Eve Kosofsky Sedgwick, "A Poem is Being Written," in *Tendencies* (Durham: Duke University Press, 1993), pp. 177–214.

13. S. R. Munt, *Heroic Desire: Lesbian Identity and Cultural Space* (New York: New York University Press, 1998).

14. For a related discussion, see my "Orifices in Space: Making the Real Possible" in Sally R. Munt, ed., *Butch/Femme: Inside Lesbian Gender* (London and Washington, D.C.: Cassell Academic/Contemporary Studies, 1998), pp. 200–209.

15. Francis Broucek, "Shame and Its Relationship to Early Narcissistic Developments," in *International Journal of Psycho-Analysis* 63 (1989):369, discussed in Sedgwick and Frank, eds., *Shame and Its Sisters*, pp. 5–6, 25.

16. Judith Butler, *Bodies that Matter: On the Discursive Limits of "Sex"* (London and New York: Routledge, 1993), p. 226.

17. See Rebecca O'Rourke, *Reflecting on "The Well of Loneliness"* (London: Routledge, 1989). Despite the fact that O'Rourke's reader response survey is now over a decade old, the novel's notoriety is still strong and it remains a crossover text for those on the cusp of a queer life.

18. Judith Butler, *The Psychic Life of Power* (Stanford: Stanford University Press, 1997), pp. 3–4.

19. Ibid., p. 7.

20. "Cutting" is common in Caribbean culture, and as Sarah Chinn has pointed out (personal communication), it was also a staple of the nineteenth-century North American novel, particularly in Henry James's *Daisy Miller*.

21. Butler, *Psychic Life of Power*, p. 18.

22. Donald L. Nathanson, "Shame and the Affect Theory of Silvan Tompkins" in Melvin R. Lansky and Andrew P. Morrison, *The Widening Scope of Shame* (Hillsdale N.J. and London: The Analytic Press, 1997), pp. 107–138. Nathanson credits this observation to a personal communication with Silvan Tompkins.

13

The Well of Loneliness as War Novel

SUSAN KINGSLEY KENT

Radclyffe Hall's *The Well of Loneliness*, the "classic story of Lesbian love," as the blurb on my 1974 Pocket Book edition describes it, first appeared in 1928.[1] Its publication occurred just as a flood of war novels and memoirs began to inundate the British public, some ten years after the conclusion of the Great War. The tale of "invert" Stephen Gordon excited comment from many quarters of Western society, but apart from its use of the war as an arena in which inverted women might find scope—and societies find use— for their hitherto wasted talents,[2] neither its author nor critics placed it alongside those myriad works that told of the agonies experienced by the war generation. Yet in its structure, conventions, motifs, and above all portrayal of a particular rendition of masculinity and male subjectivity, *The Well of Loneliness* deserves to be classified as one of the first manifestations of that genre.

Hall depicts Stephen Gordon, the tortured protagonist, in terms that we would describe as transgendered, giving her the qualities of a man trapped in a woman's body. Other inverts, such as Stephen's friend Valérie Seymour, demonstrate decidedly feminine qualities, so that inversion per se does not automatically carry with it the characteristics of maleness. Although at times Hall presents Stephen as a member of a third, or intermediate sex,

Hall's textual characterization of Stephen establishes her as an almost exclusively masculine figure in thought, in appearance, and in deed. There is nothing feminine about her.

In reproducing a manliness for Stephen Gordon to emulate, Hall, it seems to me, had to self-consciously construct a masculinity that other writers, particularly those of war memoirs, might not feel the need to articulate or elaborate upon. For those others, for whom identity and subjectivity might appear "natural," masculinity might be self-evident. Hall's writing of Stephen Gordon, in other words, affords an opportunity to examine masculinity in caricature, one whose features had to be clearly, because simplistically, drawn. It is possible, therefore, to see just what kind of male was being impersonated by Hall in her depiction of Stephen Gordon; to examine the kind of emotional valences that were attached to that concept of masculinity at that historical moment; and to ask what made that particular model of male, and not others, so compelling to Hall.

For although lesbians in Britain and elsewhere in Europe had been self-consciously donning male garb for perhaps half a century by 1928, the manliness performed by Stephen Gordon differed from that of earlier impersonations. As Martha Vicinus has shown, European women at the turn of the century participated in the creation of their own lesbian identities and articulated their sexual desires by drawing upon the *travesti* roles popular with theatre audiences.[3] Eschewing the medical establishment's definition of homosexuality as deviant *gender* behavior, these privileged and wealthy white women adopted "various male symbols" in order to represent what they understood to be a unique sexual identity deserving of cultural recognition, however circumscribed.[4] As Vicinus tells us, they seized upon the cross-dressed figures of the stage and the music hall—the "ineffectual warrior, symbolized by the Duke of Reichstadt," in the case of Parisian women, and Joan of Arc in those of the British lesbians and suffragists—as a way to present themselves to the world as androgynous. Their androgyny, she notes, partook mightily of the military.[5]

In the years prior to the First World War, the military figure was often a comic one as he/she appeared on the stage, or a chaste and spiritual one in the historical character of Joan of Arc. After the war the warrior could no longer be denoted frivolously or innocently; too many traumatic meanings had accrued to his figure in the four years of trench warfare, and too many visible reminders of the war walked the streets of Britain with their artificial limbs and their hollow stares. The notion of masculinity as military had undergone massive transformations in the years since 1914, and postwar society could no longer look at the music-hall warrior with the same eyes. The warrior figure, whose distinguishing features consisted of a uniform and the bearing of arms, could appear to Edwardians as comic or innocent, but to postwar citizens he was tragic and frightening, a man whose single greatest identifying feature was no longer a uniform but a wound. As Nicoletta Gullace has eloquently put it in another context, "the spirit of the Somme" had superceded the "levity of the music hall."[6]

Gullace has demonstrated that during the first few years of the war, women clearly identified manhood with the outward sign of the uniform, conferring their approbation on those men in khaki and their scorn on those in civilian clothes. They often mistook men out of uniform recuperating from wounds for shirkers and presented them with white feathers as a mark of cowardice. Many men resented these actions deeply, as well as the model of masculinity upon which they rested, arguing in subsequent years, as Gullace observes, that "masculinity was more than a series of external symbols but part of the essence of a man who had served or been willing to serve as a soldier or officer at the front" (201).

Personal suffering, not a military uniform, constituted the foundation of true manhood as increasing numbers of soldiers, sailors, military rejects, and conscientious objectors saw it. "As men noted," Gullace writes, "if a uniform could be taken off the wounds of battle could not. These hidden scars—clothed and covered in the romance of a uniform or the ignominious attire of civilian clothes—were the indelible marks of manhood etched deeply into the bodies and consciousness of those who fought."[7]

The wound became a predominant image and source of masculine identity in the years following World War I, and the wounded male a symbol that could be readily mobilized in narratives seeking to reestablish health, wholeness, and normalcy to societies that had undergone upheaval in virtually every area of life, not least in the realm of gender difference. The emasculated male and the robust, boyish Modern Girl exemplified for the British public the gender reversals wrought by the Great War, creating the appearance of what Lou Roberts has called for France a "civilization without sexes."[8] That civilization required the reassertion of traditional gender roles if stability, peace, and normalcy were to be restored, a process in which sexologists and psychoanalysts were prominently involved. Their pronouncements about "normal" sexual behavior, as I have argued in an earlier work, resonated in a culture that had come to associate sex with war, a culture that desperately needed peace.[9]

But Brady Brower is quick to caution us against reading a "civilization without sexes" as a "civilization without sexuality, desire, or pleasure," urging us to understand that the emasculated European male of the interwar period is not necessarily the impotent male he has been made out to be by historians. Brower comprehends "emasculation" *not* in the sense

> that men's bodies were in some way unsexed by the trench experience but that sexuality, or more specifically, erotic pleasure, had become less certain, less fixed. Gender had become more ambiguous in the wake of the war and so did the erotic body which gender pretended to signify. If we can picture the androgynous modern woman as the desired object of one type of anxious gaze, then her ambiguous counterpart, the wounded veteran, became the desired object of another.

Brower notes that the wound became eroticized in many postwar discourses, serving "as the expression for a great deal of sexual anxiety and desire. Pleasure and pain, desire and fear, dominance and submission are all forms of power that found new avenues of expression through the signifying capacities of the wounded body."[10] The point here is that wounded masculinity could take on a variety of possibilities, that personal suffering as the mark of manhood might coexist with another version that valorized polymorphous eroticism.

Prominent British lesbians such as Radclyffe Hall and Una Troubridge publicly, and Vita Sackville-West privately, embraced the postwar masculine figure as the model for their sexual identity.[11] They seem to have identified with—and did not merely perform in a theatrical sense—the wounded masculine creature of the postwar years. For by the 1920s psychologists and sexologists had succeeded in casting lesbianism as an abnormal sexual, and not just gender, practice. Finding themselves at the receiving end of society's ostracism, these women identified in the person of the wounded veteran an exemplar of themselves. Personal suffering, grievous offense, and an acute sense of dislocation in and alienation from society—these were experienced by veterans and inverts alike. So too was the sense of erotic possibility arising from the wounds of war, if the works of Magnus

Hirschfeld, Helen Zenna Smith, Mary Borden, Wilfred Owen, Siegfried Sassoon, and Radclyffe Hall—to name only a few—are any indication. In identifying with the suffering masculine antihero of the 1920s, lesbians might partake of the pleasurable as well as the painful possibilities opened up by the wound.

Hall's *The Well of Loneliness* portrays both the pleasurable and painful aspects of wounded postwar masculinity. The novel is redolent of the language of war and suffering. Homosexuality, it seems, closely resembled the condition of being wounded; the homosexual mirrored the figure of the soldier in battle. Hall refers to Stephen Gordon's inversion as "the no-man's-land of sex"—"all around here were grey and crumbling ruins, and under those ruins her love lay bleeding; shamefully wounded . . . a piteous, suffering, defenceless thing, it lay bleeding under the ruins" (203). Hall represents homosexuals as "maimed, hideously maimed and ugly (204)" in the eyes of the normal world; she uses exactly the same words to explain why England fought in the Great War as she does to articulate the struggle facing homosexuals: both are engaged in a battle for "the right to existence" (379). Inverts, declares Hall throughout, suffering from the "wound of existence" (303), are fighting a "ceaseless war for the right to existence" (379). "Over the bodies of prostrate comrades those others must fall in their turn or go on hacking—for them there was no compromise with life, they were lashed by the whip of self-preservation" (349). "Never stop fighting," one veteran of the inverts' war advises Stephen (352), who herself struggles on a daily basis to shield her lover, Mary, from being "wounded and utterly crushed" by "the whole hostile world" (371). When "the world . . . achieved its first real victory" (371) against them, when she and Mary are shunned by "normal" society in the guise of Lady Massey, Mary joins what another character, their American friend, Pat, calls "the miserable army" (356) of lesbians and gay men who inhabit the underground gay clubs of Paris. Stephen, "unwilling to visualize defeat" (376) at the hands of "those ruthless, pursuing millions bent upon the destruction of her and her kind" (379), instead "began once again to sharpen her weapon" (376)—her pen—to do battle against them. As her closeted former governess, Puddle, constantly reminds her, "work's your only weapon. Make the world respect you, as you can do through your work; it's the surest harbour of refuge for your friend, the only harbour—remember that—and it's up to you to provide it, Stephen" (339).

In Paris Stephen and Mary meet a younger generation of lesbians who engage their enemies more aggressively, a generation, as Hall describes them, "that was marching to battle with much swagger, much sounding of drums and trumpets, a generation that had come after war to wage a new war on a hostile creation. Being mentally very well clothed and well shod, they had as yet left no blood-stained footprints; they were hopeful as yet, refusing point-blank to believe in the existence of a miserable army" (381). The "as yets" in this passage make it clear that their eager battle-readiness would give way to battle fatigue and their "reckless," self-assured bravado succumb to depression, disillusionment, and despair, in a sequence that would parallel that of the men who marched off gaily to war in 1914 with visions of glory in their heads, only to become bogged down in the muddy, bloody, agony of the trenches.

It is through physical wounds that manliness is established in *The Well*. When war breaks out in the novel, Stephen longs to enlist, longs for the chance to "justify her existence." But she cannot, and "every instinct handed down by the men of her race, every decent instinct of courage, now rose to mock her so that all that was male in her make-up seemed to grow more aggressive, aggressive perhaps as never before, because of this new frustration" (267). Jonathan Brockett, on the other hand, a mincing, effeminate acquaintance of Stephen's who, we are to understand, is homosexual, whose "soft white hands," and "high little laugh" repulse Stephen, does go off to war, and she envies him his opportunity to prove his manhood, to "justify his existence, for they had not refused him when he went to enlist" (267). But after the war, as Hall makes clear, it is Stephen, and not Jonathan, despite his war service, who has proved her manliness. The war has changed him, to be sure: he has become "more robust, there was muscle and flesh on his wide, straight shoulders." His face is more lined now, especially around the mouth. "The war had left its mark upon Brockett," Stephen notices. But it has not changed the mark of his effeminacy, "those white and soft-skinned hands of a woman" (330). Stephen, always described by others as virile and manlike, leaves no doubt of her manliness when she is wounded while working as an ambulance driver at the front. Her "face was struck by a splinter of shell, and her right cheek cut open rather badly" (293). Stephen, Hall wants us to understand, is manly, Jonathan is not. She has been wounded, he has not. "Stephen's distinguished herself I see," remarks Brockett enviously upon encountering her for the first time since the war, "'Croix de Guerre and a very becoming scar. Don't protest, my dear Stephen, you know it's becoming. All that happened to me was a badly sprained ankle'; he laughed, 'fancy going out to Mesopotamia to slip on a bit of orange peel! I might have done better than that here in Paris'" (330).

As this dialogue intimates, wounds play a potentially erotic role in the narrative of the novel. In every instance some kind of wounding takes place or has taken place just as Stephen is about to enter into a sexual relationship or lose one to someone else. In some instances the wound prefigures a pleasurable experience of desire; in others a painful loss of love object. The first incident of this kind occurs when seven-year-old Stephen comes across her beloved Collins, a domestic servant whom she adores, being kissed by the footman:

> He kissed her full on the lips. Stephen's head felt suddenly hot and dizzy, she was filled with a blind, uncomprehending rage; she wanted to cry out, but her voice failed completely, so that all she could do was to splutter. But the very next moment she had seized a broken flower-pot and had hurled it hard and straight at the footman. It struck him in the face, cutting open his cheek, down which the blood trickled slowly. (28)

The second takes place when an adult Stephen first meets Angela Crossby, the woman with whom she first falls in love and has her first affair. Angela's dog, Tony, is being attacked by another dog, and in an effort to save him, Angela is bitten on two fingers and has to be seen by a doctor. Tony himself is dripping with gore (130). Later, when Stephen discovers Angela having an affair with Roger Antrim, her insufferable neighbor, she becomes hysterical. "She laughed and she laughed like a creature demented—laughed and laughed until she must gasp for breath and spit blood from her tongue, which had somehow got bitten in her efforts to stop her hysterical laughing; and some of the blood remained on her chin, jerked there by that agonized laughter" (195). During the war, working for the ambulance corp, she meets Mary Llewellen, the woman who will share her home and her bed after the Armistice. As we have seen, Stephen is struck in the face by a shell, which leaves a scar. Only one page after that incident, Mary declares her love for Stephen, at which point, "the barely healed wound across Stephen's cheek flushed darkly" (294). Six pages later, while Stephen paces the floor of her room, wracked with desire for Mary and yet fearful of acting on the impulses of her "anxious and passionate body," as Hall puts it, "the red scar on her cheek stood out like a wound" (300). Later the author allows that "the scar on her cheek" is one of the things that Mary "found so deeply appealing in Stephen" (343). And finally, Martin Hallam, a prewar friend and alter ego to whom Stephen will hand over Mary, has also been wounded in the war. "Just beside the right temple was a deep little scar—it must have been a near thing, that bullet" (412). The proximity of wounding on the one hand and the promise of erotic fulfillment or loss on the other undergirds the narrative of *The Well*.

But it is also the case—as the incidents of Stephen losing control before Collins and the footman, or becoming hysterical before Angela Crossby and Roger Antrim suggest—that wounds in relation to eroticism can signal the possibility of derangement. In these and other scenes, Hall portrays her protagonists in the language of shell shock, the quintessential condition of mental illness during and immediately following the war. She describes "the terrible nerves of the invert, those nerves that are always lying in wait" (184). Even before the war breaks out within the context of the novel, Stephen's nerves "ran like live wires through her body, causing a constant and ruthless torment, so that the sudden closing of a door or the barking of Tony would fall like a blow on her shrinking flesh. At night in her bed she must cover her ears from the ticking of the clock, which would sound like thunder in the darkness" (184–185). This passage, which relies upon the language sexologists and physicians used to describe inversion, could have been written by Robert Graves, Siegfried Sassoon, Wilfred Owen, or hundreds of other soldiers whose frontline experiences landed them in Craiglockart for the treatment of shell shock.

Later, after the war, while fighting the war for existence against "enemies" determined to snuff her and her kind out, "those treacherous nerves of hers would betray her" (379); "those nerves that were strained to breaking" (380) would cause her to strike out against Mary in an agitated fury over the slightest thing. At bars Stephen encounters soldiers of the miserable army, "battered remnants of men whom their fellow men had at last stamped under," whose eyes, "those haunted, tormented eyes of the invert," depress her deeply (387). She watches as men "of all ages, all degrees of despondency, all grades of mental and physical ill-being . . . must yet laugh shrilly from time to time, must yet tap their feet to the rhythm of music, must yet dance together in response to the band," as if these are outbursts of sound and motion over which they, like victims of shell shock, have no control. "And that dance seemed the Dance of Death to Stephen," Hall explains, in case the reader hadn't made the analogy herself.

The final action of the novel crystallizes in miniature virtually all of the elements that made up the wounded male subject of the postwar world. It consists of "a bitter and most curious warfare . . . waged between Martin and Stephen" (427) for the right to offer protection and sanctuary to Mary against a world filled with hostility and hate. Stephen's weapon in this war, her writing, seems at first to be sufficient to overcome Martin's challenge, but with every passing day, as she works in a "frenzy" to defeat Martin, "she would feel that her pen was dipped in blood, that with every word she wrote, she was bleeding!" (428). Stephen finally decides that Mary would indeed be better off with Martin, but knowing that she could never induce her loyal lover to leave, she devises a strategy that will force her away: she pretends indifference to Mary and concocts an affair with Valérie Seymour to convince Mary that she no longer loves her. "Ruthless as the world itself she became, and almost as cruel in this ceaseless wounding" of Mary, writes Hall (430). "Stephen struck at her again and again, desperately wounding herself in the process, though scarcely feeling the pain of her wounds for the misery of what she was doing to Mary" (430–431).

In the denouement, after Mary, having been convinced of Stephen's coldness and treachery, runs off, blinded by tears, into the waiting arms of Martin, Stephen suffers recriminations for having betrayed herself and her lover. She hallucinates a scene that closely resembles those described by shell-shocked soldiers who witnessed the death and destruction of men all around them and experienced the guilt of having survived when their comrades did not. "The room seemed to be thronging with people. Who were they, these strangers with the miserable eyes?" (436). As might be predicted, they are all the soldiers of the miserable army Stephen has met in Paris, come to accuse her of surrendering them to the enemy.

> They were many, these unbidden guests, and they called very softly at first and then louder. They were calling her by name, saying: "Stephen Stephen!" The quick, the dead, and the yet unborn. . . . She could see their marred and reproachful faces with the haunted, melancholy eyes of the invert—eyes that had looked too long on a world that lacked all pity and all understanding. . . . And these terrible ones started pointing at her with their shaking,

white-skinned, effeminate fingers: "You and your kind have stolen our birthright; you have taken our strength and have given us your weakness!" They were pointing at her with white, shaking fingers. . . . And the press and the clamour of those countless others—they fought, they trampled, they were getting her under. In their madness to become articulate through her, they were tearing her to pieces, getting her under. They were everywhere now, cutting off her retreat. . . . The walls fell down and crumbled before them; at the cry of their suffering the walls fell and crumbled. (436–437)

Her love, her very being, lies crumbled under the ruins produced by a world waging war against her.

A number of scholars[12] have identified the First World War as a literary and cultural watershed, an event that rendered inadequate the means by which contemporaries articulated their experiences prior to 1914 and established the need for new and different representations consonant with the upheaval and trauma produced by war. I want to extend that claim to encompass the psychic, to argue for Britain, as others have for Germany, that the Great War constituted a psychological watershed for that country as well, that it established the need to imagine a new kind of subjectivity. The conviction that permanent conflict now characterized relations between individuals, groups, classes, and nations—what Paul Fussell has described as the "modern *versus* habit: one thing opposed to another, not with some Hegelian hope of synthesis involving a dissolution of both extremes (which would suggest 'a negotiated peace,' which is anathema), but with a sense that one of the poles embodies so wicked a deficiency or flaw or perversion that its total submission is called for"[13]—permeated postwar thought. Certainly we find it structuring Hall's novel in her creation of a hostile world waging war on inverts. What we would regard as "thinking in rigid binary oppositions," as Eric Santner puts it, altering somewhat Fussell's earlier formulation, compelled Westerners to come up with a different way of conceptualizing how human beings understood themselves as subjects.[14]

What is at issue here is what Jean Comaroff has called "cultural ontology."[15] She argues that people in particular times and places arrive at various conceptualizations of selfhood that make sense within the circumstances of those times and places, that resonate with the social, economic, political, and cultural practices that prevail. In the case of Europeans, the Enlightenment male subject of prewar Western society—a rational, autonomous, and bounded whole—and his subsequent Freudian counterpart—driven by instincts and urges that were nevertheless contained within a unified tripartite structure of id, ego, and superego—no longer proved adequate to the task of representing the subject of postwar Europe. Instead, the self theorized by Jacques Lacan, whose most obvious attributes were those of the shell-shocked soldier whose symptoms we have come to call posttraumatic stress disorder, served as a far more persuasive representative of the conditions and circumstances produced by the most terrible war to date. Described as one whose mind has been shattered by the endless cycles of bombardment, terror, destruction, and death at the front, and lacking control over both his bodily and mental capacities, the post–World War I masculine archetype has perhaps best been described as one possessing, as Hal Foster terms it, a "fascistic subjectivity."[16]

Between 1914 and 1918 and again during the interwar period, the anxieties produced by the Great War were often articulated through an idiom of gendered and sexualized language that stressed the blurring of boundaries between men and women, warrior and civilian, heterosexuality and homosexuality. Carolyn Dean has argued that the blurring of identities caused by the war was reflected in and recast by the work of Lacan, in particular in his conception of the true self as an irretrievable, unsymbolizable, inaccessible other.[17] Where Freud posited that subjects attain a unified, gendered identity through the process of oedipal conflict, Lacan's theory of how the individual arrives at a sense of selfhood involves the infant perceiving himself [sic] in a mirror. The image of a whole self produced by the mirror, however, is not, according to Lacan, just imaginary; it also conjures up the fantasy of a previous moment when the body was not whole, when it was in pieces, shattered, fragmented, and fluid, vulnerable to drives that threatened to annihilate it. The ego, in this formulation, acts as a kind of armor designed to stave off the return of the body in pieces, to protect against the chaotic forces that might reduce the subject once again to fragmentation and dissolution. Those forces might be internal or external; they might be conscious or unconscious sexual desires or racial, sexual, gendered, or political "others."[18]

What Foster calls the armoring of the fascistic self by members of postwar society informs *The Well of Loneliness*. The fascistic subject seeks to preserve himself or herself as a psychic whole, as a discrete object in an environment in which the blurring of boundaries and the shattering of categories go on apace. The figure of Stephen Gordon, an anatomical female whose every thought, physical attribute, sensation, action, impulse—her very appellation, in fact—are coded as male, stands as a quintessential model of the blurring of gender and sexual lines that haunted postwar society. We see this blurring of categories and fluidity of identities in Hall's depiction of Stephen and other homosexuals in the language of shell shock, a psychological condition that Elaine Showalter and others have demonstrated to be hysteria, a disease characteristic of women up until 1914 and then of men who believed themselves to be unmanned by the terrors of war.[19]

The structure of the novel and the imagery Hall uses to claim toleration for inversion involve the process of Stephen becoming "one," of becoming integrated, whole. She spends the entire novel seeking for herself and others like her "the right to existence." Existence, the text makes clear, is intricately bound up with oneness, integrity, solidity. It also connotes naturalness, a quality that "normal" men and women possess in abundance, but one for which Stephen desperately strives. As a child and an adolescent she feels out of place, awkward around the girls of her acquaintance. She despises them for their feminine airs and their gossip, their "light-hearted conversation" (76). But she also "longed to be like them," for "they seemed very happy, very sure of themselves. . . . There was something so secure in their feminine conclaves, a secure sense of oneness, of mutual understanding" from which she was excluded by virtue of her sexual identity. Morton, her family home, also exudes "oneness" for Stephen. The garden, to which she flees in panic and revulsion after she rejects Martin Hallam's prewar proposal of marriage, seems to her a place of "communion," or "oneness," for its inhabitants, though not for her. "A mysterious and wonderful thing this oneness, pregnant with comfort could she know its true meaning" (101). Lacking "oneness" within herself and with others implies that Stephen does not understand herself to be an integrated whole; rather, she feels disintegrated. Only her wartime experiences with other inverted women provide Stephen with the sense of wholeness, of belonging and security that "oneness" promised. The war had given her and her colleagues "something terrible yet splendid, a oneness with life in its titanic struggle against death" (295). The war had also given her Mary, with whom for the first time in her life she felt "natural" and whole. "Something primitive and age-old as Nature itself, did their love appear to Mary and Stephen" (313).

The beleaguered inverts of Hall's acquaintance may well have found in the figure of the traumatized, agonized, shell-shocked veteran of the front lines—Foster's quintessential fascistic subject—the most accurate and sympathetic representation of themselves. Yet these soldiers of the miserable army are the very people from whom the traumatized, weary, heartsore, but still resolute Stephen Gordon desperately struggles to remain distinct, separate, apart. These represent the forces Foster enumerates, the ones against which the fascistic subject armors her- or himself: "sexuality and the unconscious, desire and the drives, the *jouissance* . . . that shatters the subject, that surrenders it precisely to the fragmentary and the fluid."[20] It appears that Stephen is ultimately unsuccessful in staving off the disintegrating forces that shatter the subject, as the last scene of hallucination is meant to imply: "We are coming, Stephen—we are still coming on, and our name is legion—you dare not disown us!" warn the miserable army:

> She raised her hands trying to ward them off, but they closed in and in: "You dare not disown us!"
>
> They possessed her. Her barren womb became fruitful—it ached with its fearful and sterile burden. It ached with the fierce yet helpless children who would clamour in vain for their right to salvation. (437)

And yet, in a variation on Foster's explanation of the armoring of the fascistic subject against chaos without, Stephen Gordon incorporates those fragmentary, fluid, chaotic forces within that threaten to tear her apart into a single, unitary whole with whose collective strength she faces the hostile world to demand her right to existence:

> And now there was only one voice, one demand; her own voice into which those millions had entered. A voice like the awful, deep rolling thunder; a demand like the gathering together of great waters. A terrifying voice that made her ears throb, that made her brain throb, that shook her very entrails, until she must stagger and all but fall beneath this appalling burden of sound that strangled her in its will to be uttered. . . . "Acknowledge us, oh God, before the whole world. Give us also the right to our existence!" (437)

Gathering together within the figure of Stephen Gordon, the fragmented, broken, incoherent soldiers of the miserable army utilize her singular voice to proclaim their oneness with nature, to demand their "right to existence."

In contrast to others represented as possessing a fascistic subjectivity who fought off the disintegrating forces they so feared by annihilating them, who secured their armored, unitary ego structures by destroying the "others" who appeared to threaten them, whether they be Jews, communists, women, Indians, or Irish Catholics, Stephen ultimately establishes a coherent, integrated, unitary subject position by embracing and taking within herself the potentially disintegrating forces of sexuality, desire, and pleasure. The wounded male subject, the shell-shocked, traumatized victim of wartime horrors, offered Hall a model of masculinity that best represented her struggles, her pain, her pleasures, and, above all, her courage and integrity in claiming for herself and all inverts a tolerated place in society. Critics have often derided Hall's overwrought, even hysterical, prose; they have condemned her book as a "bad" novel. By reading *The Well of Loneliness* as war novel, however, by seeing it as one of the first manifestations of the genre, we can make a case for regarding it as an exemplary expression of the twentieth-century condition.

Notes

1. All quotations from the text derive from the 1974 edition of *The Well of Loneliness* (New York: Pocket Books).

2. The scenes at the front elicited comment from the magistrate presiding over the obscenity trial of the novel. Radclyffe Hall tried to protest against his declaration that she had asserted that "a number of women of position and admirable character, who were engaged in driving ambulances in the course of the war, were addicted to this vice." See p. 45 of this volume. She was silenced by the magistrate and could not in court assert, as she had done in an "Author's Note," that "a motor ambulance unit of British women drivers did very fine service upon the Allied front in France during the later months of the war, but although the unit mentioned in the book, of which Stepehn Gordon becomes a member, operates in much the same area, it has never had any existence save in the author's imagination."

3. See Martha Vicinus, "Male Impersonation and the Private Fantasies of *Fin-de-Siècle* Lesbians,"in Richard Dellamora, ed., *Victorian Sexual Dissidence* (Chicago: University of Chicago Press, 1999).

4. Martha Vicinus, "Fin-de-Siècle Theatrics: Male Impersonation and Lesbian Desire," in Billie Melman, ed., *Borderlines: Genders and Identities in War and Peace, 1870–1930* (New York: Routledge, 1998), p. 167.

5. Ibid., p. 184.

6. Nicoletta Gullace, "White Feathers and Wounded Men: Female Patriotism and the Memory of the Great War," *Journal of British Studies* 36, no. 2 (1997), p. 201.

7. Ibid., pp. 202, 201.

8. See Mary Louise Roberts, *Civilization without Sexes* (Chicago: University of Chicago Press, 1994).

9. See Susan Kingsley Kent, *Making Peace: The Reconstruction of Gender in Interwar Britain* (Princeton: Princeton University Press, 1993), passim.

10. Matthew Brady Brower, "Re-membering the Modern Subject: The Wounded Body and the Politics of Mourning, 1917–1937," M.A. thesis, University of Colorado, 1996, ch. 3.

11. Vita Sackville-West donned the garb of a soldier and wrapped an impressive bandage around her head to signify a head wound when she ventured out with Una Troubridge. See Harold Nicolson, *Portrait of a Marriage* (London: Weidenfeld and Nicolson, 1973).

12. Paul Fussell, *The Great War and Modern Memory* (New York: Oxford University Press, 1975); Sandra Gilbert, "Soldier's Heart: Literary Men, Literary Women, and the Great War," *Signs* 8, no. 3 (1983), 422–450; Elaine Showalter, *The Female Malady: Women, Madness, and English Culture, 1830–1980* (New York: Pantheon, 1985); Samuel Hynes, *A War Imagined: The First World War and English Culture* (New York: Atheneum, 1991); Eric Leed, *No Man's Land: Combat and Identity in World War I* (Cambridge: Cambridge University Press, 1979); Kent, *Making Peace.*

13. Fussell, *The Great War*, p. 79.

14. Eric L Santner, *Stranded Objects: Mourning, Memory, and Film in Postwar Germany* (Ithaca, N.Y.: Cornell University Press, 1990), p. 2.

15. See Jean Comaroff, "Aristotle Re-membered," in James Chandler, Arnold I. Davidson, and Harry Harootunian, eds., *Questions of Evidence: Proof, Practice, and Persuasion Across the Disciplines* (Chicago: University of Chicago Press, 1994), p. 465.

16. See Hal Foster, "Postmodernism in Parrallax," *October* 63 (Winter 1993): 3–20.

17. Carolyn Dean, *The Self and Its Pleasures: Bataille, Lacan, and the History of the Decentered Subject* (Ithaca, N.Y.: Cornell University Press, 1992), p. 5.

18. Foster, "Postmodernism in Parallax," p. 8.

19. See Showalter, *The Female Malady*; Gilbert, "Soldier's Heart."

20. Foster, "Postmodernism in Parallax," p. 10.

14

War Wounds: The Nation, Shell Shock, and Psychoanalysis in *The Well of Loneliness*

JODIE MEDD

Radclyffe Hall's *The Well of Loneliness* immediately made history, many histories. As the collection of essays in this book attests, the novel's publication and legal prosecution constituted powerful nodal points in the history of sexuality, obscenity, legality, and literature. Published just ten years after the end of the Great War, *The Well of Loneliness* also boldly remade history and the languages of history by enlisting the memories of war and the rhetoric of national citizenship in the service of an antihomophobic literary project. Such a strategy contested the traditions of censorship and sexual purity campaigns that recurrently figured the threat of deviant sexuality through a rhetoric of battle and national invasion. Indeed, the moral "war" against homosexuality was vividly staged by one of Hall's most vituperative critics, James Douglas, whose editorial in the *Sunday Express* instigated the legal suppression of *The Well of Loneliness*. When Douglas attacked Hall's novel and demanded its withdrawal, he quite literally issued a battle call to the postwar British nation. "I know that the battle has been lost in France and Germany," he exclaims, "But it has not yet been lost in England, and I do not believe that it will be lost."[1] He continues with patriotic fervor, "The English people are slow to rise in their wrath and strike down the armies of evil, but when they are aroused they show no mercy, and they give no quarter to those who exploit their tolerance and their indulgence."[2] Drawing upon absolute moral oppositions characteristic of war propaganda, Douglas configures the homosexual "armies of evil" as foreign invaders, insisting that loyal British citizenship dictates militant and militaristic homophobia.[3] While Douglas incites moral panic by mobilizing nationalistic rhetoric, Hall's history-making novel reclaims the affective power of the languages of war and citizenship to render the pathos and legitimacy of homosexual identity. If we examine how *The Well of Loneliness* inscribes inversion within the cultural memory of the Great War, we find that the war is both a crucial condition of Stephen's narrative and crucially conditions the post–Great War reader's relation to the novel by offering a powerful combination of historical reference, metaphoric relation, and narrative structure.

Only recently has a move toward cultural historicism prompted greater attention to the relevance of the Great War and national identity in *The Well of Loneliness*.[4] Previous readers of the novel have predominantly focused on Hall's conspicuous, if ambivalent, reliance upon tropes of Catholic Christianity and the biological determinism of late nineteenth-century sexology to construct Stephen Gordon's sexuality as a morally irreproachable tragic necessity that is worthy of sympathy and social tolerance. According to this reading, Hall's sexological case study avoids a psychoanalytic developmental model of homosexuality because it would imply the possibility of a "cure" and render the invert morally responsible for his or her sexual deviance. While Hall clearly attempts to authorize her novel and protagonist through the transcendent claims made by sexual science, Christianity, and tragic destiny, the novel also references the forces and events of history, discourses that reconfigure the contours of a sexological-theological reading.

In her article on national service in Hall's fiction, Claire Buck eloquently argues that Hall consistently links the female invert's "emerging identity to war service."[5] In *The Well of Loneliness*, Buck specifies, the war "provides the link between citizenship and sexuality . . . by means of the language of chivalry."[6] Expanding upon Buck's attention to the connections among sexuality, gender, and national citizenship, I propose that we read *The Well of Loneliness* through the traumatic memory of the Great War in addition to the war's heroic conventions. While supplying Hall with a language of chivalry to galvanize Stephen's admirable masculine citizenship,[7] the war also provided a language of national and individual trauma that inflects Stephen's psychic narrative. The novel's paradoxical representation of the war as both "a splendid national endeavour" and "the most stupendous and heartbreaking folly of our times" functions as a national-historical allegory of Stephen's simultaneously splendid and heartbreaking narrative of sexual difference.[8] In a striking textual echo, the novel's patriotic and prosopopeitic formulation of England "fighting for her right to existence" (269) during the Great War is reinscribed in the narrative's desperate closing line, in which Stephen channels the cries of all the suffering inverts in an appeal to God (and the novel's readers) to "Give us the right to our existence!" (447). This textual repetition directly identifies the "dreadful reality" England must face in war with both Stephen's individual narrative of suffering and the collective oppression of all sexual inverts, mapping the national struggle of England onto the psychological struggle of sexual minorities.[9]

Such a textual convergence of history, nation, and psychosexuality is a reminder that Hall's attempt to write the embattled psyche of a sexual invert into English literature is implicated in a larger reconsideration of individual and collective psychology that was brought about by the war. The national destruction and individual psychological devastation wrought by the "folly" of war effected a paradigm shift in how the psyche was conceptualized in England, a change that allowed for the possibility of understanding and even sympathizing with psychological differences. Specifically, the unprecedented epidemic of "shell shock" and "war neuroses" suffered by both combatants and noncombatants during the Great War baffled traditional psychological medicine and led to a wider introduction and legitimization of psychoanalytic accounts of the traumatized psyche. Subsequently, we find that an historically specific version of psychoanalysis emerges from the novel's allusions to shell shock and provides a narrative structure of traumatic memory that operates as a compelling and suitably controversial supplement to Stephen's dominantly sexological representation.

Jean Radford and others have already appreciated the psychoanalytic resonances in the novel, from Jonathan Brockett's allusion to Ferenczi to the Gordon family's glaringly oedipal dynamics.[10] While I endorse Radford's observation that Stephen's identity is "overdetermined" by the novel's strategic combination of sexological and psychoanalytic allusions, I want to draw attention to how psychoanalysis functions in the novel through its historical connection with the war and shell shock and consider how Hall aroused her contemporary readers' *affective relation* to this history in an attempt to condition the moral evaluation of Stephen's invert narrative. *The Well of Loneliness* endeavors to render Stephen's invert identity legible and affectively accessible to a heterosexual post–Great War audience by staging it within what Lauren Berlant has termed a National Symbolic[11] that binds reader, author and protagonist together in a shared national history that includes the war, shell shock, and psychoanalysis.

Shell Shock and the Cultural Emergence of Psychoanalysis in Britain

Among its many radical disruptions of cultural experience, World War I catalyzed a revolution in psychology when traditional psychiatric medicine, which relied upon theories of inherited insanity and organic etiologies, failed to accommodate the widespread psychological casualties of war.[12] Reflecting upon the impact of shell shock, historian Martin Stone notes, "The monolithic theory of hereditary degeneration upon which Victorian psychiatry had based its social and scientific vision was significantly dented as young men of respectable and proven character were reduced to mental wrecks after a few months in the trenches."[13] Diagnoses of hereditary weakness and organic damage persisted, but proved inadequate and ideologically undesirable when applied to the psychic disorders of war, while the relatively new psychoanalytic doctrines of Freud and his British followers offered one of the only alternatives for understanding and treating the shell-shocked soldier. Avoiding Freud's connection between sexual life and the neuroses, British doctors selectively adapted Freudian concepts in their attempts to (ad)dress the psychic wounds of war. The respected and influential British shell shock doctor, W. H. R. Rivers, insisted that selective Freudianism proved "of direct practical use in diagnosis and treatment" of cases of mental disturbance presented by the war and offered a "working hypothesis. . . . to stimulate inquiry and help us in our practice while we are groping our way towards the truth concerning the nature of mental disorder."[14] Subsequently, what emerged during the war from shell shock doctors such as Rivers was an eclectic "depth psychology" that incorporated such psychoanalytic concepts as mental trauma and unconscious psychical conflict, in an approach that destabilized entrenched medical assumptions about distinct boundaries between mental health and illness.

While the phenomenon of shell shock was revolutionizing British medical psychology, it was simultaneously reverberating throughout mass culture, complete with psychoanalytic after-effects. With at least eighty thousand soldiers and officers over the course of the war rendered unfit for service by psychological crises, shell shock became a widely circulated, if relatively undefined, psychological category.[15] The influence of shell shock discourse on the public was noted by the British government's *Report of the War Office Committee of Enquiry into "Shell-Shock,"* published in the autumn of 1922. Lamenting "shell shock" as an inaccurate and overgeneralizing term, the committee recognized its popular appeal: "The alliteration and dramatic significance of the term had caught the public imagination, and thenceforward there was no escape from its use."[16] Uniting medical diagnosis with cultural poetics, shell shock was a vague but compelling term that provided a serviceable appellation for an ideologically fraught condition:

> There was much anxious solicitude as to the incapacitated, and such was the appeal of the term "shell-shock" that this class of case excited more general interest, attention, and sympathy than any other, so much so that it became a most desirable complaint from which to suffer. . . . To the public mind any condition which arose during the war and which gave rise to the assumption of irresponsibility of conduct by the individual concerned was to be ascribed to "shell-shock."[17]

Embedded in this rather cynical commentary is the official recognition that for a substantial portion of the war generation, shell shock functioned as a necessary collective belief that legitimized and exculpated soldiers' extreme psychic reactions to the nightmare of history. On the other hand, the condescending tone also conveys the suspicion with which shell shock was often regarded, particularly by officials who were intent on disciplining "cowardice" and malingering. The unresolved debates in the report indicate how shell shock elicited a range of irreconcilable ambivalent responses, bringing into question not only how to categorize the psychological wounds of war but also how to understand, represent, and account for the modern psyche. Indeed, war neuroses were not confined to combatants but were also increasingly diagnosed in the civilian population, in effect rendering the neurotic psyche as *the* paradigm of national wartime citizenship and as a model of modern, traumatized British subjectivity.[18]

In conjunction with the war's influence on notions of the psyche, psychoanalysis infiltrated the British journal-reading public. General interest journals, from the *Athenaeum* to the *Spectator*, and lay-science magazines such as *Psyche* and *Discovery*, all claimed that the mental casualties of war raised popular awareness of psychoanalysis in Britain.[19] While "extreme" Freudianism was often dismissed as inappropriately preoccupied with sexuality, the press tended to embrace the more moderate, homegrown, new British depth psychology expounded by shell shock doctors such as Rivers. Subsequently, journalists widely employed Freudian language and introduced psychoanalytic concepts to their readers. Such terms as war nerves, shell shock, hysterical symptoms, conversion, repression, sublimation, the unconscious, neuroses, flight into illness, wish fulfillment, and traumatic memory became common phrases of the media.[20] By the 1920s the press was referring to the "psychoanalysis craze" as the latest bourgeois preoccupation.[21] "A characteristic feature of the emancipated conversation of the present day," claims the *Saturday Review* in 1920, "is the popularity of the works of Freud as a dinner-table topic. . . . One can hardly read a review without finding some allusion to his discoveries, or some reference to the jargon peculiar to his disciples."[22] Similarly, *Discovery* reports that "the new psychology, or psychoanalysis . . . is made the subject of letters to newspapers, sermons from the pulpit, and discussions at afternoon tea," while *The New Statesman* asserts simply, "We are all psychoanalysts now."[23] Shell shock and its impact on discourses of the psyche had introduced Freud into the vernacular of the bourgeois reading public by the 1920s, providing the interwar generation with an appropriately modern language for categorizing and interpreting post–Great War subjectivity.

The Shell-Shocked Invert

It is within this context of the Great War, traumatic neuroses, and popularized concepts of psychoanalysis that I want to situate a reading of *The Well of Loneliness*. In writing the narrative of a 1920s female invert, Hall strategically appropriated the traumatic memory of both the war and shell shock and exploited their discursive influences on both national and individual psychic structures. In one sense Hall was faced with a dilemma comparable to that of a British shell shock doctor and responded accordingly. While Hall relied upon theories of congenital inversion to render Stephen an innocent victim of a biological necessity, she also needed to avoid negative suggestions of degeneration that accompanied such biological accounts in order to promote Stephen as a valuable national citizen of "respectable and proven character." To achieve this delicate balance, Hall supplemented established hereditary and organic psychosexual theories with a psychoanalytic narrative of trauma that gained public currency through shell shock. Just as "shell shock" exceeded its initial physiological diagnoses and functioned as an unspecific term that signified a condition brought on by an indefinable combination of "biological, psychological and social events,"[24] the term "sexual invert" in Hall's novel exceeds sexology and functions as a sign that gathers together a range of discursive explanations for socially proscribed forms of gender and desire. In another sense Hall's antihomophobic project aimed to communicate Stephen's difference while still making her affectively accessible to her readers. To this end *The Well of Loneliness* constructs the narrative and its protagonist in part on a model of shell shock, enlisting a familiar and affectively charged discourse to render homosexual difference both historically comprehensible and emotionally compelling. Such a strategy recalls "Miss Ogilvy Finds Herself," Hall's "invert" short story that she characterized as the "nucleus" for *The Well of Loneliness*.[25]

Written before but published after *The Well of Loneliness*, "Miss Ogilvy Finds Herself" constitutes an illuminating frame for the novel. In Hall's short story, the armistice requires the masculine Miss Ogilvy to abandon her fulfilling work in a women's ambulance corps and reluctantly return to her narrow spinster life in England. Her growing irritation with insufferable domestic tedium is snidely dismissed by her hysterical sisters as "shell shock," and finally Miss Ogilvy departs in search of an adventure on a coastal island, determined, she says, to "shake off all my troubles."[26] Perplexed by the uncanny familiarity of the island, Miss Ogilvy spontaneously reacts in a "sudden, inexplicable fury" when the innkeeper shows her the disinterred skull of a cave-dwelling warrior who was killed in battle on the island. "For her sense of outrage was overwhelming as she stared at those bones that were kept in the scullery" the narrator tells us, "moreover, she knew how such men had been buried, which made the outrage seem all the more shameful" (1402). These eerie memories and extreme psychological states prompt Miss Ogilvy ultimately to speculate, "Is it shell shock? . . . I wonder, can it be shell shock?" (1403). As Miss Ogilvy draws closer to "remembering" her earlier embodiment as the very prehistoric tribesman whose bones are kept in the scullery—and thus "finding" the primeval origins of her sexual inversion—shell shock offers the one culturally available concept for relating the repressed memories of her past life to the repressed homosexual desires of her present life. Shell shock, then, functions as both an intervening screen explanation for the origins of her sexual and gender dysphoria and as an accurate diagnosis—she is in fact recalling her mortal wound in combat. As an historical allusion familiar to postwar readers, shell shock provides a discourse of traumatic memory that mediates Miss Ogilvy's travel back in history—indeed, into prehistory—where she unearths the "origins" that explain and ennoble her traumatic personal history.[27] Whereas Elaine Showalter, among others, has argued that soldiers suffering from shell shock during the Great War were regarded as effeminized, hysterical men, here Hall exploits shell shock as a metaphor for female sexual inversion to render both the masculinity and the suffering of invert women legible and legitimate.[28]

The Well of Loneliness maintains, extends, subtends, and complicates such connections among the war, shell shock, and inversion. The novel not only situates Stephen Gordon within a shared national experience of the Great War, it also adopts the language of war as the grammar of Stephen's embattled existence. Metaphors of wounding, death, and battle saturate the (melo)drama of Stephen's sexual desire. When seven-year-old Stephen is in love with Collins the housemaid, she attempts to share Collins's suffering by acquiring her "housemaid's knee" and imagines herself as the mortally wounded admiral Nelson: "I'm in the middle of the Battle of Trafalgar— I've got shots in my knees!" (19). After the tragic loss of Collins, the wounded Stephen "[fights] out her battle alone" to recover from her grief (27). When she is betrayed by Angela Crossby, her suffering is figured as a landscape of destruction and mutilation: "All around her were grey and crumbling ruins, and under those ruins her love lay bleeding; shamefully wounded by Angela Crossby . . . a piteous, suffering, defenceless thing, it lay bleeding under the ruins" (206). She introjects her mutilated love as a corpse: "She had the sense of a dead thing that lay close against her heart and oppressed it. A corpse—she was carrying a corpse about with her. Was it the corpse of her love for Angela?" (198), and finally pronounces the death of her heart, "A gruesome companion to have, a dead heart" (235). Although not directly citing the Great War, this morbid metaphoricity resonates with the spectacle of destroyed bodies and ruined landscapes that characterized the Great War and its literary representation, appropriating the images of war to validate invert desire and suffering.

Indeed, a lexicon specific to the Great War encodes Stephen's sexual identity long before the war itself enters the novel as an historical event. Discussing Stephen's gender dysphoria at the age of seventeen (ten years before the war), the narrator remarks knowingly, "she had not yet learnt her hard lesson—she had not yet learnt that the loneliest place in this world is the no-man's-land of sex" (77). The late nineteenth-century concept of the "intermediate sex" finds a corroborative vehicle in the language of the battlefield, a language that communicates Stephen's tragic sexual alienation through imagining her in "no-man's-land," the uninhabitable gulf between warring front lines. Deploying this war term before it has even entered the characters' historical frame of reference, the novel proleptically figures Stephen's "not yet" discovered congenital inversion through an historical anticipation. "No-man's-land" is an ontological space that eludes Stephen as a concept because it is not yet available to her individual or historical consciousness. According to the *Oxford English Dictionary* (2d ed., 1989), the term "no-man's-land" was used for centuries before the war with the meaning of "a piece of waste, or unowned land; in early use as the name of a plot of ground, lying outside the north wall of London, as used as a place of execution"; however, its military meaning as "the terrain between the front lines of armies entrenched opposite one another" was peculiar to the twentieth century. The *OED* cites 1908 as the first usage of the term but it was not until the unprecedented publicity of the Great War, along with the war's topography of trench warfare, that the term "no-man's-land" was brought into wide public circulation.

Just as her country will eventually learn the disturbing connotations that will accrue to the phrase "no-man's-land," only later will Stephen unlock the sexological mystery of her difference.[29] Hall's contemporary postwar readers, however, are interpellated here as sharing the memory of the phrase with the narrator and are asked to transfer its affective weight onto a sympathetic appreciation of Stephen's alienation.

By the time the war arrives, Stephen has learned the "hard lesson" of her inversion and laments her inability to enlist in military service with a figurative repetition: "she was nothing but a freak abandoned on a kind of no-man's-land at this moment of splendid national endeavour" (271). Whereas in the first reference to no-man's-land, the narrator claimed an epistemological advantage over Stephen, here the phrase "no-man's-land" occurs in a passage of free indirect discourse where the narrative voice speaks for and as Stephen. This conjunction implies that Stephen catches up with what the narrator knew about Stephen's identity ten years earlier, at the very moment when England learns the meaning of "no-man's-land." Such a convergence suggests that Stephen's identity-consolidation coincides with—even requires—the cultural codes of meaning afforded by the war.

History and metaphor rejoin in the novel's representation of the actual event of war. Like "Miss Ogilvy Finds Herself," *The Well of Loneliness* configures the Great War as an emancipatory moment for female inversion, boldly declaring that "many a one who was even as Stephen" finds that her ability to "fill a man's place" is not only accepted but valued by her nation at war (274). "War and death," the novel declares, "had given them a right to life" (275). In giving female inverts life, the war also gives them a metaphor for their shared identity: "A battalion was formed in those terrible years that would never again be completely disbanded" (275). Such a line signals that the war offers the literature of homosexuality a figurative arsenal as it simultaneously supplies collective invert subjectivity with a moment of historical consolidation.

Battle metaphors continue after the war as the perpetually "wounded" Stephen and her lover Mary combat the "world's . . . onslaught upon them" (341) and the redoubtable Miss Puddleton insists to Stephen "work's your only weapon" (343). Pat, a "gloomy" member of Valérie Seymour's menagerie of ex-patriot inverts in Paris, conveys the violence of homosexual suffering by "quoting American history, speaking darkly of blood-tracks left in the snow by what she had christened 'The miserable army'" (359–360). Like Stephen, Pat identifies with a fallen war hero: "she seemed haunted by General Custer, that gallant and very unfortunate hero. 'It's Custer's last ride, all the time,' she would say. 'No good talking, the whole darned world's out to scalp us!'" (360). Pat's trope of "the miserable army" is taken up for the duration of the novel, and is even contrasted with a new generation of lesbians, "a generation that was marching to battle with much swagger, much sounding of drums and trumpets, a generation that had come after war to wage a new war on a hostile creation" (387). Here "war" first seems to refer to the event of the Great War and then "new war" returns to a metaphorics of inversion as battle, as the sentence rapidly shuttles between the war as a central historical event and as a central figurative trope in the story of sexual inversion.

The actual war and Stephen's figurative "war of existence" (338) powerfully condense in the scar she receives from a splinter of shell while she serves as an ambulance driver at the front. Stephen's fixation upon bearing the "mark of Cain" insists that we read her scar as the physical iconography of her invert suffering. Within the novel's tragic structure, Stephen first assumes the figurative mark of Cain in a melodramatic scene of anagnorisis. With her mother having just banished her from Morton, Stephen instinctively enters her dead father's study where she discovers the "truth" of her identity in his sexology books and then immediately turns from Krafft-Ebing to the Bible, "demanding a sign from heaven" (207). She opens the Bible at the words "And the Lord set a mark upon Cain," a sentence of criminality, shame, and exile that the narrative will rework for its own trajectory. As the novel's religious allusions predominantly associate Stephen with Catholic martyrs and missionaries, the shameful mark of Cain is yoked with holy martyrdom and prophecy, constituting an appropriately ambivalent figure that unites Old Testament outlaw and New Testament redeemer.

Stephen's physical scar from the war then transforms the allusions of the mark of Cain into flesh, operating as another ambivalent signifier. In making Stephen's inversion glaringly legible, the scar constitutes in one sense a nearly parodic literalization of Foucault's account of the nineteenth-century medicalization of sexual identity, in which the homosexual's shameful sexuality is "written immodestly on his face and body" as a "lesion . . . or as a symptom . . . on the surface of his skin."[30] In the novel the scar shifts the moral and pathological valence of such an inscription by visibly registering the sincerity of Stephen's internal tortured sexual desire. At the climatic moment when Mary confesses, "All my life I've been waiting for something. . . . I've been waiting for you, and it's seemed such a dreadful long time, Stephen," the narrator notes that the scar speaks for Stephen's unspeakable desire: "The barely healed wound across Stephen's cheek flushed darkly, for what could she find to answer?"[31] When Stephen furiously contemplates her desperate love for Mary, which is doomed to meet with public condemnation, her scar again leaps into sight and signification, "the red scar stood out like a wound" (303).

Corporealizing Stephen's sexual woundedness through the literal wounds of battle, the scar also condenses sexual difference and national belonging. The French doctor who stitches the gash declares, "Mademoiselle will carry an honourable scar as a mark of her courage" (295), performatively equating the very sign of sexual abjection with heroic national citizenship. When Stephen returns to Paris, the misfortune of her scar and its association with her sexual difference is immediately aligned with the dignity of her war decoration: "[Pauline the housekeeper] must . . . deplore the long straight scar upon Stephen's cheek: 'Oh le pauvre! Pour une dame c'est un vrai désastre!' But Pierre must point to the green and red ribbon in Stephen's lapel: 'C'est la Croix de Guerre!' so that in the end they all gathered round to admire that half-inch of honour and glory" (299). Pauline interprets Stephen's disfigurement as a heterosexual "désastre," "but" the passage immediately conjoins, "C'est la Croix de Guerre!" The syntactic parallel of "Pauline must deplore . . . But Pierre must point" is redoubled by Pierre's exclamation, which counters Pauline's lament while mirroring her syntax, so that the disaster of the scar is transformed by the honor of war and the redemption of the cross. Here Stephen's war wound and war decoration become interchangeable signifiers, to the point that we are left puzzling over just which "half inch of honour and glory" the house staff most admires—the cross or the scar? In a similar elision, Jonathan Brockett quips, "Stephen's distinguished herself I see—the Croix de Guerre and a very becoming scar. Don't protest, my dear Stephen, you know it's becoming" (333). The very "becoming" attractiveness of the scar's connotation of heroic service allows Stephen's traumatic inversion to "become" both legible and legitimate, by becoming history. The local baker, for example, reads Stephen's scar as both emphasizing and forgiving her gender ambiguity. "'If Mademoiselle Gordon is strange in appearance,'" he rationalizes, without locating quite where this strangeness is to be found, "'one should not forget that she served la France and must now wear a scar as well as a ribbon.' Then remembering his four sons slain in the war, he sighed" (397). Drawing the baker's suspicious heterosexual eye only to gain its approval, the disfiguring but heroic scar reconfigures and revalues Stephen's "strange appearance" to transport her from the position of failed woman to surrogate son (and honorary French citizen). The scar thus serves paradoxically both to inscribe and efface—to remember and forget—the social stigma and moral transgression of inversion, while rendering inversion as coextensive with heroic national sacrifice.[32]

At the very moment the scar conveys Stephen's radical sexual difference, then, it also functions as a point of identification for a postwar reader who, like the baker, would have admitted an affective relation to the war history that the scar inscribes. In this way the novel circumvents a direct and potentially risky identification between Stephen and the reader as sexed or gendered subjects and instead triangulates identification through the scar's connotation of national citizenship. If reader and protagonist are distanced by Stephen's homosexual difference, then they are bound together by the imagined community of the nation. But this appeal to national identification is not without irony[33]: Stephen's invert heroism and suffering, inscribed and sanctioned by a masculinizing disfigurement, derives from her work in gathering the mangled male bodies of war, so that it is precisely the shattered manhood mourned by the war generation that allows Stephen to "become" a legitimate masculine citizen. Indeed, it is the baker's *loss* of his sons that allows Stephen to take their place.

In another strategy of legitimization, the novel draws together the wounds of war and the wounds of the invert through an explicit citation of shell shock that once again conjoins historical reality with a metaphorics of embattlement. Detailing the female inverts' unique qualification to serve their country in crisis, the narrator remarks that not only does their "unorthodox" knowledge of motor cars and accounting distinguish them from "really nice women with hairpins" (275) but their psychological constitution miraculously defies war neuroses: "Their nerves were not at all weak, their pulses beat placidly through the worst air raids, for bombs do not trouble the nerves of the invert, but rather that terrible silent bombardment from the batteries of God's good people." Commending the female invert for her resilient nerves in wartime, while at the same time equating shell shock with the usual psychic condition of the invert, the novel continues to compound historical reference and metaphorics in its project of representing invert identity. This redoubled analogy—in which the invert is both like and not like a shell shock victim—exploits the ambivalence surrounding the peculiarly modern dilemma of shell shock. In one sense Stephen's congenital immunity to shell shock reinforces her claims to masculinity—her "resilient nerves" render her more of a man than many of her male compatriots; meanwhile her simultaneous invert affinity with the psychological causalities of war favorably positions her psychological "abnormality" within the trauma of history. This dual appeal to shell shock discourse is crucial to how the novel wants its readership to respond to Stephen; engaging a rhetoric of heroism and psychic resilience, it also cites a cultural knowledge of and solicits an affective response to the trauma of shell shock in its desire to explicate and exculpate Stephen's difference and render inversion intelligible, legitimate, and even sympathetic to the post–Great War generation. As Adam Parkes contends, Stephen might share a "kinship" with the "hysterics" of war, "particularly with the damaged males spawned by postwar British fiction";[34] however, Stephen's alignment with shell-shocked soldiers does not simply buttress the notion of the female invert as a pathetic figure of failed masculinity or sexuality; rather, it exploits structures of traumatic narrative as a means of justifying Stephen's difference while reinforcing her moral character. Appropriating shell shock as an objective correlative to inversion, the novel suggests that the repeatedly lamented "terrible nerves of the invert, nerves that are always lying in wait" (154, 185) are as much an effect of repeated "bombardments from the batteries of God's good people" as they are of congenital determination, and thereby encourages the reader to interpret Stephen's personal history as a series of traumas analogous to the neuroses-producing conditions of war.[35]

Like an eclectic British shell shock doctor, then, Hall layers a range of theories, explanations, and languages, including psychoanalysis, to account for her wounded protagonist. If we reread Stephen's gender and sexual narrative in light of shell shock discourse, we find the story of her youth is punctuated by a series of scenes that stage and replay her encounter with heterosexuality as moments of psychical wounding. These scenes are all linked together by overdetermined symbols in both the text and Stephen's own memory, such that hysterical symptom formation and compulsive repetition prove necessary supplements to sexological determinism. These obsessive returns to traumatic heterosexuality, then, finally prepare Stephen to assume the mark of Cain and bear the weight of her sexological-theological identity while trying to survive her personal "war of existence." The clues to Stephen's congenitally inverted "truth" are plotted through a psychoanalytically inspired structure, a structure that the discourse of shell shock would have made familiar and affectively compelling to the novel's readership. This is not to insist that Hall's contemporary readers necessarily performed a conscious psychoanalytic reading of Stephen's narrative; rather, it is to suggest that the novel's narrative structure and metaphoric web of trauma invoke a shell shock discourse historically embedded in the national consciousness—and even unconscious—of the novel's 1928 audience.

In the first of these traumatic scenes, "a really catastrophic thing happens" (24) to Stephen at the age of seven when she passes the garden potting shed and discovers Collins, her beloved housemaid, in a rough embrace with the footman. "Stephen's head suddenly felt hot and dizzy, she was filled with a blind, uncomprehending rage; she wanted to cry out, but her voice failed completely, so that all she could do was to splutter."[36] Hurling a broken flowerpot at the footman, which "struck him in the face, cutting open his cheek," Stephen wounds her rival with a mark of shameful heterosexuality in proleptic anticipation of her own honorably acquired mark of Cain in the war. Flight then follows fight: "Then Stephen turned and fled from them wildly. . . . She sobbed as she ran and covered her eyes, tearing her clothes on the shrubs in passing, tearing her stockings and the skin of her legs as she lunged against intercepting branches" (24). This distressing scene of unassimilable recognition uncannily echoes Miss Ogilvy's reaction to seeing the Neanderthal skull. Just as Stephen grows "hot and dizzy" and is "filled with a blind, uncomprehending rage" at the sight of the servants' embrace, Miss Ogilvy loses her sense of hearing, "for the pounding of the blood in her temples" and is "filled with a sudden, inexplicable fury" and an "overwhelming" "sense of outrage" upon seeing the warrior skull (1402). As rage turns to "a terrible unassuageable grief," Miss Ogilvy, like Stephen, flees from the scene. While Stephen sobs blindly in her flight, Miss Ogilvy retires to her room muttering, "Is it shell shock?" (1403) This scene not only gestures intertextually to Miss Ogilvy, and by extension to shell shock, but within the novel it becomes an intratextual refrain, compulsively repeated in the plot, in Stephen's memory, and in the very language of the text.

Years later, when Martin Hallam confesses to Stephen that he is in love with her, his passionate lover's plea is suddenly stopped short by Stephen's outraged reaction to yet another heterosexual confrontation:

And then, as though she had suddenly struck him, he flinched: "Good God! What's the matter, Stephen?"

She was staring at him in a kind of dumb horror . . . while gradually over her colourless face there was spreading an expression of the deepest repulsion—terror and repulsion he saw on her face, and something else too, a look as of outrage. . . . She wheeled round and fled from him wildly. (96–97)

Stephen's literal assault on the footman returns as a figurative violence against Martin, so that "as though she had suddenly struck him, [Martin] flinched." Again inarticulate in her "dumb horror," but still fully expressing her terror, repulsion, and outrage, Stephen "fled from him wildly," the language exactly repeating the moment in the potting shed. Like the servants before him, Martin is banished from Morton, and Stephen is left in her deepest quandary about her sexual identity. Ruminating in the garden, she is revisited by traumatic memories:

And now she was passing the old potting shed where Collins had lain in the arms of the footman. . . . The potting shed smelling of earth and dampness, sagging a little on one side, lop-sided—Collins lying in the arms of the footman, Collins being kissed by him, wantonly, crudely—a broken flower pot in the hand of a child—rage, deep rage—a great anguish of spirit—blood on a face that was pale with amazement, very bright red blood that kept trickling and trickling—flight, wild, inarticulate flight, away and away, anyhow, anywhere—the pain of torn skin, the rip of torn stockings— (101)

This moment of spontaneous and unwilled associative memory gestures toward Freudian psychoanalytic narratives of trauma, symptom formation, and free association. The memories accumulate through repetition and association, as each recalled element is embroidered with affective details. Stephen's dawning realization of her desire is thus represented as a repressed traumatic memory: "She had not remembered these things for years, she had thought that all this had been quite forgotten. . . . Strange how these memories came back this morning. . . . But the garden was full of a new memory now; it was full of the sorrowful memory of Martin" (101). As Stephen associates these embattled experiences through memory, she draws closer to suspecting the sexological "truth" that the novel purports to hold at its core, just as Miss Ogilvy's memories compel her toward the prehistoric "truth" of her identity.

Finally, Stephen's love affair with Angela Crossby ends in a scene that returns again to Collins, a memory now entrenched in Stephen's mind as symbolic of base heterosexuality. After restlessly spending a "long night of vigil" away from Angela, Stephen returns in the early morning "to stand and keep watch in [Angela's] garden" (197, 196), only to encounter another heterosexual shock when she spies Angela and Roger Antrim, her childhood rival, clasped in a coarse embrace, "drunk with loving." Stephen's hysterical reaction is as much to the memory that the scene arouses as it is to the scene itself:

> Then, as sometimes happens in moments of great anguish, Stephen could only remember the grotesque. She could only remember a plump-bosomed housemaid in the arms of a coarsely amorous footman, and she laughed and she laughed like a creature demented—laughed and laughed until she must gasp for breath and spit blood from her tongue, which had somehow got bitten in her efforts to stop her hysterical laughing; and some of the blood remained on her chin, jerked there by that agonized laughter. (197)

Here the force of "grotesque" memories drives Stephen to an hysterical and gruesome spectacle; however, its staging within a structure of shell shock trauma (amplified by Stephen's bloodied face) invites the reader to engage sympathetically with Stephen's invert woundedness. This moment also catalyzes a series of "bombardments" by God's good people that culminates in Stephen claiming an identity as a sexological invert. Stephen's hysteria so frightens Angela that she betrays Stephen to her husband, who in turn informs Stephen's mother, which finally results in Stephen's banishment from Morton. This chain of betrayals compels Stephen into her father's library, where she discovers the "answer to the riddle of her unwanted being" (206), realizes the extent of his paternal failure to convey this knowledge, and assumes the mark of Cain.

Once finally discovered, the sexological diagnosis locked within Philip Gordon's bookcase then offers a difficult but welcome answer to the neurotic questions posed by the garden scenes. In this way the traumatic scenes and their memories provide the conditions of possibility for Stephen's, and the reader's, acceptance of her sexological-theological sentence. That is, the master narratives of sexology and the Bible require the supplementary discourse of traumatic memory afforded by the war, shell shock, and psycho-analysis. Whereas Adam Parkes reads these scenes as "sexual failures" and Stephen's repeated flight as an attempt to flee the history of social conditions that entrap her,[37] I propose that by structuring Stephen's narrative according to a traumatic discourse of shell shock, the novel attempts to render Stephen a deeply sympathetic invert who is betrayed by others and whose identity and identification with her readers are only made possible by and through history and memory—both personal and national.

But what does it mean for homosexuality in this text to be structured as a traumatic memory? Although the traumatic experiences Stephen suffers prepare her for the moment of invert revelation in her father's library, by taking a psychoanalytic route they destabilize the authoritative claims of a sexological model. Whereas Miss Ogilvy's memories purport to arrive at a primary and "primitive" originary scene of invert identity, Stephen's memories recede back only to refuse a final, determinate point of reference. Stephen's discovery of Collins with the footman operates not as a stable founding moment but as an event whose repetition in memory ultimately gestures beyond itself, so that Stephen's sexuality—like shell shock, perhaps—both does and does not have a traumatic point of origin, both is and is not a congenital condition. Consequently, these memories invoke another Freudian structure and function as screen memories that reference a phantasmatic primary scene of invert sexual and gender identity that itself can never be known or represented.[38] Within a structure that appeals to the national memory of shell shock, these scenes that replay in Stephen's memory and the memory of the text cite an originary moment of inversion that can only ever be phantasmatic, a space in memory where the diverging discourses that structure Stephen's story and condition its reception—sexology, theology, psychoanalysis, history, and metaphor—can meet.

Notes

I extend my sincerest thanks to Ellis Hanson, Molly Hite, Biddy Martin, Gabrielle McIntire, and Petra Rau for their intellectual support and for their valuable suggestions for improving both the form and content of this essay. The editorial comments of Laura Doan and Jay Prosser were also incredibly helpful and greatly appreciated.

1. Quoted in Vera Brittain, *Radclyffe Hall: A Case of Obscenity?* (New York: A. S. Barnes, 1969), p. 55.

2. Ibid.

3. This tradition in England of equating homosexuality with national sedition was vividly demonstrated in a number of scandalous trials, including Oscar Wilde's trial for "gross indecency"; Roger Casement's trial for his involvement in the 1916 Easter Uprising, in which his private journals revealing homosexual encounters were used to support charges of political treachery against him; and the sensational 1918 trail in which the dancer Maud Allan charged Noel Pemberton-Billing, a reactionary scandalmonger, with libel for his suggestion that her performance in Oscar Wilde's *Salome* was implicated in a plot of German invasion through homosexual seduction. For a comprehensive discussion of these trials, see David Boxwell, "'Between Idealism and Brutality': Desire, Conflict, and the British Experience of the Great War" (Ph.D. diss., Rutgers University, 1995), chap. 1. My own as yet unpublished work is an attempt to analyze Pemberton-Billing's trial within the terms of national fantasy.

4. See for example, Claire Buck, "'Still Some Obstinate Emotion Remains': Radclyffe Hall and the Meanings of Service," in Suzanne Raitt and Trudi Tate, eds., *Women's Fiction and the Great War* (Oxford: Clarendon Press, 1997), pp. 174–196; Adam Parkes, *Modernism and the Theater of Censorship* (New York and Oxford: Oxford University Press, 1996); David Boxwell, "Between Idealism and Brutality"; and Jaime Hovey, "Imagining Lesbos: Identity and National Desire in Sapphic Modernism, 1900–1930" (Ph.D. diss., Rutgers University, 1995).

5. Buck, "Still Some Obstinate Emotion Remains," p. 181.

6. Ibid., p. 188.

7. In addition to Claire Buck, see also Claire M. Tylee, *The Great War and Women's Consciousness* (Iowa: University of Iowa Press, 1990), pp. 176–179.

8. Radclyffe Hall, *The Well of Loneliness* (1928; reprint, London: Virago, 1982), p. 271 and p. 297. All subsequent references to *The Well of Loneliness* will be from this edition, with page numbers cited in parentheses.

9. Jaime Hovey discusses this repetition in "Imagining Lesbos," pp. 165, 170.

10. See Jean Radford, "An Inverted Romance: *The Well of Loneliness* and Sexual Ideology," in Radford, ed., *The Progress of Romance: The Politics of Popular Fiction* (London and New York: Routledge and Kegan Paul, 1986), pp. 97–111.

11. As Jaime Hovey elucidates, Lauren Berlant's notion of the National Symbolic "yokes together Benedict Anderson's idea of the nation as an 'imagined community' with the Lacanian subject-in-language" (Hovey, "Imagining Lesbos," p. 8). Hovey specifically discusses Hall's writing and the National Symbolic in her chap-

ter 3). Berlant defines the National Symbolic as "the order of discursive practices whose reign within a national space produces, and also refers to, the 'law' in which the accident of birth within a geographic/political boundary transforms individuals into subjects of a collectively-held history. Its traditional icons, its metaphors, its heroes, its rituals, and its narratives provide an alphabet for a collective consciousness or national subjectivity; through the National Symbolic the historical nation aspires to achieve the inevitability of the status of natural law, a birthright" (Lauren Berlant, *Anatomy of National Fantasy* [Chicago: University of Chicago Press, 1991], p. 20). On the relation between fantasy and national consciousness, see also Jacqueline Rose, *States of Fantasy* (Oxford: Clarendon Press, 1996).

12. See Ted Bogacz, "War Neuroses and Cultural Change in England, 1914–1922: The Work of the War Office Committee of Enquiry into 'Shell-Shock,'" *Journal of Contemporary History* 24 (1989): 277–256; Chris Feudtner, "'Minds the Dead Have Ravished': Shell Shock, History, and the Ecology of Disease-Systems," *History of Science* 31 (1993): 377–420; Janet Oppenheim, *"Shattered Nerves": Doctors, Patients, and Depression in Victorian England* (Oxford: Oxford University Press, 1991); Elaine Showalter, "Male Hysteria: W. H. R. Rivers and the Lessons of Shell Shock," in *The Female Malady: Women, Madness and English Culture 1830–1980* (Virago: London, 1985); Martin Stone, "Shellshock and the Psychologists," W. F. Bynum, Roy Porter, and Michael Shepherd, eds., *The Anatomy of Madness*, vol. 2 (London: Tavistock, 1985), pp. 242–271; Ruth Leys, "Traumatic Cures: Shell Shock, Janet, and the Question of Memory," *Critical Inquiry* 20, no. 4 (1994): 623–62.

13. Stone, "Shellshock and the Psychologists," p. 245. Joanna Bourke, however, argues in response to Stone that "the Victorian theory of hereditary degeneracy as a central explanation for psychiatric disorders may have been dented by ideas about shell-shock, but after the war such lessons were placed to one side." See Joanna Bourke, *Dismembering the Male: Men's Bodies, Britain, and the Great War* (Chicago: University of Chicago Press, 1996), p. 120.

14. W. H. R. Rivers, "Freud's Theory of the Unconscious," *The Lancet* (June 16, 1917): 914. Allan Young convincingly argues that Rivers's similarities to and interest in Freud have been overemphasized by medical historians. However, the popular journals after the war repeatedly refer to Rivers as the British doctor responsible for making Freudian psychoanalysis respectable in Britain and useful for treating war neuroses. While Rivers was indebted to many thinkers other than Freud, he became a representative figure of the judicious incorporation of psychoanalysis into British psychology. See Allan Young, *The Harmony of Illusions* (Princeton: Princeton University Press, 1995), chap. 2.

15. The statistics are from Chris Feudtner, "Minds the Dead Have Ravished," p. 377.

16. *Report of the War Office Committee of Enquiry into "Shell-Shock,"* Accounts and Papers (London, 1922), p. 5.

17. Ibid., p. 6.

18. On civilian war neuroses, see Trudi Tate, *Modernism, History, and the First World War* (Manchester: Manchester University Press, 1998), pp. 10–40.

19. See "Disorders of the Mind," *Athenaeum* (October 3, 1919): 979; "Madness and Society," *Athenaeum* (February 20, 1920): 245–246; "The A B C of Psycho-Analysis" *Spectator* (February 12): 196–197 and (February 19): 228–229; "The Evolution of Instinct from the Standpoint of Psycho-Analysis," *Psyche* 3 (July 1922): 4–12; "Editorial," *Discovery* 2 (December 1921): 305.

20. See "A Balanced View of Mind-Cure," *Review of Reviews* (December 15, 1922): 673; and "Kleptomania" in the same number, p. 647; "Psychoanalysis A La Mode," *Saturday Review* (2 February, 1921): 129; "The A B C of Psycho-Analysis," "Disorders of the Mind," and "Madness and Society."

21. Edward Clodd, "The Psycho-analysis Craze," *Sphere* (November 22, 1924): 218.

22. Editorial, *Saturday Review* (September 4, 1920): 191.

23. Joan Cornie, "What is the Nature of the Unconscious Mind?," *Discovery* (May 1921): 132; Raymond Mortimer, "New Novels," *New Statesman* (28 April 1923): 82.

24. Feudtner, "Minds the Dead Have Ravished," p. 380.

25. Hall refers to the story as the "nucleus" for *The Well of Loneliness* in her author's forenote. Hall, *Miss Ogilvy Finds Herself* (New York: Harcourt, Brace, 1934), p. 2.

26. Radclyffe Hall, "Miss Ogilvy Finds Herself" in Sandra Gilbert and Susan Gubar, eds., *The Norton Anthology of Literature by Women* (New York and London: Norton, 1996), p. 1401. Subsequent references to the story will be cited directly in the text, in parentheses.

27. For related readings of "Miss Ogilvy Finds Herself," see Parkes, *Modernism and the Theatre of Censorship*; Hovey, *Imagining Lesbos*, and Buck, "Still Some Obstinate Emotion Remains."

28. See in particular Showalter, "Male Hysteria," and Sandra Gilbert and Susan Gubar, *No Man's Land: The Place of the Woman Writer in the Twentieth Century*, vol.2 (New Haven, Yale University Press, 1989), chap. 3.

29. Eric Leed analyzes "No Man's Land" as a space of marginality, liminality, and unreality: "Astonishing numbers of those who wrote about their experience of war designate No Man's Land as their most lasting and disturbing image. This was a term that captured the essence of an experience of having been sent beyond the outer boundaries of social life, placed between the known and the unknown, the

familiar and the uncanny" (Leed, *No Man's Land: Combat and Identity in World War I* [Cambridge: Cambridge University Press, 1979], p. 15).

Gilbert and Gubar deploy No Man's Land as a dominant trope for their analysis of early twentieth-century writing and gender relations. They refer to No Man's Land as a place of "muck and blood" (260), a site of "reverses and reversals" (263), "a land that was not, a country of the impossible" (267), and as a space that "was real in its bizarre unreality" (286). While Gilbert and Gubar might overinvest in the connotations of the term, they do indicate its metaphorical power and its centrality to the Great War imaginary. See Gilbert and Gubar, *No Man's Land*, vol. 2.

30. Michel Foucault, *The History of Sexuality, Volume 1*, trans. Robert Hurley (New York: Random House, 1978), pp. 43, 44.

31. Hall, *Well of Loneliness*, p. 295. Notably, Mary also "stroke[s] the new Croix de Guerre" (295) before confessing her love to Stephen.

32. Stephen's scar inevitably invites readings about castration, narcissistic wounding, and Stephen's "masculinity complex." For a psychoanalytic interpretation that engages with and complicates these associations, see Teresa de Lauretis, *The Practice of Love: Lesbian Sexuality and Perverse Desire* (Bloomington: Indiana University Press, 1994), chap. 6. While recognizing the density of the scar's connotations in relation to invert or lesbian identity, I want to maintain a focus on the scar's historical significance and its relation to the other wounds—and glories—of war. Although it is tempting to equate wounded soldiers with damaged masculinity, Trudi Tate argues for a more nuanced interpretation that recognizes the limitations of "castration" or "emasculation" for analyzing war wounds. The war's creation of groups of men as injured soldiers adds an historically specific valence to visual wounds (and their relation to theories of sexuality and gender) and suitably inscribes Stephen's "masculinity" within an historical moment when masculinities were being contested and explored. See Tate, *Modernism, History, and the First World War*, chap. 4.

33. Notably, even this national identification is triangulated through the French ally.

34. Parkes, *Modernism and the Theater of Censorship*, p. 160.

35. For the novel's references to Stephen's invert "nerves" and sensitivity see also pp. 43, 111, 256, 376, 385, 414.

36. This is a classic moment of trauma, which Cathy Caruth defines as "the response to an unexpected or overwhelming violent event or events that are not fully grasped as they occur, but return later in repeated flashbacks, nightmares, and other repetitive phenomena." (Caruth, *Unclaimed Experience Trauma, Narrative, and History* [Baltimore: Johns Hopkins University Press, 1996], p. 91.) I will complicate this notion of trauma as event later in this essay. See also Freud's postwar text

on the death drive, *Beyond the Pleasure Principle* (first published in English 1922, trans. James Strachey [New York: Norton, 1961]), which begins with a discussion of war neuroses.

37. Parkes, *Modernism and the Theatre of Censorship*, pp. 160–161.

38. My thanks to Biddy Martin for her suggestion that I consider the operation of screen memories.

15

Of Trees and Polities, Wars and Wounds

TREVOR HOPE

"Do you believe in God, Martin?"

And he answered: "Yes, because of His trees. Don't you?"[1]

Not a woman of them all but felt vaguely regretful in spite of the infinite blessing of peace, for none could know what the future might hold of trivial days filled with trivial actions. Great wars will be followed by great discontents—the pruning knife has been laid to the tree, and the urge to grow throbs through its mutilated branches.

For these roots, neglected by this blind and impotent system, have everywhere developed wild, as best they could, yielding good fruit in a few who were inspired by God, but evil fruit in the majority. . . . We can spare ourselves the wearisome task of dismembering [zergliedern] the inner sap and veins of a tree whose fruit is now fully ripe and lies fallen before the eyes of all, proclaiming most clearly and distinctly the inner nature of its progenitor.[2]

As buds give rise by growth to fresh buds, and these, if vigorous, branch out and overtop on all sides many a feebler branch, so by generation I believe it has been with the great Tree of Life, which fills with its dead and broken branches the crust of the earth, and covers the surface with its ever-branching and beautiful ramifications.[3]

This is the dawn. Womanhood shakes off its bondage. It asserts its right to be free. In its freedom, its thoughts turn to the race. Like begets like. We gather perfect fruit from perfect trees. The race is but the amplification of its mother body, the multiplication of flesh habitations—beautified and perfected for souls akin to the mother soul.[4]

The spectacle of the British Tree of Knowledge guarded by the flaming swords of Mr. James Douglas, Sir William Joynson-Hicks and Sir Chartres Biron may be delightful, but it is scarcely one which a self-respecting nation can permanently afford.[5]

There is something vaguely, or perhaps even persistently, regretful about nineteenth-century Romantic organicisms and their resonances through Darwinism and post-Darwinian thought. The grand arborescent genealogies of organicist and evolutionary thought turn out, after all, less to present a triumphalist narrative of the struggle and survival of a continuist archilegitimate genus than to reveal the extent to which any *biotope*—or, following Darwin's consistent references to the "polity of nature," it's difficult not to insist: *biopolis*—is haunted by the specter of morbidity. The vestiges of those "branches" that have sheared away from the core of the *genus*, those buds or "scions" blighted by the genealogical play of "overtopping," superseding, *succeeding*, bear witness to the fraught logic of a Malthusian scarcity economy that, by means of a benevolent pruning, will magically conjure bounty out of loss, vigor out of morbidity, variety out of extinction. To reread the epigraph from Darwin cited above is, after all, to acknowledge the primacy of the dead and broken over and above those beautiful ramifications by which they are to be overtopped; the necessity, even, of a morbid crust that must, according to this topographic and temporal priority *underlie* the present-participiality of an *ever-branching* polity of surface; the necropolis as grounding architectural principle of the biopolitical edifice; the tragically belated branch as foundation for, guarantor of, the univalent trunk and its frayed rhetoric of rootedness. The *biopolis* becomes a beautiful (not to say, sublime?) *corpus socians* by reference to the *corpse/s* (copses?) it must persistently outgrow, overtop—according to a logic both botanical and political, *crown*. Sovereignty, according to a tradition that makes Darwin the semilegitimate scion of Hobbes, sprouts precariously above the wretched foment of generalized struggle.[6] And precarious, indeed, must be the logic that forges the sovereignty of type out of the furnace of an ever-ramifying generality. What necromancy is it that can conjure the very principle of filial legitimacy out of such a murderous constitution?

> And we have seen in the chapter on the Struggle for Existence that it is the most closely-allied forms,—varieties of the same species, and species of the same genus or of related genera,—which, from having nearly the same structure, constitution, and habits, generally come into the severest competition with each other; *consequently, each new variety or species, during the process of its formation, will generally press hardest on its nearest kindred, and tend to exterminate them.*[7]

Lest we allow the familial rhetoric here to naturalize the animus of endogenous propinquity, however, we must also remember the exceptional, exogenous (and quintessentially colonial) location of type:

> By considering the nature of the plants or animals which have in any country struggled successfully with the indigenes and have there become naturalized, we may gain some crude idea in what manner some of the natives would have to be modified, in order to gain the advantage over their compatriots.[8]

If, as Foucault notoriously proclaimed, the nineteenth century discovered the homosexual as *type*, then this essay is an attempt to explore the extremely concrete ways in which Hall conceives of her inverts in ontological, ontogenic, phylogenic, pathogenic terms: as a species thrown up from a profoundly challenged natural "order," as "representative" of an order of which they appear simultaneously to stand for the archi-essential exception and the quintessential symptom.[9]

Afflicted Member #1: Housemaid's Knee

Before turning to Hall's arboreal imagery of patrilinear descent and dissent with its figuration of the invert as noble scion and monstrous and perverse *graft*, I think it is useful to consider another scene of a different kind of *graft* in the novel's account of the natural history of the female invert:

> Collins was what was called "second of three"; she might one day hope for promotion. Meanwhile she was florid, full-lipped and full-bosomed, rather ample indeed for a young girl of twenty, but her eyes were unusually blue and arresting, very pretty inquisitive eyes. Stephen had seen Collins sweeping the stairs for two years, and had passed her by quite unnoticed; but one morning, when Stephen was just over seven, Collins looked up and suddenly smiled, then all in a moment Stephen knew that she loved her—a staggering revelation! (13)

Collins (who is never granted an appellation beyond her presumed patronym—which yet turns out to be cryptically maternal, as we shall see), like all good symptoms, must be read according to a peculiarly recursive temporality: it is after two years of daily, one might say ritual, contact that Stephen discovers, thanks to the swift blow of Freudian *Nachträglichkeit*, that she is (or rather *always has been?*) in love.[10] If Collins has been overlooked for so long, taken to be a mere part of the domestic scenery, this is surely owing to her class status, but also because she has already been encoded as ground rather than figure: in fact, quite literally, she has been landscaped in two ways. First, etymologically (Latin *collis*: hill), her name takes us back to the romanticized landscape of the Malvern Hills. Her "full-bosomed" figure also binds her doubly to maternity (specifically to Lady Anna, Stephen's mother) and to a conventionally Romantic vision of a naturalized national body:

> From her favorite seat underneath an old cedar, [the pregnant Anna] would see these Malvern Hills in their beauty, and their swelling slopes seemed to hold a new meaning. They were like pregnant women, full-bosomed, courageous, great green-girdled mothers of splendid sons! (8–9)[11]

The first blush of love, however, is rapidly recoded as shame:

> She had always said: "Good morning, Miss Stephen," but on this occasion, it sounded alluring—so alluring that Stephen wanted to touch her, and extending a rather uncertain hand she started to stroke her sleeve.
>
> Collins picked up the hand and stared at it. "Oh my!" she exclaimed, "what very dirty nails!" Whereupon their owner flushed painfully crimson and dashed upstairs to repair them. (13)

There follows a story of the attempted repair (not to say reparation!) with scissors, the angry intervention of the nurse, and the punishment of Collins. Then ensues a narrative of hygienic discipline qua religious penance qua masochistic eroticism of dizzying recursivity. The scissors in themselves, of course, perform as a wonderfully ambivalent prosthesis: the self must be *repaired* through an intervention that comes to figure as a further wounding, even as that further surgical wounding may operate economically as a defense (a screen) against the knowledge of the cryptic wound it re-presents.[12] In a narrative straight from *Beyond the Pleasure*

Principle, the symptom may be tended to, indeed nursed, in order cryptically to preserve the culpable pleasure for which it is supposed to denote atonement; the symptomatic wound is guilty pleasure: guilt *at* pleasure, guilt as displaced and preserved pleasure, pleasure *in* guilt, all in one. In *The Well's* rendition of invert as aristocrat (placing the novel in the tradition of literature of familial degeneracy culminating in the eclipse of the patronym in the final emasculated scion, but also binding this narrative to that of sterile hereditary antitype or "sport") the eroticization of the working-class body may even exploit the notion that the "object" is so *essentially* debased as to constitute, fantastically, the complex of pleasure and atonement peculiar to the notion of "slumming."

The figuration of the maid's body as wounded and hence desirable (or, rather, available as symptomatic surface within which to find one's desire cryptically rendered back to one?) is further intensified through the very literal accession to a symptomaticity that rerenders her occupation and class corporally legible:

> But one day, when Collins had been crosser than usual, she seemed to be filled with a sudden contrition. "It's me housemaid's knee," she confided to Stephen. "It's not you, it's me housemaid's knee, dearie."
>
> "Is that dangerous?" demanded the child, looking frightened.
>
> Then Collins, true to her class [!], said: "It may be—it may mean an 'orrible operation, and I don't want no operation." (17)

In an access of morbid religiosity Stephen gravely expresses the desire to "catch" the symptom in order to be "awfully hurt" for Collins "the way that Jesus was hurt for sinners." After Collins has "displayed the afflicted member," Stephen dreams both of acquiring the symptom in order to have the operation in Collins's stead and of performing the operation herself in the guise of Messianic surgeon, "cutting off her knee with a bone paper-knife and grafting it on to her own" (18). It is the encapsulation of the symptom within this abyssal play of excision and graft, amputation and prosthesis, that I want to pursue in various other cryptic figurations in the novel, but, to conclude this episode, it should, perhaps, be explained that the ever-resourceful Stephen finally manages perfectly to capture the compromise-formation of the symptom by herself displacing it into a ritual of atonement surely far racier than any "actual sex" to be found in the novel:

> There were endless spots on the nursery carpet, and these spots Stephen could pretend to be cleaning; always careful to copy Collins' movements, rubbing backwards and forwards while groaning a little. (19)

And now we surely realize the importance of a detail regarding the moment at which Stephen acknowledged her erotic attachment to Collins, a moment in which Collins was—as she ritually was obliged to do, as she "always already" (or at least for two years!) had been doing—*sweeping*, Stephen arguably recognized and realized the narrative of guilt and atonement for which there was not yet (and never will have been) any prior "transgression."[13]

Afflicted Member #2: Boughs and Breaches

"Twilight of the Father" might almost make an adequate title for Hall's entire novelistic oeuvre. Above and beyond the standard sexological representations of inversion inherited from Krafft-Ebing, Havelock Ellis, and their cohorts, Hall's female inverts are often specifically presented as somewhat mournful inheritors of the paternal legacy.[14] We first witness the narrative of "patrilinear deviation" through Anna Gordon's eyes:

> It would seem to Anna that she must be going mad, for this likeness to her husband would strike her as an outrage—as though the poor, innocent seven-year-old Stephen were in some way a caricature of Sir Philip; a blemished, unworthy, maimed reproduction. (11)

And later, in the wake of the passing of the paternal "original," she will accuse:

> And this thing that you are is a sin against creation. Above all is this thing a sin against the father who bred you, the father whom you dare to resemble. You dare to look like your father, and your face is a living insult to his memory, Stephen. (203)

The logic of the parodic copy is familiar terrain in the land of deconstruction and the antifoundationalist critique of gender.[15] On the one hand, Stephen's body *is* the memorial encryptment of an immemorial lineage of (presumptively male) Gordons:

> To these things she belonged and would always belong by right of those past generations of Gordons whose thoughts had fashioned the comeliness of Morton, whose bodies had gone to the making of Stephen. (107)

And on the other, she must be disavowed as illegitimate variation upon the theme of legitimate typological filiation:

> Yes, she was of them, those bygone people; they might spurn her—the lusty breeders of sons that they had been—they might even look down from Heaven with raised eyebrows, and say: "We utterly refuse to acknowledge this curious creature called Stephen." But for all that they could not drain her of blood, and her blood was theirs also, so that do what they would they could never completely rid themselves of her nor she of them—they were one in their blood. (107)

Morton itself proves to be the archetypal patriarchal haunt, complete with aristocratic familial portrait gallery "in which hung the funny old portraits of Gordons—men long dead and gone but still wonderfully living, since their thoughts had fashioned the comeliness of Morton; since their loves had made children from father to son—from father to son until the advent of Stephen" (103).[16]

The perverse offshoot weighs heavily upon the old familial stock and becomes a blight to the stem according to the peculiar retroactivity of the symptom (as archi-essential swerve that actually *founds* or *roots* the thrown linearity of generation and genealogy):

> She would notice with a sudden pain in her heart that he stooped when he walked, not much yet, but a little. And she loved his broad back, she had always loved it—a kind, reassuring protective back. Then the thought would come that perhaps its great kindness had caused it to stoop as though bearing a burden; and the thought would come: "He *is* bearing a burden, not his own, it's someone else's—but whose?" (85)

Somewhere between the anthropomorphizing of a tree and the "arborification" of the human, the (patriarchal) biopolitical order is ripe for tragedy:

> The gardens lay placidly under the snow, in no way perturbed or disconcerted. Only one inmate of theirs felt anxious, and that was the ancient and wide-boughed cedar, for the weight of the snow made an ache in its branches—its branches were brittle like an old man's bones; that was why the cedar felt anxious. (113)

Sir Philip is to be crushed by the weight of that fretful bough even as he supervises the gardeners in the attempt to relieve it of its affliction. Finally, he traces a moribund arborescent Gestalt upon the snow-covered ground: "Sir Philip lay very still on the snow [cf. above: "the gardens lay placidly *under* the snow"], and the blood oozed slowly from between his lips. He looked monstrously tall as he lay on that whiteness, very straight, with his long legs stretched out to their fullest." (114)

Stephen immediately takes charge, and it becomes clear that the dismembering (Fichte's polysemantic *Zergliederung*) of the cedar prefigures a more volatile sense of amputation within the family. As Stephen tends to her father as father had tended to tree, and as she, branch or scion, thus attempts to staunch (and supplement?) the loss of blood /sap from the familial stem (*Stamm*)—that blood, we must remember, that cannot be drained from her, that binds her to the tree from which she has branched— a dizzying logic of sympathy, hygienic intervention, identification, and supersession renders her now a live ramification overtopping the morbid vestige of the morbid stock (parasitically, or even vampirically, if we conjure the cannibalistic image of the botanical "sucker"?), now the melancholic embodiment in the present of the totality of the genealogical descent: tree to the paternal branch that must be sundered (sacrificed?) as "afflicted member." One might even say that it is actually through the sundering of the paternal limb and the freeing up of libido formerly bound to the bough, the withdrawal of the libidinal sap/blood from the afflicted member to the wounded/cauterized trunk, that the *filial* scion performs an attachment back to the stem/*Stamm* of the familial through the mourning of the father: an attachment that must, nonetheless, remain riven and scarred by a graft that encrypts the paternal absence: a persistent melancholic "gnarl."[17] Interestingly, then, as one attachment is forged (that of branch to tree), another is breached (that of Stephen *as* arborescent totality to her membral *parts*, her limbs, earlier location of her erotic shame, wound, symptom). On the principle of an aptly reversed legacy, her hands belong to Daddy:

> She kept wiping the blood away from his mouth, and her fingers were stained; she looked at her fingers, but without comprehension—they could not be hers . . . they must surely be somebody else's. (115)

Afflicted Member #3: War and the Bleeding Polity

The *topoi* of woundedness—of the loss of sap and the attempt to staunch that flow, of sacrificial and hygienic amputation, of attachment *to* and *through* loss—will be amply played out, once again, at the level of the national body politic, and I want to insist, indeed, that these earlier avatars of the afflicted member must already be read as embedded within the national narrative, even as, in true Fichtean manner, the narrative of the many-limbed phylogenic "whole" recapitulates the ontogenic narrative of its individual members.

The grand figure for the traumatization of the national body politic/*biopolis*, in the novel is the war:

> England, the land of bountiful pastures, of peace, of mothering hills, of home. England was fighting for her right to existence. Face to face with dreadful reality at last, England was pouring her men into battle, her army was even now marching across France. . . . Morton was pouring out its young men, who in their turn might pour out their life-blood for Morton. (269, 270)

As England lies bleeding, the invert must necessarily reconsider her biological function: Stephen's attention is drawn, interestingly, to the same limbs upon which she earlier bore the mark of infantile shame and the blood of undone/resutured familial attachment:

> She stared at her bony masculine hands, they had never been skillful when it came to illness; strong they might be, but rather inept; not hands where-

with to succour the wounded. No, assuredly her job, if job she could find, would not lie at the bedsides of the wounded. And yet, good God, one must do something! (271)

Stephen will ultimately join an ambulance unit, and at one intriguing moment, when a bandage staunching the flow of blood from the gaping wound in the stomach of a French *poilu* has slipped, will step protectively between that wound and Mary, her feminine lover, making a hasty readjustment. The dedication of the "battalion" of inverts stems from a sense of a "stigma" to be "lived down," and, when Stephen (inevitably!) is wounded, she "cashes in" this mark of Cain for an "honourable scar," a "mark of courage" that will, revealingly, flush darkly when Mary declares her love. Not only, it seems, does this new displacement and recathexis of the symptom represent a libidinal reconciliation (or at least a cease-fire?!) with her own bodily ego, but the assumption of the wound surely pays a libidinal debt that staunches the wounds of the nation, is credited, one might say to a National Libidinal Debt, even as her own patriotic libidinal attachment is rendered incarnate (as debit) upon her own (now nationalized) body. In other words, the invert's putative exclusion from the biopolity is only mitigated by her accession to it insofar as she bears the mark of excision upon her own body. She may either *become* the national lost object or herself *bear* the signs of the nation's loss, paying the price, say, of a cryptic wound or of a mortified limb. The polity demands of the invert that she either *be* its symptom or that she *have* it.

The nationalization of the invert clearly partakes of a far-reaching eugenic rendition of the national body politic. As men (and even male inverts) are poured into the calamity of war, the female invert's place initially seems uncertain:

> She felt appalled at the realization of her own grotesqueness; she was nothing but a freak abandoned on a kind of no-man's-land at this moment of splendid national endeavour.[18]

And yet, clearly, in the "universal convulsion" of war, a new space *is* opened up for the invert within the national *biopolis*:

> For as though gaining courage from the terror that is war, many a one who was even as Stephen, had crept out of her hole and come into the daylight,

come into the daylight and faced her country: "Well, here I am, will you take me or leave me?" And England had taken her, asking no questions—she was strong and efficient, she could fill a man's place. . . . England had said: "Thank you very much. You're just what we happen to want . . . at the moment." (274)

In this emergence of the inverts from their subterranean existence (their encryptment, Antigone-like, in the necropolis of a submerged national archive?) we might, in fact, read a kind of shaking loose (precisely a decrypting) of the invert as melancholic symptom of a national body that, through her banishment, has attained a fantasy of hygienic self-sufficiency. The anamnesis of this disavowed *member* of the national polity constitutes a momentary re-membering of the exceptionally Other that, like a phantom limb (or a dead branch?), phantasmatically limns the contours of the national ego ideal.[19]

The logic that makes of the invert a kind of national monument (one of what Quentin Crisp has called "England's stately homos"!) depends on a particular ambivalence of memory mapped simultaneously onto the ambivalence that surrounds limbs as liminal parts of a bodily ego and onto those "dead and broken branches" of Darwin. If Freud has maintained that the ego might be nothing but the precipitation of accumulated lost objects with which the self is melancholically identified, then we might understand the peculiar status of the invert as lost/repudiated national treasure. The mobility of the synecdochic symptom (the invert may herself have—and contain—the symptom or may stand in her entirety for the symptom of the national body) is related to the fact that, as she is encrypted *within* the national body, the invert also represents to it the place where its loss is sustained, conserved, contained, and hence undecidably assuaged and preserved. What might then strike us as a radical possibility within Darwin— one that potentially brings him into the same productive deconstructive territory around melancholic subject-formation so brilliantly explored by Judith Butler—is that, far from representing a purely triumphalist narrative of survival, the evolutionary concept of the genus is irreparably caught up in the paradoxical preservation of those branches that have fallen from the tree as the very core—the trunk or stem—of its self-identity. It is key to my reading here of the "management" of the libidinal economy of loss and nostalgia (an economy rendered concrete, in the novel's terms, as sap and blood) that we read the memorial both in conventional terms as a place of recuperation and preservation and also as a more ambivalent space of "archiving"; in the guise of archive, the memorial, the symptom, can become places of the foreclosure of interest and even places where a work of active amnesia is performed: the self is relieved of its ghosts by burying them in "outlying territory," the space of a prosthetic or "supplementary" memory.[20]

There is, of course, something both very disturbing and terribly apt about the converging logic of Darwinian and imperialist *Lebensraum* in the novel's depiction of war as *struggle*. Eugenics, even before the First World War, had further turned the logic of imperialism in upon itself, sustaining the Darwinian insistence on competition with what he, too, as we have seen, termed "compatriots."[21]

> When they got up to go, [Brockett] relented: "War is surely a very necessary evil, it thins down the imbecile populations who have murdered the most efficacious microbes. People will not die, very well, here comes war to mow them down in their tens of thousands. At least for those of us who survive, there will be more breathing space, thanks to the Germans—perhaps they too are a necessary evil. (273)

There may be a sense in which placing such forthright eugenic proclamations in the mouths of its characters actually allows the novel to distance itself from (though obviously not to purge itself hygienically of) a thoroughgoing endorsement of eugenics, and yet the text cannot escape the logic that makes of this "general convulsion" the medium of inverted life. To return to the epigraph I used to index the relationship between arborescent polity and national morbidity:

> Not a woman of them all but felt vaguely regretful in spite of the infinite blessing of peace, for none could know what the future might hold of trivial days filled with trivial actions. Great wars will be followed by great discontents—the pruning knife has been laid to the tree, and the urge to grow throbs through its mutilated branches. (298)

The pruning knife, of course, evokes the paper knife that Stephen has once dreamed of taking to Collins's leg (in order to transplant it to her own): an action that, once again, vacillates strangely between plain sacrifice—the amputation of what is diseased—and *self*-sacrifice, as the melancholic incorporation/encryption of the affliction upon her own body. Likewise, in the strange patriotism of the text, the invert becomes simultaneously metonym of the national body and figure for its woundedness. Perhaps there is even, between or beyond these two options, an identification between the invert and the cut itself. According to this reading, the general convulsion that rends the biopolity and bares the necropolis of symptoms upon which it is founded, momentarily forces those identified with the community of the living to exhume its dis(re-)membered parts, to ache or throb with a morbid quickening, to re-member themselves in the image of the invert:

> And now because they were not prepared to slink back and hide in their holes and corners, the very public whom they had served was the first to turn round and spit upon them; to cry: "Away with this canker in our midst, this nest of unrighteousness and corruption!" (412)

Afflicted Member #4: The Canon

For the city, as you yourself see, is now too sorely vexed and can no longer lift her head from beneath the angry waves of death. A blight is on her in the fruitful blossoms of the land, in the herds among the pastures, in the barren pangs of the women. And that flaming god, the malign plague, has swooped on us and ravages the town; by him the house of Cadmus is made waste, but dark Hades rich in groans and tears.[22]

I have seen the plague stalking shamelessly through great social assemblies. I have heard it whispered about by young men and young women who do not and cannot grasp its unutterable putrefaction. . . . The contagion cannot be escaped. It pervades our social life.[23]

To read Hall's rendition of inversion as symptomatic spur to a splendid vital sociality—as allied with that "bitter and ruthless potion of war that spurred and lashed at their manhood" (*The Well* 268)—is inevitably, in the context of this volume, to conjure up the judgment of James Douglas and, above all, his likening of the novel to a moral poison, a phial of prussic acid. While he evokes the image of "healthy boy" or "healthy girl" in this context (perhaps unconsciously avowing that in cases of children already afflicted, the poison might turn cure?), his is generally a vision of a national literary culture that is to be defended—"literature as well as morality is in peril" (38)

> In order to prevent the contamination and corruption of English *fiction* it is the duty of the critic to make it impossible for any other novelist to repeat this outrage. I say deliberately that this novel is not fit to be sold by any bookseller or to be borrowed from any library. . . . The challenge is direct. It must be taken up courageously, and the fight must be fought to a finish. If our bookshops and our libraries are to be polluted by fiction dealing with this undiscussable subject, at least let us know where we are going. (36,37)

Yet, as the prophetic visions of the haunting plague cited in the epigraph at the beginning of this section make clear, "the contagion cannot be escaped," since it "pervades our social life." Beyond questions of the *palate*, then, arguably, according to this rhetoric, the poison has already been *stomached*, taken in, even if, as supplement, to ensure a hygienic purgation. "Perhaps it is a blessing in disguise or a curse in disguise," Douglas equivocates, "that this novel forces upon our society a disagreeable task which it has hitherto shirked, the task of cleansing itself from the leprosy of these lepers, and making the air clean and wholesome once more" (37).

Uncannily echoing the novel's own thematic deployment of World War I, Douglas (fancying himself, perhaps, as "flaming god" and only unwittingly casting himself thereby as plague?) couples images of national struggle with those of Holy War on sexual infidels:

> I know that the battle has been lost in France and Germany, but it has not yet been lost in England, and I do not believe that it will be lost. The English people are slow to rise in their wrath and strike down the armies of evil, but when they are aroused they show no mercy. (37)

Finally, it seems, even as England must expunge itself internally of its afflicted member, casting out the *xenoi* from within, it ends up sundering itself from the polity of Europe. Douglas, in attempting to close the archive of national fiction, forecloses the fiction *of* nation in a fantasy of totality that, disavowing the contingency of the polity, refusing the most rudimentary hospitality due to one's ghosts, must surely identify the nation ever more resolutely with the forces of death. The death drive, after all, is not the property of the afflicted member; rather, it belongs to the symptomatic body that imagines that through a sundering—a dis(re-)membering that is also an archiving—it might return to its imagined pristine (originary, unmined) ground of plenitude.

Notes

1. The first two epigraphs are from Radclyffe Hall, *The Well of Loneliness*, p. 93 and p. 298. All citations in the text, unless otherwise indicated, are from *The Well*, and all italics, likewise unless otherwise stated, are my own.

2. Johann Gottlieb Fichte, *Addresses to the German Nation*, p. 12. I have slightly amended the translation, substituting the more literal (and felicitous) "dismembering" for Jones and Turnbull's "analyzing." Fichte's "tree-totality" is the "national self"; its branches and fruit are citizens.

3. Charles Darwin, *The Origin of Species*, 171.

4. Margaret Sanger, *Woman and the New Race*, p. 233. It is worth noting, in the context of this essay, that Sanger's treatise both represents a direct response to World War I and also takes up the image of warfare in the struggle for sexual enlightenment and the forging of a new "race."

5. Conclusion to an unsigned article appearing in *Time and Tide*, November 23, 1928. Cited in Vera Brittain, *Radclyffe Hall: A Case of Obscenity?* p. 109

6. My thanks go to Richard Juang for edifying conversations on Darwin as political theorist.

7. Darwin, *Origin*, p. 142.

8. Ibid., p. 147.

9. I believe I am in fact following Jay Prosser's corrective to the Foucauldian narrative here. Prosser's work has very powerfully argued that it is more specifically the *invert*, rather than the Foucaultian homosexual, that the nineteenth century thus added to its cosmogony of type and antitype (fruit and freak?). See Jay Prosser, "'Some Primitive Thing Conceived in a Turbulent Age of Transition': The Invert, *The Well of Loneliness*, and the Narrative Origins of Transsexuality," in *Second Skins*, pp. 135–169. On the quintessential symptom, cf. Mikkel Borch-Jacobsen: "Like Freud, Le Bon uses 'pathological' states as the key to decoding 'normalcy.' The two share a common conviction (along with the vast majority of late-nine-

teenth-century psychologists) that the pathological return to a previous state bears witness to the existence of a state of ontogenetic and phylogenetic development that has been surpassed (that is, integrated and by the same token recovered). 'Pathological,' in this sense, does not mean abnormal; on the contrary, it is archi-normality itself, primary normality. And the origin (the essence) can thus be read in the symptom." (135)

10. Is it reasonable to propose that even the detail of her "rank," the "second of three," indicates something of her suspended temporality: neither first nor third, neither alpha nor omega, yet the supplement that binds the archetype to its pheno-typical form in a rather unstable trinity? If we read her as avatar of the maternal, then is number one also the mother as *genitrix*, and would the third of the three hence be the (inverted) daughter in such a manner as to represent an imbrication of the Trinity with the iconography of Virgin and child (Stephen so often in the novel figuring as sacrificial lamb and savior of her people), with Collins as perverse usurper and mediator of the filial bond?

11. The precise rendition of this "race mother" ("he came of a race of devoted mothers") is, however, fraught with ambivalence. We are immediately informed, at the beginning of the novel, that Anna, as well as being "the archetype of the very perfect woman" is also "lovely as only an Irish woman can be." Both mother and daughter are said to have "warm Celtic blood" flowing in their veins. I hope that, as my reading of the symptom in *The Well* unfolds, it will become clear how a sentimentalized Celticness can figure as the quintessence (the melancholic core) of Englishness. The name "Collins" is further overdetermined by the evocation of Michael Collins, leader of Sinn Féin and signatory of the treaty founding the Irish Free State in 1921. For insight into the significance of Celticism to Hall's narratives of race and nation, I am highly indebted to Margot Gayle Backus's essay "Sexual Orientation in the (Post)Imperial Nation: Celticism and Inversion Theory in Radclyffe Hall's *The Well of Loneliness*," which offers both an important cultural-historical contribution to Hall scholarship and also a beautiful close reading of the novel.

12. I'm reminded here of Nietzsche's definition, in *On the Genealogy of Morals*, of *ressentiment* as a "desire to *deaden pain by means of affects*": "or every sufferer instinctively seeks a cause for his suffering; more exactly an agent . . . some living thing upon which he can, on some pretext or other, vent his affects . . . for the venting of his affects represents the greatest attempt on the part of the suffering to win relief, *anaesthesia*—the narcotic he cannot help desiring to deaden pain of any kin" (127, emphasis in the original). This opens up onto my discussion of memory and/as foreclosure below: the symptom that encrypts both preserves and mortifies.

See Wendy Brown on this passage on Nietzsche, and on attachment and wounding in the relations between citizens and states. My later discussion of polity tries to keep open a discussion with radical-democratic political theory.

13. Another last note on the vicissitudes of the symptom, or, how to double your fetishistic options: "Collins now had a most serious rival, one who had lately appeared at the stables. He was not possessed of a real housemaid's knee, but instead of four deeply thrilling brown legs—he was two up on legs, and one up on a tail, which was rather unfair on Collins! . . . She would say: "Come up horse!" in the same tone as Williams; or, pretending to knowledge she was far from possessing: "Is that fetlock a bit puffy? It looks to me puffy; supposing we put on it a nice wet bandage" (36–37).

14. This is true also, for example, of Miss Ogilvy in "Miss Ogilvy Finds Herself" and Joan Ogden in *The Unlit Lamp*.

15. See especially Judith Butler's "Imitation and Gender Insubordination." For an antifoundationalist deployment of melancholia see her "Melancholy Gender—Refused Identification" in *The Psychic Life of Power*.

16. I should acknowledge here that, while I think it is amply justified (even demanded) by the novel, the account I am providing here of the "patrilineal" filiation of the female invert does not exhaust the narrative of the familial matrix in Hall's fiction. Esther Newton dwells on the mother-daughter bond in "The Mythic Mannish Lesbian" (pp. 89–108 in this volume), as do I (primarily in the context of *The Unlit Lamp*) in "Mother, Don't You See I'm Burning?"

17. On the narcissistic withdrawal of libido onto the wounded ego, see the second section of Freud's "On Narcissism."

18. Hall, *Well of Loneliness*, p. 271. It's perhaps worth noting here that the *place* in which Miss Ogilvy (as the title of Hall's short story has it) finds herself, is on the beach as she heads back from the war in which she too has served as an ambulance driver. It might almost be said that she springs autochthonously from this ambiguous ground, and when she is repatriated to tiny England she immediately ex-isles herself off the Cornish coast, as if only able to survive in the *limina* of nationhood. See Darwin (pp. 138–139) for a discussion of islands as isolated polities in which "anomalous forms"—"living fossils," indeed—tend to be preserved. Miss Ogilvy and Stephen are repeatedly cast as primitive visitations, forms, one might say, that have returned from the archives of national history.

19. My evocation of the "exceptionally other" (*exceptio*, scapegoat), as quintessential (even cryptically *sovereign*) part of the polity is influenced by René Girard and Giorgio Agamben among others. For a more specific commentary on the foreclo-

sure/preservation (encryptment/entombment) of the feminine as *ground* of the polity, see Luce Irigaray's reading of Hegel on Antigone in "The Eternal Irony of the Community."

20. Again, for her reading of those two other nineteenth-century melancholics Nietzsche and Freud, see Butler's *The Psychic Life of Power*. My reading here of the play of prosthetics and memory in relation to the bodily ego is also very much influenced by Elizabeth Grosz, who notes in *Volatile Bodies* that "the phantom can indeed be regarded as a kind of libidinal memorial to the lost limb" (41). Miss Ogilvy might again figure as the quintessential reminder of the possibility of a revivification of the "lost limb," the return of the prodigal national invert. On the prosthetic workings of memory see Jacques Derrida's *Archive Fever*.

21. Darwin, it should perhaps be remarked, without exiting the logic of eugenics, considered war *dys*genic: "The shorter and feebler men, with poor constitutions, are left at home, and consequently have a much better chance of marrying and propagating their kind." Cited in Paul Crook, *Darwinism, War, and History*, p. 24.

22. Sophocles, *Oedipus the King*, p. 78.

23. James Douglas's editorial in the *Sunday Express*, August 19, 1928, p. 37 in this volume. All further page references for Douglas's editorial are to this volume.

Works Cited

Agamben, Giorgio. *Homo Sacer: Sovereign Power and Bare Life*. Trans. Daniel Heller-Roazen. Stanford: Stanford University Press, 1998.

Backus, Margot Gayle. "Sexual Orientation in the (Post)Imperial Nation: Celticism and Inversion Theory in Radclyffe Hall's *The Well of Loneliness*." *Tulsa Studies in Women's Literature* 15, no. 2 (Fall 1994): 253–263.

Borch-Jacobsen, Mikkel. *The Freudian Subject*. Trans. Catherine Porter. Stanford: Stanford University Press, 1988.

Brittain, Vera. *Radclyffe Hall: A Case of Obscenity?*. London: Femina Books, 1968.

Brown, Wendy. "Wounded Attachments," *States of Injury: Power and Freedom in Late Modernity*. Princeton: Princeton University Press, 1995.

Butler, Judith. "Imitation and Gender Insubordination." In Diana Fuss, ed., *Inside/Out: Lesbian Theories, Gay Theories*. New York: Routledge, 1991. 13–31.

———. *The Psychic Life of Power: Theories in Subjection*. Stanford: Stanford University Press, 1997.

Crook, Paul. *Darwinism, War, and History: The Debate over the Biology of War from the "Origin of Species" to the First World War.* Cambridge: Cambridge University Press, 1994.

Darwin, Charles. *The Origin of Species.* 1859. Reprint, New York: Random House, 1993.

Derrida, Jacques. *Archive Fever: A Freudian Impression.* Trans. Eric Prenowitz. Chicago: University of Chicago Press, 1996.

Fichte, Johann Gottlieb. *Addresses to the German Nation.* Ed. George Armstrong Kelley. New York: Harper & Row, 1968.

Freud, Sigmund. *Beyond the Pleasure Principle.* Vol. 18. *The Standard Edition of the Complete Pyschological Works of Sigmund Freud.* Trans. James Strachey. London: Hogarth, 1953–1974.

———. "On Narcissism: An Introduction." Vol. 14. *Standard Edition.*

Girard, René. *Violence and the Sacred.* Trans. Patrick Gregory. Baltimore: John's Hopkins University Press, 1977.

Grosz, Elizabeth. *Volatile Bodies: Toward a Corporeal Feminism.* Bloomington: Indiana University Press, 1994.

Hall, Radclyffe. "Miss Ogilvy Finds Herself." *Miss Ogilvy Finds Herself.* New York: Harcourt Brace, 1934.

———. *The Unlit Lamp.* 1924. Reprint, London: Virago, 1981

———. *Well of Loneliness.* 1928. Reprint, London: Virago, 1982.

Hope, Trevor. "Mother, Don't You See I'm Burning? Between Female Homosexuality and Female Homosociality in Radclyffe Hall's *The Unlit Lamp.*" In Mandy Merck, Naomi Segal, and Elizabeth Wright, eds., *Coming Out of Feminism?* Oxford: Blackwell, 1998: 123–153.

Irigaray, Luce. "The Eternal Irony of the Community." *Speculum of the Other Woman.* Trans. Gillian C. Gill. Ithaca: Cornell University Press, 1985: 214–226.

Newton, Esther. "The Mythic Mannish Lesbian: Radclyffe Hall and the New Woman." *Signs* 9, no. 4 (1981): 557–576.

Nietzsche, Friedrich. *On the Genealogy of Morals. On the Genealogy of Morals and Ecce Homo.* Trans. and ed. Walter Kauffman. New York: Random House, 1989.

Prosser, Jay. *Second Skins: The Body Narratives of Transsexuality.* New York: Columbia University Press, 1998.

Sanger, Margaret. *Woman and the New Race.* New York: Truth Publishing Company, 1920.

On Location

16

"I Want to Cross Over into Camp Ground": Race and Inversion in *The Well of Loneliness*

JEAN WALTON

White Patrons and Black Bottoms

The Well of Loneliness is not just a novel with a lesbian protagonist, it is a political manifesto, fashioned explicitly as a literary attempt to give a collective voice to a hitherto voiceless social constituency. It is seen as emerging from an important historical moment, the interwar decade of the 1920s, when campaigns for sexual freedom meant not only challenges to women's oppression but also the destigmatization of same-sex desire. But what if we were to recontextualize *The Well* by recalling that the twenties was also known for widespread white patronage of African American literary, artistic, and musical expression on both sides of the Atlantic? What if we were to remember that modernism relied for its understanding of "modernity" in part on an often racialized distinction between the "primitive" and the "civilized," a distinction elaborated in one form or another in the multiple discourses that intersected with and informed literary production of the decade: from anthropology and psychoanalysis to sexology and eugenics? What if we were to recognize that by the time Radclyffe Hall's novel emerged on the scene, it had become almost routine for white writers of the twenties to include some strategically located fantasy of racial blackness in their work as a means to facilitate the development of their white protagonists? If Hall's novel is most productively read as an important site for the discursive production of sexuality in the late twenties, I would suggest that such readings must now be complicated by inquiring how sexuality is simultaneously racialized in the process.

I will begin by dramatizing a crucial historical moment, the phenomenon of white patronage of African American artistic production, and then move on to a key scene in *The Well of Loneliness* that resonates with this historical moment and compels us to remark the whiteness of this novel's sexual project.

It is the summer of 1927. Taylor Gordon and J. Rosamond Johnson have just arrived in London, by way of Paris, to begin a series of concerts in private homes that will culminate in their appearance at the Coliseum, which Gordon refers to as "the world's largest variety house."[1] The year before, Johnson and his brother, James Weldon Johnson, had published *The Book of American Negro Spirituals*, which contained Rosamond's arrangements of the spirituals and a substantial preface by Weldon. After getting their start in the home of Carl Van Vechten (whom Gordon dubbed "the Abraham Lincoln of Negro art"), Johnson and Gordon performed these spirituals in a number of private residences in New York, then in public venues around the United States.

The public performance of spirituals (and its dependence on white patronage) had by this time become the site of much larger political questions pertaining to racial oppression and the institution of colonialism, as evidenced in the case of the Hampton choir during its controversial European tour. This all-black, classically trained choir, under the direction of African American composer/conductor Nathaniel Dett, toured Europe and England in 1930, presenting a program of European choral music and Dett's arrangements of Negro spirituals. While Dett wished to foreground the choir's classical training, intending to "vindicate the Negro" by showcasing his own sophisticated arrangements of the spirituals, his white sponsors at the Hampton Institute pressured him to allow the choir to perform the spirituals without direction, to give a more "spontaneous" effect.[2] The request that the spirituals be sung without direction was in keeping with the Hampton Institute's stated intention behind the tour: to set an example to Europeans for the effective management of blacks in their colonial outposts, an intention wholly endorsed by Dett's white benefactor, George Peabody. Peabody's goal was to "demonstrate to Europe what Negroes were capable of accomplishing 'under true leadership'—ultimately white leadership (since whites ran Hampton Institute and had trained and provided opportunities for Dett)" (46). If the British could educate the Africans of their colonies after the model by which the white-administered Hampton Institute trained Negroes in America, the result, Peabody thought, would be "'the evolution of the African into modern civilization,' a civilization of their own which would be more closely aligned with their alleged natural qualities" (46). Thus, by the late twenties, programs of Negro spirituals in England and Europe were necessary sites of political contestation: enabled by white patronage, they were expected to demonstrate how members of the "inferior races" could benefit from white guidance and leadership. But directed by an African American professional who sought to undermine essentialist presumptions about Negro music and musicianship, such performances could also be sites for anticolonialist, antiracist cultural work.

It was in this climate that Johnson and Gordon embarked on their London tour. They began at the home of Somerset Maugham, who "had in his drawing-room the cream of England to listen to us" (204). At first Gordon writes of being favorably impressed by the white socialites he meets in London: "It was the first time in my life since I had been a man that I had met a large Group of Caucasians that really knew they were white and didn't feel that contact with an Ethiopian could taint their chastity" (204–205). These people "were not afraid to talk to me, or ask me anything they thought I might know about. The women didn't have to have men standing by their sides to be at ease while we had a little chat" (205). While Gordon is pleasantly surprised not to be treated as though he poses a threat to white women, he nevertheless finds himself the target of white sexual projection just the same:

> I was introduced to Lady Oxford, one of the most fascinating, energetic ladies one would want to meet. After learning my name, the first question she asked me was, "Have you got a good black bottom?" Before I could answer, she turned to the lady sitting at the piano, not three feet from me, and said, "Play the music we dance our black bottom to." The lady struck up that syncopated melody of *ta*-tata-*ta*-tata, and Lady Oxford turned toward me with her eyes staring toward my feet, which remained motionless. When

I didn't start to dance, she looked at me with great disappointment. "Oh, aren't you going to teach me your step?" she asked. (205–206)

Seemingly oblivious to the racialized sexual overtones of her evocation of a "good black bottom," Lady Oxford (Margot Asquith)[3] presumes a tone of informality with Gordon, in spite of the fact that he has been invited to give a performance of sacred music. Gordon not only refuses to play the role she expects of him (that of the accommodating native informant/travelling minstrel) but also recounts the event in ways that expose the racialized sexual aggression underlying Lady Oxford's "innocent" request. "I was all balled up," he writes, "I did want to show her my black bottom then, but you know I had gone to this party with singing on my mind, and to do the best I knew how." The implication here is not so much that he would like to dance for her, but that he'd like to expose his backside to her. To do so would be to respond to the sexual invitation in her request and to expose the exploitative nature of that invitation; it would be to call her bluff, in other words. Indeed, he figuratively shows her his "black bottom" before the exchange is over: pretending to be apologetic, he says, "I'm very sorry to disappoint you at the present time. I have been congratulated for having a good black bottom, but critics say singing spirituals is my specialty— although if you care to wait until later on, I will gladly display it" (206). If Lady Oxford presumes that his "black bottom" is available for public display on demand, his response is to remind her that he does perform in public, but only to sing the spirituals he has prepared as a professional interpreter

I recount this anecdote to give a sense of what the cultural context for the interpretation of spirituals looked like to at least one African American performer in England, a performer who it might be supposed shared with Radclyffe Hall the experience of "representing" a "people" through an artistic production presumed to be inherently expressive of that people. Gordon sings Negro spirituals and is called upon to display his "black bottom;" Hall was in the process of writing the novel of the invert, a novel that would ensure that her body be hitherto as sexually marked as Gordon's body was racially marked. But my intention here is not merely to evoke Gordon as offering a racial analogue to Hall's sexual politics. For, as we shall see, these "parallel lives" were literally to cross paths in such a way that Gordon's performances of spirituals was to become the raw material for a scene in the novel Hall was composing. After his debut at the home of Somerset Maugham, Gordon's next engagement, it turns out, was at the Hall-Troubridge residence on Holland Street.

Hall had just been awarded the Prix Femina in May, and had been receiving much acclaim for her novel *Adam's Breed*. Biographer Sally Cline writes: "Suddenly it was July, and though she was approaching exhaustion there was still the party she and Una had planned to give. It seemed from the guest list that half of London's literary establishment were coming to Holland Street to hear Rosamond Johnson and Taylor Gordon sing Negro spirituals." Cline lists the many distinguished members of the literati who attended the party, then remarks that "the press couldn't get enough of it. John wore a man's dinner jacket and Mrs Galsworthy favoured a crinoline skirt; each had their followers, enabling the press to report that 'half the ladies present favoured the masculine mode and half the latest Victorian effect.'"[4] Diana Souhami adds that the party lasted until two-thirty in the morning and included Florence Mills (who was appearing at the Strand Theatre with her Blackbirds at the time) among the performers. Souhami notes that "Deep River, My Home Is over Jordan" and "Oh What a Shame I Ain't Nobody's Baby" were among the numbers performed.[5]

Gordon's account of the party does not contradict those of Hall's biographers; rather, it emphasizes different aspects. He begins by recalling his impressions of his hostesses, remarking that Troubridge "is what I always had in mind an English Lady should be like. I can't say why any particular contour of the face and body should have come to me to be what a native of any country should be like, but she fills the bill on the female side." He then goes on to say that "Radclyffe Hall is equally as striking, and the kind of person that is always so attractive in her manner" (214). One wonders if Hall "fills the bill" on the "male" side of what an English "native" should be like; in any case, what Gordon emphasizes in his account is not the way in which his hostesses are gendered but how they in some way represent their Englishness. After an appreciative description of their garden and pond, and an account of dinner during which he reminisces about the American West with Robert Cunningham Grahame (Gordon had grown up in Montana), Gordon gives a brief account of the after-dinner concert. From him, we discover that he, Johnson, and Mills are not the only musical entertainers for the evening: "Ursula Greville, who can sing old Irish and Scotch Folklore better than anyone I have ever heard, held all spellbound, and our spirituals were well received" (215). It would appear that Hall and Troubridge decided to celebrate Hall's success by arranging an evening of folk-based songs, exhibiting not only an African American tradition but also the Celtic traditions of those nearer geographical locales under English colonial domination. Only from Gordon's account do we have a sense of the African Americans as consumers as well as producers of ethnic or national cultural commodities.

Hall, already a year into the composition of *The Well of Loneliness*, drew upon the details of this party in order to dramatize a scene that, at first glance, might be discounted as inconsequential to the advancement of the plot, the development of the characters, or even the elaboration of the novel's sexual politics. In an attempt to make life less lonely for Mary, Stephen introduces her, through Valérie Seymour, to the circle of sexual exiles who inhabit Paris and who find community with each other. For these "men and women who must carry God's mark on their foreheads," Valérie Seymour creates an "atmosphere of courage." It would seem that, in spite of their rejection by English high society, Mary and Stephen have been welcomed into the expatriate community of Paris, a group of people linked by the marks of abnormality that set them apart from the normal world.

Once this emergent exilic community has been established in the novel, the scene that most concerns us is introduced. Jamie, who has been studying at the conservatory, announces that she has met a pair of "Negro brothers" there and plans to bring them home to perform spirituals for a gathering of Valérie Seymour's coterie of sexual exiles.[6] The two short chapters that dramatize this event are clearly a fictionalization of the evening of spirituals hosted by Hall and Troubridge in the summer of 1927, with significant displacements and embellishments. A close reading of these chapters, considered in relation to the actual musical evening in Hall's home, will help to understand how Hall sought to portray the "voice" of Negro suffrage in order to find a "voice" that could make the case for sexual suffrage.

The Negro Brethren Come to Sing

The Negro brothers are invited to Jamie's apartment primarily as representatives of a folkloric musical tradition, one rooted in an historical struggle for freedom. As we shall see, however, they are also invited as specimens of a racial category, a category that necessarily inflects the politics they represent. Hall introduces them to us as follows:

> They were very unlike each other, these Negroes; Lincoln, the elder, was paler in colour. He was short and inclined to be rather thick-set with a heavy but intellectual face—a strong face, much lined for a man of thirty. His eyes had the patient, questioning expression common to the eye of most animals and to those of all slowly evolving races. He shook hands very quietly with Stephen and Mary. Henry was tall and as black as a coal; a fine, upstanding, but coarse-lipped young Negro, with a roving glance and a self-assured manner. (362)

If a difference is detected between these two "Negroes," it is understood to be a difference in racial blackness. Where the one is "paler in colour" with an "intellectual face," the other is "black as a coal" and "coarse-lipped." The lighter-toned Lincoln is restrained and respectful, knowing to shake hands "very quietly" when introduced. The darker Henry is introduced as "fine, upstanding," but his "coarse lips," "roving glance," and "self-assured manner" call into question these apparently positive qualities. Indeed, the self-assurance is understood to be out of keeping with his position in this social situation; we are told he "plumped himself down at Mary's side, where he started to make conversation, too glibly" (362).

Most revealing about the passage, however, is the reference to Lincoln's eyes, described as having a "patient, questioning expression," which is first compared to the eyes of animals then to those of "all slowly evolving races." This description reminds us that the lightness of Lincoln's skin is an indicator of his relative position on an evolutionary scale; if he has intellectual eyes, knows to shake hands quietly, and is, as we find out in the next paragraph, a "little self-conscious," it is because the white admixture in his blood has brought him to an evolutionary stage that is nearer than Henry's to that of his white audience members. His virtue lies in the fact that he exhibits "patience" in the face of his slow evolution; he is willing to wait politely, using the little "consciousness" of the self that his semiwhiteness has given him to keep to his proper place.

It is important that Henry, on the other hand, be portrayed as truly black and therefore more clearly immured in a state of racial primitivity. If he (impatiently) engages in "civilized" behavior, this is understood to be merely a premature façade, which will fall away whenever his natural blackness reasserts itself. By the same token, however, his musical genius is understood to stem precisely from his primitive status: as a direct expression of his nature, it grips its audience more firmly and deeply—indeed, affects them on a spiritual level. Consider this passage, in which Hall describes what happens to Henry as he performs:

> He was not an exemplary young Negro; indeed he could be the reverse very often. A crude animal Henry could be at times, with a taste for liquor and a lust for women—just a primitive force rendered dangerous by drink, rendered offensive by civilization. Yet as he sang his sins seemed to drop from him, leaving him pure, unashamed, triumphant. He sang to his God, to the God of his soul, Who would some day blot out all the sins of the world, and make vast reparation for every injustice: "My home is over Jordan, Lord, I want to cross over into camp ground." (363)

Henry, as the coal-black Negro, is the truly "primitive" of the two; if he is, like Lincoln, compared to an animal, it is not because his eyes reveal his "patience" in the face of slow evolution but because he is inevitably susceptible to his bestial appetites. Further back on the evolutionary scale than Lincoln, he is merely "rendered offensive" by civilization, not given self-consciousness by it. The "sins" that seem to drop from him seem intimately bound up in the way his race precludes his proper relation to civilization; if his desire for and consumption of a "civilization" that is not meant for him (because it belongs more properly to whites, who have "evolved" more quickly) renders him "dangerous" and "offensive," the singing of spirituals would seem to result in his transcendence of the very distinction between the civilized and the primitive.

But it is precisely his lack of self-consciousness, rooted in his primitivity, that makes his singing so powerful. If it overtakes his audience with primitive emotion, it is because it has overtaken him: "Once started they seemed unable to stop; carried away they were by their music, drunk with that desperate hope of the hopeless" (363). Singing is here presented not as the result of a consciously attained musical education but as the authentic primal expression of primitive blackness, where the primitive takes on the connotations of the sanctity of innocence.

That Henry is entirely fabricated out of the flotsam and jetsam of early twentieth-century racial ideology becomes obvious if we compare Hall's fantasy of his primitivity with the remarks made by Taylor Gordon about his own musical performances. Gordon, as the tenor in the singing duo, is presumably the model for Henry. His relationship to his music, however, is much more a matter of conscious practice and training than of unconscious expression. "I wouldn't call myself a natural musician," he writes. Unlike his brother, George, who "can go to a show and come back and play the tunes he heard there on the piano," Gordon has "had to study hard the music I have learned" (193). Elsewhere he remarks that "I have been around lots of music and I notice that music has a peculiar effect on people. I think this reaction alone has held my interests more than anything else" (191). Gordon positions himself here as an observer of audiences, one who understands his performances as a matter of conscious manipulation of the emotions of his listeners. Having witnessed once how a violin made "a room full of women cry one afternoon at Stanley Spiegelberg's Fifth Avenue apartment," he begins to "watch closer the effect of the spirituals on people" (191):

> I have grown to really enjoy singing them, even if I do have to concentrate hard on dead people (chiefly my mother) so I can get their interpretation. The dead people I think of sang them in true Christian belief. A spiritual makes some people cry, others laugh, and arouses another's passion. All these things can be done with one song. I don't know any other music that can get the same results. (191)

In Hall's account, the singer is imagined to be unconsciously channeling the despair and hope of his dead ancestors; his blackness makes him one of them in a mystical way, regardless of the fact that he is of a generation that postdates slavery, may not have grown up in the South, and may come from a very different cultural background than the slaves who originated the spirituals. It is as though his spiritual singing is something he is racially programmed to do. Gordon, on the other hand, very consciously learns the spirituals he sings, must "concentrate hard on dead people" to give them the most effective interpretation, and is not, like the dead people he conjures, particularly driven by "true Christian belief." Whether Hall really believed Gordon's singing talent to be a "natural" component of his racial makeup is in some sense not important; what interests us is the necessity, in her fiction, to produce a figure of the Negro whose singing ability is not a matter of expertise and conscious training but of instinctual expression. This helps us to understand how race inflects the effect that Henry's singing has on his white audience.

As he sings, "all the hope of the utterly hopeless of this world, who must live by their ultimate salvation, all the terrible, aching, homesick hope that is born of the infinite pain of the spirit" seems to "break from [Henry] and shake those who listened, so that they sat with bent heads and clasped hands . . . as they listened" (362–363). His singing is something that comes from beyond him; it is as though he channels the voices of the "hopeless," so that these voices mysteriously interpellate the listeners in such a way that they spontaneously clasp hands with each other, acknowledging their shared status with the "hopeless." As though to suggest how these particular listeners might identify with rather than pity the "hopelessness" expressed in the songs, Hall gives us brief reaction shots of each individual in the audience, reminding us of the pathos that marks each character's plight. Jamie's eyes ache from "unshed tears," the "gentle" and "learned" Adolphe Blanc ponders "many things deeply," Pat remembers her lost love, Brockett thinks of unrecorded "brave deeds that even he . . . had done out in Mespot," and Wanda plans an "enormous canvas depicting the wrongs of all mankind." The passage ends with an emphasis on the lesbian couples in the room: "Stephen suddenly found Mary's hand and held it in hers with a painful pressure, while Barbara's tired and childish brown eyes turned to rest rather anxiously on her Jamie," and we are told that "not one of them all but was stirred to the depths by that queer, half defiant, half supplicating music" (363). An obvious point of identification is being established here between the plight of black people and that of the listening inverts.

So far, it seems that both groups are presented as oppressed by suffering and that in both cases, that suffering seems as much to do with a congenital defect of the body (racial, sexual) as it does with political oppression. But as soon as this shared suffering is evoked, Hall reminds us that only the African Americans are understood to have at their disposal a "native" form with which to express that suffering and to call out for "delivery." The spirituals thus function in two ways: they spontaneously emerge from the singers' racial primitivity, and they also index a certain history of oppression based on that primitivity. If Henry and Lincoln are able to induce a sense of community in their audience (as signaled by their listeners' "bent heads and clasped hands"), it is because they have at their disposal a musical form that has passed down through generations, as though through a bloodline of descent; a musical form that, by the late twenties, signifies to its white audiences something at once indigenous to its racially defined "other" and somehow evocative of the white audience's own "primitive" roots. It is the means by which the white subject, suffering from the fragmentation, industrialization, and depersonalization of modernity might experience a "return" to an idealized, premodern state.

It is worth stressing that Hall has transformed Johnson and Gordon into "brothers" for the purpose of her story, as though to emphasize that their presence signifies "kinship": the kinship of racial determination, the kinship of shared oppression, and the kinship of spiritual supplication. This last aspect of kinship is signaled in the passage that describes the shift in their tone from despair to bold defiance:

> And now there rang out a kind of challenge; imperious, loud, almost terrifying. They sang it together, those two black *brethren*, and their voices suggested a multitude shouting. They seemed to be shouting a challenge to the world on behalf of themselves and of all the afflicted. (363, emphasis mine)

To use the term "brethren" instead of "brothers" is to inflect this "natural" kinship bond between them (the bond of blood, of race) with the connotations of religious righteousness. The rules of kinship (one must care about, care for, one's blood relations) are called upon to be extended, metaphorically, to a "people." One must care for one's "people" as one would for one's blood brother. As spiritual "brethren," they speak not only on behalf of their "people" but of all who are "afflicted:"[7]

> The eternal question, as yet unanswered for those who sat there spellbound and listened. . . . "Didn't my Lord deliver Daniel, then why not every man?"
> Why not? . . . Yes, but how long, O Lord, how long? (364, Hall's ellipses)

This eternal question, it turns out, has two parts: the first is contained within the quotation marks that identify it as belonging to the lyrics of the song, asking if Daniel was delivered, then "why not every man?" The second part of the question is also part of the song, but here it is posed without quotation marks, "Yes, but how long, O Lord, how long?" To leave off the quotation marks is to indicate that the song's lyrics have been internalized by the consciousness of the narrator of the novel and redeployed in order to express the plight not just of the African Americans but also of their invert audience. This is the point at which the novel appropriates the spirituals, borrows them to "speak" on behalf of its white protagonists. Indeed, once introduced via this racialized origin, the phrase "How long [O Lord]" will be reprised later in the novel to explicitly address the question of sexual oppression:

> How long was this persecution to continue? How long would God sit still and endure this insult offered to His creations. How long tolerate the preposterous statement that inversion was not a part of nature? (404–405)

This appropriation is necessary because the inverts apparently do not yet have a music, a voice, an expressive vehicle, for proclaiming their oppression. They do not yet, like Henry and Lincoln, share with each other the status of "brethren." Indeed, throughout the novel, we have seen Stephen struggle to find just such a form, though in earlier scenes, before she has been introduced into the community of inverts, and before these inverts have had their identificatory moment with the Negro brothers, this struggle for form has been perceived by Stephen as an individual matter. When Stephen feels frustrated about the progress of her second novel, for instance, she attributes her sense that there is "something wrong with it" to the fact that she has never experienced sexual fulfillment: "Why have I been afflicted with a body that must never be indulged, that must always be repressed until it grows stronger much than my spirit because of this unnatural repression? . . . I shall never be a great writer because of my maimed and insufferable body" (217). Even when Stephen has finally found sexual fulfillment (through Mary), there remains the imperative to link her singular body to a collective body that would constititute her "people." While Paris has by this historical moment become a geographical space for the congregation of these bodies (the space for sexual expatriates), there is not yet an artistic or rhetorical space of shared inhabitation. I would suggest that Hall presents the Negro spiritual as a kind of model for this shared psychic space, a space that is also an indigenous form for the expression of one's oppression. By having the Negroes present a model that will inform Stephen's discovery of the form for which she has been searching as invert-novelist, Hall employs a cultural ventriloquism that has by now become a familiar trope in a white modernist tradition that is characterized by its invention of, and fascination with, the "primitive."

Obstreperous Negroes

Before continuing with this analysis of the spirituals scene, it will be instructive to contemplate at least one other significant instance in which Radclyffe Hall attempted to represent racial difference. If Una Troubridge's account is to be trusted, it would seem that Hall was no stranger to dominant white presumptions about the sexuality of African Americans. Troubridge writes that when traveling in the United States in her twenties, Hall and her cousin Jane Randolph kept "a revolver handy for obstreperous Negroes," presuming that, as white women traveling alone, the greatest danger they might encounter would be aggressive black men.[8] In the mid-teens, Hall made this figure of the "obstreperous Negro" the basis for a short story. In "the Career of Mark Anthony Brakes," a young black man is presented as having separated himself from his "people" by becoming educated, practicing as a lawyer, and presuming to take on a white woman as a client.[9] This narrative is a rich resource for understanding something about how what Toni Morrison calls "American Africanism" functioned within British literary history.[10]

The "pure black" but highly educated Mark Anthony Brakes has ambivalent feelings about other African Americans, aspiring instead to whiteness:

> He missed some quality in his own people, they seemed to him childish and limited. His allegiance went out to the master race, the race whose skin was white. The old slavish instinct of his fore-fathers stirred in him, side by side with the longing for a larger life that the Emancipation had made possible. (3–4)

Imitating the white man's speech, clothing, and hairstyle (4), he is disdainful of his fellow college students' lack of a proper "attitude towards the white race" (6). Moreover, he laments the "grotesque and insufferable things" his male peers do: "following unprotected white women through the darker streets of the town at night" and "swaggering insolently, crudely self-assertive, if by chance they found themselves together with white people" (6–7). Finding their "coarseness . . . almost brutish at times," Brakes feels "near despair," asking himself how he could "ever hope to attain where others had failed? After all, their blood was his blood, and it was rotten" (7).

This notion of race as a matter of "rotten" blood, intrinsic to the body and at war with an overlay of rationalism (a metonym both for whiteness and civility) pervades the entire story, and, as we have seen, survives into Hall's composition of *The Well* over a decade later. While Brakes is able to succeed as a lawyer and is acknowledged in the press for having won a case on behalf of a white woman (his first white client), it turns out that this "rotten" blood will be his downfall after all. Feeling "instinctively that marriage with a woman of his own race must degrade him" (12), he falls in love with his white client. Although he is assailed by doubt that their blood "would not, could not mix" and experiences a "horror of such an union, a horror bred of the remembrance of the disastrous illicit experiences of those bygone days of slavery," he nevertheless proposes to her (17–18). But this "rotten blood," no matter how desperately he tries to repress it, reemerges in the story's climactic scene. The white woman ridicules him and, overcome by shame and desire, he reverts to his "true" racial state, a reversion that is indexed by two symptoms: the disruption of his educated speech by "the old tricks of intonation and dialect that were usually so carefully hidden" and his recourse to violence when the white woman spurns him (20). While he restrains himself from killing her, he understands himself to have committed a "murder" nevertheless. He reflects that his "blood," which he has "subdued so long," has "driven [him] to commit this unspeakable crime" and "conquered [him] in the end." "You were born black," he reminds himself, "and black you have always remained. You have murdered your own ideal" (22). At the story's conclusion, he takes a revolver from his drawer and walks out into the night with the purpose, we are to presume, of committing suicide.

It would seem, thus, that Hall has constructed the perfect "obstreperous" Negro in this story, perfect in the sense that, having recognized the danger he poses to the white world, he is prepared to do away with himself with his own revolver. More important for our purposes, however, it could be suggested that Hall is less interested in the painful paradoxes produced by racism in this story and more interested in the opportunity it offered to explore the disastrous implications of a sexual proclivity that refuses to be repressed. Hall failed to find a publisher for the story in 1915, when she was looking for venues for her short fiction. Later, when she was a successful novelist and had the opportunity to publish "Mark Anthony Brakes" with other earlier short stories, she chose not to. Troubridge gives this explanation:

> [Hall] decided that whatever might be its merits of style and construction, what had, when she wrote it, been the originality of its theme: the sudden and disastrous breakdown of civilization and self-control in an educated Negro under the stress of sexual emotion, had since been treated and exhausted by other writers, both white and coloured, and that her story had definitely missed the boat. (40)

We need not, however, take this explanation at face value. I would suggest that the story, though not published in its original form, is transformed into something else by the time Hall writes *The Well*. By the late 1920s the Harlem Renaissance had brought African American music, literary, and visual arts to white audiences in England, and Radclyffe Hall would undoubtedly have been aware of black literary and artistic production. If her narrative of Mark Anthony Brakes was in some sense an early substitute for the novel of the invert, which she was now ready to write, she would no longer need to publish her short story, especially since African Americans were speaking for themselves. But the character of Brakes (and the presumptions about blackness and primitivity he embodies) was nevertheless redistributed into the characters of Stephen, on the one hand, and the Negro spiritual singers on the other.

Nobody's Baby

We now return to the scene of the spirituals concert in *The Well of Loneliness*. As we have seen, Hall presents the Negro brethren as spontaneously evoking a sense of shared community in their listeners, so that the inverts experience an emotionally charged moment of identification with the performers. Yet I would suggest that this point of identification also produces an unacknowledged racial anxiety that must, in turn, be contained by the novel; as soon as Hall raises the possibility that her white protagonists might recognize something of themselves in the mirroring offered by the Negro brothers, she runs the risk that inversion, which she is attempting to positively valorize, will become "tainted" by the racial blackness to which it is being compared. In order to avert this risk, then, whiteness-as-(over)-civilization must be stressed here, so that it will contrast clearly with blackness-as-primitivity.

To this end, the racially based distinction between the performers and their listeners is remarked emphatically in the passages that follow the concert. When they have finished, the "brethren" bow and thank their audience, after which the narrator comments that "it was over. They were just two men with black skins and foreheads beaded with perspiration. Henry sidled away to the whisky, while Lincoln rubbed his pinkish palms on an elegant white silk handkerchief" (364). Once the state of transcendence is broken, the performers (like Mark Anthony Brakes) revert to the specificity of their bodies, bodies whose racial features are emphasized (the "black skins" and the "pinkish palms," not to mention the appetite for whisky). Not surprisingly, they have had a loosening effect on their white listeners, who "quite suddenly" all "become merry, laughing at nothing, teasing each other." Even Valérie Seymour (who is the least tolerant of drinking and debauchery among the group) "unbent more than was her wont and did not look bored when Brockett chafed her" (364). The presence of the black performers turns Jamie's studio into a temporary refuge from the strictures of white, civilized modernity and gives license to emote, to indulge, to party long into the night.

At the same time, it is as though Hall is at pains to remind us that the extent to which whiteness may be "infected" by blackness is limited. After supper, the white musicians at the party put on performances of their own, performances that contrast sharply with Henry and Lincoln's: "Jamie played the overture to her opera, and they loudly applauded the rather dull music" (364). It is as though her whiteness preordains that Jamie's music sound "so scholarly, so dry, so painfully stiff, so utterly inexpressive of Jamie" (364). While Henry's expressiveness is a natural outgrowth of his innate primitivity, an unconscious channeling of his racial kinship with his "people," Jamie's "utterly inexpressive" music is the sterile result of conscious "scholarly" instruction. If she cannot express herself, she can never hope to give voice to the "people" to whom she is linked by virtue of the specificity of her body (whether that be its whiteness or its sexual proclivity). Wanda in turn evinces a learned "skill" in handling her mandolin, but must be released by brandy from the strictures of whiteness in order to sing her ethnically inflected love songs. In the end, as a result of her artificially induced "fierceness," she seems to be destroyed along with her instrument and ends up "sprawled out" upon the floor. The white inverts appear to be racially ill equipped to give voice to their collective angst.

By the end of the evening we are presented with a detail that evokes Taylor Gordon's account of his exchange with Lady Oxford. As the guests are drunkenly getting ready to leave at four in the morning, we are told that:

> As for Henry Jones, he started to sing at the top of his lungs in a high falsetto:
> *"Oh, my, help, help, ain't I nobody's baby?*
> *Oh, my, what a shame, I ain't nobody's baby."* (365)

This fragment of a popular tune is presented as the secular counterpart to the spirituals that had been performed earlier in the evening. Insofar as it, too, belongs to a racially inflected musical genre (an African American jazz or blues tradition), it is understood to issue as spontaneously from Henry as had the spirituals. Hall's fictional Negro here doesn't even need to be asked to give a performance in keeping with white expectations of his racial talents; he will readily display his "black bottom" at the point in the narrative where it is most needed: to indicate the "darkness" that underlies the apparent frivolity of the party. His "high falsetto" voice signals that, even as he and Lincoln have infected the whites with their blackness, they in turn have infected him with their inversion. And while the slang lyrics of the popular tune ostensibly bewail the protagonist's lack of a lover (he or she is "nobody's baby"), they also resonate with the theme of kinship that has been running throughout the chapter. To be "nobody's baby" is to be orphaned, to lack the kin ties that locate one in a community of others. Once again Hall uses Henry to ventriloquize the plight of the disparate, white inverts, bereft of a sense of kinship upon which to base a plea for salvation. Moreover, the easy slippage between sacred and profane modes of expression, and the fact that the spirituals and the popular songs erupt almost indistinguishably and somewhat compulsively from the place of "blackness" in this scene, establishes a racially based ground from which Stephen's voice of the invert will emerge in the novel's conclusion.

Ma Soeur, Mon Frère

Up to this scene, we have only seen Stephen and her newly discovered group of exiled friends gathered at Valérie Seymour's, where drinking is forbidden, the level of discussion remains distinctly highbrow, and the inverts seem somehow sheltered from recognition of their "lower" natures. The evening of the spirituals functions as a transitional scene, a kind of early introduction to later episodes in the novel that take place in what is construed as a depraved, public atmosphere. It is no doubt the presence of the New York Negroes in Jamie's apartment, and especially Henry's fondness for whisky and his introduction of the jazz lyrics, that makes the community of exiles seem for the first time to be tinged by the questionable ambience of the nightclub. Only a few short chapters later, having been rebuffed by the respectable world represented by Lady Massey, our heroines make "their first real acquaintance with the garish and tragic night life of Paris that lies open to such people as Stephen Gordon" (378). After a series of visits to clubs and cafés, each more squalid than the last, Stephen and Mary find themselves in "Alec's," the seediest of all the nightspots, populated by the most depraved and hopeless of the inverts. Here, a youth with a "grey, drug-marred face" and a "mouth that tremble[s] incessantly" whispers "Ma soeur" to Stephen (388). After some initial repulsion, Stephen recognizes in this youth the frightened eyes of the fox from her hunting days. Identifying with these eyes, she mutters "Mon frère" in reply (389). In this scene the youth mobilizes the very trope that had structured the earlier spirituals passage: he interpellates Stephen as sister, making claim to a kinship with her. The "brothers" of the spirituals scene have established the trope of sibling kinship as a necessary ground for the development of this scene in the club, where Stephen comes to acknowledge herself as "sibling" to other inverts, as a member, therefore, of a people linked by their peculiarly marked bodies.

Stephen's resignation to her inclusion as a "sibling" is thus far presented as an admission of self-degradation; insofar as she is among the "hunted," she can deny no longer her abject status. It is no accident that, as soon as she acknowledges her "frère," she is approached by "a quiet, tawny man with the eyes of the Hebrew; Adolphe Blanc, the gentle and learned Jew" (389). His appearance is designed to transform her abjection into resolution. To be "brothers" with the abject invert is not enough; she must strive, after the model of Henry and Lincoln, to shift the kinship metaphor into the realm of spiritual righteousness and join the other inverts as a community of "brethren." "I am glad you have come to this place," Blanc says to her, "because those who have courage also have a duty" (389). In the course of their brief conversation, Blanc urges Stephen to consider that medical books about inversion (which are only read by students and which represent only the plight of the "neurasthenics") are not adequate to make "thoughtless" people regret the injustice of their persecution of the sexually oppressed. The "whole truth" can be represented only by "the normal invert. The doctors cannot make the ignorant think, cannot hope to bring home the sufferings of millions; only one of ourselves can some day do that" (390).

It is important to recapitulate how this scene in the nightclub relies on the spirituals scene for part of its coherence. Both scenes elaborate the theme of voice and ventriloquism: the Negro brothers give voice to all their black "brethren" in suffering; moreover, through processes of identification, the brothers' voices are invested by the white inverts with the power to express their own abject plight. The brethren are being made, by Hall, to draw upon a tradition of Negro spirituals in order to give voice to more than one "people." In this sense, a familiar appropriation occurs, where an African American musical tradition is incorporated into a white European context so as to procure an emotional response (in Hall's characters, as well as in her reading audience insofar as they identify with these characters) that, it is presumed, could not be produced in any other way. It is their "race," indeed the fact that they are singing "racial" music, that defines Henry and Lincoln as the site where an authentic natural/spiritual affect will be best accessed and afterward mobilized for political purposes. They set an example that Stephen, at the behest of Adolphe Blanc (who shares with Henry and Lincoln the status of a "raced" character, with his "tawny" skin and "eyes of the Hebrew"), is encouraged to follow by the novel's conclusion.

Stephen Finds Her Voice

In the final scene of the novel, in which Stephen experiences a complex vision as a result of having sacrificed Mary to Martin Hallam, the trope of the voice, which was introduced in the spirituals chapter, is given its ultimate elaboration. Stephen has just witnessed Mary, "the sun falling full on her hair," run into the arms of Hallam, telling him why she has "fled from that thick, awful darkness" (436). Mary's running out into the sun, her passing "under the archway" with the man she loves, signifies her passing into a world at once heteronormative and white, while Stephen remains behind in the "awful darkness" of the world of the invert. As soon as she is alone, however, Stephen experiences a long and elaborate hallucination.

The room seems to be "thronging with people," all of them inverts, her friends Jamie, Barbara, and Wanda, as well as "those lost and terrible brothers from Alec's." There are multitudes of these "unbidden guests," surrounding Stephen with their "marred and reproachful faces with the haunted, melancholy eyes of the invert" and beseeching her to "speak with your God and ask Him why He has left us forsaken!" (436). In the next moments she experiences "rockets of pain, burning rockets of pain—their pain, her pain, all welded together into one great consuming agony" (437). Moreover, she seems literally to be attacked by these crowds of spirits as "they fought, they trampled, they were getting her under. In their madness to become articulate through her, they were tearing her to pieces, getting her under" (437). The fantasy of being attacked becomes explicitly sexual in the next paragraph, making it seem as though Stephen is experiencing her surrender to this mob as a kind of gang rape, a forced violation that will result in the "articulation" the spirits are struggling for:

> They possessed her. Her barren womb became fruitful—it ached with its fearful and sterile burden. It ached with the fierce yet helpless children who would clamour in vain for their right to salvation. They would turn first to God, and then to the world, and then to her. They would cry out accusing: "We have asked for bread; will you give us a stone?" (437)

These hallucinated spirits are reminiscent of the throng of voices conveyed by the "two black brethren" of the spirituals chapter, whose "voices suggested a multitude shouting . . . a challenge to the world on behalf of themselves and of all the afflicted" (363). In the final scene we are to understand that Stephen is now being endowed with the same capacity of the spirituals singers to convey the suffering of a "multitude," that she is on the threshold of launching a tradition of expression that will do for inverts what spirituals have done for Negroes. Insofar as the scene that inaugurates this tradition is figured as an imagined rape leading to her "barren womb" becoming "fruitful," the already racialized motif of kinship appears once more to be evoked: having admitted to being a "sister" to the "lost and terrible brothers from Alec's," Stephen now appears paradoxically to become their sexual partner (insofar as they "possess" her) and their mother (insofar as she will give birth to them). The result will be that when she next speaks, she will by virtue of this fantasy of overdetermined kinship be able to make claims on behalf of her "people." "And now there was only one voice," we are told:

> one demand; her own voice into which those millions had entered. A voice like the awful, deep rolling of thunder; a demand like the gathering together of great waters. A terrifying voice that made her ears throb, that made her brain throb, that shook her very entrails, until she must stagger and all but fall beneath this appalling burden of sound that strangled her in its will to be uttered. (437)

In this voice Stephen demands from God, before the "whole world," that inverts be given the "right to our existence!" To undergo the transformations necessary to be able to take up her role in giving voice to a people, it is almost as though, through the tutoring devices of the Negro brethren and the Jewish Adolphe Blanc, Stephen has inevitably been "raced" by the end of the novel.

This is not to say that her whiteness, or her Englishness, has become visible as a racial trait; rather, her claim to race-less-ness (that is to whiteness, which is still seen by this novel as transcendent of race, as universal) is understood as compromised, in spite of Hall's attempts to maintain distinctions between black primitive and white civilized characters. Mary, even with her Welsh background, can finally "pass" as white through her heterosexual union with Martin Hallam. But Stephen is presented as one who is denied access to the heteronormative kinship system that would guarantee her status as white; instead, she becomes "impregnated" by her invert peoples and will, we presume, give birth to their voice when she finally writes the book that will speak on behalf of sexual inversion in a way that medical books have not been able to. Like racial difference, sexual difference is thus depicted as bound up with questions of reproduction, blood relations, the dissemination of physical or embodied traits from within a counterkinship system. If the novel's ostensible tone of hope and defiance is haunted by undertones of anxiety in the end, I would suggest that this is in part due to its inability to fully dispel the implication that to be sexually aberrant is also to be racially suspect. In depicting sexual suffrage through the images of impregnation, birth, and kinship—thus mobilizing many of the same tropes bound up with miscegenation and racial brotherhood—Hall might seem also to be implying that an alleviation of the plight of the invert includes not only the inception of a world where homoerotic desire may circulate without repercussion but also the restoration of whiteness to the bodies whose sexual marks had seemed to betoken racial marking as well. The implication is that if inverts have suffered in part from their misassociation with blackness, there is hope for them to attain whiteness in the future. What Hall might have intended to be read as an attempt at an alliance with Negro and Jewish suffrage proves, after all, to privilege whiteness in the service of sexual suffrage.

Notes

1. Taylor Gordon, *Born to Be* (1929; reprint, Lincoln: University of Nebraska Press, 1995), p. 216.

2. Jon Michael Spencer, *The New Negroes and Their Music* (Knoxville: University of Tennessee Press, 1997), p. 49.

3. My thanks to Lucy Bland for identifying Lady Oxford for me.

4. Sally Cline, *Radclyffe Hall: A Woman Called John* (New York: The Overlook Press, 1997), pp. 220–221.

5. Diana Souhami, *The Trials of Radclyffe Hall* (New York: Doubleday, 1999), p. 160.

6. Radclyffe Hall, *The Well of Loneliness* (1928; reprint, New York: Anchor Books, 1990), p. 361. All further references in this text.

7. It should be noted that Hall stresses the spiritual connotations of the trope of brotherhood at the expense of its more political connotations at the time: the 1920s was the decade that saw the birth of the Brotherhood of Sleeping Car Porters and Maids, whose unionizing efforts were considered to be dangerously radical. In

emphasizing the spiritual connotations of "brethren," Hall situates both her black and her white protagonists' struggles in a genealogy of supplication rather than of militancy.

8. Una, Lady Troubridge, *The Life of Radclyffe Hall* (New York: Arno Press, 1975), p. 19.

9. Radclyffe Hall, "The Career of Mark Anthony Brakes," unpublished typescript. Courtesy of the Harry Ransom Humanities Research Center, the University of Texas at Austin.

10. Indeed, it should take its place in an archive of similar instances within the literary trajectories of white queer writers of the early twentieth century: alongside Hall's "The Career of Mark Anthony Brakes," we should consider the likes of Stein's "Melanctha," H.D.'s poetry and films featuring Paul Robeson, Van Vechten's *Nigger Heaven*, and other moments when blackness is made to figure within a white writer's developing sense of an aesthetics and politics of homoeroticism. For more on "American Africanism," see Toni Morrison, *Playing in the Dark: Whiteness and the Literary Imagination* (New York: Vintage, 1992).

17

"Something Primitive and Age-Old as Nature Herself": Lesbian Sexuality and the Permission of the Exotic

SARAH E. CHINN

Considering the accusations of obscenity that dogged the book, very little sex happens in *The Well of Loneliness*.[1] There is the fetishistic worship of the housemaid Collins by a six-year-old Stephen Gordon, some fevered kissing (but no more) between teenage Stephen and Angela Crossby, and some rather more restrained kisses bestowed by Stephen on Mary Llewellyn until the fateful night in which "they were not divided."[2] Like Stephen herself, the novel maintains a rigid physical self-control that only intensifies the roiling emotions kept by sheer force of will under the surface.

The one place that lesbian sexuality has permission to emerge, and Stephen can let down her guard, is at the Villa del Ciprés on the Canary Island of Tenerife. Tenerife, the largest of a cluster of about half a dozen islands and six more subislands off the border coast of Morocco and what is now Western Sahara, was—as it still is—a Spanish colony with an already long history of tourism in the 1920s.[3] Five centuries of Spanish occupation of and involvement in transcontinental trade in the Canary Islands had created a hybrid culture of indigenous Guanche, Spanish, North African, and sub-Saharan cultures and populations.[4] The islands' landscapes are dramatic, dotted with mountains and volcanoes. Some of the smaller islands are densely rocky; others, like Tenerife, are lush and fertile—not surprisingly, since the islands lie less than ten degrees North in longitude from the Tropic of Cancer.

In this essay I want to explore *why* Tenerife is the only possible site for the expression of an untroubled lesbian sexuality in *The Well of Loneliness*. The logic of novel makes it clear that Morton, the Gordon family estate, cannot be such a site. Nor can Stephen's home in London, tenderly maintained by the protoinvert Puddle. In fact, Europe as a whole cannot bear the lightness of a lesbian sexuality that is not freighted with anxiety, decadence, self-doubt, and strict self-control (or its complement, anarchy). Instead, Hall—comfortably equipped with the imperialist discourses of exoticism and orientalism—constructs an imaginary space of "the primitive" that allows Stephen and Mary to consummate their love by "going native" (all the while maintaining their status as white bearers of modernity).

Tenerife is explicitly envisaged as an escape both from the modernity of Europe and from Stephen's painful entrance into lesbian adulthood, most poignantly represented by her mercy killing of her horse Raftery.[5] In London Stephen is as aggressively modern as she is masculine: not only does she cut her hair short, she also becomes an urban creature. Her skin becomes "paler than it had been in the past, it had lost the look of wind and sunshine—the open-air look"; her fingers are "heavily stained with nicotine—she was now a voracious smoker"; most important, she casts off the rhythms of rural life for the nocturnal existence of the city (*Well* 210). She embraces the isolation of modernity as well as the friendship of the utterly "kaleidoscopic" Jonathan Brockett, whose analysis of the horrific means that achieve the exquisite ends of pâté de foie gras—"I wish I knew the esoteric meaning of these mixed emotions!"—might well be read as the rallying cry of modernism itself (*Well* 230).

Although queer life is very much in evidence in Paris, particularly with Jonathan Brockett as tour guide, the evidence is modernity's open secret. Jonathan's invocation of Marie Antoinette and her rumored love affair with Marie-Thérèse Louise, Princesse de Lamballe, provides a direct link between the origins of the modern era and the duplicity of homosexuality:

> Those two would often come here at sunset. Sometimes they were rowed along the canal in the sunset—can't you imagine it, Stephen? They must often have felt pretty miserable, poor souls; sick to death of the subterfuge and pretences. Don't you ever get tired of that sort of thing? My God, I do! (*Well* 239)

As Terry Castle has argued, Marie Antoinette was a "cult figure . . . in works of fiction written by and about lesbians in the first decades of the twentieth century."[6] According to Castle, Marie Antoinette offered a very modern mode of self-imagination: "a poetics of possibility. . . . Marie Antoinette functioned as a kind of lesbian Oscar Wilde. . . . She gave those who idolized her a way of thinking about themselves. And out of such reflection . . . something of the modern lesbian identity was born."[7]

That "modern lesbian identity," manifested as inversion theory within *The Well of Loneliness*, both enables and hamstrings Stephen. On the one hand, it allows her to recognize herself as a type rather than a freak as she pores over the pages of Krafft-Ebing in the Morton library, and it gives her at least temporary refuge in the louche social circle of Valérie Seymour, filled with "men and women who must carry God's mark on their foreheads" (*Well* 352). But Stephen Gordon's modernity—and is this not modernity's self-image, after all?—is profoundly sterile, atomized, incorporeal. The most powerful feelings are despair and ennui or a brittle pleasure brought on by extravagance, such as Stephen's luxurious gifts to the impoverished lesbian couple Jamie and Barbara.

London and Paris are represented in contrast to two locales that are equally (and mutually) opposite to each other: Morton and Tenerife. Where the cities are profoundly imbricated with an urban, modern aesthetic, both Morton and Tenerife are defined by their pre- or extramodernity and drenched in the immediacy of the natural world. However, as Gillian Whitlock has shown, at Morton "all relationships to nature are heterosexual and rigidly policed in terms of gender."[8] The natural world in Morton is hyperbolically fertile, the Malvern Hills "like pregnant women, full-bosomed, courageous, great green-girdled mothers of splendid sons!" (*Well* 13). Even the animals diagnose Stephen as inadequate, from Peter the imperious male swan to the thrush that, after Stephen rejects her suitor Martin, sings "Stephen, look at me, look at me. . . . I'm happy, happy, it's all very simple" (*Well* 97).

Morton is also the site of Stephen's parents' marriage, which is explicitly represented as both sacred and paradigmatic. As a child Stephen walks with her father, Sir Philip, through the countryside surrounding Morton. Sir Philip is so closely linked to the natural world of Morton that he "knew all about wild flowers and berries, and the ways of young foxes and rabbits and such people" (*Well* 25). Similarly, in one of the few moments of intimacy

Stephen shares with her mother Anna, the two walk through a meadow: "The scents of the meadows would move those two strangely—the queer, pungent smell from the hearts of dog-daisies; the buttercup smell, faintly green like the grass; and then meadowsweet that grew close by the hedges" (*Well* 32).

Stephen's relationship with her parents can be partially mediated by the natural world of Morton only before she reaches adulthood—specifically, sexual maturity. Although she nurtures the fantasy that she and Angela Crossby are "both filled with the old peace of Morton," she could not be more wrong (*Well* 145). Every moment in which Stephen is initiated into the next step of adulthood—her first hunt, her first love affair, shooting Raftery—she is pulled further away from Morton.

But Morton is more than an always-already lost Eden. After all, Stephen's desire to feel at home there is hardly effortless. The natural world continually reminds Stephen of how she does not quite fit into the social: it is "a reminder of her failure to fulfill norms of femininity that seem to be 'natural.'"[9] In fact, Morton is, as Margot Gayle Backus has shown, *the* signifier for an impossible but uncomplicated, heterosexualized, aristocratic Englishness (it is no coincidence that Angela Crossby is not just queer but also *American*). Hall's construction of Stephen not simply as masculine but as the apogee of the "English gentleman" is a defensive gesture that privileges the "English reader's belief . . . in the innate superiority of the English in general and the English gentleman in particular [over] the reader's equally firm conviction that lesbianism is unthinkable and immoral."[10] Backus argues that the Celticness of Anna Gordon (Irish) and Mary Llewellyn (Welsh) is constructed as the sensual feminized "other" to Stephen's insistent English erectness.

Stephen's ambivalent relationship to Celticness reveals that the "otherness" of "the Celt" is always partial and shifting. It is what causes her mother to reject her (as opposed to her father's English rationalism, which helps him understand her), but it is also what connects mother and daughter in their meadow walks; it links Mary and Stephen by genealogy even as it separates them by temperament. Hall may, as Backus argues, represent Anna Gordon as "occupying the extralinguistic, sensual, emotional, feminine, and also vindictive and childlike or child*ish* realm that Victorian and Edwardian culture . . . associated with 'the Celt.'"[11] But Stephen is part Irish herself, her mother's daughter. She is caught between two "racial" temperaments: rational, decorporealized, masculine Englishness and sensual, embodied, feminine Celticness. The merging of these two identities within her body insists on a genealogical heterosexuality, articulated through the landscape of Morton, that works to deny the legitimacy of inversion.

It is in Tenerife that this conflict is, however temporarily, resolved. Like Morton, the Villa del Ciprés is old, "older than the oldest villas on the hill. . . . It was so old indeed, that no peasant could have told you precisely when it had come into being; the records were lost, if they had ever existed" (*Well* 304–305). And like the landscape around Morton, Orotava is insistently fecund in prelapsarian terms: the villa's garden is "a veritable Eden of a garden, obsessed by a kind of primitive urge towards all manner of procreation" (*Well* 305). But whereas in Morton nature is the medium for the disciplining of Stephen's body, however unsuccessfully, to conform to rigid codes of masculinity and femininity, the natural world of Tenerife is hybrid, multigendered, mysterious. The flowers—usually gendered feminine—have "virile growth," and the fragrance of the trees is "disturbing" (*Well* 305).

At Orotava Mary finally confronts Stephen, pushing beyond her gentlemanly reserve and aristocratic disembodiedness. This is a gradual process, however. Stephen affects a kind of obtuseness, refusing to understand Mary's requests for intimacy as what they are. The atmosphere at Orotava exacerbates the tension between them, until Mary threatens to go home to England. The confrontation ends in Stephen's confession of love and the sexual consummation of their relationship, which transforms the rest of their time on Tenerife into an idyll. The Orotava episode, which takes up much of book 4 of the novel,[12] is the elaboration of this narrative that moves from Stephen's brittle rejection of Mary "for her own good" to the two women's integration into the natural world of Tenerife through their sexual union. It is larded with dense descriptions of vegetation and transcriptions of folk songs, reported conversations with Orotavans, and accounts of sightseeing trips to give the reader a sense of the environment that so fully absorbs Stephen and Mary. Throughout this section of the novel, Hall (re)creates a fantasy world that constructs a Tenerife imagined as the opposite (and hence image) of modernity.

What defines Tenerife is its *difference*: from the city, from the English countryside, from the idea of Englishness, from the sexual economy in which Stephen has so far been bad currency. Orotava is "primitive" (a word Hall uses several times to describe it), and it allows Stephen and Mary to be primitive too, in a cultural imaginary in which "primitive" means sensual, "natural," uncomplicated, emotionally unstable, both inscrutable and wholly predictable. Indeed, Hall describes Stephen herself as "primitive" at key moments of the novel, particularly times of intense emotion. Provoked to childhood rage by her neighbor Roger Antrim, Stephen's masculinity leaps off her face, "grotesque and splendid, like some primitive thing conceived in a turbulent age of transition" (*Well* 52). In this episode Stephen's rage distances her from rational Englishness and aligns her with the primitive (the child, the Celt, the Tenerifan, the natural). Primitiveness is, in this novel, the sign of excess physicality, directly contrasted with the understated sophistication of the modern world.

The analogizing of uncontrollable emotion, unorthodox and unfettered sexuality, and anthropological primitivism was a significant part of the sexological literature in which Hall immersed herself. Richard von Krafft-Ebing, one of the Virgils to Hall's inverted Dante, explicitly linked inversion to arrested sociological (as well as psychological) development. Sexual difference and heterosexuality were, he argued, more dominant in more evolved cultures: "The psycho-physical sexual difference runs parallel with the high level of the evolving process. . . . The individual being . . . is originally bisexual, but in the struggle between the male and female elements either one or the other is conquered, and a monosexual being is evolved which corresponds with the type of the present stage of evolution."[13]

Within the more evolved culture of Western Europe, Stephen and Mary must maintain both rigidified gender identities and disembodied sexual selves. Tenerife, however, throws these assumptions into question. White and European in an African island, Stephen and Mary find that the terms on which gender and sexuality have been constructed for them are reconfigured by their encounter with the "less evolved" Canarian "natives": just as, according to Edward Said, Western imperialists imagined the Middle East as an erotic playground (and also a place in which gender became blurred through the feminization of the "Oriental" man), Tenerife is "a place one could look for sexual experience unobtainable" in Europe.[14]

Hall sets up a complicated series of analogies and oppositions, mediated by sexology and imperialist racism (an invert's "Orientalism," to use Said's influential term), in which Tenerife, representing one set of terms, is transformed into a combination of Garden of Eden, tourist resort, and colonial plantation, and Stephen and Mary—embodying the other side of the opposition—are lesbianism's First Parents, sightseers, and blissfully unaware imperialists. Stephen's modernity in particular is predicated (as was the modernity of the high modernists such as T. S. Eliot and the U.S. imagists) on heroic self-control.[15] This focus on restraint connects directly to Krafft-Ebing, for whom the most dangerous manifestation of inversion was uncontrollable masturbation, which led inexorably to neurasthenic decline. The primitive atmosphere of Orotava allows Stephen to loosen her self-control, to give in to the primitive self that has previously surfaced only at times of extreme stress. Moreover, Tenerife's exoticism allows Mary to push beyond the sexual limits of British femininity and Stephen to experience desire in an untroubled way for the first time. But the efflorescence of lesbian desire depends upon representing Orotava and its inhabitants as actors within the script of colonial desire, reducing them to stock figures who provide the colorful backdrop for the *real* action.

Tenerife had already been the object of orientalist fantasy in Britain for centuries before Hall wrote *The Well of Loneliness*. The "Peak of Teneriffe," the highest of a series of mountains on the island, was used by Samuel Johnson as a symbol for complete self-removal from the world in his 1748 allegorical tale, *The Vision of Theodore, Hermit of Teneriffe*. In the eighteenth century, many European intellectuals believed the peak, at twelve thousand feet, to be among the tallest in the world. More importantly, the peak had been imagined as "a designation of immense height for English writers as early, at least, as the seventeenth century."[16] By the 1920s, however, Tenerife was more than an object of fantasy. It was a popular holiday spot for the well-to-do; indeed, Ramon, the gardener at the Villa del Ciprés, "spoke English passably well; he had picked it up from the numerous tenants" of the villa, and Ramon's assistant, Pedro, made extra money "driving his father's mules for the tourists" (*Well* 306).[17]

Hall's account of Orotava is a mix of ethnography, botany, light comedy, and fantasy. She lists by name a large number of different plants, flowers, and trees on the island, describes the folkways of the Orotavans, and transcribes some of the songs sung by the local people.[18] The staff at the Villa are described as mildly ridiculous; they are comic relief to the serious business of Mary and Stephen's burgeoning love affair. Hall speaks in generalizations about the island people and outlines the best way to handle the servants (speaking through Ramon), who are irrational but pleasingly predictable:

It was better to take Pedro and none other as your guide, for thus would be saved any little ill-feeling. It was better to let Concha do all the shopping—she was honest and wise as the Blessèd Virigin. It was better never to scold Esmeralda, who was sensitive on account of her squint and therefore inclined to be easily wounded. If you wounded the heart of Esmeralda, she walked out of the house and Concha walked with her. The island women were often like this; you upset them and per Dios, your dinner could burn! They would not even wait to attend to your dinner. (*Well* 306)

The Canarians linger in the background of the novel: they are upstaged by the forces of nature that define Tenerife for Hall. The most salient natural characteristic of Orotava is sensual abundance. The island is overgrown with flowers and fruit trees, fragrance and flavor. For dinner they eat "large baskets of fruit; loquats still warm from the tree that bred them, the full flavoured little indigenous bananas, oranges sweet as though dripping honey, custard apples and guavas" (*Well* 307). The garden is "bountiful" (*Well* 313) and filled with "urgent sweetness" (*Well* 308). This sense of plenty is typical of European representations of the tropics as "bountiful places offering travelers an escape from everyday realities and a temporary materialisation of what is imagined to be the 'good life.'"[19]

This bounty is implicitly and explicitly linked with sexuality and uncontrollable fertility of both land and people. As Ann Stoler has observed, "the tropics provided a site of European pornographic fantasies long before conquest was underway,"[20] and these fantasies were only strengthened by the colonial experience. In *Confessions of an Opium Eater*, Thomas DeQuincy imagined Asia as "swarming with human life," a site of "luxuriant or virulent productivity"; he characterized the "uncivilised world" through its "unlimited, ungovernable fertility."[21] The colonial enterprise entailed more than economic gain or the structured production and imposition of systems of knowledge (although it did rely upon both these things and more)—it also fed into and nourished a variety of fantasies of "the East" or "Africa" or "the South Pacific" as places powered by jungly overgrowth of all kinds. As Edward Said argues, "the East" (and here "Africa") represented "not only fecundity but sexual promise (and threat), untiring sensuality, unlimited desire, deep generative energies."[22]

What is most fascinating about the Tenerife episode is what happens with gender, particularly given Krafft-Ebing's emphatic links between societal evolution and strictly defined binary gender. Throughout *The Well of Loneliness*, as in any popular romance novel,[23] gender expression is unambiguously linked to sexual attraction: Stephen is masculine and she seeks out feminine lovers, from the bruised and Erasmic-scented Collins to the shopworn Angela Crossby to the ingenue-like Mary. But on Tenerife, gender shifts around. Mary is subtly masculinized. There is "something in the quality of Mary's youth," that appears in Orotava, "something terrible and ruthless as an unsheathed sword" that is as phallic as the scar on Stephen's cheek or the horses she rides or the swords with which she fences (*Well* 308). Along with the "unsheathed sword" of her youth, Mary takes on the role of lover rather than beloved: as Loralee MacPike points out, it is Mary who initiates almost all the physical contact between Stephen and herself, and Mary who forces the confrontation that leads to their first sexual encounter.[24] Momentarily their roles are reversed, and "Mary is the pursuer, Stephen the hesitant and fearful pursued."[25]

This reversal does not complete the metamorphosis Mary and Stephen experience on the island, however. Rather, Mary's masculinization acts as a chrysalis for the development of transformed identities, just as Stephen's masculine modernity (the cigarettes, the tailored suits, the imperiousness) is a tough carapace for the tender inverted heart within. On the one hand, as Jean Radford and Ann Rosalind Jones have argued, this interior/exterior contrast has been and remains a staple of romantic fiction:[26] the harsh, dark, aristocratic hero is rendered helpless by his desire for the blushing young heroine. But this opposition does not define the connection between Stephen and Mary, and the novel (one might say despite itself) cannot sustain the binary gendering of the lovers in the face of what Hall represents as the overwhelming fecundity of Orotava, itself gendered insistently, primitively, female.

Hence the terms of masculinity and femininity shift away from the bodies of Mary and Stephen and onto the collective body of the Orotavans. While Mary and Stephen may be gendered oppositely (that is to say, complementarily) in the metropolis—masculine/feminine, English/Celtic, aristocratic/petty bourgeois are all terms that operate on the same gendered axis in this novel—femininity is unmoored from Mary's body and translated onto the exoticized corporeal and geographic bodies of the tropics. Hall literalizes both Ann McClintock's argument that within nationalist discourse, "women are represented as the atavistic and authentic 'body' of national tradition (inert, backward-looking, and natural)"[27] and Edward Said's and Sander Gilman's careful documentation of how one of the processes of "othering" a colonized population is by imagining the men as feminized, sensual, atavistic, and indistinguishable from the natural world. But she inverts the terms: the national tradition of the Canarians is represented as atavistically and authentically female; the natural world creates a group of people indistinguishable from it. The "natives" in *The Well of Loneliness* are identified with "the heart of the island": they are as pragmatic and as romantic as children, as static and authentic as women in the national imagination (*Well* 310). For Hall, the island, its flora and fauna, and its people are all part of the lush tropical world of Orotava.

Stephen is part colonial aristocrat, part eager tourist, seeking to immerse herself in the "authentic" natural world of the island that provides the template for an unfettered sexuality.[28] This is the world that gives permission to lesbian sexuality, even as it allows Stephen and Mary (and Hall) to imagine that the sexuality permitted is not lesbian but something else, something "primitive and age-old as Nature herself" (*Well* 313). Here, Hall takes Krafft-Ebing's claim that the more primitive a culture the less it operates within the heterosexual matrix and transforms it from a condemnation to an explanation for the sexual freedom Tenerife offers. At the same time Orotava is Edenic because it reproduces itself effortlessly, and folds them into the procreative process; it is paradise because, having shunted femininity (as identified with naïveté and primitivism on the one hand, and boundless fertility on the other) onto the Canary Island(er)s themselves, Hall can imagine Stephen and Mary *without* gender—an unashamed, undifferentiated nakedness that extends beneath the skin. Now that Stephen and Mary have traversed the island, eaten its bounty, interacted with natives, and distanced themselves from the urban modernity that defines them and that they seek to escape, they can fantasize themselves as caught up in the force of Tenerife, "in the grip of Creation, of Creation's terrific urge to create" (*Well* 313).

At Orotava Stephen and Mary can imagine themselves beyond the confines of binarized gender *because of* their identities as white colonizers/ tourists *and* inverts. They can also occupy an identity that is not modern lesbianism, or inversion, but that is instead imagined as a totalizing emotional experience that exists on multiple levels, invoking parent-child dependency, the erotic exchange of lover/beloved, and the mutuality of friendship:

> And Stephen as she held the girl in her arms, would feel that indeed she was
> all things to Mary; father, mother, friend and lover, all things; and Mary all
> things to her—the child, the friend, the beloved, all things. (*Well* 314)

In a final transposition of race, gender, and sexuality Hall reverses the cause
and effect of nature and lesbian sexuality. At the beginning of the Tenerife
episode nature (which, of course, includes the people of Orotava) produces
abundance and fertility. Nature's generative powers give permission to the
engendering of Stephen and Mary's degendered (although not totally
mutual, as the quotation above indicates) relationship. By the end of their
time at Orotava, the direction of permission has changed, a process traced
in the final paragraph of the Tenerife section:

> They no longer felt desolate, hungry outcasts; unloved and unwanted,
> despised of the world. They were lovers who walked in the vineyard of life,
> plucking the warm, sweet fruits of that vineyard. Love had lifted them up as
> on wings of fire, had made them courageous, invincible, enduring. Nothing
> could be lacking to those who loved—the very earth gave of her fullest
> bounty. The earth seemed to come alive in response to the touch of their
> healthful and eager bodies—nothing could be lacking to those who loved.
> (*Well* 317)

Mary and Stephen have so absorbed the generative powers of the island
that they nourish the earth, not the other way around. Their immersion
into the "primitive" has resulted not just in suntans and fresh guavas but,
ironically, in their rendering the earth itself dependent upon them for its
abundance. In surrendering to nature, they end up mastering it.[29]

The irony here is that Stephen and Mary never quite give up their identities as moderns. Despite the metamorphoses they both experience (and
that Hall and her lover Mabel "Ladye" Batten seemed to undergo during
their visits to Tenerife), the hierarchies of colonial imperialism and the
sophisticated heteropatriarchy that is imperialism's other half remain in
palimpsest form: hazy, to be sure, but still there. Stephen is still "father and
mother" to Mary, for example. More important for my argument, the
divide between Europe and Africa, culture and nature, although reversed
and transformed, does not wholly dissolve. Stephen and Mary are not just
changed by Tenerife. Rather, the text assures us, they end up changing it:

"The earth seemed to come alive in response to the touch of their healthful and eager bodies." Although they adjust to island life, in the final analysis the natural world of the island becomes (in the logic of this sentence) shaped to their experiences and their needs, just as economic conditions demand that a beach or rain forest or mountain be physically or imaginatively shaped to fulfill the needs of its visitors, whether colonists or tourists.

What kind of visitors are Stephen and Mary? Certainly, the difference between the tourist and the colonizer is that the tourist expects to leave. The paragraph above can be read as the narrative of lesbian tourists looking through the discourse of orientalism at an "exotic" location to which they can flee from the insults of modernity. As their visit winds to a close, it is increasingly clear that Stephen is not the aristocratic colonizer but simply a consumer, renting the experience of Tenerife as she rents the Villa del Ciprés. She and Mary go on more sightseeing trips around the island and up the Peak, "trying to impress such pictures on their minds, because all things pass and they wished to remember" (*Well* 316). The more intense the experience, the more profoundly it is understood as wrapped "in a cloud of illusion and glory" (*Well* 317).

It is, of course, the very existence of the modern category of "tourist"— and of "invert"—that makes Hall's fantasy of Tenerife, and the experience of her lesbianism, possible. As Dean MacCannell astutely observes, "the best indication of the final victory of modernity . . . is not the disappearance of the nonmodern world, but its artificial preservation and reconstruction in modern society."[30] Stephen and Mary's love appears "as primitive and age-old as Nature herself" because to them, as moderns, it *is*—not because their love is so ancient but because such a belief in Nature as primitive is so acutely modern. The triumph of the urban worldview in the twentieth century cemented the idealized fantasy of "Nature" as a place to escape to, a place in which one could really be oneself and hence the *need* to maintain "unspoiled" natural sites (whose very unspoiledness is due to human intervention). Tourism is the extension of this worldview, an invention of the modern imagination in which urban and suburban subjects can experience an "authentic" nature that has been created for them to consume *as* tourists and is only successful when it disguises its constructedness.[31] That lesbianism is yoked to Krafft-Ebing's evolutionary theory of sexuality only reinforces the "naturalness" of the homologous categories of primitive, invert, and Nature.

"Tourists," McCannell argues, "are purveyors of modern values the world over."[32] And is the same not true of inverts? As *The Well of Loneliness* shows us, the category of inversion creates the narrative that Stephen can then deploy to understand her own life. Similarly, imperialist and consumerist categories of modernity create the fantasy of Tenerife as authentic, exotic, and permissive. Stephen's lesbianism may in some way authorize our own, but it also requires the gestures of white supremacy and primitivism to operate most fruitfully, just as the modernists required African masks, or the working classes, or Tahiti, to offset their own sense of anomie on the one hand and overweening desire for (self-)control on the other.

This is not to negate the power of *The Well of Loneliness*. It is a profoundly moving text, not least because Hall recognizes—however fitfully—that the authenticity of Orotava is always already a fantasy (some of the locals speak English, for example; they recognize the value of money; ultimately, they don't care about Stephen and Mary). As lesbian readers, we might find it hard to resist that fantasy; as conscious, feminist readers, we need to see it for what it is.

Notes

Thanks to Sarah Kelen, Jay Prosser, and Laura Doan for their help in polishing this piece. Thanks, too, to Kris Franklin, whose generosity of time created out of chaos the space for this work and whose generosity of spirit has been my sustenance.

1. In fact, as Leigh Gilmore shows, "obscenity" did not necessarily mean sexual explicitness; instead, it referred to any text that had the tendency, in the words of *Regina v. Hieblin* (a landmark British obscenity ruling in 1868) "to deprave and corrupt those whose minds are open to such immoral influences," Gilmore, "Obscenity, Modernity, Identity: Legalizing *The Well of Loneliness* and *Nightwood*," *Journal of the History of Sexuality* 4, no. 4 (April 1992): 606.

2. Radclyffe Hall, *The Well of Loneliness* (1928; reprint, New York: Anchor Books, 1990), p. 313 (hereafter cited in text as *Well*).

3. At the beginning of this project I thought I should acquaint myself more with Tenerife and the Canary Islands more generally. As well as reading historical and anthropological materials, I searched the World Wide Web, to see what contemporary image of the islands themselves wanted to present. The vast majority of the web-

sites I found (there were about two dozen) was geared towards tourists, touting golf courses and resorts as well as the dramatic mountain landscapes. A good online portal to information about the Canary Islands is *canary-guide.com*, 1997–99, Canary-guide s.l., 1 October 1999 <http://www.canary-guide.com>.

4. For an analysis of early colonization of the Canary Islands, see John E. Kicza, "Patterns in Early Spanish Overseas Expansion," *William and Mary Quarterly* 49, no. 2 (April 1992): 229–253.

5. Although Stephen had been banished from Morton after the revelation of her affair with Angela Crossby three years earlier, it is Raftery's death that heralds "the end of Morton" for her (*Well* 224). Later in the novel Stephen meditates on the meaning of Raftery's death in terms of the painful freedom of modernity: "Raftery was dead, there was nothing to hold her, she was free—what a terrible thing could be freedom. Trees were free when they were uprooted by the wind; ships were free when they were torn from their moorings; men were free when they were cast out of their homes—free to starve, free to perish of cold and hunger" (*Well* 234–235).

6. Terry Castle, *The Apparitional Lesbian: Female Homosexuality and Modern Culture* (New York: Columbia University Press, 1993), p. 140.

7. Ibid., p. 149.

8. Gillian Whitlock, "'Everything Is Out of Place,': Radclyffe Hall and the Lesbian Literary Tradition," *Feminist Studies* 13, no. 3 (Fall 1987): 565.

9. Ibid., p. 566.

10. Margot Gayle Backus, "Sexual Orientation in the (Post)Imperial Nation: Celticism and Inversion Theory in Radclyffe Hall's *The Well of Loneliness*," *Tulsa Studies in Women's Literature* 15, no. 2 (1993): 257.

11. Ibid., p. 255.

12. The first half deals with Stephen and Mary's experiences as ambulance drivers in WWI—a harsh reminder of the destructive powers of modernity that are healed by the premodern idyll of Orotava.

13. Richard von Krafft-Ebing, *Psychopathia Sexualis: With Especial Reference to the Antipathic Sexual Instinct. A Medico-Forensic Study*, trans. Franklin S. Klaf (New York: Bell Publishing, 1965), p. 227.

14. Edward W. Said, *Orientalism* (New York: Vintage Books, 1979), p. 190.

15. Of course, where Stephen's self-mastery is corporeal and sexual, the high modernists' self-control is rooted in the text itself.

16. Gwin J. Kolb, "*The Vision of Theodore*: Genre, Context, Early Reception," in James Engell, ed., *Johnson and His Age* (Cambridge: Harvard University Press, 1984), p. 118.

17. Hall herself had spent three months on the island in 1910 with her then lover Mabel "Ladye" Batten, a sojourn Hall's biographer Sally Cline describes as "rapturous." In her memoir of Hall, Una Troubridge mentions several trips Ladye and Hall took to the Canary Islands in the 1910s. See Troubridge's *The Life and Death of Radclyffe Hall* (London: Hammond, Hammond and Co., 1961). In a recent biography Diana Soulami characterizes the stays in Tenerife as both emotionally and professionally fulfilling for Hall and Ladye: "Both declared that they had never been so happy in their lives before [their visit] and that this was their one great love." *The Trials of Radclyffe Hall* (London: Weidenfeld and Nicolson, 1998) p. 48.

18. The Canary Islands have been an important site for ethnomusicologists, since the oral tradition lasted through to the 1960s, particularly in terms of song. At the same time that Hall was writing about Tenerife, Spanish anthropologists began collecting the ballads of the Canary Islands, so there was clearly a sense in the 1920s that Canarian culture was worth preserving (even as tourism and the lure of the peninsula were eroding it).

Strikingly, ethnographers then and now found a variety of cultural influences on the ballad tradition in the Canaries. Sources stretched as far away as sub-Saharan Africa and the Middle East, particularly Sephardic Jewish song patterns. For a discussion of Canarian balladry, see Maximiano Trapero, "Hunting for Rare Romances in the Canary Islands," *Oral Tradition* 2, no. 2–3 (1987): 514–546.

19. Brian E. M. King, *Creating Island Resorts* (London: Routledge, 1997), p. 1.

20. Ann L. Stoler, "Making Empire Respectable: The Politics of Race and Sexual Morality in 20th-Century Colonial Cultures," *American Ethnologist* 16, no. 4 (November 1989): 635.

21. Robert J. C. Young, *Colonial Desire: Hybridity in Theory, Culture, and Race* (London: Routledge, 1995), p. 98.

22. Said, *Orientalism*, p. 188.

23. For a discussion of *The Well of Loneliness* as participating in the romance genre, see Jean Radford's "An Inverted Romance: The Wall of Loneliness and Sexual Ideology" in Jean Radford, ed., *The Progress of Romance: The Politics of Popular Fiction* (London: Routledge, 1986), pp. 97–111.

24. Loralee MacPike, "Is Mary Llewellyn an Invert? The Modernist Supertext of *The Well of Loneliness*," in Elizabeth Jane Harrison and Shirley Peterson, eds., *Unmanning Modernism: Gendered Re-Readings* (Knoxville: University of Tennessee Press, 1997), pp. 73–89.

25. Ibid., p. 79.

26. Radford discusses this in the introduction to *The Progress of Romance*, cited above. See also Ann Rosalind Jones's essay "Mills and Boon Meet Feminism" in the same volume, pp. 195–218.

27. Anne McClintock, "Family Feuds: Gender, Nationalism and the Family," *Feminist Studies* 44 (Summer 1993): 364.

28. For a discussion of the meaning of "authenticity" in the tourist experience, see Dean MacCannell, *The Tourist: A New Theory of the Leisure Class* (New York: Schocken Books, 1976).

29. This process is deeply reminiscent of Ralph Waldo Emerson's approach to the natural world in his landmark essay *Nature* (1837). While "man" touches the sublimity of the Supreme Being through nature, he is ultimately nature's master, using "her" to construct meaning for himself through art, language, and social structures.

30. MacCannell, *The Tourist*, p. 8.

31. Hence the tourist's desire to experience the "back regions" of a tourist site, where things are "intimate and real" rather than for show (MacCannell 94). As MacCannell further explains, the term "tourist" is used most deprecatingly by tourists themselves, who pride themselves on getting access to "an *authentic* and *demystified* experience," on being more ethnographers than "mere" tourists (94–95).

32. MacCannell, *The Tourist*, p. 5.

18

Once More unto the Breach:
The Well of Loneliness and the Spaces of Inversion

VICTORIA ROSNER

The problem with prefaces is that they come first but inevitably are written last, so that only at the end of the writing process does the writer decide how to bring the reader into the beginning of the work. Radclyffe Hall must have experienced this problem to a prodigious degree as she considered how to preface *The Well of Loneliness*, the first English novel to present a fully realized depiction of what had recently been termed "sexual inversion." As she warned Una Troubridge, publishing "such a book might mean the shipwreck of her whole career."[1] Hall believed that in presenting the reading public with sexual inversion "as a fact of nature," her novel was attempting something truly new; as she wrote to one prospective publisher, "Nothing of the kind has ever been attempted before in fiction."[2] How to introduce such a work to her readers?

The *Well* opens with two pieces of front matter, as well as a dedication.[3] The first, entitled "Commentary," tries to ward off critics with the endorsement of a respected authority. Hall had invited psychologist Havelock Ellis's comments in the hope of preventing the novel from being read, as she wrote to Ellis, as a "salacious diversion."[4] In his remarks Ellis briefly attests to the truthfulness and tact with which the author set forth her primary subject matter: "one particular aspect of sexual life as it exists among us today."[5] Hall also wrote a preface of her own, an "Author's Note." Contrary to what one might expect, here Hall ignores the issue of sexuality in the novel. After a boilerplate statement that all characters in the work are "purely imaginary," Hall disclaims further:

> A motor ambulance unit of British women drivers did very fine service upon the Allied front in France during the later months of the war, but although the unit mentioned in this book, of which Stephen Gordon becomes a member, operates in much the same area, it has never had any existence save in the author's imagination.

Taken together, Ellis and Hall's prefaces are a bit disorienting, for they point the reader in opposing directions. Set against Ellis, Hall's note diffuses the novel's source of controversy, shifting the reader's attention away from sexual matters and toward questions of verisimilitude. There's more to this story than the scandalous tale of an invert, the author seems to be pointing out. The two prefaces also disagree about the novel's relation to the real world; for Ellis the *Well* is possessed of "a notable psychological and sociological significance"; for Hall it is, "purely imaginary."

To the contemporary reader, both prefaces may seem inadequate. Ellis praises the representation of "sexual life" in a novel famously lacking in sex. Hall insists that the ambulance unit is her own invention, while in fact her account is drawn in spirit and detail from the historical record. Hall's preface turns the reader's expectations away from sexuality and toward what has been substituted for that absent but anticipated subject, toward what might be called the spaces of inversion. In lieu of actually showing us physical love between women, Hall locates historically the site of this emerging sexual identity in the early years of the twentieth century, finding it not just on the World War I battlefields but also in the gay bars of Paris, in Natalie Barney's Paris salon, on the island of Tenerife, and in other locations. As the *Well* will itself demonstrate, creating the space for same-sex desire is as much the condition of its possibility as the sexological explanation provided by Ellis. In the space between Ellis's reference to "sexual life" in a work that omits sex and Hall's repudiation of the ambulance unit she will anatomize fully, the hide-and-seek of representing what had been thought unrepresentable takes shape.

The *Well* has often been read as a somewhat conservative work, depicting a world in which inverts are punished for their desires. While indis-

putably conservative in many regards, including its conventional style and
form, as well as its inability to imagine a lasting love relationship for its central character, the *Well* is at its most inventive with its assertion that uncon-
ventional gender and sexual identities are best given expression in uncon-
ventional spaces.[6] Victorian domestic spaces such as Morton, the Gordon
family seat in the *Well*, often served to contain or control sexuality, but the
Well articulates an alternative spatial rhetoric, one that offers a sexual poetics of emancipation through the use of a variety of spatially transgressive
strategies, including renovation, squatting, tourism, and demolition—a
veritable guide to the creation of what would now be termed queer space.
Through both seeking out and creating spaces of inversion, the *Well* attends
to the production of such space and can be usefully brought to bear on the
contemporary project that Elspeth Probyn advances: "to think about how
space presses upon bodies differently; to realize the singularities of space
that are produced as specific bodies press against space."[7]

By connecting the expression of inversion to decidedly post-Victorian
spaces, Hall affiliates herself with more categorically modernist writers and
artists.[8] An evidently modernist work such as Virginia Woolf's *A Room of
One's Own*, published in the same year as the *Well*, shares with it the
assumption that embarking on a self-consciously modern life requires a
change in the way space, and domestic space in particular, is organized and
allocated.[9] Reading the *Well* spatially allows us not only to make sense of its
careful recreation of Victorian mores but also to see how those concerns are
finally subordinated to a new impulse to clear the ground for new definitions of gender and sexuality. What renders these spaces modern, I would
argue, is that they provide a place in the public social order for the figure of
the invert, made newly legible to heterosexual society by the contemporary
sexological discourses in which the *Well* is so explicitly invested.

The first half of the *Well* is set exclusively in Stephen's family home,
Morton, the most retrograde of settings, while the second half moves
among a host of locations, each of which contributes to the project of quite
literally "constructing" the identity of the female invert. If Morton's gender-
segregated rooms force Stephen to wander unplaced, "between the
spheres," the spaces of the book's second half do the opposite: they often
actively encourage or at least willingly overlook the expression of female
masculinity or of same-sex desire between women. Traditional domestic
spaces such as those at Morton prove incapable of adequately domesticat-

ing Stephen's sexuality; rather, the values promulgated by such spaces are threatened by the insurgence of her same-sex desire. In these spaces Stephen is able to consolidate her masculine identity rather than sending it into hiding.

In short, the *Well* develops its representation of sexual inversion by first establishing the hegemony and near-ubiquity of heterosexual space and then going in search of spaces of reconceived domesticity that encourage greater sexual freedom. Far from acting as a simple backdrop to events, these are spaces that play a direct role in inventing the public and private identity of the invert. Just as Morton is a rigidly heterosexual space, the locations where Hall sends her heroine in the second half of the novel are spaces of inversion, based on actual places. As such, the *Well*, a work termed "purely imaginary" by its author, contains a documentary account of various spaces of inversion in England and France in the first part of the twentieth century. I begin this essay with an analysis of the spatial organization of sexuality put forward by country houses such as Morton and go on to show how in the second half of the novel, after her eviction from Morton, Stephen constructs and inhabits alternative spaces that enable her to come into her own sexuality and gender identity. Between Ellis's preface and Hall's is a fair preparation for the novel after all: a move from sexuality into history that defines the two interrelated focal points of the *Well*.

The setting for the first half of the *Well* is the Gordon family home, an old-fashioned dwelling that provides uneasy shelter for Stephen, its unquestionably modern heir. Morton is an extraordinarily nostalgic space, harking back to the classic traditions of English country houses, homes that were built to preserve strict gender divisions.[10] The novel begins with an extended description of the house and its grounds: "Not very far from Upton-on-Severn—between it, in fact, and the Malvern Hills—stands the country seat of the Gordons of Bramley; well-timbered, well-cottaged, well-fenced and well-watered, having, in this latter respect, a stream that forks in exactly the right position to feed two large lakes in the grounds."[11] The forked stream and two lakes imply that gender is formally presented by Morton as a choice between two opposite positions, with Stephen somehow caught between these two spaces: "Then that part of Stephen that she still shared with Morton would know what it was to feel terribly lonely, like a soul that wakes up to find itself wandering, unwanted, *between the spheres*" (35, emphasis mine). Stephen is crucially caught between the spheres of gender, a lonely space indeed.

As the novel's first sentence forecasts, Stephen's dilemma is all about being in-between. Gender dysphoric (as we might now say) from childhood, she feels trapped and out of place in her woman's body.[12] The text explains Stephen as an "invert," a blanket term that broadly referred to cases of one sex taking on the appearance or behavior of the other. For Sandra Gilbert and Susan Gubar, Hall's subject is a "congenitally masculine girl born to a father who confirmed her inversion by treating her as the son he wanted."[13] Stephen's troubles are caused by her feeling that she is neither one sex nor the other but some combination of the two—the classic dilemma of the invert.[14] Yet as the *Well* makes clear, the world that Stephen lives in is literally built around a clear division between the genders, without accommodation for any in-between position.

This binary structure of gendered space was hardly Hall's invention; it was typical of English country-house architecture.[15] Floor plans for such homes often show the house divided into male and female zones, with designations such as "Young Ladies' Entrance," "Bachelors' Stairs," "Gentleman's Room," "Gentleman's Dressing Room," and innumerable other variations on the theme, carefully demarcating who belonged where. Acute specialization and segregation in the division of space characterized the country houses. Writers on architecture and interior design in the late nineteenth century describe gendered staircases, closets, bedrooms, and dressing rooms. Even those rooms not apparently marked by gender on floor plans, such as the billiard room, were often implicitly intended for men or women only. The gender divisions in Morton's interior design are most clearly evinced by the opposition between Sir Philip and Lady Anna's rooms, a study and a drawing room, respectively. Both accord with the nineteenth-century design tenets expressed by influential architects and designers such as Robert Edis and Robert Kerr. The drawing room is a shrine to upper-class femininity, and Lady Anna is its choicest ornament: "In the vast drawing-room so beautifully proportioned, so restfully furnished in old polished walnut, so redolent of beeswax and orris root and violets—all alone in its vastness would Anna be sitting, with her white hands folded and idle" (79). This room is Lady Anna's feminine stronghold, the place to which she righteously calls Stephen to banish her from Morton.

Anna sits alone in this scented shrine to femininity because her husband and daughter are always in the study together, living the life of the mind, which in this house pertains only to the life of the male body. Sir Philip's study is squarely within the country-house tradition, presented as a private space above all else, a sanctuary within the home that is dedicated to one person, generally the master of the house. Studies were the house's nerve center, where servants were hired and fired, sensitive business transacted, and important papers kept. Sir Philip's study is described as large, grave, and quiet. It has a desk with a locked drawer that contains a gun, and many bookcases, at least one of which can also be locked. It contains writing materials and a distinguished library—"one of the finest libraries in England" (26)—as well as an old armchair, in which its owner is generally seated. At Morton the drawing room and the study form the architectural binary templates for gender between which Stephen is expected to choose.

When Stephen reaches the age at which she is expected to start acting "like a lady," she must move into a drawing room, like her mother, or a study, like her father; predictably, she seeks the latter. Stephen and her father sit together for hours in the study, discussing "the feel and the smell and the essence of books" (86), an odor that provides a sensual alternative to Lady Anna's beeswax and violets. Lady Anna is excluded from this space by the lack of education that is also the basis for her husband's affections: she is "very far from learned—that, indeed, was why Sir Philip had loved her" (80). Stephen's deviant gender behavior is depicted as growing out of her unwavering identification with her father, and the study is key to that identification. This room serves as the mold for Stephen's masculine identity: a masculinity that in its architectural inception is always already mismatched and unhoused. Against the backdrop of gendered architectural space, Stephen's ambiguous status is accentuated, but also completely submerged, as her inversion becomes her family's deepest secret. Her misfit status is underlined by her exclusion from the secret that underwrites the study's authority. For Sir Philip's study contains a secret that is essential to Stephen: a hidden collection of books, which her father can only read in private. "Alone in that grave-looking, quiet study, he would unlock a drawer in his ample desk, and would get out a slim volume recently acquired, and would read and reread it in the silence. The author was a German, Karl Heinrich Ulrichs" (26). Ulrichs was the first to describe the phenomenon of sexual inversion and, as Philip reads, he makes tiny marginal notes about his daughter. Thus Stephen's marginal gender status finds a textual mirror in actual marginalia, with the study, masculinity's stronghold, chosen as the repository for a secret that undermines the very authority of the space.

The secret of Stephen's inversion is one that Philip is at pains to keep all his life. After his death Stephen is discovered by her mother to have fallen in love with another woman and on that basis is exiled from Morton. Leaving Anna in the drawing room, Stephen retreats to her father's study to think things over.

> As though drawn there by some strong natal instinct, Stephen went straight to her father's study; and she sat in the old arm-chair that had survived him; then she buried her face in her hands. . . . Getting up, she wandered about the room, touching its kind and familiar objects; stroking the desk, examining a pen, grown rusty from long disuse as it lay there; then she opened a little drawer in the desk and took out the key of her father's locked bookcase. . . . She had never examined this special book-case, and she could not have told why she suddenly did so. . . . Then she noticed that on a shelf near the bottom was a row of books standing behind the others; the next moment she had one of these in her hand, and was looking at the name of the author: Krafft Ebing—she had never heard of that author before. (203–204)

Inscribed in the pages of what is most likely *Psychopathia Sexualis*, Stephen finds her own name and quickly realizes the implications. This troubling inheritance, bequeathed not by a death but by an eviction, launches Stephen's adult life. Esther Newton writes that Stephen is necessarily denied "patriarchal legitimacy" because she is a daughter and not a son; whatever else she inherits from her father, "she cannot be his true heir."[16] The books which are all the inheritance that Stephen can claim confirm what she has sensed all along: Morton was not built to house her. But even after leaving Morton, Stephen clings to the architectural template for masculinity that Morton has shown her: the study and the secrets it keeps.

In spite of her fidelity to this model, the architecture of gender offered by Morton proves an inadequate base for Stephen's nascent identity in her new, independent home. The novel moves directly from the study at Morton to Stephen's first study in London. Like her father's, Stephen's study is a working room, as she has chosen to become a novelist. Unlike her father's study, however, Stephen's first study is ugly. After a fruitless day's writing, she regards her surroundings. "It came upon her with a slight sense of shock that she was seeing this room for the first time, and that everything in it was abnormally ugly" (233). Attempting to imitate her father, Stephen produces a bad copy and realizes that Morton itself is an inadequate model for the work of self-invention she must now undertake. "Stephen had tried to feed her inspiration upon herbage, the kind, green herbage of Morton" (234), but she finally admits that such food has never nourished either her creativity or her sense of her own identity.

Having realized that her study is ugly, Stephen abruptly decides to forsake England and move to Paris. In the search for a place where Stephen can more visibly construct her emerging sexual identity, the Paris of her time is an obvious and excellent choice. Under English law male homosexuality was illegal, but the Napoleonic code of France did not ban homosexual practices. The city was occasionally referred to as "Paris-Lesbos" because of its reputed lesbian population, and same-sex desire was considered moderately fashionable in upper-class Parisian circles (though laws against female cross-dressing were still enforced).[17] Paris was far from being a paradise for lesbians, who risked their families, social standing, and livelihood by making their sexual preferences known, but to a greater degree than London, Paris provided a space for the potential expression of same-sex desire. This context is communicated to Stephen by her friend and fellow invert Brockett, who quietly installs within his guided tour of Paris hints of a submerged inverts' history, hints that "stirred [Stephen's] imagination" (240). Living in Paris opens possibilities unavailable at home.

Stephen's most important discovery of a sexually transgressive space in Paris comes with her first visit to Valérie Seymour's salon. Like all the spaces Stephen explores in the second half of the novel, this salon has a specific historical referent: Natalie Barney's much-celebrated salon in Left Bank Paris, which Barney began in 1909 and continued for decades. Barney took full advantage of the freedoms that the city allowed; as she wrote, "Paris has always seemed to me the only city where you can live and express yourself as you please."[18] Her salon attracted well-known writers, scholars, and artists from France and America, including Radclyffe Hall, Renée Vivien, Mata Hari, Isadora Duncan, Gertrude Stein, and Colette.[19] Amateur theatricals were staged in Barney's garden for the enjoyment of a largely female, bohemian audience.[20] Shari Benstock describes Natalie Barney as "the most active and candid lesbian of her day,"[21] and the salon was overtly geared toward the interests of the Paris lesbian community.

Hall's recreation of the Barney salon exudes aesthetic decadence: rich scents mingle in the air, antiques and musical instruments are scattered about, and gossip abounds. For the self-hating Stephen, such a space presents possibilities that both disturb and entice. Valérie's rooms offer a fully developed alternative to the domesticity of Morton. Morton's grace and order present gender as a tidy binary, but Valérie's rooms offer "splendid disorder" and are "blissfully unkempt," a gorgeous mess that permits gender categories to blend and blur, a place where such blurring seems the rule rather than the taboo exception. "For Valérie, placid and self-assured, created an atmosphere of courage; everyone felt very normal and brave when they gathered together at Valérie Seymour's" (352). This atmosphere repels Stephen to a certain extent, yet so impressed is she by Valérie that during that first visit to her salon, Stephen spontaneously decides to move permanently to Paris. Valérie recommends a house for Stephen on the rue Jacob, the street where Barney's salon was actually held (Hall has relocated Valérie's salon to the quai Voltaire). Benstock writes of the important specificity of a rue Jacob address for Barney: "It was located in the heart of the intellectual and artistic quarter of Paris, a place whose traditions are associated with the classical divisions of learning . . . rather than with inherited titles and property."[22] Life on the rue Jacob for Stephen means forsaking the beloved traditions of aristocratic Morton to begin to build her own traditions. By having Stephen do so at Natalie Barney's address, Hall draws on the cultural history of the Paris lesbian community and acknowledges its existence. Moreover, by placing her heroine within that history, she quietly connects Stephen to views at odds with Stephen's own attitudes toward her sexuality. Living in her father's house, Stephen may see herself as "maimed, hideously maimed and ugly" (204), but once she comes to dwell in the house of Barney in Paris, a possible happiness and the semblance of a stable independent life slowly gather momentum around her.

Rather than build a new structure, Stephen renovates the old house on the rue Jacob, the age of which is implied by its lack of bathrooms, stone staircase, and ruined garden temple. The renovation design is all her own, as she seeks out "one of those very rare architects who refrain from thrusting their views on their clients" (249), an architect who carries out Stephen's plan to "preserve the spirit of the place intact, despite alterations" (250). This plan finds a parallel in Stephen's attempts to model her masculine identity on her father's, though necessarily with "alterations." Her effort in both cases is directed at taking older forms unsuited to modern life (the country gentleman, the ancient, ruined house) and updating them to render them suitable for her own use. The study is the first room to be planned; as at Morton, it is the symbolic center of the house. While Stephen, imitating her father, chooses a study for her main living space, she designs it after her own tastes, in the Empire style: "She decided to have an Empire study with grey walls and curtains of Empire green, for she loved the great roomy writing tables that had come into being with the first Napoleon" (250). The Empire style, which combines classical and imperial elements, well embodies Stephen's strong, even military sense of her masculinity, but the invocation of Napoleon (like her childhood identification with the naval commander Nelson, who lost an eye and an arm in battle) casts her once again in the role of a man *manqué*. In Stephen's repeated casting of the invert as "maimed," we can trace her identification with both Nelson and Napoleon: hypermasculine, yet physically somehow lacking—a role that seems within her reach.

Stephen's renovation is aimed at producing a negotiated stance, simultaneously looking forward and looking back. It is inspired by Valérie's self-acceptance of her sexual identity, yet it renders Stephen no more content with her perceived sexual abnormality. It holds Stephen's first successful study, the appropriated architectural crucible of her emergent masculine identity, but that study continues to be built around the closeted sexological texts bequeathed by her father, deferring to a heterosexual taboo.

Stephen also rejects, at least initially, the Paris community but finds community again, despite herself, through wartime service as World War I enters the *Well*. From the moment that war is declared in the novel, Stephen's sense of manliness propels her toward serving her country. As the novel demonstrates, traditionally feminine women have defined methods of national service: they can sacrifice their sons, like Stephen's housekeeper Pauline; they can volunteer their homes, like Stephen's mother; or they can nurse, like her childhood friend Violet. Stephen rejects all these options, seeking a masculine engagement in the war:

> all that was male in her make-up seemed to grow more aggressive. . . . She was nothing but a freak abandoned on a kind of no-man's-land at this moment of splendid national endeavour. England was calling her men into

battle, her women to the bedsides of the wounded and dying, and between these two chivalrous, surging forces she, Stephen, might well be crushed out of existence. (267)

Stephen is once again caught between the spheres of gender, with her secret gender inclinations pulling in one direction and her official gender affiliation in another. Hall's assignment of Stephen to "a kind of no-man's-land" makes an explicit comparison between the unassigned, constantly shifting place where Stephen stands and the actual battlegrounds of the war in which no-man's-land is the war's contested terrain. The struggle to claim and define these plots of ground becomes Stephen's own battle, as she fights for a space that will take account of her difference. In the context of wartime, to stand in no-man's-land means that rather than being invisible, as she was at Morton, Stephen is tremendously visible. She is a target, but at least she has an official location, in a new, third kind of space.

 Morton never offered a third space of any kind, but World War I does proffer such an alternative, for Stephen, as for many women involved in the war effort. Hall asserts that the war created valuable openings for women like Stephen, who suddenly were offered a socially acceptable outlet for their masculine feelings:

> For as though gaining courage from the terror that is war, many a one who was even as Stephen, had crept out of her hole and come into the daylight, come into the daylight and faced her country: "Well, here I am, will you take me or leave me?" And England had taken her, asking no questions—she was strong and efficient, she could fill a man's place. (271)

The masculine qualities that were lifelong liabilities for women like Stephen are suddenly transformed into assets, as national priorities and individual desires are suddenly, albeit briefly, brought into alignment. As in the description of Stephen's location as a "no-man's-land," the image of women coming into the daylight is one of enhanced visibility. The war allowed masculine women to become permissibly visible, even speakable. It praised women for assuming roles and activities previously assigned exclusively to men, as factory workers, administrators, and ambulance drivers.[23]

Within the range of positions that women broke into through war work, it might fairly be said that none was more restricted than service at the front. The physical site of "no-man's-land" was above all no place for women—it was considered far too dangerous for anyone but (male) soldiers. Yet the front was where many women, emphatically including Stephen, wanted to be. "Stephen was obsessed by her one idea, which was, willy-nilly, to get out to the front" (270). Gilbert and Gubar argue that the war front was, oddly enough, a much better place for women like Stephen than the home front: "For many women, but perhaps in particular for women . . . whose refusal to identify with conventional 'femininity' had always made gender an issue for them, the war facilitated . . . an unprecedented transcendence of the profounder constraints imposed by traditional sex roles."[24] This certainly turns out to be the case for Stephen, who finds at the front a sense of purpose and community previously unavailable to her.

Stephen makes her way to the French front as a member of Mrs. Breakspeare's British ambulance unit. This episode is of course the subject of the *Well*'s preface, with its disclaimer of any real-world basis for the ambulance unit depicted in the novel. But the Breakspeare Unit is modeled very closely, in both substance and spirit, on the record of the Hackett-Lowther Ambulance Unit, the only British women's unit to serve on the front in France. Hall's choice of the unit as a model no doubt sprung from her friendship with the unit's co-commander, Barbara "Toupie" Lowther. Hall met Lowther around 1910, and their friendship continued intermittently through the late twenties. Lowther regaled Hall with tales of her adventures in the war, and Hall was envious of Lowther's achievements, having herself been unable to take an active part in the conflict.[25]

Leaving aside the serendipity of Hall and Lowther's personal relationship, there were a number of reasons why the Hackett-Lowther Unit offered an appealing model for the *Well*'s war scenes.[26] The service performed by an ambulance unit on the war's front lines is comparable to Stephen's social negotiations on the home front. A wartime ambulance unit exists to rescue the injured men with whom Stephen identifies, as she repeatedly describes inverts as "maimed." The war zone is where maimed men belong: they are generated by the practice of war and are intrinsic to it: no able-bodied man even appears in this part of the novel; all are reified into wounded and maimed bodies needing transport. In fact, men as individuals seem nonexistent in this section of the novel, as the front is presented as a female world. Thus, once she arrives on the French front, Stephen finds herself doubly at home for the first time in her life, identified both with the members of the unit and with the men whom she rescues.

Records of the Hackett-Lowther Unit suggest that the problems and challenges confronted by both its leader and its members resonate with Stephen's experience. Lowther organized the volunteer unit around a single ambition: "to form an ambulance section on exactly the same lines, subject to the same conditions as the allied men's sections."[27] The Hackett-Lowther Unit, which served at the end of the war in 1917–18, became the only women's unit attached to the French army to serve at the front. Unlike the women ambulance drivers serving in Britain, the Hackett-Lowther was affiliated with the French army itself and not with the Red Cross. Its members replaced actual soldiers and were given the same wages as the French *poilus*. Thus, more than perhaps any other women active in the war zone, the members of the Hackett-Lowther were serving as honorary men, an important specificity for Hall's purposes.

Moreover, Toupie Lowther's own background and gender identity seemed to resemble those of Stephen Gordon. Like Stephen, Lowther had an aristocratic background (she was the oldest daughter of an earl) and loved athletics, particularly fencing and tennis. Tall and muscular, Lowther cultivated a masculine appearance: an apocryphal story frequently repeated about her describes how crossing the French-Italian border she was arrested for impersonating a man, and on her return journey was again arrested, this time for impersonating a woman. Lowther's gender ambiguity could seem threatening to law and order, but in World War I she found acceptance from forces that at any other time would have deemed her a threat. For Lowther, the war was "the high point of her life."[28] Unsurprisingly, she does not allude to the sexual preferences of members of her unit in her brief official memoir, but she does give some sense of how both she and the unit seemed to challenge the army's ideas about women and soldiering, as in the description of her confrontation with one high Army official who was blocking the unit's transfer to the front lines. Bursting into the commandant's office, she finds him surrounded by his entire, male staff. She recalls, "They were all seated at various tables staring at me and I am sure regarding me as some extraordinary bold freak who had dared under some mad impulse to beard [the commandant] in his den." Lowther succeeded largely because of her perceived freakishness—the commandant hardly knew how to understand her and what she wanted, much less how to refuse her repeated requests to go to the front. The unit was eventually sent to the Compiègne front, where Stephen's unit is also headquartered, after which several of its members were awarded the Croix de Guerre, a citation Stephen also receives.

Memoirs by some of the unit's twenty-one members accord closely in spirit and detail with Hall's Breakspeare Unit. Mary Dexter, an American woman serving with the unit, wrote to her mother about the unit's quarters:

> Yesterday we moved, bag and baggage, to the château where we are billeted, about two kilomètres away. It is a typical French house, large and square, standing among poplars. . . . In our château we have only a moderate log fire in the dining room on very cold days—and the rest of the house is exactly like outdoors, only even damper. There are broken panes of glass in the windows.[29]

In her description of the Breakspeare Unit's housing, Hall conforms exactly to the specifications of Dexter's descriptions but adds additional layers of significance:

> The room had once been the much prized salon of a large and prosperous villa in Compiègne, but now the glass was gone from its windows; there remained only battered and splintered shutters which creaked eerily in the bitter wind of a March night in 1918. The walls of the salon had fared little better than its windows, their brocade was detached and hanging, while a recent rainstorm had lashed through the roof making ugly splotches on the delicate fabric—a dark stain on the ceiling was perpetually dripping. The remnants of what had once been a home, little broken tables, an old photograph in a tarnished frame, a child's wooden horse, added to the infinite desolation of this villa that now housed the Breakspeare Unit—a Unit composed of Englishwomen, that had been serving in France just over six months, attached to the French Army Ambulance Corps. (277)

The location, the house, the broken windows, and the damp cold are all drawn from the historical record, but Hall goes further in depicting the unit's headquarters as a ravaged domestic scene, where everyday family life has been blown out of existence. The devastated château reveals the potential fragility of stately homes that, like Morton, uphold seemingly timeless social and sexual mores. Morton evicted Stephen, whose desires could not be housed by its traditional forms. But the comparably luxe French villa, blasted apart by war, provides the meeting-ground for Stephen and her chief love interest in the novel. In this ruined home Stephen meets her lover, Mary Llewellyn, as the instability of the spaces of war allows her—as the unit's name signals—to break out of the spheres of gender between which she has thus far been caught. The destroyed salon suggests that because the war has destroyed domesticity, it has opened a space for women like Stephen to begin to create relationships that such domesticity made impossible and to construct a new way of life built around these new relationships and new subjects of modernity.

In the *Well*, the woman who leads the Breakspeare Unit suggests that the emotional stresses of life on the front can itself foster lesbianism. She calls Stephen to her quarters to tell her to drive with other partners than Mary: "These are strenuous times, and such times are apt to breed many emotions which are purely fictitious. . . . I'm sure you'll agree with me, Miss Gordon, in thinking it our duty to discourage anything in the nature of an emotional friendship, such as I fancy Mary Llewellyn is on the verge of feeling for you" (289). Hall implies, here and elsewhere, that the war provides both special opportunities for inverts to express their natures and also the space for same-sex intimacies to develop.[30] Like Valérie Seymour's salon in Paris, the château and surrounding war zone are spaces that make the expression of transgressive gendered and sexual identity allowable—and even encouraged. And again, Hall brings lesbian history to light to show that although Stephen may be unique in literature, her real-life fellows are more ubiquitous than the heterosexual world may imagine. The novel brings together two seemingly incommensurate topographies: that of the opposing spheres of gender and that of the opposing trenches of war. Between both of these rigidly defined and oppositional spaces, Hall suggests, is a third space—no man's land—which is dangerous, constantly shifting, and definitionally unstable.

Although I cannot discuss them in detail here, a number of other such permissive spaces figure in the novel's final section, including the villa at Orotava where Stephen and Mary spend their first night together as lovers,[31] the studio at which Negro spirituals are sung, and the gay bars of Paris that Stephen and Mary visit. Gilbert and Gubar have argued about these spaces that "the only social milieu within which Stephen and Mary can shed the secrecy of their lives is depicted as ghettoized and therefore sadly limited and self-destructive."[32] But the novel's progression from the rigid hierarchy of gender at nineteenth-century Morton to the excitement and gender anarchy of a diverse range of spaces offers the spectacle of the invert, newly visible to the public gaze (if primarily through medical and juridical frameworks), as part of a progression away from self-destruction. When Stephen sits in a gay bar, depressed over the tragic decrepitude of her fellows, she is chided by a friend with words that seem to be "speaking her thoughts": "You are wrong, very wrong—this is only the beginning. . . . From their very degradation that spirit will rise up to demand of the world compassion and justice. . . . There is no destruction" (390).[33] Rather than simply a scene of self-destruction and limitations, the bar (like the war front) is also an important site of contest and of change, a space that has only recently been carved out from the heterosexual monopoly. The notion of a ghetto put forward by Gilbert and Gubar implies that the invert community has simply been relegated to society's margins, where they can be subordinated and ignored. Rather, locations of community such as the bar, or Valérie Seymour's salon, or even the headquarters of the Breakspeare Unit (all chosen, I would argue, for their links to the historical record of real communities) are engaged in the project of expanding the range of possible gender and sexual identities and, by extension, calling into question the dualistic gender scheme represented in exaggerated form by life at Morton.

The *Well* is, in a very real sense, a novel about the shifting location of inversion in early twentieth-century England. Having worked its way from the tight confines of the locked bookshelf in the study through a diverse array of more accommodating spaces, inversion has literally moved out of the closet (as the first studies were called)[34] and into the street, where its subjects can recognize each other and be recognized more widely. Inversion, Hall suggests, is too big a secret to remain safe with the doctors, or the fathers: it will collapse the boundaries that seek to render it marginal or abject and in so doing will undermine the stability of architecture itself. In the novel's final scene, the community of inverts populating Stephen's imagination pushes through every obstacle toward open space: "They were everywhere now, cutting off her retreat; neither bolts nor bars would avail to save her. The walls fell down and crumbled before them; at their suffering the walls fell and crumbled: 'We are coming, Stephen—we are still coming on, and our name is legion—you dare not disown us!'" (437). The cry of the inverts is powerful enough to knock down the walls that, at places such as Morton, serve to uphold and inculcate the gender binary. The revelation of the inverts' existence undermines the architecture of gender and clears the ground for spaces yet to be built.

Notes

I gratefully acknowledge the enthusiastic assistance of the librarians of the Imperial War Museum in London. This essay also benefited greatly from the careful reading and insights of Douglas Brooks, Laura Frost, and Jay Prosser.

1. Una Troubridge, *The Life and Death of Radclyffe Hall* (London: Hammond, Hammond & Co., 1961), p. 82.

2. Radclyffe Hall to Newman Flower, 16 April 1928. Qtd. in Sally Cline, *Radclyffe Hall: A Woman Called John* (London: John Murray, 1997), p. 235.

3. In the first edition of the novel, published by Jonathan Cape in 1928, an additional authorial inclusion was a brief epigraph on the title page: "nothing extenuate, nor set down aught in malice" (William Shakespeare, *Othello* V:ii).

4. Radclyffe Hall to Havelock Ellis, 18 April 1928. Qtd. in Cline, *Radclyffe Hall*, p. 236. It is not clear whether it was Hall's or Cape's decision to print Ellis's comments as a preface to the *Well*.

5. Ellis's original wording had been more explicit: "various aspects of sexual inversion," but this was changed at the publisher's request, since it could be interpreted as referring to male homosexuality, an illegal act. Cline, *Radclyffe Hall*, pp. 237–238.

6. In a larger sense, this argument can be seen as an extension of Stephen Kern's claim that between the years 1880 and 1918 the perception of space was marked by what Kern calls "the leveling of traditional spatial hierarchies" (8). *The Culture of Time and Space 1880–1928* (Cambridge: Harvard University Press, 1983).

7. Elspeth Probyn, "Lesbians in Space: Gender, Sex, and the Structure of Missing," *Gender, Place and Culture* 2, no. 1 (1995): 83. See also Gill Valentine, "(Re)Negotiating the 'Heterosexual Street': Lesbian Productions of Space," in Nancy Duncan, ed., *BodySpace* (London and New York: Routledge, 1996), p. 146–155; and Sally R. Munt, *Heroic Desire: Lesbian Identity and Cultural Space* (New York: New York University Press, 1998).

8. For another discussion of the *Well*'s modernist aspects, see Loralee MacPike, "Is Mary Llewellyn an Invert? The Modernist Supertext of *The Well of Loneliness*," in Elizabeth Jane Harrison and Shirley Peterson, eds., *Unmanning Modernism: Gendered Re-Readings* (Knoxville: The University of Tennessee Press, 1997), pp. 73–89.

9. Jane Marcus discusses other aspects of the *Well*'s influence on *A Room of One's Own* in "Sapphistory: Narration as Lesbian Seduction in *A Room of One's Own*," in *Virginia Woolf and the Languages of Patriarchy* (Bloomington: Indiana University Press, 1987), pp. 163–188.

10. According to Jean Radford, Hall's depiction of Morton was also a way of conforming to the conventions of romantic fiction in the period. Jean Radford, "An Inverted Romance: "*The Well of Loneliness* and Sexual Ideology," in Radford, ed., *The Progress of Romance: The Politics of Popular Fiction* (London: Routledge & Kegan Paul, 1986), pp. 97–112.

11. Radclyffe Hall, *The Well of Loneliness* (1928; reprint, New York: Anchor Books, 1990), p. 11. Further page references to this work will be given parenthetically in the text.

12. The *Well* has long been read by critics as a lesbian novel—as *the* lesbian novel; indeed, the cover of my edition dubs it "A 1920s Classic of Lesbian Fiction." However, Jay Prosser offers a compelling reading of the *Well* as a transsexual narrative. As Prosser states, "Read in situ, as a fictional consequence of inversion's case histories, *The Well* comes into focus as not only not a lesbian novel, not only our first and most canonical transsexual novel, but as a narrative that itself contributed to the formalization of transsexual subjectivity." For Prosser, Stephen Gordon's persistent male-identification, her failed lesbian relations, and her yearning for a man's body all place the narrative squarely in a transsexual context—before that term was invented. (The word "lesbian" is also absent from the text.) For the purposes of my discussion, I will use the terminology the book itself relies on, that of the "invert." Jay Prosser, *Second Skins: The Body Narratives of Transsexuality* (New York: Columbia University Press, 1998), p. 140.

13. Sandra M. Gilbert and Susan Gubar, *No Man's Land: The Place of the Woman Writer in the Twentieth Century*, vol. 2, *Sexchanges* (New Haven and London: Yale University Press, 1989), p. 354.

14. Esther Newton writes that "the true invert was a being between categories, neither man nor woman." Esther Newton, "The Mythic Mannish Lesbian: Radclyffe Hall and the New Woman," p. 97 in this volume.

15. The other structuring binary of the country houses was class; the servant's quarters typically formed almost a separate house, also divided along gendered lines. Thus, with Stephen's early crush on Collins the housemaid, she is violating two architecturally entrenched divisions, of both gender and class. For example, "ladies'" rooms on the family side are distinguished from "women's" rooms on the servant side. Sonja Ruehl considers the connections between sexuality and class in the *Well* in "Inverts and Experts: Radclyffe Hall and the Lesbian Identity," in Judith Newton and Deborah Rosenfelt, eds., *Feminist Criticism and Social Change: Sex, Class and Race in Literature and Culture* (New York: Methuen, 1985), pp. 165–180, esp. 170–174.

16. Esther Newton, "The Mythic Mannish Lesbian: Radclyffe Hall and the New Woman," *Signs* 9, no. 4 (1984): 569.

17. Shari Benstock, *Women of the Left Bank* (London: Virago, 1987), p. 47.

18. Elyse Blankley, "Return to Mytilène: Renée Vivien and the City of Women," in Susan Merrill Squier, ed., *Women Writers and the City* (Knoxville: University of Tennessee Press, 1984), p. 47.

19. Karla Jay, *The Amazon and the Page: Natalie Clifford Barney and Renée Vivien* (Bloomington: Indiana University Press, 1988), p. 25.

20. Blankley, "Return to Mytilène," p. 48.

21. Benstock, *Women of the Left Bank*, p. 8.

22. Ibid., p. 80.

23. Such change met with great opposition. Jenny Gould writes, "Women in military organizations were a target . . . and it was not uncommon during the First World War for women who joined the military services to be regarded as peculiar at least, if not downright immoral." Even as the massive demands of the war encouraged women to offer themselves for service, the women who answered the call found themselves under suspicion as unwomanly women. Jenny Gould, "Women's Military Services in First World War Britain," in Margaret Higonnet et. al., eds., *Behind the Lines: Gender and the Two World Wars* (New Haven and London: Yale University Press, 1987), pp. 118, 120.

24. Gilbert and Gubar, *No Man's Land*, p. 297. Making a similar case about the role of the war in Hall's work, Sharon Ouditt argues that in Hall's short story "Miss Ogilvy Finds Herself," "the war, at last, provides a space in which [Miss Ogilvy] can act authentically. . . . The lesbian 'hero' thus finds liberation in a masculine subject position." Ouditt, *Fighting Forces, Writing Women: Identity and Ideology in the First World War* (London and New York: Routledge, 1994), p. 25.

25. For an account of this friendship, see Michael Baker, *Our Three Selves: The Life of Radclyffe Hall* (London: Hamish Hamilton, 1985), pp. 125–127. Also see Troubridge, *Life and Death of Radclyffe Hall*, p. 113.

26. Claire Buck discusses the significance of wartime service in Hall's works in her "'Still Some Obstinate Emotion Remains': Radclyffe Hall and the Meanings of Service," in Suzanne Raitt and Trudi Tate, eds., *Women's Fiction and the Great War* (Oxford: Clarendon Press, 1997), pp. 174–196.

27. Barbara "Toupie" Lowther, "Account of Motor Ambulance Section Commanded by Toupie Lowther," unpublished memoir, May 20, 1928, Imperial War Museum, London.

28. Baker, *Our Three Selves*, p. 126.

29. *In the Soldier's Service: War Experiences of Mary Dexter, Edited by her Mother* (Boston and New York: Houghton Mifflin, 1918), p. 177.

30. Jane Marcus argues that Helen Zenna Smith's *Not So Quiet . . .* (1930) was written to exonerate English women ambulance drivers from the allegation of lesbianism scandalously advanced by the *Well*. Marcus, "Corpus/Corps/Corpse: Writing the Body in/at War," in Helen M. Cooper, Adrienne Auslander Munich, and Susan Merrill Squier, eds., *Arms and the Woman: War, Gender, and Literary Representation* (Chapel Hill and London: University of North Carolina Press, 1989), p. 154.

31. Around 1908 Hall visited Orotava for the first time in the company of her long-time lover, Mabel Veronica Batten. At Batten's prompting, Hall studied Spanish, and the two eventually took several enthralling trips to Tenerife, in the Canary Islands, on the slopes of the Teide volcano. Cline, *Radclyffe Hall*, pp. 63–66.

32. Gilbert and Gubar, *No Man's Land*, p. 219.

33. Marcus discusses some of the bars and clubs that Hall frequented, arguing that the *Well* takes its name from one such place, called The Cave of Harmony. Marcus, "Sapphistory," p. 167.

34. See Eve Sedgwick's discussion of the etymology of "closet" in her *Epistemology of the Closet* (Berkeley: University of California Press, 1990).

19

Great Cities: Radclyffe Hall at the Chicago School

JULIE ABRAHAM

Neither the criminal, the defective, nor the genius has the same opportunity to develop his innate disposition in a small town that he invariably finds in a great city.

—Robert Park, *"The City: Suggestions for the Investigation of Human Behavior in the Urban Environment"*

So now they were launched up the stream that flows silent and deep through all great cities.

—Radclyffe Hall, The Well of Loneliness

No one goes to Chicago in *The Well of Loneliness*. New York, London, and particularly Paris all make their contributions to Radclyffe Hall's story of lesbian life. Nevertheless, as a young Chicago woman explains in Floyd Dell's 1921 novel, *The Briary-Bush*, "We're all a little . . . queer" here. Moreover, she continues, Chicago "is beginning to realize that it needs us. Chicago wants to be a metropolis. And all the stock-yards in the world won't make a metropolis. Enough of us, given a free-hand—can. And Chicago knows it."[1]

That queers are to be found in cities is a lesson that predates both *The Well of Loneliness* and Chicago's metropolitan aspirations—a lesson that has been being invoked by sexologists and gay advocates as well as commentators on urban life since the first discussions of modern homosexualities. It is moreover a lesson that embraces many cities. Paris was already being denounced by journalists as a haven for sodomites in the mid-nineteenth century.[2] In the 1890s Havelock Ellis was quoting "a well-informed American correspondent" on "The great prevalence of sexual inversion in American cities."[3] At that same moment John Addington Symonds was insisting that "the pulse" of "this passion" could be felt in "London, Paris, Berlin, Vienna, . . . Constantinople, Naples, Teheran, and Moscow."[4]

Magnus Hirschfeld, who was both gay advocate and sexologist, offered the first gay urban study, of Berlin, in 1904.[5]

Scholars in contemporary lesbian/gay/queer studies assume that urbanization was necessary for the development of modern understandings of homosexuality. But there has been little examination of that connection. Queer presence in cities is almost invariably explained as a result of the social and therefore sexual opportunities of urban life, with vague reference to historical identifications of the city with freedom and with vice. Discussions of urban "freedom" focus on anonymity. Discussions of urban "vice" focus on sex. And once freedom and vice have become anonymity and sex, the analysis too often devolves into an argument about the role of anonymous sex in gay male urban experience.[6]

The city in which lesbians have most often appeared in contemporary scholarship is Paris, in large part because of Hall's novel but also because of the two generations of middle- and upper-class lesbians who went to Paris—mostly from North America—from the 1900s through the 1930s, whose lives, legends, and literature have been being recovered by biographers and critics for the past three decades.[7] These studies of Gertrude Stein, Natalie Barney, Renée Vivien, Romaine Brooks, Janet Flanner, Margaret Anderson, Djuna Barnes, etc., however, when not focused on their subjects' art, focus on their salons, social networks, and romantic lives.[8] Paris serves as an exotic backdrop for their stories, as it does in the broader Anglo-American cultural tradition in which sexuality and sophistication are projected onto the French—and the French capital in particular.

In *The Well of Loneliness* Hall acknowledges the city as a sexualized space but resists the narrative logic whereby her heroine should find sex there. Likewise she acknowledges the rewards of salon life but embeds the salon in a complex account of homosexual urbanity. Paris is sexualized from the moment Stephen Gordon arrives: Jonathan Brockett insists to Stephen, "You've got to have an affair with Paris!"[9] Stephen recognizes that the city offers sexual permission: "There was many another exactly like her in this very city, in every city; and they did not all ... deny ... their bodies ... [and] becom[e] the victims of their own frustrations" (299). But Stephen neither meets a lover nor begins her sexual life in Paris. Similarly, when Hall sends Stephen to Valérie Seymour's salon, she offers us a fictional portrait of Natalie Barney. But this salon, as I shall discuss further later, is not the sum of lesbian life in the novel's city. Nor is Hall's Paris exotic. Throughout the novel she insistently generalizes from "this very city" to "every city" (299).

The familiar accounts of vice, anonymity, and Paris do not begin to account for *The Well*. It is, moreover, certainly time for a new argument about homosexualities and cities, an argument not limited by gender nor limited to particular cities. I am therefore taking Radclyffe Hall to Chicago, and particularly to the fledgling University of Chicago sociology department where Robert Park, Louis Wirth, Ernest Burgess, and their students were producing influential paradigms for the investigation of metropolitan life, even as Hall was writing her paradigmatic lesbian novel.[10]

While this might seem an incongruous move, what becomes apparent when Hall's novel is read in the context of Chicago School urban studies are the striking congruities between Hall's and the Chicago School's accounts of homosexuality and the city. These congruities are the result of a larger cultural history—reading Hall alongside the Chicago School offers one window onto that history—in which modern understandings of cities and homosexualities developed not only simultaneously but interdependently. This interdependent development has produced a fundamental congruence between modern homosexual and modern urban types. Modern homosexuals emerge, in fact, as model citizens of the modern city.

All it takes to be "a little . . . queer" in Floyd Dell's 1920s Chicago is to not "want to make a million dollars" (34). But the thoroughgoing "queer" who prompts his novel's discussion of queers and the metropolis is Paul, a "shrill" (33) fellow, a theatrical set designer who speaks with a "mincing accent" (31) in an "unnatural and 'prissy' voice" (32), has "graceful . . . and beautifully manicured" hands he "wave[s] . . . helplessly," and lives in a room with "tattered Persian rugs" on the walls, "bronze figures" on the shelves, and books on the floor (32). What is particularly telling, though, is that Paul sounds as if he comes from London, although he is actually in flight from Arkansas.[11]

Quite specific messages are being conveyed about queers as well as about cities, when anyone declares all of the citizens of a city "a little . . . queer" or proposes that queers might "make a metropolis." If everyone in the city is "a little . . . queer," then some degree of queerness is necessary to urban life. If queers might "make a metropolis," queers produce urban life. If "Chicago wants to be a metropolis. And all the stock-yards in the world won't make a metropolis" but "Enough" queers "can," then the metropolitan status that queers can confer is opposed to the specificity of any particular place. Queers supersede stockyards. They generalize the city, producing or at least signifying an urban space that exceeds local and even national allegiances. Hence the London accent of Paul from Arkansas, living in Chicago.

Dell's character's statements about queers and cities are, of course, a novelist's invention. However, literary works have been among the key sources of the interdependent development of modern understandings of homosexuality and the city. Novels are still assumed to be reliable sources of information about urban life, lesbian/gay/queer life, and specifically lesbian/gay/queer urban life, in urban studies, in lesbian/gay/queer studies, and particularly in lesbian/gay/queer urban studies.[12] That assumption can be traced to the work of influential urban commentators such as the Chicago School's Robert Park and influential lesbian/gay/queer novelists such as Hall, who shared a faith in fiction as a source of information, whether about cities or homosexualities. Park, a devotee of Whitman, acknowledged prominently, "We are mainly indebted to writers of fiction for our more intimate knowledge of contemporary urban life."[13] And Hall, in *The Well*, places squarely in Stephen Gordon's hands the novelist's "duty" of explaining the invert to the rest of the world.

My own interest in reading literary and sociological texts simultaneously is based in part on this history of interdependence. But my goal is not to pursue the sociological value of the literature, or the literary value of the sociology, much less the "truths" either might reveal. I want to begin to describe a web of shared interests and assumptions that have shaped the development of literary, sociological, and consequently popular representations of homosexualities and cities.

Hall and the Chicago School shared not only a faith in fiction but also an international language of "great cities." This shared language reflected a shared interest in the paradigmatic, whether cities or queers. The Chicago School studied Chicago for what could be learnt about "great cities" as a form, developing, in the process, the analyses of a previous generation of German sociologists: Robert Park was especially indebted to Georg Simmel's work on the modern metropolis, which grew out of Simmel's observations of Berlin.

While the Chicago School bridged the Atlantic, Hall bridged the Channel. For reasons I will discuss later, Hall sends her lesbian to Paris in

The Well of Loneliness, even though she herself stayed in London. But as I have suggested, throughout her novel "this very city," whether London or Paris, is also "every city" (299): the invert is isolated in Paris "as in all the great cities of the world" (406); the homosexual society of Paris is represented as "the stream that flows . . . through all great cities" (356). In fact Hall presents Paris as a representative city whenever she invokes it as a setting for gay life. For Radclyffe Hall as for Floyd Dell, the city the queer inhabits is a generalized metropolis, a great city.

For the purposes of this essay I have juxtaposed *The Well* with Robert Park's landmark essay, "The City: Suggestions for the Investigation of Human Behavior in the Urban Environment" (1915–1925). My reading of Radclyffe Hall at the Chicago School has two parts. I begin by describing the ways in which Park's and Hall's shared investment in the "difference" of cities and homosexuals frames their accounts of the city and the invert so that Hall's invert can emerge as a model citizen of Park's great city. I go on to discuss the ways in which their emphases on difference play out in their accounts of "communal life"—when negotiating "communal life" is presented as the definitive dilemma of urban citizens and homosexuals alike.[14]

What I hope to produce here is a reading of a sequence of interlocking arguments that turn on the two subjects that Hall and Park share—cities and deviance—by mapping the shifting relations between Park's and Hall's texts. Homosexuals are obviously not the only deviant individuals who find their way to great cities. Nevertheless my argument here presupposes that some deviants exemplify the urban better than others. As I will demonstrate, homosexuals exemplify the urban best of all.

The Criminal, the Defective, and the Genius

Both Park and Hall believed that literature was true but it was science that they believed would give their analyses credibility. Park wanted to claim for urban study the "patient methods of observation" and the credit granted "anthropologists like Boas and Lowie" (92); he wanted to "make of the city a laboratory or clinic in which human nature and social processes may be conveniently and profitably studied" (130). Hall likewise believed in the "laboratory or clinic" as the ultimate source of validation for her work, asking Havelock Ellis to comment on her novel and then publishing *The Well* prefaced by his guarantee of its "notable psychological and sociological significance."[15] But in order to secure the justification of scientific authority, both Park and Hall had to claim for their subjects a distinction that would justify scientific study. They had, that is, to emphasize the difference of the city and the homosexual. The difference of Park's city became in part the difference of the city's homosexual inhabitants; the difference of Hall's homosexuals became in part the cities they inhabited.

Park claimed the status of anthropologist by asserting an analogy between "Boas and Lowie['s] . . . study of the life and manners of the North American Indian," and his and his colleagues "investigation of . . . Little Italy on the lower North Side in Chicago, or . . . the more sophisticated folkways of the inhabitants of Greenwich Village . . . New York" (92–93).[16] But Greenwich Villages were of much more use than ethnic enclaves in his pursuit of scientific credibility. Like a laboratory, the "great city," he believed, "spread out and lay bare to the public view . . . all the human characters and traits." This the city could do "because of the opportunity it offers . . . to the exceptional and abnormal types of man" (130). The "exceptional and abnormal" became then the fulcrum of Chicago School readings of the city. It was their presence that turned the city into a "laboratory or clinic."

Hall makes a parallel move. The difference of life in the city gives structure and substance to the portrait of homosexual difference that justifies her scientific claims. If gender inversion and same-sex desire are the origins of homosexuality in Hall's narrative, a homosexual life is built out of the lesbian's inevitable journey from a family identified with the countryside to the others of her kind she will find in the city. Stephen Gordon's growth from uncomprehending boyish-girl to self-consciously inverted masculine-woman is inextricable from her exile from a home county dedicated to the heterosexuality of the Anglo-Saxon aristocracy to a foreign city where Jews and Negroes as well as inverts gather. Lest there be any doubt about the significance of the city in Stephen's history, her exile to London, and so to Paris, is prompted by her romantic passion for Angela Crossby, who seems just a country neighbor but has already been corrupted by New York. The city is the focus of all of the other homosexual lives in the novel as well. Almost every lesbian and gay person introduced has come to the city from elsewhere. Jamie and Barbara, whose grim fates epitomize lesbian suffering, die together in Paris largely because of their exile from the small Scottish village where they grew up in love together. By contrast, the American

Valérie Seymour's supreme comfort with her own lesbianism is mirrored in her identification with Paris.

That Hall sends everyone, in the end, to Paris rather than London underlines her own interdependent investments in the difference of homosexuality and of the city. London could not represent the difference of the city for a character of Hall's protagonist's class background. Stephen Gordon's visits to that city, before she leaves home, reflect a historical continuity between the county and the city, the countryside and London, for the English gentry. She can meet a gay man, in London, who will lead her on to the gay world of Paris. But London cannot be Stephen's queer city because it is culturally too close to home.

For Park as much as Hall, the great city was a city of newcomers, and not only newcomers but—to emphasize the difference of the city—newcomers who had come from afar, psychologically and/or geographically. Consequently they were both interested in emphasizing the difference between "great" cities and all other places. Park's analysis rested on a reading of "smaller communities" where "intimate and permanent associations" (126) are built at the cost of surveillance and repression. In smaller communities "no individual is so obscure that his private affairs escape observation and discussion" (124), and because of this proliferation of observation, "exceptional and abnormal . . . human characters and traits . . . are ordinarily obscured and suppressed" (130). In case we are in any doubt, Park makes clear that smaller communities are the home of the "normal man," the place where "the normal man, the man without eccentricity or genius . . . seems most likely to succeed" (130).

In *The Well* Hall heightens the difference of the great cities in which the adult Stephen will take refuge by emphasizing the country setting of her childhood and adolescence. The surveillance and the hostility to difference Park ascribes to "smaller communities" are everywhere to be found in Hall's countryside, where Stephen is subject to years of suspicious observation by the local worthies before she is driven to the city.

But Hall's invert is more than just one of the multitude of newcomers to Park's great city. In Park's schema, the paradigmatic urban newcomer is the person with the most to gain from the city, one of those least favored in the country, the not "normal," "the criminal, the defective . . . [and] the genius" (126). While "the small community often tolerates eccentricity," Park observes, "the city . . . rewards it" (126). That rewarding of the deviant is, in fact, key to the difference that defines his city. As one among "the criminal, the defective . . . [and] the genius" or—from different perspectives—all three, Hall's queer as urban immigrant, Stephen Gordon, lives at the center of Park's great city.

Stephen is representative of Park's urban newcomer not only because abnormality is rewarded by the city but also because hers is the quintessential abnormality rewarded there. Park distinguishes between smaller communities and great cities in sexual terms. Park's small communities are the sites of heterosexuality and reproduction, which are, in turn, actively threatened by the city. "Metropolitan life," according to Park, "inhibit[s] and suppress[es] . . . natural impulses and instincts": "in the country" marriage occurs earlier and children "are counted as an asset," whereas "in the city" children are "a liability. . . . Marriage takes place later." Sometimes in fact, it "doesn't take place at all" (129). *The Well's* opening description of the Gordon family home begins to make much the same argument. An ideally manly man, Sir Philip Gordon, marries an ideally womanly woman, Lady Anna—a marriage that culminates in Stephen's birth—amidst the natural beauties of the surrounding landscape: the countryside is firmly identified with heterosexual love and reproduction. The novel's conclusion completes Hall's version of Park's analysis, with Mary Llewellyn's final flight from our heroine, from lesbianism, and from Paris into the wide open arms of Martin Hallam and the wide open spaces of the Canadian prairie—where she will undoubtedly have the babies Stephen cannot provide.

Not only does Hall's invert fit neatly within Park's analysis of the great city but Park's and Hall's stories of the city and of the invert, focused as they both are on newcomers, share the same central preoccupation, a preoccupation with becoming, whether the "becoming" in question is becoming urban or becoming gay. The question underlying both of their analyses is about the degree to which the "becoming" they are interested in is a process: are urban persons, or are homosexuals, made or born? Insofar as both of their answers are "born," they are both concerned with the degree to which their subjects are "natural."

Modern urban commentators and modern lesbian/gay/queer advocates have all long wrestled with the charges that cities and homosexuals both are unnatural. It could be argued that cities have been and continue to be represented as unnatural spaces because the city is taken to be the home of unnatural persons such as homosexuals. Certainly both Park and Hall had to contend with prior representations of their subjects as "unnatural."

However, Park and Hall were both invested in the "naturalness" of their subjects. Paradoxically, despite Park's belief in the city's suppression of natural instincts, he and his Chicago School colleagues were committed to the concept of the great city as "organic," as "a living entity" (93), "a product of nature, and particularly of human nature" (91). Equally paradoxically, while Hall's opening identification of heterosexuality with the natural world of the countryside implies a corollary identification of homosexuality with the unnatural, the one subject on which Hall's opposed avatars of modern homosexuality, Stephen Gordon and Valérie Seymour, agree, is that homosexuality is a natural phenomenon. Stephen, protesting "the preposterous statement that inversion [is] not a part of nature"—"since it exist[s] what else could it be?"—declares the invert "God's . . . creation" (405). Valérie presents "Nature" as a feminine life force "trying to do her bit." "Inverts," she argues, are "being born in increasing numbers" (406).

Park's theory of the organic city depends on two interdependent propositions: first, that the city's population naturally organizes itself into particular forms; and second, that while the city might reward the abnormal, it does not produce their abnormality but merely fosters the "innate dispositions" they bring with them from the countryside and/or smaller communities they are fleeing. These propositions are interdependent because the characteristic site of naturally occurring social organization in Park's account of the city is the "moral region." According to Park, individuals naturally and therefore inevitably segregate themselves into moral regions based on shared interests or passions. And the quintessential form of the moral region is the "vice district," a "detached milieu . . . in which vagrant and suppressed impulses, passions, and ideals emancipate themselves from the dominant moral order" (128). For Park "the forces which in every large city tend to develop these detached milieus," if they are to be understood as natural, must be a product of the "latent impulses of men" (128). That is, the "reward" the city offers to Park's criminals, defectives, and geniuses is "the . . . opportunity to develop [their] innate disposition[s]" (126). To "become" urban might be "to develop," but only to develop a possibility already present in the self, already produced by nature.

Consequently, the city's relation to nature depends, for Park, on the relation to nature of the city's "abnormal" residents, people such as the city's queers. The right relation to nature of the invert guarantees the city's right relation to nature. But the "right" relation in each case is reversed. The question of the "naturalness" of cities merges with the question of the "naturalness" of homosexuality; Park's argument for a natural city is in this sense supported by Hall's natural-born homosexual. However, Park's organic city is flexible, "rooted in the habits and customs of the people who inhabit" the city (93), "habits and customs" shaped by as well as shaping even material conditions. "The city possesses a moral as well as a physical organization," he observes, "and these two mutually interact in characteristic ways to mold and modify one another" (93). But unlike Park, for Hall, to be natural is to be fixed. Stephen's and Valérie's natural homosexuality is "born"; it simply "exists." By all rights, the fixity of Hall's invert ought to make her an alien creature in Park's organic city. Nevertheless, not only are Park and Hall discussing similar subjects similarly but in the end Hall's portrait of the natural invert is a description of precisely the urban citizen Park needs. It is, paradoxically, precisely because of her fixity that Hall's natural homosexual not only belongs in Park's organic city but is required by it, for Park's vision of a flexible, living city is based on his belief in a fundamentally fixed human nature.

At the same time Hall was invested in a vision of a natural city to support her portrait of the natural homosexual. As I have noted, she focused on the French capital rather than London as the ultimate setting for her representative lesbian because Paris was some distance for her elite Englishwoman to travel. But there is at least one other reason Stephen Gordon lives on the Left Bank rather than by the British Museum. The distinction Hall establishes between the city in which Stephen settles and the other great cities in her novel lies in their relations to nature. New York and London are commercial and/or industrial centers: Angela Crossby tramps the "long, angular streets, miles and miles of streets" (179) of Manhattan in search of employment; Stephen finds smokestacks belching soot over the river and trees of London. But no one works for a living in Hall's Paris (except Stephen's servants, in what seems to be a semifeudal arrangement). No industrial processes impose themselves upon the landscape. Without commerce or workplaces, Paris can serve as the focus of her presentation of the queer "great city" as a natural setting, where the urban homosexual world Stephen and Mary join can be described as a "stream that flows silent and deep" (356).

In the end, in both Park's and Hall's accounts, the city becomes its own peculiar natural world, with inverts as its denizens. Park concludes that "We must . . . accept these . . . more or less eccentric and exceptional people . . . as part of the natural, if not the normal, life of a city" (130). The city, "every city," becomes the space in which Stephen Gordon and "many another exactly like her" can live "natural lives—lives that to them [are] perfectly natural" (299).

Finally however, despite Park's commitment to a city that merely fosters innate differences, and Hall's insistence that homosexuals are born and not made, neither could sustain such commitments to fixity against the pressure of the urban life each had invoked. Neither Park nor Hall could deny the possibility that the organic city might itself produce deviants. Park admitted that "great cities have always been . . . melting pots. . . . Out of the vivid and subtle interactions of which . . . have come . . . the newer social types" (125), "not merely vocational, but temperamental types" (125). What, then, we might ask, is the relation of these "newer. . . . temperamental types" to the "innate dispositions" of urban immigrants? That question arises also in *The Well*, in the persons of those many lesbians in the great city whose nature is unaccounted for, and even more dramatically, those whose nature seems malleable.

Communal Life

The underlying subject of Park's arguments about naturally occurring segregation and the moral regions such segregation produced—the subject that Chicago School urban studies set out to address—was the problem of communal life. This problem, in their view, had two dimensions: the isolation experienced by individuals in the city and the forms of association the city offered. "Communal life" was also the central dilemma of the invert's existence, in Hall's analysis, and has for her invert the same two dimensions: isolation and association. In neither case do the opportunities for association offered by the city ease the experience of isolation.

As I noted earlier, according to Park, "What . . . makes the city what it is," is the "absence" of the "amazing amount of personal information afloat among the individuals" within "small communities" (124). That absence of information means also the absence of "the more intimate and permanent associations of the smaller community" (126). Personal information, that is, is the source of intimacy and the basis of permanent connections. The individual in Park's great city is not known and consequently is not intimately or securely connected to others. Instead, in the great city "the individual's status is determined to a considerable degree by conventional signs—by fashion and 'front'—and the art of life is largely reduced to a skating on thin surfaces and a scrupulous study of style and manners" (126).

Hall's account of the invert in the city is similarly organized around both isolation and an emphasis on "style and manners." "Here, as in all the great cities of the world," Stephen declares bitterly, inverts are "isolated until they . . . [go] under" (406). At the same time she is constantly subject to the attentions of strangers. "In the restaurants" and on the streets, "people would stare" (241) at Stephen alone. When Stephen and Mary go out together, "people . . . stare at the tall, scarred woman in her well-tailored clothes and black slouch hat. They would stare first at her and then at her companion. . . . There would be a few smiles" (326).

In fact the invert brings this dimension of urban experience with her. Stephen is both isolated and judged by her appearance before she reaches the great city. As a member of Park's class of "the exceptional and abnormal," she is deprived from the outset of access to the "intimate and permanent associations" that smaller communities provide the normal. For the invert, the very relationship Park posits between personal information and intimacy and permanent associations is, as it were, inverted. Although her family and neighbors have information about Stephen, only her father translates that information into knowledge, and he does not tell anyone—including his daughter—what he knows. When her mother gains this knowledge she explicitly denies her daughter intimacy and permanent association. At the same time, in *The Well* the world of the invert is always, like the city, dominated by appearances. From Stephen's childhood on she is subject to her own as well as others' obsessive interpretations of her "signs," "style and manners." As a despairing young woman, she examines her own body in the mirror for signs of her stigma.

Hall's insistence that homosexuals convey their abnormality through their distinctive style and manners converges with peculiar force with the urban focus on style and manners Park describes. Even in the lesbian/gay/queer social world Stephen eventually finds in Paris, people look at her "curiously; her height, her clothes, the scar on her face riveted their attention" (348). Those assessing Stephen in the public places of the city are confident of their ability and their right to define her by reading her appearance. And after all, their confidence is justified. The narrator herself catalogues the lesbians of Paris largely in terms of their looks, "the build of an ankle, the texture of a hand, a movement, a gesture" (352). Her admission that "the grades were so numerous and so fine that they often defied the most careful observation" (352) only underlines her commitment to the visual sign. In London, "People stared at the masculine-looking girl. . . . And someone, a man, laughed and nudged his companion: 'Look at that! What is it?' 'My God! What indeed?'" (165). The smiles of those who observe Stephen and Mary on the streets of Paris confirm the implication of the Londoner's question. Even in the city she is read as an abnormal person, which is how both Park and Hall needed her to be read.

The city is nonetheless a place of community—the only place for community, according to both Park and Hall—for the abnormal and exceptional such as Stephen. Hall's Paris is Park's "spontaneously" divided city in which "the population tends to segregate itself, not merely in accordance with its interests, but in accordance with its tastes or its temperaments" (128). When Valérie Seymour declares that "nearly all streets in Paris lead sooner or later to Valérie Seymour" (298), she is asserting the centrality of her lesbian self to Paris. But as even Valérie admits, there are some streets that do not lead to her. As Park observes, "the segregation of the urban population. . . . establishes moral distances which make the city a mosaic of little worlds which touch but do not interpenetrate" (126).

Hall dramatizes the segregation of the great city by offering many different versions of Paris in *The Well*. The first Paris described is the "tourist Paris" to which the flamboyantly gay Jonathan Brockett initially introduces Stephen, leading her "through the galleries of the Luxembourg and the Louvre; up the Eiffel Tower . . . down the Rue de la Paix" (241). The last Paris is the heterosexual Paris to which "the thoroughly normal" Martin Hallam introduces Stephen and Mary, a city of fashionable restaurants where "neat, well-tailored men; pretty, smartly dressed women . . . laughed and talked, very conscious of sex and its vast importance" (417).

The novel's city centers on the gay milieu Brockett has brought Stephen to Paris to join. Stephen insists that homosexuals isolated in the great city have only one option: "in their ignorance and resentment, they turn . . . to the only communal life a world bent upon their destruction had left them; . . . to the worst elements of their kind, to those who haunted the bars" (406). But despite Stephen's grim conviction that bars are the only form of gay communal life, so "great" a city is Paris that Hall offers an alternative to the bars in Valérie Seymour's salon.

In this regard Hall complicates Park's picture of "detached milieus . . . emancipate[d] . . . from the dominant moral order" (128) by acknowledging the workings of class and gender distinctions. The bars are public, commercial, and presided over by men who are heterosexual and/or drug dealers. People "of all ages, all degrees of despondency, all grades of mental and physical ill-being . . . laugh shrilly . . . [and] dance together" (387). Theirs is the democracy of misery. But Valérie's salon, private rather than either public or commercial, and presided over by a woman who is also a lesbian, is a genteel haven for the elite. There is neither alcohol nor dancing at Valérie's. Lesbian and gay "writers, painters, musicians and scholars" (349) mingle with tolerant heterosexuals, while "Valérie, placid and self-assured, create[s] an atmosphere of courage" (352).[17]

Nevertheless, the emphasis on difference that guides Hall's work weights her novel toward the bars, just as Park weights his analysis of the city toward the criminal, the defective, and the genius. Valérie, a "charming and cultured woman" creates a setting in which "everyone [feels] very normal" (352). The pseudonormality of Valérie's salon is available to Stephen because of her class and her gender, but neither protects her from having to identify with the misery of the bars. It is at the grimmest of these bars, at Alec's, that Stephen must come to terms with her abnormality: challenged by a "youth" with "a grey, drug-marred face" who addresses her as "Ma soeur," she acknowledges their connection when she responds, "Mon frère" (388).

There still remains a fundamental contradiction between the emphases on isolation and on community in both Park's and Hall's works. How can urban experience be characterized, simultaneously, in such opposed terms? Why do the great city's isolated individuals not simply take up appropriate communal lives? In the end Park needs "the criminal, the defective, . . . [and] the genius" to resolve these questions at the heart of his account of the city. *The Well* suggests why. As Stephen Gordon's lesbian story illustrates, the deviant experience both of the dimensions of urban life most intensely. They bring their isolation to the city with them and continue to be isolated, to be marked out as different, even on city streets. Meanwhile their need for community is proportional to the degree of their isolation— the reward of the city is peculiarly theirs. But most important, they experience the loneliness of the city and its embrace simultaneously, because of the experience of deviance.

In *The Well*, as in Park's great city, the reward of Paris is "communal life" (406), but this reward depends on the deviant's acceptance of herself as deviant, and her deviance as defining her self. As Stephen acknowledges, "in Paris I might make some sort of a home, I could work here—and then of course there are people" (248). "People" make possible Stephen's home and work in Paris; her meeting Valérie Seymour prompts her to stay in the city, and Valérie literally finds her a home. Nevertheless it is a grim moment, when Stephen Gordon "turn[s] at last . . . to her own kind," and launches herself and Mary Llewellyn upon "the stream that flows silent and deep through all great cities, gliding on between precipitous borders, away and away into no-man's land—the most desolate country in all creation" (356).

Hall introduces the prospect of community as a loss. Stephen's former governess, Puddle, who first accompanies her to London and Paris, inveighs against "like to like": "No, no. . . . Stephen was honourable and courageous; she was steadfast in friendship and selfless in loving; intolerable to think that her only companions must be men and women like Jonathan Brockett" (242). To take up with such companions—by definition neither "honourable" nor "courageous," "steadfast" nor "selfless"—is, Puddle implies, to move definitively out of the normal moral world. Park's analysis confirms her fears. Once "the poor, the vicious, the criminal, and exceptional persons generally" have joined with their own kind, he observes, "social contagion tends to stimulate . . . the[ir] common temperamental differences and to suppress characters which unite them with the normal types about them" (129).

Stephen's profound ambivalence about lesbian/gay/queer communal life is based in her sense of her self. She worries "that [Valérie] liked me because she thought me—oh, well, because she thought me what I am" (248). In order to consider the friendship of those "like" herself, she has to acknowledge "what" she is. That is, she has to admit a stigmatized identity and to admit that stigmatized identity as defining. But intimacy might still be elusive; she might be "liked" by those "like" herself only for "what" she is. Such a connection would inevitably be superficial, insofar as she understands herself as having a self that exceeds her deviance.

Hall's and Park's works, perhaps because they were each negotiating social hostilities—to homosexuality and to the city—finally converge on the ground of ambivalence. Valérie completes the novel's identification of normality with the countryside and the invert with the great city, when she proposes to Stephen, "you don't belong to the life here in Paris. . . . you've the nerves of the abnormal with all that they stand for . . . [but] you've all the respectable county instincts of the man who cultivates children and acres" (407). Apparently Stephen cannot be fully abnormal, which is to say fully urban, given her instincts as a county gentleman. But Stephen does remain in the city. Which points to a further paradox in Park's analysis: it is those who remain at odds with the city, who remain isolated as well as engaged in communal life, who are in the end the most properly urban. Stephen, in her ambivalence, remains a model urban citizen.

The metropolitan aspect of *The Well* that matches in such a complex fashion the patterning of Park's urban sociology can, in the end, never be separated from Hall's use of the city in the service of an individual as well as a generic narrative. Valérie's verdict also suggests the degree to which it is in the nature of Stephen's particular deviance that she will be ambivalent about the urban communal life to which she might belong. Because she is a masculine woman, she is abnormal and therefore urban, but because she cannot abandon the understanding of gender that her masculinity represents, she resists both abnormality and urbanity. At the same time Hall's gay Paris is also always "every city." We can see in *The Well* the beginning of the process whereby the city itself begins to take on the burden of the stigma of homosexuality.

The convergence of Radclyffe Hall's and Robert Park's interlocking representations of "great cities" in the 1920s, across the distance between Paris and Chicago, illustrates one phase of the history of the interdependent development of modern understandings of homosexualities and of cities. That modern understandings of homosexualities and of cities *did* develop interdependently is my underlying thesis in this essay. Clearly, there is much more to be said on this subject. Reversing Dell's novelistic declaration that queers make a metropolis, Alfred Kinsey, by mid-century, could allude to "a widespread theory among psychologists and psychiatrists" that cities make queers, "that the homosexual is a product of an effete and overorganized urban civilization."[18] At the end of the twentieth century we still live with and within the shared history of homosexuals and cities. Model citizens of the modern metropolis, we still, in a postmodern world, read *The Well of Loneliness*, and many of us still live in cities.

Notes

1. Floyd Dell, *The Briary-Bush*, p. 34. All further references to this text.

2. Michael D. Sibalis, "Paris," pp. 10–38, 10.

3. Havelock Ellis, *Sexual Inversion*, p. 351.

4. John Addington Symonds, *A Problem in Modern Ethics*, pp. 77–113, 78–79.

5. David Higgs, *Queer Sites*, p. 190.

6. Higgs's *Queer Sites* demonstrates this pattern clearly. More specific, often neighborhood-based work is being done under the rubric of "queer space" in collections such as Gordon Brent Ingram, Anne-Marie Bouthillette, and Yolanda Retter, eds., *Queers in Space*. For another alternative see Kath Weston, "Get Thee to a Big City."

7. Sally R. Munt's analysis of the contemporary lesbian as flâneur, in *Heroic Desire*, suggests alternatives to the Paris/lesbian focus.

8. Studies of the expatriate lesbian community in Paris range from Gayle Rubin's "Introduction" to Andrea Weiss's *Paris Was a Woman*.

9. Radclyffe Hall, *The Well of Loneliness*, p. 238. All further references to this text.

10. On the Chicago School, see Fred H. Matthews, *Quest for an American Sociology* and Martin Bulmer, *The Chicago School of Sociology*. Chicago School research into lesbian/gay/queer life is discussed by David K. Johnson, in "The Kids of Fairytown" and Allen Drexel, in "Before Paris Burned."

11. See Marilee Lindemann on "queer" in the 1920s in *Willa Cather: Queering America*.

12. See Elizabeth Wilson, *The Sphinx in the City*; Marshall Berman, *All That Is Solid Melts into Air*; Richard Sennett, *Flesh and Stone*; and Higgs, *Queer Sites*, pp. 191–192.

13. Robert E. Park, "The City," pp. 91–130, 93. All further references to this text.

14. In this essay I choose from among a range of terms for individuals who pursue, identify with, or are identified with same-sex desire. I use "lesbian/gay/queer" in relation to contemporary materials; "invert," "lesbian," or "homosexual" when referring to *The Well*; and "homosexual" as the broadest term for my historical frame.

15. Havelock Ellis, "Commentary," p. 35 in this volume.

16. Park notes that "Every large city tends to have its Greenwich Village" ("The Urban Community," pp. 3–20, 6). These "villages" all have their "distorted forms of sex behavior" (Harvey Warren Zorbaugh, *Gold Coast and Slum*, p. 100).

17. Nowhere in Hall's account of the city is there any mention of the street-oriented public sex scenes that are routinely the focus of descriptions of gay male urban life.

18. "The failure to make heterosexual adjustments is supposed to be consequent on

the complexities of life in our modern cities; or it is a product of a neuroticism which the high speed of living in the city imposes upon an increasing number of individuals" (Alfred C. Kinsey, Wardell B. Pomeroy, and Clyde E. Martin, *Sexual Behavior*, p. 455).

Works Cited

Berman, Marshall. *All That Is Solid Melts into Air: The Experience of Modernity*. New York: Penguin, 1982.

Bulmer, Martin. *The Chicago School of Sociology: Institutionalization, Diversity, and the Rise of Sociological Research*. Chicago: University of Chicago Press, 1984.

Dell, Floyd. *The Briary-Bush*. New York: Alfred A. Knopf, 1921.

Drexel, Allen. "Before Paris Burned: Race, Class, and Male Homosexuality, 1935–1960." In Brett Beemyn, ed., *Creating a Place for Ourselves: Lesbian, Gay, and Bisexual Community Histories*, pp. 119–144. New York: Routledge, 1997.

Ellis, Havelock. "Commentary." In Radclyffe Hall, *The Well of Loneliness*. 1928; reprint, New York: Doubleday, 1990.

———. *Sexual Inversion*. In *Studies in the Psychology of Sex*, vol.1, New York: Modern Library, 1942.

Hall, Radclyffe. *The Well of Loneliness*. 1928; reprint, New York: Doubleday, 1990.

Higgs, David, ed. *Queer Sites: Gay Urban Histories Since 1600*. New York: Routledge, 1999.

Ingram, Gordon Brent, Anne-Marie Bouthillette, and Yolanda Retter, eds. *Queers in Space: Communities/Public Places/Sites of Resistance*. Seattle: Bay Press, 1997.

Johnson, David K. "The Kids of Fairytown: Gay Male Culture on Chicago's Near North Side in the 1930s." In Brett Beemyn, ed., *Creating a Place for Ourselves: Lesbian, Gay, and Bisexual Community Histories*, pp. 97–118. New York: Routledge, 1997.

Kinsey, Alfred C., Wardell B. Pomeroy, and Clyde E. Martin. *Sexual Behavior in the Human Male*. Philadelphia: W. B. Saunders, 1948.

Lindemann, Marilee. *Willa Cather: Queering America*. New York: Columbia University Press, 1999.

Matthews, Fred H. *Quest for an American Sociology: Robert E. Park and the Chicago School*. Montreal and London: McGill-Queen's University Press, 1977.

Munt, Sally R. *Heroic Desire: Lesbian Identity and Cultural Space*. New York: New York University Press, 1998.

Park, Robert E. "The City: Suggestions for the Investigation of Human Behavior in the Urban Environment." In Richard Sennett, ed., *Classic Essays on the Culture of Cities*, pp. 91–130. New York: Appleton-Century-Crofts, 1969.

———. "The Urban Community as a Spatial Pattern and a Moral Order." In Ernest W. Burgess, ed., *The Urban Community*, pp. 3–20. Chicago: University of Chicago Press, 1926.

Rubin, Gayle. "Introduction." In Renée Vivien, *A Woman Appeared to Me*, pp. iii–xxxvii. Trans. Jeannette H. Foster. Tallahassee, Fla.: Naiad Press, 1976.

Sennett, Richard. *Flesh and Stone: The Body and the City in Western Civilization.* New York: Norton, 1994.

Sibalis, Michael D. "Paris." In David Higgs, ed., *Queer Sites: Gay Urban Histories Since 1600*, pp. 10–38. New York: Routledge, 1999.

Symonds, John Addington. *A Problem in Modern Ethics: Being An Inquiry into the Phenomenon of Sexual Inversion* (1896). In John Lauritsen, ed., *Male Love: A Problem in Greek Ethics and Other Writings*, pp. 77–113. Foreword by Robert Peters. New York: Pagan Press, 1983.

Weiss, Andrea. *Paris Was a Woman: Portraits from the Left Bank.* San Francisco: Harper Collins, 1995.

Weston, Kath. "Get Thee to a Big City: Sexual Imaginary and the Great Gay Migration." In *Long Slow Burn: Sexuality and Social Science*, pp. 29–56. New York: Routledge, 1998.

Wilson, Elizabeth. *The Sphinx in the City: Urban Life, the Control of Disorder, and Women.* Berkeley: University of California Press, 1991.

Zorbaugh, Harvey Warren. *Gold Coast and Slum: A Sociological Study of Chicago's Near North Side.* Chicago: The University of Chicago Press, 1929.

20

Well Meaning: Pragmatism, Lesbianism, and the U.S. Obscenity Trial

KIM EMERY

Before *The Well of Loneliness*, popular conceptions of female homosexuality in the United States were vague and varied, to the extent that they existed at all. The growing medical literature on lesbianism was characterized by disagreement and divergent approaches (ranging from noninterference to "cold sitz baths" to surgical "asexualization"[1]). Other professional discourses offered everything from sensationalism to silence. But with *The Well*, "an abrupt locking into place of meaning"[2] circumscribed the emerging discourses of female homosexuality within constraints now so pervasive they pass almost unnoticed.

Most readers contend that this is a predictable effect of the publicity generated by the obscenity trials and assume that the relatively more stable notion of female homosexuality that emerged is an extension of Radclyffe Hall's established belief in sexological theories of congenital inversion. Teresa de Lauretis voices the overwhelming critical consensus when she describes the book as "drawing its view of homosexuality from the late-nineteenth-century sexology of Krafft-Ebing and Havelock Ellis" and explains that "it was intended, and in the main received, as a plea for social acceptance or toleration of sexual deviance cast in terms of divine compassion and liberal humanism." Because the terms of that toleration seem to require a narrow conception of lesbianism as gender inversion and "the repudiation of lesbianism as such," most critics concur that the novel simply "confirm[s its protagonist's] view of herself as a 'freak,' 'nature's mistake'—a masculine woman."[3] Although Esther Newton defends this strategy on the grounds that it made possible the imputation of desire and sexual agency to an upper-class white female protagonist, others have concluded that the costs were too high. Catharine Stimpson calls the book "a parable of damnation,"[4] while Newton herself acknowledges that even the novel's appeal may lie in the supposedly damning stereotypes it appears to promote:

> *The Well* has continued to have meaning to lesbians because it confronts the stigma of lesbianism—as most lesbians have had to live it. . . . As the Bowery bum represents all that is most feared and despised about drunkenness, the mannish lesbian, of whom Stephen Gordon is the most famous prototype, has symbolized the stigma of lesbianism . . . and so continues to move a broad range of lesbians.[5]

And that's the thing: for all its narrowness, negativity, self-pity, and repudiation, *The Well has* continued "to move a broad range of lesbians" *and* to deeply affect the conditions and conceptions of lesbian possibility in twentieth-century Anglo-America.

Canadian novelist Jane Rule has called it "*the* lesbian novel, a title familiar to most readers of fiction, either a bible or a horror story for any lesbian who reads at all."[6] U.S. historian Blanche Wiesen Cook acknowledges that "*The Well* was banned in England only to become throughout western civilization the archetype of all things lesbian—the 'butch,' the tears, the despair of it all."[7] So how can a novel so "trite, superficial," "dull," "unduly long," "melodramatic," "inflated and sentimental" have such staying power?[8] Why would its influence be so profound? Although many have attributed the book's impact to its notoriety in a context offering very few public images of lesbianism,[9] and some, such as Newton, have suggested that the book's supposed faults actually underlie its success, these accounts don't fully explain how one book can be both "Bible" and "horror story"— and don't even attempt to address the discrepancy implied in Cook's observation that the book was banned *only* to become an "archetype." More to the point, Newton's insight that the novel's impact might somehow be related to its reliance on negative stereotypes might be usefully extended to examine the role Hall's novel has played in *shaping* the particular "stigma of lesbianism" it has come to symbolize.

Ironically, the idea that an appeal to liberal humanism must be a quality of the text itself is *itself* an assumption "cast in terms" of liberal foundationalism. Not coincidentally, it is also consistent with the reading of Stephen as an unproblematic example of congenital inversion. By this understanding, the book's influence is overt and unidirectional; the novel affects society exactly to the extent that readers accept and adopt the understanding of female homosexuality depicted within (and presumably exemplified by Stephen). "Society" can act on the novel, in contrast, only by suppressing (censoring) or accepting the terms it sets out. This situation parallels exactly the relationship drawn between the congenital invert and the society (fictional or otherwise) in which she appears: others may accept or reject, deny or expose the truth she embodies, but her sexuality is understood to be an integral and incontrovertible quality of the invert herself.

I wish to suggest an alternative possibility. From a pragmatic perspective, the "abrupt locking into" (congenital) identity of (lesbian) desire appears an effect less of text (Hall's or those that influenced her) than of the particular historical circumstances through which *The Well* was introduced to the United States. Hall's novel entered this country via a legal system itself in the throes of a paradigm shift. One result, I believe, was that what Leigh Gilmore calls "the mutuality between literary and legal production" of lesbian identity[10] was paradoxically cemented, in the United States, in a legal preference for understanding female homosexuality as congenital inversion—and a cultural tendency to see lesbians' legal standing as rooted in this foundationalist identity. So while Americans continue to argue whether "real" lesbians are necessarily born that way, a more fundamental presumption has settled into the national conviction that there is a meaningful distinction to be drawn between "status" and "conduct." Whether revered or reviled, disdained or desired, Stephen Gordon has been codified as the quintessential congenital butch—and the example of her experience has contributed to the development of an American mindset marginally more comfortable with homosexual identity than with homosexual activity (evidenced, for example, in the oddity of increasing civil rights protections enacted against a backdrop of enduring sodomy laws).[11] Interestingly, *The Well*'s journey through the U.S. legal system marks a juncture at which a very different understanding of lesbianism very nearly entered mainstream discourse, had the book been positioned less precisely within the shifting legal discourses that determined its reception.

In August 1928 the *New York Times* reported that a reputable U.S. publisher was "TO PRINT BANNED BOOK HERE." The brief item, datelined London, describes Hall's novel as "the book on sex matters suppressed by its publishers here on the request of the Home Secretary, after a newspaper controversy."[12] Needless to say, the particular publication history of this particular novel positioned it to enter U.S. discourses in particular ways.

First published in England by Jonathan Cape, the book had come out on July 27, 1928, to mixed, but generally respectful reviews; the *Saturday Review*, the *Sunday Times*, and the *Nation and Athenaeum* all applauded the book's sincerity and seriousness but, to varying degrees, also suggested that the novel's polemic at times overpowered its art.[13] Leonard Woolf was among the harsher critics, describing the story as "extremely interesting" and admitting that "it is written with understanding and frankness, with sympathy and feeling," but concluding nevertheless that "the book fails completely as a work of art."

> Miss Hall loses the whole in its parts, and is so intent on the stars that she forgets the heavens. Her book is formless and therefore chaotic. . . . The first 150 pages are good . . . but after the death of Sir Philip the novel becomes a catalogue, almost a ragbag. Incident is added to incident, and character to character, and one sees the relevance which Miss Hall intended each to have to the theme of the book. But their relevance is intellectual, not emotional, and therefore not artistic. They remain discrete patches which never join to form a pattern.[14]

Woolf's criticisms were mild, however, compared to the attack that appeared on August 19 in the *Sunday Express*. Under the banner headline "A Book That Must Be Suppressed," James Douglas's article denounced *The Well* for promoting perversion. "I say deliberately," he wrote, "that this novel is not fit to be sold by any bookseller or to be borrowed from any library. . . . I would rather give a healthy boy or a healthy girl a phial of prussic acid than this novel. Poison kills the body, but moral poison kills the soul."[15]

On August 20 the *Daily Express* printed Cape's rebuttal—and his offer to forward copies of the book to the home secretary and the director of public prosecutions for review. Remarkably, he volunteered to discontinue publication and destroy the printing plates at their request. By subjecting the book's future to the discretion of noted reactionary William Joynson-Hicks, the British home secretary (a move made, incidentally, without con-sulting—or even informing—author Radclyffe Hall), Cape virtually ensured *The Well*'s suppression in England.

The publisher attempted to redeem himself by shipping molds of the text to Paris's Pegasus Press before destroying the plates and by advertising the resultant Paris edition to English booksellers. But it was too late for England. When shipments of the Paris edition were seized by English cus-toms and declared obscene, Cape's initial acquiescence came back to haunt him. Both the publisher's voluntary withdrawal of the novel and his appar-ent duplicity in reintroducing the book via this French connection helped to discredit the project—and, hence, Hall's purpose—in the eyes of the law. After a well-publicized and well-attended trial, Bow Street Magistrates Court declared *The Well of Loneliness* officially obscene on November 20, 1928. The perfunctory appeal was lost on December 19, with the court's conclusion that *The Well* was "a disgusting book [and] prejudicial to the morals of the community."[16]

Almost as if anxious to exert influence similar to that exhibited by the English press, the *New York Times* opportunistically (and inaccurately) characterized *The Well* as a "SEX NOVEL" in both the headline and the copy of their second article about the novel's suppression.[17] Although this article also mentions that "it is understood that the book either is published or will be published in the United States by Alfred Knopf," the Knopfs had in fact already rescinded their offer, on the excuse that Hall had violated her contract by allowing Cape to bring the book out in England well in advance of the planned simultaneous publication date. Back in July Alfred Knopf had written to Hall that he was "rather disturbed to learn . . . that Cape is publishing before the end of this month." In the same letter, however, he concludes only that "under the circumstances I fear we will probably have to rush the book out early in the Fall" and promises that as long as the proofs are gotten "back to us at once all will be well." At this date Alfred Knopf claimed to "feel very happy indeed that we are to publish [*The Well of Loneliness*]," describing it as "a very fine book indeed" and professing to "have very great hopes for its success."[18] Indeed, at least as late as September 5, production seemed to be proceeding apace, as Alfred Knopf's secretary wrote to acknowledge a letter from Hall and to assure her "that the corrections you give there have been made in our copy of THE WELL OF LONELINESS."[19]

On September 20, however, Blanche Knopf wrote with disturbing news. "Dear John,"[20] she said,

> When I was in London I was inclined to feel as you did, that there would be no difficulty in the way of THE WELL OF LONELINESS over here. Now that I have been back at the office for a week and have got in touch with the situation here I find it much more serious than I had suspected.

According to this letter, the "seriousness" of the situation involved several related factors, including "a lot of very unfortunate publicity in the American press," quantities of orders "not . . . from the better type of book seller but rather from dealers who expect a sensational demand for the book from people who expect something very s[a]lacious," and Cape's irresponsible handling of affairs in England. Blanche Knopf came down especially hard on this lattermost point:

> Our decision not to publish [The Well of Loneliness] will I am sure, come as a great shock to you but you must view the situation from our point of view. We are . . . faced with the hopeless prospect of attempting to defend a book which had not been defended in its author's own country.
>
> I must point out in this connect[ion] that while it would have been difficult to foresee the English fate of THE WELL OF LONELINESS the unfortunate American situation of the book would have been completely avoided had we been protected, as we should have been, by being able to effect simultaneous publication with Cape. When our deal went through it was certainly on the assumption that we would be so protected. . . . [W]e feel we were definitely sacrificed to Cape's convenience and this is the result.

Although she offered to turn her firm's type over to another U.S. publisher at cost, Blanche Knopf implored her friend John "to keep the book entirely out of the American market," claiming that "no American publisher could now handle it except as pornography."[21]

Fortunately for Radclyffe Hall, this warning proved false. Forewarned by the fiasco in England, Covici-Friede took a proactive approach to the obscenity issue when they published the first U.S. edition of *The Well of Loneliness* in December 1928; as soon as the book was selling well, partner Donald Friede telephoned the New York Society for the Suppression of Vice to turn himself in.[22] New York police dutifully seized 865 copies of the U.S. edition's sixth printing, and charged Friede with violating prohibitions against "lascivious" literature. On February 21, 1929, the case was heard in the City Magistrates Court (Borough of Manhattan, Seventh District), Judge Hyman Bushel presiding.

So *The Well* entered American consciousness framed within the context of its alleged obscenity. The relevant section of New York Penal Law stipulated that "a person who sells * * * or has in his possession with intent to sell, * * * any obscene, lewd, lascivious, filthy, indecent or disgusting book * * * is guilty of a misdemeanor." In this case, however, even the prosecution agreed that the novel under indictment "contains no unclean words"—and Judge Bushel concurred. And in fact, *The Well* is a singularly unsexy book, devoid not only of "lewd" language but of any direct description of sexual activity.[23]

Because the book could not be characterized as lewd, lascivious, filthy, or disgusting, Bushel based his judgment against the publishers not in the novel's language but in his estimation of its possible effects. From this perspective it could be considered potentially indecent and obscene. To legitimate this decision, Bushel was reduced to relying on an 1868 English case for precedent. The ruling in *Regina v. Hicklin* held that the test of obscenity should be "whether the tendency of the matter charged as obscenity is to deprave or corrupt those whose minds are open to such immoral influences, and who might come into contact with it." In their memorandum to the court of appeals, Friede's defense lawyers dismissed this rationale as an "ancient test of obscenity" and denounced it as "patently unfair, unreasonable, and unsound," arguing that "it sought to gauge the mental and moral capacity of the community by that of its dullest-witted and most fallible members, and . . . to withhold from society any material which might conceivably injure its lowest and most fatuous element."[24] Bushel, however, would admit only that this test of immoral influence is "not sole and exclusive"—and concluded that it nevertheless "may be accepted as a basis for judicial decision" in the case of *People v. Friede*. In his view, *Hicklin* is a test that *The Well of Loneliness* obviously fails.

This judgment is of course based in Bushel's understanding of the novel, which he summarizes as follows:

> The book here involved is a novel dealing with the childhood and early womanhood of a female invert. In broad outline the story shows how these unnatural tendencies manifested themselves from early childhood; the queer attraction of the child to the maid in the household; her affairs with one Angela Crossby, a normally sexed, but unhappily married woman. . . . The book culminates with an extended elaboration upon her intimate relations with a normal young girl, who becomes a helpless subject of her perverted influence and passion.[25]

That "the author has treated these incidents not without some restraint" is irrelevant to the test applied. What *is* central to the question at hand is that "the unnatural and depraved relationships portrayed are sought to be idealized and extolled." Bushel takes issue not with the letter of the text but with its implications—not with the words used or even the objects they denote but with the book's potential to shift the terms of social judgment. What's objectionable, from this perspective, is the way "the characters in the book who indulge in these vices are described in attractive terms," the way in which "it is maintained throughout that they be accepted on the same plane as persons normally constituted, and that their perverse and inverted love is as worthy as the affections between normal beings."

To prove his charge, Bushel points to a passage about halfway through the lengthy book: the scene in which Stephen finally first stands up for herself, defending her life and her love against her mother's charge that she is "unnatural," an "insult" to her father's memory, and "a sin against creation."[26] Bushel singles this section out as exemplifying the text's objectionable "theme":

> An idea of the moral tone which the book assumes may be gained from the attitude taken by the principal character towards her mother, pictured as a hard, cruel and pitiless woman because of the abhorrence she displays to unnatural lust and to whom, because of that reaction, the former says: "But what I will never forgive is your daring to try and make me ashamed of my love. I'm not ashamed of it, there's no shame in me.[27]

Significantly, the first half of the book is suffused with shame and confusion. Recall Stephen's guilty, thrilling crush on the unworthy Collins. Because Collins has involved seven-year-old Stephen in an insignificant deceit involving dirty fingernails, the child's ardor is shot through with shame and ambivalence:

> Oh, Collins, Collins, with those pretty blue eyes and that funny alluring smile! Stephen's own eyes grew wide with amazement, then they clouded with sudden and disillusioned tears, for far worse than Collins' poorness of spirit was the dreadful injustice of those lies—yet this very injustice seemed to draw her to Collins, since despising, she could still love her. (17–18)

Indeed, Hall makes clear that such love as Stephen feels is in fact inseparable from the act of despising: "Stephen brooded darkly over Collins' unworthiness; and yet . . . she still wanted Collins . . . thinking about her made Stephen go hot down her spine" (18). In a move calculated, it would seem, to communicate the sensation of sexual desire to her adult audience, Hall plays on the culture's own intense ambivalence about sex. By thus commingling shame and excitement in her description of the child's emotions, Hall imputes a precocious—almost incongruously Freudian—sexuality to her seven-year-old protagonist. But this section, like others less evocative but more explicit, was not singled out by the censors. Like many literary critics, legal judges of the text's obscenity seem to have had fewer problems with the first half of the book than with the second—even though much of the most explicit description of lesbian sexual expression is found early on—for example, such descriptions as "Stephen took Angela into her arms, and she kissed her full on the lips, as a lover" (146). Of course, Stephen's affair with the married and capricious Angela Crossby is also suffused with a sense of shame.

I would suggest that the early imbrication of Stephen's sexual identity with shame, guilt, and ambivalence is consistent with Hall's evident emphasis on creating a readily recognizable lesbian for a protagonist. In this she was prescient: to this day historians sometimes confuse lack of shame in expression of passionate attachment with evidence of an absence of sexual activity between, for example, nineteenth-century "Romantic Friends." By infusing her protagonist's erotic identity with shame and ambivalence, Hall established her sexual agency and rendered recognizable an actively lesbian orientation. Not coincidentally, contemporary critics including Leonard Woolf and L. P. Hartley also applauded "the first 150 pages" of the novel while dismissing the remainder as too "polemic."[28] Michael Baker continues this tradition in his critical biography of Hall, summing up his assessment of

The Well in a single sentence: "The early promise of the story, with its powerful depiction of a sensitive child's growing years, too quickly deteriorates into an assortment of stereotypes representing the Tragic Invert."[29] What is revealing about this reading is the way it ignores and in effect inverts the actual strategic distribution of stereotypes within Hall's text. The first half of the novel is rife with stereotypical images of gender inversion and sexual shame, creating, if we are to accept the critics' judgment, a "convincing" portrait of an acceptable invert. One begins to suspect that it is precisely the sense of shame permeating these pages that makes for good literature, in the critics' opinion, and good influence, from the judges' perspective. In this, as in general, Bushel would seem to follow Sir Chartres Biron, the English magistrate who similarly seized on the *Hicklin* test to support his judgment—but although the similarities are striking, Bushel's decision was rendered in a different context, with distinct stakes and implications.

The British Common Law system required strict reliance on judicial precedent, whereas Bushel was obligated to balance *Hicklin*'s example against both explicit constitutional guarantees protecting freedom of speech and freedom of the press, and more extensive legislative codification. Local differences in the development of case law also contributed to the distinct circumstances of Bushel's decision. In England, "any one passage in [a] book, indeed one word, which could be judged obscene, was enough to condemn the whole book; it did not have to be read as a whole."[30] The best refuge of literary freedom in early twentieth-century New York, in contrast, was the established standard of judging works in their entirety instead of on impressions of isolated passages. But, ironically, because *The Well of Loneliness* contained no "unclean words" and no indecent episodes, a judgment of obscenity could not have been placed on *any* of its parts per se. Taken as a whole, however, Hall's novel certainly could be held, as Bushel phrased it, "to debauch public morals." In a sense, as the judge recognized, this was the book's basic raison d'être:

> The theme of the novel is not only anti-social and offensive to public morals and decency, but the method in which it is developed, in its highly emotional way attracting and focusing attention upon perverted ideas and unnatural vices and seeking to justify and idealize them, is strongly calculated to corrupt and debase those members of the community who would be susceptible to its immoral influence.[31]

Because U.S. precedent required that the novel be judged "as a whole," a verdict of "obscene" could be returned on a book containing "no unclean parts."

On entering the U.S. legal system, moreover, Hall's novel was caught up in a field of contestation in which not simply its own alleged obscenity but the very logic and nature of legal judgment were open to question. In the United States at this time, a forward-looking progressive jurisprudence was building on its successes of the very early twentieth century to profoundly challenge classical legal theory. Legal historians describe this move away from precedent-based jurisprudence and toward a results-oriented practice as consistent with the larger Progressive movement and what historian Morton White has termed the "Revolt against Formalism." Roscoe Pound spoke for many of his contemporaries when he identified this change in legal reasoning with a larger cultural shift, writing in 1909 that "jurisprudence is the last in the march of the sciences away from the deduction from predetermined conceptions." Championing a "sociological" jurisprudence that would advance "the adjustment of principles and doctrines to the human conditions they are to govern rather than to assumed first principles," Pound applauded the trend he termed "the movement for pragmatism as a philosophy of law."[32] The description is apt. Like philosopher C. S. Peirce, progressive or sociological jurisprudes (and, after them, in a fashion, the so-called "legal realists") tended to seek meaning in effects instead of sources and saw abstractions as (relatively) derivative, with historical, material foundations. In his 1921 *The Nature of the Judicial Process*, Justice Benjamin Cardozo famously observed that law "is not found, but made"— and argued that "its truth is relative, not absolute."[33]

As Leigh Gilmore observes, under *Hicklin*, "obscenity was determined through a 'test' rather than as a quality in the material."[34] Interestingly, this distinction legitimizes precisely the segregation that progressive jurisprudence sought to trouble. In the context of British common law, Gilmore is probably right to insist that "in the absence of a legal definition of what obscenity *is*, obscenity's criminality exists wholly in relation to what it threatens." But her claim is descriptive, not definitive—and in the United States, at this time, pragmatism seemed to promise a different way of thinking about the relationship between what something *is* and the effects that it has. Following the pragmatic insights of Peirce, jurists such as Oliver Wendell Holmes sought out the relations that informed identity, recognizing that the "qualities" identified by legal categories were the effects of interactions rather than essential, inborn traits. Holmes's landmark opinion in the *Lochner* case, for example, had turned on his insight that the "right" to "freely" contract one's labor was always already restricted by one's situation relative to capital. By recognizing that history and whole sets of relations inhere in what the law recognizes as individuals—and hence in such concepts as "civil liberties" and "natural rights"—progressive jurists such as Holmes brought pragmatism into the courtroom.

Although Bushel drew on *Hicklin* to frame his objections to *The Well of Loneliness*, his discussion of the novel suggests a somewhat more nuanced sense of the relations between text and context, cause and effect, identity and interaction. His reasoning is not exactly pragmatic (and his conclusions were hardly progressive), but Bushel seems to have hit upon an intersection between conservative condemnation and progressive semiotics. As Gilmore explains, *Hicklin* held that "the problem with obscenity lay in its potential—what would obscenity *do*?" Similarly, the founding insight of pragmatism was that meaning could be understood as a function of function; or, as Peirce himself put it: "Consider what effects that might conceivably have practical bearing you conceive the object of your conception to have. Then your conception of those effects is the WHOLE of your conception of the object."[35] Like the *Hicklin* test, pragmatism looked to potential effects; but unlike *Hicklin*, pragmatism did not separate effects from essence.

In the context of U.S. progressive jurisprudence, then, *The Well*'s contested "obscenity" presented an opportunity to reconsider the connections among identity (what it *is*), function (what it *does*), and relation (upon what is it contingent?). And indeed, Bushel's argument appears to turn not on the fear that Hall's novel would directly incite lesbian desire but on an intuition that the book could contribute to a change in conditions conducive to lesbian existence. As he saw it, *The Well* was not calculated to seduce individual readers into lesbian activity; instead, it threatened to *recast the terms* through which homosexuality was conceived—and historically condemned.

In saving *The Well* from censorship, unfortunately, the Court of Special Sessions missed this opportunity for pragmatic reevaluation and firmly returned legal conceptions of lesbianism to a logic bounded by firm distinctions between action and essence. Acting within a frame identical to that outlined by Bushel, the three-judge panel nonetheless returned the opposite judgment, concluding "that the book in question is not in violation of the law" only "after a careful reading of the entire book."[36] The crux of their interpretation is evident in the opening lines of the opinion:

> The book in question deals with a delicate social problem, which, in itself, cannot be said to be in violation of the law unless it is written in such a manner as to make it obscene * * * and tends to deprave and corrupt minds open to immoral influences.

The vague language of this decision exploits the inherent ambiguity of relevant legal precedent in order to clear semantic space for the existence of a text inoffensive in its manner but potentially unsettling in its theme. By separating the book's "theme" from its "manner" and isolating a "tendency to corrupt" as yet an *additional* condition of obscenity (as opposed to an effect of theme and manner), the court was able uphold the principle of free expression and rule in the publishers' favor. As this ruling makes clear, however, "careful reading of the entire book" is not the same as evaluating its cumulative character; the brief opinion suggests that the charge to judge the text "as a whole" was here taken to require only thorough evaluation of all of its parts.

Implicit in the higher court's rejection of the *Hicklin* test is a repudiation of the semiotics at the heart of progressive jurisprudence. Uninterested in moral censure, the Court of Special Sessions wisely refuses speculation about what the text might *do* and restricts itself to an examination of what it *is*. But the court's assumption that the letter of the text can be read without regard to the connections among its parts betrays an atomistic logic— the idea that meaning is additive not integrative—and affirms the liberal attachment to identity independent of (inter)action.

That this indisputably essential victory for freedom of expression was achieved at the cost of both intellectual rigor (in the interpretation and rearticulation of the letter of the law) and deeper understanding (of the complex cultural effects of legal and literary interventions) points to tensions fundamental to contemporary U.S. law and culture—and, relatedly, to the making and meaning of lesbian subjectivity in the U.S. Whatever Hyman Bushel's faults, he proves a peculiarly astute reader—and a more attuned interpellant of cultural processes than his colleagues on the higher court. In understanding *The Well* to embody much more than the mimetic representation of a "delicate social problem" or a straightforward plea for compassion toward congenital inverts, Bushel seems to have intuited the pragmatic significance of Stephen Gordon. Considered in isolation, Stephen the congenital butch represents no more threat to the established order than does the unobjectionable language Hall uses in *The Well of Loneliness*. Stephen as a representative manifestation of larger lesbian possibility, however, is another story altogether—and makes *The Well* a different novel. Stephen becomes the spokesperson, the visible index, of a whole host of inarticulate, effectively unrealized others—"the quick, the dead, and *the as yet unborn*" (436, emphasis mine).

In predicating their protection of free expression on an essentialist understanding of lesbian possibility as an isolable, innate, individual trait fundamentally unrelated to social conditions and historical circumstance, the "progressive" jurists on the Court of Special Sessions contained this threat, conceptually severing lesbian realization from the conditions of its own possibility. It is unfortunately characteristic of the era that this separation was carried out with such success and so little self-consciousness; as the pragmatic intuitions of progressive jurisprudence hardened into the positivistic technology of legal realism, the "individual" conceived by law was increasingly alienated from the network of semiosic relations that sustains subjectivity. To this day readers tend to celebrate or criticize Stephen Gordon's congenital masculinity without exploring the complexity of Hall's representation—perhaps because, in the course of its trials, the book's existence came to require such rigid interpretation. But the connection between civil liberties and foundationalist philosophies is neither necessary nor self-evident—and as the essays in this volume demonstrate, *The Well of Loneliness* has richer legacies to leave.

Notes

This essay, a shortened version of chapter 3 in my book The Lesbian Index: Pragmatism and Lesbian Subjectivity in the Twentieth-Century United States, *is reprinted by permission of State University of New York Press (c) 2002, State University of New York. All Rights Reserved. I am also grateful to Laura Doan and Jay Prosser for their excellent editorial advice; to Elizabeth Dale, Danaya Wright, and Karen Young for assistance in negotiating the strange domain of U.S. legal history; and to Kathryn Baker, just in general.*

1. Xavier Mayne (Edward I. Prime Stevenson), *The Intersexes: A History of Similisexualism as a Problem in Social Life* (privately printed, c. 1908); James G. Kiernan, "Insanity. Lecture XXVI—Perversion," *Detroit Lancet* 7, no. 11 (May 1884): 483–484; F. E. Daniel, "Castration of Sexual Perverts," *Texas Medical Journal* (Austin, August 1893): 255–271; all quoted in Jonathan Ned Katz, *Gay American History*, rev. ed. (New York: Penguin, 1992), pp. 146–48, 134–137.

2. Leigh Gilmore, "Obscenity, Modernity, Identity: Legalizing *The Well of Loneliness* and *Nightwood*," *Journal of the History of Sexuality* 4, no. 4): 603–623.

3. Teresa de Lauretis, *The Practice of Love* (Bloomington: Indiana University Press, 1994), pp. 204, 212.

4. Catharine R. Stimpson, "Zero Degree Deviancy: The Lesbian Novel in English," in Elizabeth Abel, ed., *Writing and Sexual Difference.* (Chicago: University of Chicago Press, 1982), p. 249.

5. Esther Newton, "The Mythic Mannish Lesbian: Radclyffe Hall and the New Woman," p. 90 in this volume.

6. Jane Rule, *Lesbian Images*, p. 78 in this volume.

7. Blanche Wiesen Cook, "'Women Alone Stir My Imagination': Lesbianism and the Cultural Tradition," *Signs* 4, no. 4 (Summer 1979): 718.

8. "A ridiculous book, trite, superficial" (Romaine Brooks, quoted in Lillian Faderman, *Surpassing the Love of Men: Romantic Friendship and Love Between Women from the Renaissance to the Present* [New York: William Morrow, 1981], p. 322); "a meritorious, dull book" (Virginia Woolf, as recounted in Rule, *Lesbian Images*, p. 80 in this volume); "As a novel, written in a language which is unfalteringly clear, sometimes beautiful and often irritatingly Biblical, it is unduly long and overburdened with detail frequently irrelevant to the story's progress" (Vera Brittain, *Time and Tide*, August 10, 1928, p. 59 in this volume); "melodramatic" (Cyril Connolly, *The New Statesman*, August 25, 1928, p. 68 in this volume); "inflated and sentimental and diffuse as it sometimes is, one cannot deny the earnestness" (L. P. Hartley, *Saturday Review*, July 28, 1928, p. 51 in this volume).

9. Or as Blanche Wiesen Cook puts it, "most of us lesbians in the 1950s grew up knowing nothing about lesbianism except Stephen Gordon's swagger, Stephen Gordon's breeches, and Stephen Gordon's wonderful way with horses" (p. 719).

10. Gilmore, "Obscenity, Modernity, Identity," p. 604.

11. By way of comparison, I would venture that in the U.K. distinctions between sin and crime, or between private morality and public decency—also of continued relevance in the U.S., of course—may have became somewhat more culturally central than the status/conduct distinction. The Wolfenden Report, for example, specified that "there must remain a realm of private morality and immorality which is not the law's business," while maintaining the state's duty to "preserve public order and decency" (*The Report of the Committee on Homosexual Offences and Prostitution*, Cmnd 247 [London: HMSO, 1957], p. 10)—but the absence of U.S.-style sodomy prohibitions (an effect of post-Wolfenden reforms) did not prevent the passage of Section 28's prohibition against the "promotion" of homosexuality in 1988. For further discussion, see David T. Evans, "(Homo)sexual Citizenship: A Queer Kind of Justice," in Angelina R. Wilson, ed., *A Simple Matter of Justice? Theorizing Lesbian and Gay Politics* (London: Cassell, 1995), pp. 110–145. For more general discussion of *The Well*'s significance for U.K. readers, see Rebecca O'Rourke, *Reflecting on The Well of Loneliness* (New York: Routledge, 1989).

12. *New York Times*, August 30, 1928, p. 6, col. 2.

13. L. P. Hartley in the *Saturday Review*, July 28, 1928, pp. 50–51 in this volume; Ida Wylie in the *Sunday Times*, August 5, 1928, p. 55 in this volume; Leonard Woolf in the *Nation and Athenaeum*, August 4, 1928, pp. 52–54 in this volume. For further discussion of early English reviews, see Michael Baker, *Our Three Selves: The Life of Radclyffe Hall* (New York: Morrow, 1985), pp. 220–229.

14. Leonard Woolf, pp. 53 and 54 in this volume.

15. James Douglas, "A Book That Must Be Suppressed," *Sunday Express*, August 19, 1928, pp. 36 and 38 in this volume.

16. Baker, *Our Three Selves,* pp. 223–228, 239–245.

17. *New York Times*, October 6, 1928, p. 6, col. 4.

18. A. A. Knopf to Radclyffe Hall, July 19, 1928 (Knopf Collection, Harry Ransom Humanities Research Center [HRHRC], University of Texas, Austin, Texas).

19. Knopf Collection, HRHRC.

20. Among friends, Radclyffe Hall was customarily called "John."

21. Blanche Knopf to Radclyffe Hall, September 20, 1928 (Knopf Collection, HRHRC).

22. According to legal historian Edward de Grazia, Friede took this action because he "wished to avoid the situation in which some defenseless clerk in a bookstore would be arrested and perhaps frightened into a guilty plea or led to make an inadequate defense"—and perhaps because "provoking a successful test case would also

build up sales." (Edward de Grazia, *Girls Lean Back Everywhere: The Law of Obscenity and the Assault on Genius* [New York: Random House, 1992], p. 98).

23. *New York Miscellaneous Reports* 133: 612–613.

24. *Regina v. Hicklin*, L.R. 3 Q.B. 360; quoted in defense memorandum. "Memorandum submitted on behalf of the defendants," *People v. Friede* (HRHRC, Radclyffe Hall collection), n.p.

25. *New York Miscellaneous Reports* 133: 612–613.

26. Radclyffe Hall, *The Well of Loneliness* (1928; reprint, New York: Doubleday, 1990), p. 200; all subsequent citations are to this edition.

27. *New York Miscellaneous Reports* 133: 613.

28. See note 13.

29. Baker, *Our Three Selves*, p. 220.

30. Richard du Cann, "Appendix," to Brittain, *Radclyffe Hall*, pp. 159–178, p. 164. This standard was amended with the passage of the Obscene Publications Act of 1959.

31. *New York Miscellaneous Reports* 133: 615, 613.

32. Roscoe Pound, "Liberty of Contract," *Yale Law Journal* 18 (1909): 464.

33. Benjamin Cardozo, *The Nature of the Judicial Process* (New Haven, Conn.: Yale University Press, 1921), p. 102.

34. Gilmore, "Obscenity, Modernity, Identity," p. 606.

35. C. S. Peirce, *The Collected Papers of Charles Sanders Peirce*, 2d ed., ed. Charles Hartshorne and Paul Weiss (Cambridge: Harvard University Press, 1963), 5:422 (originally published as "What Pragmatism Is," *The Monist* 15 [1905]: 161–181.)

36. Quoted in " 'Well of Loneliness' Cleared in Court Here," *New York Times*, April 20, 1929, p. 20, col, 2.

21

Writing by the Light of *The Well*: Radclyffe Hall and the Lesbian Modernists

JOANNE WINNING

It is the lesbian in us who drives us to feel imaginatively, render in language, grasp, the full connection between woman and woman. It is the lesbian in us who is creative, for the dutiful daughter of the fathers in us is only a hack.
—Adrienne Rich, "It is the lesbian in us . . . "[1]

Whatever support Virginia Woolf might publicly have lent the cause célèbre of *The Well of Loneliness* in 1928, it is clear that in private, had she had the opportunity (through some strange Orlandian leap of time . . .) to consider the division Adrienne Rich draws above between lesbians who create and daughters who hack, she would have committed Radclyffe Hall firmly to the latter category. In a letter to Ottoline Morrell at the time of the obscenity trial, Woolf writes: "The dulness of the book is such that any indecency may lurk there—one simply can't keep one's eyes on the page."[2] As one of the thirty-nine witnesses committed to defending the literary merit of the book in court, Woolf was not alone in her private derision of its style. There is palpable unease among these eminent witnesses about how *good* a novel it might, or might not, actually be. Of course, in 1928, at the height of literary modernism, questions about the value of a literary text inevitably center around divisions between traditional literary forms and the revisionist, experimental forms of modernist writing. It is clear that in her criticisms of *The Well*, Woolf attempts to draw a line between this "meritorious, dull book" and other, more innovative literature being produced around it.[3] Ultimately, Woolf's criticism is not of Hall's decision to represent lesbian sexuality and its genesis so much as the textual manner in which she chooses to do it. Yet such a demarcation between *The Well* and its modernist peers is perhaps not quite as neat as Woolf might have wished it. There are, indeed, profound resonances between Hall's realist novel and its infamous censorship at the hands of the British establishment, and the texts produced by the group of female modernists writing at this time.[4] The first, of course, is lesbian sexuality itself. What is remarkable about this group of women, who have until so recently existed in the canonical wilderness, is the curiously lesbian inflection of their modernism. Both in terms of their literary experimentation (so many of their texts inscribe lesbian desire, however complexly or codedly) and in terms of its cultural production (so many of the key editors, patrons, and mentors of modernism were either lesbian or bisexual), lesbian sexuality is central to this period in women's literary history. Indeed, as Makiko Minow noted in 1989, given the artifacts being unearthed by the exploration of this literary grouping in the 1980s, it might well become necessary to institute the term "lesbian modernism."[5] Such a term, along with its cognate "Sapphic Modernism," is only now beginning to be theorized, at least a decade after the recuperation of female modernism.[6] This delay is partly due to the difficulty in defining both terms since, as Shari Benstock argues: "we are saddled with inadequate definitions of modernism and restrictive notions of lesbianism."[7] Undoubtedly the project of mapping the compelling correlations between modernism and lesbian sexuality requires increasingly refined theoretical tools. Not least, as Marianne Dekoven argues in relation to female modernism as a whole, we need to move beyond a discussion based simply in terms of gender or sexuality and to begin to construct an understanding of the period through "a much broader historical provenance and a much wider range of cultural work."[8] In this sense, reworking *The Well* back into its literary context is of crucial importance. While modernism has always been perceived as a reaction against popular and mass cultural forms, an exploration of Hall's text, and its swift prosecution, alongside lesbian modernist texts suggests an infinitely more complex relation between high and low forms of culture.

For its part, *The Well* has always stood outside this exclusive circle of texts, existing in a space beyond this heady intellectual milieu and (in)famous for its subject matter rather than its style. Beverley Brown offers a typical assessment of its literary worth when she calls it a rather "middle brow novel . . . not unrelated to other attempts [in the 1920s] to introduce a note of 'post-war realism' to the popular love story."[9] Yet, even on a constitutive level, there has always been a compelling mutuality between *The Well* and lesbian modernist texts. The worlds of *The Well* and lesbian modernism are populated by the same key figures. Natalie Barney, for instance, appears as Valérie Seymour in Hall's text and as Dame Evangeline Musset in Djuna Barnes's satirical *Ladies Almanack*.[10] Hall herself appears in Barnes's text, alongside Una Troubridge, recast as Tilly-Tweed-In-Blood and Lady Buck-and-Balk. In more complex textual terms too, this middlebrow novel of little literary influence, can be seen to operate upon the same sets of discourses and indeed to inflect some of the highbrow experiments of lesbian modernism in unexpected and profound ways. As Nicky Hallett notes, the struggle to write and to be lesbian are, in this historical period, commonly correlated.[11] Like so many of its lesbian modernist counterparts, *The Well* is a bildungsroman in which Stephen Gordon's coming to writing also teleogically structures her coming into lesbian identity.[12] It is *writing*, as Puddle assures Stephen at the moment of rupture with her mother, Anna Gordon, that will both make and sustain her: "You've got work to do—come and do it! Why, just because you are what you are, you may actually find that you've got an advantage."[13]

In *The Archaeology of Knowledge*, Foucault argues for the intrinsic intertextuality of books, writing that "the frontiers of a book are never clear-cut: . . . it is caught up in a system of references to other books, other texts, other sentences: it is a node within a network."[14] By a Foucauldian reckoning then, even if it does employ a "disappointing" literary style, *The Well* could never exist outside the realm of lesbian modernism and should not now be consigned to a kind of literary exile beyond other early twentieth-century lesbian texts. The "fame" it attracts through its public prosecution, indeed, gives it a central place among the proliferating discourses of lesbian subjectivity at the beginning of the twentieth century. For lesbians themselves, these discourses (both fictional and scientific) are profound and formative influences. In his *Sexual Inversion*, Havelock Ellis discusses the autobiographical narratives of inverts and notes the curious power of textuality:

> there is no doubt that inverts have frequently been stimulated to set down the narrative of their own experiences through reading those written by others. But the stimulation has, as often as not, lain in the fact that their own experiences have seemed different, not that they have seemed identical.

The histories . . . serve as models in the sense that they indicate the points on which information is desired.[15]

To *read* about one's self, then, however one may dislike the terms in which such a narrative is expressed, becomes a powerful prompt to *write* about oneself, even if one chooses to do it in a different way. How might *The Well* become such a model for other writers attempting to construct narratives of lesbian sexuality? How, indeed, might both the text and the event of its prosecution, rather than being a literary diversion from "clever" avant-garde happenings, actually represent one of the primary cultural contexts of lesbian modernism?

This essay seeks to trouble the neat dichotomy between *The Well* and its lesbian modernist counterparts, suggesting that in fact Hall's main purpose, to represent lesbian identity and develop her own discourses about its origins, is shared by other writers such as Woolf, Barnes, Dorothy Richardson, Bryher, H.D., and Gertrude Stein. It argues that where Hall "fails" to find safe passage for her text across the rocky and risky social climate of the 1920s, these lesbian writers avoid censure by employing the fragmented, dissimulating techniques of modernism (a project upon which they are already engaged) as a kind of "escape route" for lesbian representation. While there are many points of comparison to be made between *The Well* and its lesbian modernist counterparts, I intend to take only two in this essay: Woolf's *Orlando* and Richardson's *Dawn's Left Hand* and *Clear Horizon* from her *Pilgrimage* series, both produced in and around the time of *The Well*'s infamous trial. In the first instance, Woolf's *Orlando* provides a compelling example of the way in which lesbian modernism attempts to write the same story as *The Well*, while using modernist techniques as a kind of "cover" to avoid censure. In the second, a reading of two of Richardson's novel-chapters from her *Pilgrimage* series suggests how both the narrative of *The Well* and its prosecution inflects the writing practices of the lesbian modernist.

"Type-casting" the Lesbian:
Orlando and *The Well of Loneliness*

Writing in the *Daily Telegraph*, the reviewer "M. M." asserts: "As in all works of true art, subject and treatment are inseparably bound together in this book."[16] Evidently pondering this review of *The Well*, and the larger question of whether writing and content can be neatly dichotomized, Woolf writes in her diary at this time: "What is obscenity? What is literature? What is the difference between the subject and the treatment?"[17] Sir Chartres Biron, the prosecuting magistrate, provides a very public answer to Woolf's privately expressed question. In his summary of *The Well*'s misdemeanors he argues that: "the proposition that the book is well written and therefore should not be the subject of these proceedings is quite untenable."[18] Literature or not, then, the lesbian text (which seeks to defend rather than parody or pathologize lesbianism) is proscribed, dangerous, immoral. Yet, trying to estimate what representational space can be prized open between the subject and its treatment is evidently of great concern to Woolf, as modernist and sometime Sapphist. In a letter written with E. M. Forster after Home Secretary Sir William Joynson-Hicks's dictate on *The Well*'s withdrawal, Woolf argues that the Hall trial signals the dawning of a repressive climate:

> novelists in England have now been forbidden to mention it [lesbianism] by Sir W. Joynson-Hicks. May they mention it incidentally? Although forbidden as a main theme, may it be alluded to, or ascribed to subsidiary characters . . . ?
>   . . . writers produce literature, and they cannot produce great literature until they have free minds. The free mind has access to all the knowledge and speculation of its age, and nothing cramps it like a taboo. A novelist may not wish to treat any of the subjects mentioned above but the sense that they are prohibited or prohibitable, that there is a taboo-list, will work on him and will make him alert and cautious instead of surrendering himself to his creative impulses. And he will tend to cling to subjects that are officially acceptable, such as murder and adultery, and *to shun anything original lest it lead him into forbidden areas.* (emphasis mine)[19]

Despite the sharp irony employed in this potshot at the Establishment, Forster and Woolf's use of the term "original" is instructive. Coming from these signatories we might well read "original" as "experimental" or even "modernist." Thus there is some kind of equivalence being weighed here between modernism (or new literary forms) and the "forbidden" area of lesbianism. There is a subtle double bluff at work in this sardonic comment, since Hall's text, in Woolf's judgment, is far from "original." It is its realism, its legibility that commits it to so terrible a fate. Indeed, given what happens in so relentless and so public a way to *The Well*, it would seem that textual "originality" might be the only way to inscribe lesbian subjectivity and, at the same time, subvert censure.[20]

At the time of this letter Woolf herself is heavily invested in the question of how to write lesbian subjectivity as she completes her sixth novel, *Orlando*. In critical discussions *Orlando* has often been linked with *The Well*; it was published three months after *The Well* appears.[21] Critics have rightly argued that even if it wasn't clear at the time, *Orlando* is another story about lesbian desire and identity, inspired by and dedicated to the "pronounced Sapphist" Vita Sackville-West.[22] Such critical readings have located its difference from *The Well* in its "subversiveness," its attempt to trouble the boundaries of gender rather than to concretize them, and in its fey conceit of turning biography into fantasy.[23] These terms would suggest that in its aims as well as its form, it is a very different book from *The Well*; yet a reading that places key elements of both texts alongside each other suggests in fact that they seek to tell the same story, and indeed rake over the same discursive ground. Lillian Faderman has argued that due to the prescriptive climate in 1928, Woolf is unable to present a fictional account of her lover, Sackville-West, with "honesty."[24] It is certainly true that Woolf expresses concerns about exposure in her diary, stating: "I am writing *Orlando* half in a mock style very clear & plain, so that people will understand every word. But the balance between truth & fantasy must be careful."[25] Yet Faderman's argument problematically overlooks Woolf's avowed modernism. Part of *Orlando*'s "cover" is surely the way it makes use of certain experimental literary tropes and deconstructs the reader's expectations of straightforward narrative and content in order to slyly inscribe lesbian subjectivity. As Bonnie Kime Scott has argued, in such a proscriptive climate, writers such as Woolf and Barnes develop a strategic textual "playfulness."[26] While Woolf's modernism is clearly her primary literary mode (and had been since the early 1920s), we must not underestimate, I think, how such a mode offers a kind of "safe haven" during the 1920s. Through this period, as the trial of *The Well* proves, the lesbian's attempt at autonomous self-definition becomes increasingly overwritten by social and cultural prohibitions, even as the proliferating scientific and medical discourses seek to cast the lesbian "type" definitively.

In his discussion of the trial and vilification of Oscar Wilde in the 1890s, Alan Sinfield explores the ways in which effeminacy and homosexuality become amalgamated within the cultural consciousness.[27] This coalescence of the previously disparate cultural signifiers of decadence and sodomy is embodied in the figure of Wilde himself. As such, Sinfield suggests, Wilde's career and prosecution act as a kind of cultural "faultline" across which the persona of the modern-day camp gay man, codified by his blending of masculinity and femininity, is constructed. Sinfield himself notes that the something similar happens during the obscenity trial of *The Well of Loneliness*. Through the cultural spectacle of her novel's withdrawal and its prosecution, Hall herself becomes a cultural signifier, mapping signifiers of class, dress, and corporeal appearance on to the previously invisible category of "the lesbian."[28] Such an image passes into cultural consciousness primarily through the vehicle of media representation. Alongside his inflammatory editorial in the *Sunday Express* (August 19, 1928), James Douglas prints part of a photograph of Hall (the whole actually showing both Hall and Troubridge "at home" in August 1927) in smoking jacket and bow tie, with slicked hair and holding a cigarette. This masculine image thus accompanies his moral outrage at the subject of her novel, binding lesbianism and an aping of masculinity together. Covering Joynson-Hicks's ruling on the novel in a front-page report on August 23, 1928, the *Evening Standard* prints a photograph of Hall from 1926, which shows her in the masculine garb of sombrero, frilled shirt, and black overcoat. At the end of the *The Well* debacle, the *Evening Standard* (December 15, 1928) concludes its coverage with a report on the failure of Hall's appeal against Chartres Biron's decision to ban the book. Again an image of Hall supports this copy; this time the same smoking-jacket photograph that Douglas had used in his editorial in August. Such media coverage constructs a discourse in which Hall's "look" comes to codify and embody lesbian subjectivity in the consciousness of people who had no other experience (to their knowledge) of lesbianism. Hall's "look" had, of course, already been lampooned a couple of years earlier in popular satirical magazines such as *T.P.'s Weekly* and the *Popular Pictorial*.[29] The real newspaper photographs thus only serve to substantiate these earlier caricatures that inscribe Hall as pseudo-male. Furthermore, in relation to the sexological schema to which she makes appeal in the novel, Hall herself appears to fit the type of the masculine invert. By the 1920s medical, sexological, and psychoanalytic discourses had already, within their own terms, successfully mapped masculinity (in various complex and sometimes conflicting forms) on to the lesbian body.[30]

Hall herself carefully utilizes these discourses in order to validate the existence of inversion, simultaneously constructing, as Jean Radford notes, her own set of Foucauldian "reverse discourses."[31] To the public, the trial of *The Well of Loneliness* opens up the same kind of cultural "fault line" as Wilde's trial, instituting a codified lesbian identity that passes into cultural consciousness and against which the internalized landscapes of the lesbian psyche must measure itself. In addition, this lesbian identity becomes indelibly conflated with the notion of obscenity and necessary censure.

One of *The Well*'s most important scenes occurs after Stephen learns she has lost Angela Crossby to her hated childhood rival, Roger Antrim. This loss (unmitigated by a costly shopping spree for accoutrements of the masculinity she does not possess) precipitates a corporeal crisis in Stephen who proceeds to take a long, hard look at her self in the mirror:

> That night she stared at herself in the glass; and even as she did so she hated her body with its muscular shoulders, its small compact breasts, and its slender flanks of an athlete. All her life she must drag this body of hers like a monstrous fetter imposed upon her spirit. This strangely ardent yet sterile body that must worship yet never be worshipped in return by the creature of its adoration. (188)

This scene has been compellingly interpreted in recent criticism in two opposing ways. Jay Prosser, in his exploration of *The Well* as a transsexual narrative, locates this scene as an expression of the typical anguish experienced by the transsexual subject trapped within the wrong biological sex.[32] By contrast, Judith Halberstam, constructing female masculinity as a constitutive lesbian gender, regards the subjectivity expressed in this scene as a kind of precursor of a stone-butch identity of the mid twentieth century.[33] Certainly, as both theorists note, it is crucial to read the gender dysphoria of the scene in terms of the complex conflation of transsexual and lesbian subjectivities in the early twentieth century. What is common to so many of the private and public discourses written by lesbian and bisexual women at this time is a sense of anxiety about the boundaries of their gender identities. The social and sexual polarities of "femininity" and "masculinity" make it difficult for them to read their own complex subjectivities. For Hall, following sexological notions of inversion, Stephen occupies a third space between this binary, her body being at once both male and female.

This central scene from *The Well* is matched by a pivotal scene in *Orlando*, in which Woolf offers us another "mirror-scene":

> He stretched himself. He rose. He stood upright in complete nakedness before us, and while the trumpets pealed Truth! Truth! Truth! We have no choice left but to confess—he was a woman.
>
> The sound of the trumpets died away and Orlando stood stark naked. No human being, since the world began, has ever looked more ravishing. His form combined in one the strength of a man and a woman's grace. . . . Orlando looked himself up and down in a long looking-glass, without showing any signs of discomposure, and went, presumably, to his bath.[34]

Unlike Stephen, Orlando here surveys her/his corporeal nature not with anxiety but with indifference. Woolf circumvents abjection by parodying the "concreteness" of the binary division of masculinity and femininity in the ultimate trangressive act of changing bodily sex. The figure of Orlando has traditionally been read as a signifier of androgyny, yet it seems to me that here Woolf inaugurates something rather different—a lesbian gender identity similar to that articulated in *The Well*. In this moment of "sex-change," Orlando, if s/he is lesbian, seemingly fits no "type" and refuses to be "cast" in her/his bodily role by dominant discourses. S/he need not "drag'" her/his body through the three hundred years of its existence; it is simply "changed" for her/him by the Ladies of Purity, Chastity, and Modesty—at the appropriate moment. This fantastical, irreverent moment masks a more complex articulation of subjectivity. Does this transsexual moment work *with* the binary of sex or *against* it? Orlando, the narrator assures us, has become "a woman," yet his "form" is strangely doubled, combining the "strength of a man and a woman's grace." Thus Orlando is in fact a transgendered figure, occupying a third space in exactly the same way as Stephen. Where this transformative switch between bodies seems to confirm for the reader that all is normal and legible within heterosexual terms, in fact lesbian gender is subtly rendered as a mutable, doubled identity. Later in the text, as Orlando is slowly acculturated into a female role (while still retaining her/his body-memories of masculinity), the arch narratorial voice tells us reassuringly: "the difference between the sexes is, happily, one of great profundity," but then, within the same paragraph, opts for a rather more complex line on the binary of gender:

Different though the sexes are, they intermix. In every human being a vacillation from one sex to the other takes place, and often it is only the clothes that keep the male or female likeness, while underneath the sex is the very opposite of what is above.[35]

As she conceives *Orlando*, Woolf explains to Sackville-West that the book will be "all about you and the lusts of your flesh and the lure of your mind. . . . Also, I admit, I should like to untwine and twist again some very odd, incongruous strands in you."[36] It is tempting to interpret these "very odd, incongruous strands" as a reference to gender identity and to Sackville-West's sense of her own transgendered nature. Suzanne Raitt, reading Sackville-West's suppressed autobiographical account of her affair with Violet Trefusis, notes the terms of "duality" with which she understands her subjectivity. As Raitt notes, this "duality" is expressed as an "alternation" between femininity and masculinity in both psychic and relational terms.[37] This transgendered sense of being "both" is revisited time and again in both the public and the private texts of lesbian modernism. In Bryher's *Two Selves* (1920), for instance, the protagonist, Nancy, is described as: "Two selves. Jammed against each other, disjointed and ill-fitting."[38] In *Orlando*, Woolf inscribes this dysphoria without alarming the reader, through dissimulation. A key component of this inscription is effected through visual signification, with the printing of three photographs of Sackville-West that are taken by Woolf herself (to some degree, then, also codedly inscribing the desirous lesbian gaze). Thus, in the same way as the photographs and cartoons of Hall, so within *Orlando* the lesbian becomes visible, embodied. These photographs of Orlando as a "woman" sit strangely and uncomfortably beside other versions of Orlando as a "boy" and as a "man." Adam Parkes has argued that *Orlando* constructs a narrative of gender identity that, though it clearly predates a Butlerian notion of performativity, nevertheless suggests that gender identity is based upon performance. As such, in Parkes's view, Woolf does away with the body as a signifier of the terms of gender identity.[39] Yet, I would argue, through the constant destabilization of both the corporeal boundaries of its central character and also the solidity of the binary between male and female, the text in fact *centralizes* the body in its discourses on lesbian subjectivity. Orlando is *embodied* in both internal (corporeal) and external (social) terms, thus recording the acute confusions of early twentieth-century lesbian subjectivity. It is Orlando's body, like Stephen's body, which troubles and disrupts any literal interpretation of her/his development, becoming the site of the ultimate unruliness of lesbian gender with its twists and its turns.

In much the same way as Hall, then, Woolf makes her own intervention in the proliferating discourses of lesbian subjectivity. Both *The Well* and *Orlando* are legible as "reverse discourses" that seek to record their own versions of the lesbian life-story and delineate what Puddle in *The Well* calls her "niche in creation" (153). Like Hall, this involves Woolf in making a decision about the appropriate form through which to inscribe the development of the lesbian subject. As Hermione Lee notes, Woolf, as Orlando's "biographer," is "preoccupied with questions of how lives can be written."[40] Plundering the discourses of sexology, psychoanalysis, and medical science and their competing notions of the essentialist or constructionist origins of homosexuality, Hall locates the pro forma of the case history as the most useful frame for *The Well*, melding the bildungsroman form to represent Stephen's coming to identity. Thus her "story" begins in childhood and goes on to offer a detailed chronological account of her adolescence and adulthood. While we do not follow Stephen through to old age, the temporal frame of the novel is neatly bounded by the parameters of the human life span. Within this chronology, either essentialist or constructionist interpretations of her "nature" might stand. She is born a "narrow-hipped, wide-shouldered tadpole" of a baby, yet her psychic profile is also formulated out of complicated oedipal beginnings (9). In seeming contrast, Orlando's "story," in true modernist form, deconstructs human time by expanding to fill three hundred years' worth of history. Her/his narrative defies the notion of legible chronology through its ellipses and inconsistencies. Such a temporal frame makes the complexities of Orlando's figure illegible to a reader versed only in realism. In a pleasing piece of synchronicity, Arnold Bennett (perhaps the ultimate realist reader) reviews *Orlando* in the *Evening Standard* on November 8, the day before the paper carries its report on the opening of *The Well* hearing. Bennett's review, titled "A Woman's High-Brow Lark," argues that *Orlando* is "a very odd volume" that contains strange elements such as "realistic photographs" and an index.[41] Such features are, of course, more compatible with biographical form than novelistic form (this is part of Woolf's conceit), yet they also, to some degree, invoke the discursive form of the case history, suggesting that this text is a study of the figure "Orlando." Taking the form so favored by the "biologists and psychologists" who speculate endlessly on the "odious subjects" of sex and sexuality as a base model, Woolf turns the notion of the case history on its head.[42] In addition to its structural elements, the temporal frame of *Orlando* seems to parody the localized narrative of the case history, manipulating the notion of a "lifespan" by expanding the "life" under scrutiny to seemingly fantastic proportions.[43] In the same way as Stephen's "story," we cannot easily read the reasons for Orlando's "nature"; this, as the narrator is so quick to remind us, is because although the remit of the "biographer" (for which read "sexual theorist") might ostensibly be to "plod, without looking left or right, in the indelible footprints of truth," such a practice inevitably fails, particularly when it comes to questions of sex. Here, as we witness when it comes to questions of "sex-change," it is necessary "to speculate, to surmise, and even to make use of the imagination."[44] Woolf thus parodies the supposed scientific objectivity of the theorist of inversion (in addition to Victorian notions of the biographer), deconstructing the kinds of interpretive certainties of the case history. Describing *Orlando* to Sackville-West, Woolf writes: "it sprung upon me how I could revolutionize biography in a night."[45] Yet she also, within the text of *Orlando*, appears to revolutionize the typical autobiographical narrative of the invert, so often an integral component of sexological case histories, which, as Prosser notes, becomes the key trope for sexual histories in the early twentieth century. Ultimately then, though it utilizes differing literary techniques, *Orlando* is derived from the same sources as *The Well* and, playing with similar discursive forms, strives toward the same representational end.[46]

Writing Love's Loss: *Pilgrimage* and *The Well of Loneliness*

Further developing a sense of the kinds of mutualities that exist between *The Well* and lesbian modernism, I would like to explore another key intertextual resonance between *The Well* and one of the most extensive modernist texts, Dorothy Richardson's thirteen-novel series, *Pilgrimage*. Begun in 1913, the series charts the personal and artistic development of the main protagonist, Miriam Henderson, a fictionalized version of Richardson herself. Like *Orlando*, *Pilgrimage* records lesbian sexuality in complex textual terms, using modernist practices as a similar "cover" for the inscription of desire and identity.[47] The novel-chapters written between 1913 and the early 1930s contain compelling resemblances to the formulations of lesbian identity expressed in *The Well*; here Richardson, like Hall and Woolf, works over the same primary discourses of inversion and psychoanalysis. Miriam occupies the same place within the "no-man's land of sex" that Stephen inhabits in *The Well*, articulating a similar gender dysphoria.[48] Stephen's positionality, Puddle assures her, allows her to "write both men and women from a personal knowledge" (208). In *The Tunnel*, the fourth novel of the *Pilgrimage* series, Miriam describes herself as being "somewhere between a man and a woman, looking both ways."[49] Like Stephen's "personal knowledge," Miriam experiences both these gender identities through compelling and binding identifications with both: "Feeling so identified with both, she could not imagine either of them set aside."[50] Such a gender identity has a causative link to Miriam's sexuality that while at times directed towards men, finds its main impulsion in her intense emotional connections with women.

While this account of lesbian gender identity represents one important point of connection with *The Well*, perhaps the most arresting resonance between the texts is what can be seen as a parallel narrative development to *The Well*, which occurs in the tenth and eleventh novel-chapters of *Pilgrimage*: *Dawn's Left Hand* and *Clear Horizon*. In *Dawn's Left Hand* Miriam meets and falls in love with an enigmatic young Frenchwoman, Amabel, during Miriam's time in London. Like Stephen's eventual sacrifice in *The Well*, Miriam ultimately orchestrates a marriage between Amabel and her own failed suitor, Michael Shatov. Most important to a comparative analysis of *Pilgrimage* and *The Well*, these novel-chapters are written or planned in the late 1920s, during the period in which *The Well* comes to trial.[51] What is clear from the time it takes to produce these two texts is that Richardson experiences great difficulty in reworking this period of her life—her relationship with the real-life Veronica Leslie-Jones—into fictional form. While she never refers to the trial in her correspondence, it is difficult not to conjecture that her own disavowals of lesbian sexuality, which make this life-material so difficult to record, are also overwritten by the spectacle of *The Well*'s prosecution.[52] From the outset Miriam is deeply attracted to Amabel, feeling her own "self" come into being through their contact and, despite her continuing involvement with Hypo Wilson (the fictional counterpart of H. G. Wells), they embark upon a mutually compelling affair. As the novel progresses, however, Miriam begins to feel trapped within a role, a social space that she fears will subsume her whole life. Distraught, she casts around for a solution, which is finally detailed at the beginning of *Clear Horizon*. She introduces Amabel to Shatov and, in a complex sacrificial manipulation, orchestrates a marriage between them into which Amabel reluctantly enters for Miriam's sake. The complicated emotional terms of this sacrifice mirror Stephen's "release" of Mary from the tragic life of the invert to the expectant, heterosexual arms of Martin. Like Shatov, Martin is, of course, a former suitor, whose offer of marriage as sanctuary from "difference" has been rejected. Yet, where Hall's text is explicit about the reasons for Stephen's decision, Richardson's text overwrites the real factor of social prohibition through complex imagery and textual dissimulation, both of which encode the lesbian content within dense modernist prose:

> But her shocked consciousness pulled her up in the midst of relief, insisting that she should drive away the subtly attractive picture while it stood clear in her mind, and use its suspicious fruit, the aroused state of her whole being, to discover its secret origin and thereby judge its worth. *Isolated with possible motives, she found herself in a maze whose partitions were mirrors.* (emphasis mine)[53]

Here Miriam is split by the possibility of releasing Amabel to Michael, feeling at the same time a sense of "relief" and yet the trauma of her "shocked consciousness." Enacted within the psychic drama of this splitting is the decision whether to concede to social pressure or resist it. Like Stephen, Miriam is reluctantly driven to these actions. In seeking out her motives for imagining this alarming solution, Miriam becomes "isolated" within a "maze" in which she can only see her mirrored self. The partitions of this "maze," which reproduce and reflect her "self" back at her at every turn, deny escape. Suggestively reminiscent of Stephen's "mirror-scene" in which she observes her "poor, most desolate body," here Miriam's *physicality*, her lesbian body, becomes the reason why Amabel must marry Michael (188). This body, rendered so different and dislocated by prevailing social terms, thus symbolizes the impossibility of living out lesbian desire.

As well as sharing the enactment of a kind of sacrificial release, both texts identify a compulsion in these actions; for both Miriam and Stephen such a compulsion is prefigured by a sense of the predestination of their actions. In both texts this predestination, while unidentifiable to each of them, is textually constructed as the direct influence of the social prohibition against lesbianism. Miriam identifies "something" at work both upon her and the situation, the strength of which overrides her own emotional ambivalence about her decision:

> Something far away below any single, particular motive she could search out, had made the decision, was refusing to attend to this conscious conflict and was already regarding the event as current, even as past and accomplished. This complete, independent response, whose motives were either undiscoverable or non-existent, might be good or bad, but was irrevocable.[54]

In *The Well*, this predestination is figured as a kind of "dreaming" in which Stephen cannot control her actions, though she is prompted by it throughout to complete them. Her deep ambivalence at her own actions is dealt with through the assumption of another "self" who carries out the "necessary" actions of handing Mary over to Martin:

> In a kind of dream she perceived these things. In a dream she now moved and had her being; scarcely conscious of whither this dream would lead, the while her every perception was quickened. And this dream of hers was immensely compelling, *so that all that she did seemed clearly predestined; she could not have acted otherwise*, nor could she have made a false step, although dreaming . . .
> In obedience to the mighty but unseen will that had taken control of this vivid dreaming, she ceased to respond to the girl's tenderness. . . . Ruthless as the world itself she became. (emphasis mine) (439)

This climactic sacrifice, the socially determined end to lesbian desire, prompts a crisis in both Stephen and Miriam about the inferiority of lesbian gender identity. Both explore an anguish about their lack of status in comparison to men. Stephen submits to the realization that whatever male role she may have attempted to play, protecting and providing for a number of women from an early age—her mother, the housemaid Collins, the married Angela Crossby and finally her first lover, Mary—she cannot fulfill the promise she makes them. She has attempted to assume a male role, but she

remains psychologically and corporeally female. Though she may "perform" masculinity in her aping of male fashion, the punishment for such
impersonation is the denial of emotional happiness and sexual fulfillment.
At this moment in the text, it is Martin who becomes the "real" man, a figure sure enough of his place and identity to inspire awe in Stephen, *his*
masculinity being premised upon a fundamental "right" to this identity:

> And suddenly Martin appeared to Stephen as a creature endowed with
> incalculable bounty, having in his hands all those priceless gifts which she,
> love's mendicant, could never offer. Only one gift could she offer to love, to
> Mary, and that was the gift of Martin. (438–439)

For Miriam too, the handing over of Amabel to Michael is accompanied by
a chastened admiration of his masculinity and its status. Her ambivalence
at the solution she seeks out is swiftly overwhelmed by the pressing reality
of the "weakness" of her own gender position, in comparison with the position that Michael can offer Amabel as a man. In the face of her "failure"
Miriam smites herself and her "lack": "*it was she herself and not Michael,
who was the pathetic fragment,* so cut off and resourceless as to delight in
the *mere reproduction* of social rituals and *the illusory sense of power*"
(emphasis mine).[55] In the guise of the lesbian, she becomes a "pathetic fragment." Her attempted "masculinity," like Stephen's, can only ever be a
"copy." It is the realization that she can perform what she calls "the mere
reproduction of social rituals," and that her experience of power, in a man's
world, can only ever be "illusory" that provokes the decision to bring
Amabel and Michael together, and *through* Michael, vicariously experience
social and sexual union with Amabel which she herself desires.[56]

Here *The Well* and *Pilgrimage* part narrative company. Hall ends
Stephen's tragic narrative with existential anguish and polemical social
plea, whilst Richardson, in the novel-chapters that follow through the late
1930s and 1940s writes on into Miriam's future toward an "end" that figures
an intense spiritual and emotional union with a woman called Jean.[57] Yet,
during the period in which these texts enter the same orbit, both the fate of
The Well and its emotional texturing of Stephen's "story" can be seen to
inflect the events of *Pilgrimage*. Like Woolf, Richardson chooses to embed
her lesbian narrative in the textual densities of modernism, refusing perhaps to take the inherent risk of rendering it explicit in the same way as

Hall; nevertheless, its narrative provides some kind of model by which to record her own lesbian "story."

Placing these lesbian modernist texts alongside *The Well* and mapping the traces of influence across seemingly sealed literary boundaries suggests that it is time for *The Well* to be brought in from the literary cold. In the cases of both *Orlando* and *Pilgrimage*, it is clear that the text itself, the sources it uses, and its fate at the hands of the censors cast a deeply influential light over the period of the 1920s. As Benstock has argued, one of the first ways of defining Sapphic modernism is to discard the question of a text's "formal properties, aesthetic purity, or artistic programs" and to turn instead to the question of whom it seeks to "address." In this way, she suggests, "we might better be able to suggest the reasons why some lesbian writers of the period embraced Sapphic modernism and others fled from it."[58] Hall never proclaimed herself either a modernist or an avant-garde experimenter (despite her often precious defense of her own literary ability), and her avowed aim, in the case of *The Well*, was to offer an otherwise ignorant audience an insight into the tragic fate of the sexual invert. As Troubridge explains, the aim was to produce a book that "would be accessible to the general public who did not have access to technical treatises."[59] Such a remit might well place *The Well* outside what has traditionally been conceived of as the intellectually rigorous terms of modernist experimentation, but it does not seal off its influence upon such texts. Indeed the case of *The Well* and its cumulative impact of lesbian modernism suggests that the rigidity of these terms must shift. In formulating an understanding of lesbian modernism, it is crucial to recognize that texts such as *Orlando* and *Pilgrimage* cannot, and indeed do not, function independently of the important cultural context that *The Well* constitutes; that they may, in fact, be addressing themselves to the same audience in a different way. As we discover, these texts share both its sources and its intention to inscribe the lesbian's life story amidst a dominant culture that would rather do it for her in its own terms. Acknowledging the intertextual dialogue between *The Well* and lesbian modernism, the crossings of the literary tracks, is to finally reinstate it in its rightful place, within the network of lesbian textualities of the early twentieth century.

Notes

1. Adrienne Rich, "It Is the Lesbian in Us . . . ," in *On Lies, Secrets, and Silence* (London: Virago Press, 1986), p. 201.

2. Letter dated early November 1928, in Nigel Nicolson and Joanne Trautmann, eds., *A Change of Perspective: The Letters of Virginia Woolf*, vol. 3, *1923–1928* (London: Hogarth Press, 1977), p. 556.

3. Entry dated August 31, 1928, in Anne Olivier Bell, ed., *The Diary of Virginia Woolf*, vol. 3, *1925–1930* (London: Hogarth Press, 1980), p. 193.

4. Two important critical readings that open up a dialogue between *The Well of Loneliness* and its modernist counterparts are Jane Marcus, "Sapphistory: The Woolf and the Well," in Karla Jay and Joanne Glasgow, eds., *Lesbian Texts and Contexts* (London: Onlywomen Press, 1992), pp. 164–180 and Bonnie Kime Scott, *Refiguring Modernism*, vol. 1, *The Women of 1928* (Bloomington: Indiana University Press, 1995).

5. Makiko Minow, "Versions of Female Modernism: A Review Article," *News from Nowhere* 7 (Winter 1989): 67.

6. As Erin Carlston notes, Sapphic Modernism is "a highly contested term." For some of these "contestations" see Shari Benstock, "Expatriate Sapphic Modernism: Entering Literary History," in Jay and Glasgow, eds., *Lesbian Texts and Contexts*, pp. 183–203; Erin Carlston, *Thinking Fascism: Sapphic Modernism and Fascist Modernity* (Stanford: Stanford University Press, 1998); Corinne E. Blackmer, "Lesbian Modernism in the Shorter Fiction of Virginia Woolf and Gertrude Stein," in Eileen Barrett and Patricia Cramer, eds., *Virginia Woolf: Lesbian Readings* (New York: New York University Press, 1997), pp. 78–94; Diana Collecott, *H.D. and Sapphic Modernity* (Cambridge: Cambridge University Press, 1999); Nicky Hallett, *Lesbian Lives: Identity and Auto/biography in the Twentieth Century* (London: Pluto Press, 1999); Joanne Winning, *The Pilgrimage of Dorothy Richardson* (Madison: University of Wisconsin Press, 2000).

7. Benstock, "Expatriate Sapphic Modernism," p. 185.

8. Marianne Dekoven, "'Excellent Not a Hull House': Gertrude Stein, Jane Addams, and Feminist-Modernist Political Culture," in Lisa Rado, ed., *Rereading Modernism: New Directions in Feminist Criticism* (New York: Garland Press, 1994), p. 321.

9. Beverley Brown, "'A Disgusting Book When Properly Read': The Obscenity Trial," *Hecate* 10, no. 2 (1984): 13.

10. See Djuna Barnes, *Ladies Almanack* (1928; reprint, Elmwood Park, Ill.: Dalkey Archive Press, 1992).

11. Hallett, *Lesbian Lives*, p. 67.

12. See, among others: Bryher's *Development* (1920) and *Two Selves* (1923); H.D.'s *Her* (1981); Dorothy Richardson's *Pilgrimage* (1913–1954); Virginia Woolf's *Orlando* (1928), and Djuna Barnes's *Nightwood* (1936).

13. Radclyffe Hall, *The Well of Loneliness* (1928; reprint, London: Virago, 1990), p. 208. All subsequent citations are to this edition.

14. Michel Foucault, *The Archaeology of Knowledge* (New York: Pantheon Books, 1972), p. 23.

15. Havelock Ellis, *Studies in the Psychology of Sex*, vol. 1 (New York: Random House, 1942), p. 90.

16. "M. M.," *Daily Telegraph*, August 17, 1928, p. 65 in this volume.

17. Woolf, *Diary*, vol. 3, p. 207.

18. Quoted in Vera Brittain, *Radclyffe Hall: A Case of Obscenity?* (London: Femina Books, 1968), p. 92.

19. E. M. Forster and Virginia Woolf, "The New Censorship," *Nation and Athenaeum*, September 8, 1928, p. 726.

20. We might also say, though there is not space to develop the argument further here, that this equivalence suggests a compelling correlation between the representation of an identity fractured by modernity and a lesbian identity fragmented through cultural mediation and intervention.

21. *Orlando* was published on October 11, between the withdrawal of *The Well* in August and Chartres Biron's eventual ban of the book in November.

22. Entry dated February 19, 1923, in Anne Olivier Bell, ed., *The Diary of Virginia Woolf*, vol. 2, *1920–1924* (London: Hogarth Press, 1978), p. 235.

23. See, for instance, Sherron E. Knopp, "'If I Saw You Would You Kiss Me?': Sapphism and the Subversiveness of Virginia Woolf's *Orlando*," *PMLA* 103, no. 1 (January 1988): 24–34 and Adam Parkes, "Lesbianism, History, and Censorship: *The Well of Loneliness* and the SUPPRESSED RANDINESS of Virginia Woolf's *Orlando*," *Twentieth-Century Literature* 40, no. 4 (Winter 1994): 434–460.

24. Lillian Faderman, "Love Between Women in 1928: Why Progressivism Is Not Always Progress," in Monica Kehoe, ed., *Historical, Literary, and Erotic Aspects of Lesbianism* (New York & London: Haworth Press, 1986), p. 27.

25. Woolf, *Diary* vol. 3, p. 162.

26. See Scott, *Refiguring Modernism*, p. 257.

27. See Alan Sinfield, *The Wilde Century: Effeminacy, Oscar Wilde, and the Queer Moment* (London: Cassell, 1994).

28. For an excellent discussion of the complex relationship between cultural images of female masculinity and lesbian identity in the 1920s, see Laura Doan, "Passing Fashions: Reading Female Masculinities in the 1920s," *Feminist Studies* 24 (Fall 1998): 663–700.

29. See Michael Baker, *Our Three Selves* (London, Gay Men's Press, 1985) for reproductions of these cartoons. What is notable here, however, is the difference between these publications. Both the *Daily Express* and the *Evening Standard* were tabloid newspapers, thus Hall becomes a cultural cipher of "the lesbian" to a much wider (and more working-class) audience at this point.

30. These discourses might be typified by the corporeal "masculinity" that Ellis identities in the female invert in his *Sexual Inversion* and the psychic "masculinity" that Sigmund Freud locates in the development of the homosexual girl of his last case history. See Ellis, *Studies in the Psychology of Sex*, vol. 2, *Sexual Inversion* (1897; reprint, Philadelphia: F. A. Davis, 3d. ed., 1921) and Freud, "Psychogenesis of a Case of Homosexuality in a Woman" (1920), in *Case Histories II: "Rat Man," Schreber, "Wolf Man," Female Homosexuality* [Pelican Freud Library, vol. 9] (Harmondsworth: Penguin, 1979), pp. 367–400.

31. Jean Radford, "An Inverted Romance: *The Well of Loneliness* and Sexual Ideology," in Radford, ed., *The Progress of Romance: The Politics of Popular Fiction* (London: Routledge & Kegan Paul, 1986), p. 106. Though, as Jay Prosser has convincingly argued, given the use of case history as empirical data for sexological theory, and the ways in which sexology literally takes the (autobiographical) words out of the mouths of its subjects of study, it is difficult to say just who it is who writes these dominant discourses into being. See Jay Prosser, *Second Skins: The Body Narratives of Transsexuality* (New York: Columbia University Press, 1998), pp. 144ff.

32. See Prosser, *Second Skins*.

33. See Judith Halberstam, *Female Masculinity* (Durham, N.C.: Duke University Press, 1998).

34. Virginia Woolf, *Orlando* (1928; reprint, Harmondsworth: Penguin, 1993), pp. 97–98.

35. Ibid., pp. 132–133.

36. Letter dated October 9, 1927, in *The Letters of Virginia Woolf*, vol. 3, p. 429.

37. Suzanne Raitt, "Sex, Love, and the Homosexual Body," in Lucy Bland and Laura Doan, eds., *Sexology in Culture: Labelling Bodies and Desires* (Oxford: Polity Press, 1998), pp. 152ff.

38. Bryher, *Two Novels: Development and Two Selves*, intro. Joanne Winning (1920 and 1923; reprint, Madison: University of Wisconsin Press, 2000).

39. See Parkes, "Lesbianism, History, and Censorship."

40. Hermione Lee, *Virginia Woolf* (London: Vintage, 1996), p. 523.

41. Arnold Bennett, "A Woman's High-Brow Lark," *Evening Standard*, November 8, 1928, p. 7.

42. Woolf, *Orlando*, p. 98.

43. Another lesbian modernist text that parodies the case history with great relish is Barnes's *Ladies Almanack* in which the question of "origins" is so satirized. Lady Evangeline Musset, we are told, "developed in the womb of her most gentle Mother to be a Boy, when therefore, she came forth an Inch or so less than this, she paid no Heed to the Error" (Barnes, *Ladies Almanack*, p. 7). Barnes's text is another rich source of resonances with *The Well*.

44. Woolf, *Orlando*, pp. 47, 84.

45. Woolf, *Letters*, vol. 3, p. 429.

46. See Prosser, *Second Skins*, pp. 149 ff.

47. For a more detailed exploration of Richardson's recording of lesbian identity and desire see my *The Pilgrimage of Dorothy Richardson*.

48. Hall, *The Well of Loneliness*, p. 77. Miriam's gender dysphoria is also discussed by other critics, see Jean Radford, *Dorothy Richardson* (Hemel Hempstead: Harvester Wheatsheaf, 1991) and Kristin Bluemel, *Experimenting on the Borders of Modernism: Dorothy Richardson's Pilgrimage* (Athens: University of Georgia Press, 1997).

49. Dorothy Richardson, *Pilgrimage*, vol. 2 (London: Virago, 1979), p. 187.

50. Ibid., vol. 3, p. 250.

51. Richardson began writing *Dawn's Left Hand* in 1927 after the publication of *Oberland* in the same year. The novel presented her with the greatest of difficulties and took five years to write, finally appearing in 1931. *Clear Horizon* caused her similar problems, taking another four years and appearing in 1935.

52. Richardson herself did indeed orchestrate a marriage between Veronica Leslie-Jones and Benjamin Grad. The terms of Richardson's relationship with Leslie-Jones are complicated; it is not possible to describe it simply as lesbian. Yet, reading the intertextual echoes of Stephen's "rationale" in *The Well* in Miriam's internal reasoning in *Pilgrimage*, the "hidden" signifier of *The Well* as lesbian artifact makes it hard not to infer a lesbian element in this relationship.

53. Richardson, *Pilgrimage*, vol. 4, p. 285.

54. Ibid., p. 285.

55. Ibid., pp. 285–286.

56. Ibid. As Halberstam argues, in cultural terms "female masculinity [is] framed as the rejected scraps of dominant masculinity in order that male masculinity may appear to be the real thing" (*Female Masculinity*, p. 1). Here both Hall and Richardson seem to record (and ultimately reject) this commonplace dominant cultural construction of female masculinity as a "failed copy."

57. This relationship is detailed in the final, unfinished novel-chapter, *March Moonlight*.

58. See Benstock, "Expatriate Sapphic Modernism," p. 187.

59. Una Troubridge, *The Life and Death of Radclyffe Hall* (London: Hammond Hammond, 1961), p. 81.

Afterword: It Was Good, Good, *Good*

TERRY CASTLE

Oh god not again: *The Well of Fucking Loneliness.* When will the nightmare stop? Here we are again, asleep and fitfully dreaming: it's the final play before the buzzer at the Greatest Lesbian Writers of the World Basketball Championship. The stands are packed; the fans screaming; and the hometown team—the Tasteful-and-Artistic-Ones—are struggling desperately to hold on. There they all are: stylish V. Woolf, gallantly fronting the squad, of course; "Shoot It Slant" Dickinson and Willa "Big Gal" Cather, sprightly Colette and "Playmaker" Yourcenar, Djuna the Jumping Jockette, S. Bedford, J. Flanner, P. Highsmith, B. Brophy, E. Bishop, A. Rich, J. Winterson . . . Hell, we've even got some great *guys* on the bench: Chuck Baudelaire, Marcel the Proust, Henry "Awesome" James, the small but wily D.H.L. . . . (Remember that hot sapphic scene in *The Rainbow*?) But **NO!** Here **SHE** comes! Radclyffe "Sterile Kisses" Hall! Star Forward of the Terrible-Legion-of-the-Inverts! the Original Butch Horror! Franchise Player to the Suicidal! the Maimed One herself! "John" to her Friends! Trundling up the court in huge baggy men's underpants, a piece of the True Cross around her neck, and that godawful mopey look on her face! Crowd's going nuts, shouts *Defense Defense* in rhythmic unison; but it's no bloody good—she's *coming up inside*! Only one player can stop her now! Gert!! Where are you? (Down with a groin pull and unable to get a word out! Tiny trainer Alice B. runs out . . .) Help! Help! *She's* powering in on her weird "tadpole" hips! She's making us all look *bad*! She wants to be the Man! She's a freakin' Third Sex Machine! She's making us all feel *miserable*! She shoots! SHE **SCORES!!! SHE'S DONE IT AGAIN!!!** (groans, tears, cries of disbelief)

How bad, bad, bad is Radclyffe Hall's *The Well of Loneliness*? Like many bookish lesbians I seem to have spent much of my adult life making jokes about it, as if to fend it off once and for all. After all, it *is* quite possibly the worst novel ever written, crammed full with so many ghastly passages one is hard-pressed to choose one's favorite hideousness among them. The opening paragraphs, for example—in which Hall describes the idyllic courtship of Lady Anna and Sir Philip, the aristocratic parents of the book's haplessly homosexual heroine, Stephen Gordon—have a kind of enunciatory awfulness that is hard to beat:

> To Morton Hall came the Lady Anna Gordon as a bride of just over twenty. She was lovely as only an Irish woman can be, having that in her bearing that betokened quiet pride, having that in her eyes that betokened great longing, having that in her body that betokened happy promise—the archetype of the very perfect woman, whom creating God has found good. Sir Philip had met her away in County Clare—Anna Molloy, the slim virgin thing, all chastity, and his weariness had flown to her bosom as a spent bird will fly to its nest—as indeed such a bird had once flown to her, she told him, taking refuge from the perils of a storm.(11)[1]

Dear Lady Anna: not just perfect, but *very* perfect!

Yet specimens of gruesomeness abound. Many an indulgent gal pal have I regaled with my celebrated frothing-at-the-mouth impersonation of the "terrible nerves of the invert"—that frightful affliction first mentioned in the following description of Stephen's little spinster governess, Miss Puddle. The wee Puddle, it transpires, has divined her youthful charge's "abnormal" attraction to her own sex and sympathizes with her in secret:

> For none knew better than this little grey woman, the agony of mind that must be endured when a sensitive, highly organized nature is first brought face to face with its own affliction. None knew better the terrible nerves of the invert, nerves that are always lying in wait. Super-nerves, whose response is only equalled by the strain that calls that response into being. Puddle was well-acquainted with these things—that was why she was deeply concerned about Stephen. (155)

Blast those wretched super-nerves!

And likewise: who could forget (ever) *The Well*'s celebrated love scenes—turgid, pimple-ridden, sumptuously ungrammatical, yet all too apt to peter out in feeble redundancies just when everything is hotting up?

When they were alone and in comparative safety, there would be something crude, almost cruel in their kisses; a restless, dissatisfied, hungry thing—their lips would seem bent on scourging their bodies. Neither would find deliverance nor ease from the ache that was in them, for each would be kissing with a well-nigh intolerable sense of loss, with a passionate knowledge of separation. (189)

Never before had they done such a thing as this, they had never dined all alone at a wayside inn miles away from their homes, just they two, and Stephen stretched out her hand and covered Angela's where it rested very white and still on the table. And Stephen's eyes held an urgent question, for now it was May and the blood of youth leaps and strains with the sap in early summer. The air seemed breathless, since neither would speak, afraid of disturbing this thick, sweet silence—but Angela shook her head very slowly. Then they could not eat, for each was filled with the same and yet with a separate longing; so after a while they must get up and go, both conscious of a sense of painful frustration. (190)
"I love you—I love you so much . . . " she stammered; and she kissed Mary many times on the mouth, but cruelly so that her kisses were pain—the pain in her heart leapt out through her lips: "God! It's too terrible to love like this—it's hell—there are times when I can't endure it!"

She was in the grip of strong nervous excitation; nothing seemed able any more to appease her. She seemed to be striving to obliterate, not only herself, but the whole hostile world through some strange and agonized merging with Mary. It was terrible indeed, very like unto death, and it left them both completely exhausted. (371)

Cue to TC and other Sapphocomic thespians: imitate painful "scourging" lip movements, debilitating effects of saplike blood in summertime, strange agony while merging, etc. etc.

At the same time I cannot help but acknowledge—ruefully—that the will to jape conceals some rather more complex feelings too. Paradoxical though it may seem, the urge to mock has always coexisted in me with a fierce annoyance whenever I hear someone *else* disparaging *The Well*. Not its most extreme abusers, I hasten to explain: those who find in Hall's depiction of love between women some "pestilential" moral anathema and go on to blare about it. Perusing the fascinating original 1928 reviews of *The Well of Loneliness* reprinted in this volume, I am struck by how oddly impervious I am to the fantastically harsh moral judgments of female homosexuality set forth in many of them. James Douglas's famous diatribe in the *Sunday Express* (August 19, 1928), in which he castigated the novel for its sympathetic treatment of "hideous and loathsome vices" and called (successfully) for its suppression by the home secretary, seems to me merely risible and quaint—just as the more absurd outpourings of certain religious fanatics do today. W. R. Gordon's complaint in the *Daily News and Westminster Gazette* (August 23, 1928) that Hall's novel polluted one's sense of the "innocent, cheerful affectionate relationships" of women by introducing "the wandering dragon of lust" into them seems to me a piece of dated "period" silliness, a kind of comic Blimpishness, with nothing to do with me. No: far more liable to upset me are animadversions upon the novel by those writers whom I respect and admire. Virginia Woolf's often-quoted description of *The Well* as "a meritorious, dull book" never fails to irritate me in some obscure fashion; likewise the young Cyril Connolly's epicene dismissal of it in the *New Statesman* (also from 1928) as "long, tedious and absolutely humourless." Given my own compulsive waggery I have little right to complain, but I find Connolly's all-too-predictable sniping at Hall's expense somehow grating nonetheless:

> The most embarrassing parts are the sentimental animal passages. In particular the episode of the old hunter that Stephen insists on taking down in agony, all the way from London to Worcestershire, so that he may be shot outside his own loose-box, seems ridiculous in the extreme. No county family could be expected—quite apart from morals—to regard as normal such a crank as that. (68)

Connolly is right—exquisitely so—when he observes that "homosexuality is, after all, as rich in comedy as tragedy, and it is time it was emancipated from the aura of distinguished damnation and religious martyrdom which surrounds its so fiercely aggressive apologists." Sappho, he concludes, "had never heard of the mark of Cain, she was also well able to look after herself, but never did she possess a disciple so conscious of her inferiority as Stephen Gordon, or so lacking—for 15s.!—in the rudiments of charm." Elegantly put, one must concede: sense wins out over super-nerves, good taste saves the day. And yet! Even as one makes sport of *The Well*—exults over the sheer ineptitude of it all—one may also have a creeping sense of bad faith, the niggling feeling that one is being unjust and possibly even dishonest. Is charmlessness the sum of it? Is *bad, bad, bad* really all there is to say about Hall's incorrigible (yes), invidious (yes), still wrenching piece of work?

The essays on *The Well of Loneliness* collected in this volume have helped me to sort out these contradictory emotions and to find my way back—not to any untroubled intellectual endorsement or critical complacency—such I suspect will never come—but to something far more meaningful and profound: my embarrassing, possibly adolescent, yet nonetheless intransigent love for this book and its author. Love is hardly too strong a word here. Indeed, only by an avowal of love I find can I counter an aesthetic shame-reflex so fierce and heavy-breathing—nay positively glandular—as to make my computer screen fog up as I type these words. But there it is: I threw my hat into *The Well* long ago, and despite any lingering pretensions to fastidiousness, must remain bareheaded and admiring in the book's strange, compelling presence.

Which isn't to say there is anything maudlin or cloying about the illuminating essays assembled here. Their authors are all in varying degree skeptical, uncompromising, and quick to acknowledge their own frustrations with Hall's often monstrously overwrought parable of homosexual *Bildung*. (As indeed they are quick to acknowledge their frustrations with fellow readers and critics. If one of the signal attributes of a living artwork is how fiercely it promotes argument—opens itself to the rough scarifications of controversy and dissent—then all of the peculiar polemical debate that has swirled around *The Well of Loneliness* since its fraught first appearance is embodied here, in the roiling yet fascinating interrelationships obtaining between various essays, in the odd rhetorical fervor that sometimes erupts in the midst of otherwise dispassionate investigation.) No one tries to hide it: the book has its mortifications and one must wrestle with them as best one can.

Some of the problems are purely intellectual: witness the intense disagreement among contributors to this volume about the precise nature of Stephen Gordon's sexual unorthodoxy. When it comes to identifying Stephen's problem, her creator, one must confess, does not always give the impression of thinking clearly. Though we customarily speak of *The Well* as a lesbian novel, Hall never once uses the word *lesbian* or *homosexual* in its pages. Instead, drawing on the pseudoscientific nomenclature of early twentieth-century sexologists such as Havelock Ellis, Hall inevitably describes her misfit heroine as a "sexual invert." Yet as the fiction unfolds the latter term becomes increasingly (and bewilderingly) unclear. Does being an invert mean wanting to be a man? Certainly Stephen seems to yearn—excruciatingly—for some kind of real or symbolic "manhood." How does this yearning relate to her equally powerful craving for the sexual love of other women? Is being an invert the same as being a lesbian? What about characters in the work—and Stephen's "femme" lover Mary Llewellyn is a good example—who seem to desire sex with other women but evince no corresponding desire to be men? And what does it mean to "want to be a man" anyway? To wish outright for a male body? Or merely for the social and psychic freedom to dress and behave mannishly? Even as Hall foregrounds these questions with anxious compulsiveness, she seems painfully unsure about the precise relationship between body and desire, gender identity and sexual orientation. The result, intellectually speaking, is a kind of diagnostic balls-up.

Other mortifications are more metaphysical—even spiritual. As Susan Kingsley Kent and Jodie Medd capture so well in their essays on images of wounding in *The Well*, Hall's outlook on homosexuality is often morbidly kitsch, as when, for example, she somewhat tastelessly equates the pain felt by the sexual invert in a hostile society with the mental agony of World War I soldiers suffering from shell shock. She is prone to a kind of sickly, regurgitant religiosity: as Sally Munt suggests in a gruffly personal piece on the novel and Catholic guilt, Hall seems to revel perversely in "shaming" her heroine, even as she forces Stephen to do heavy symbolic duty as a kind of unwilling Christ-figure and sexual martyr. And hardly surprisingly, for a woman of her time and class and racial background (wealthy, white, and privileged), Radclyffe Hall is seldom insightful on social and political realities that don't particularly concern her. Her portraits of black characters in *The Well*, as Jean Walton points out, leave much to be desired; ditto her treatment of the various servants who bustle in and out of Stephen's life, such as the "exotic" Orotavans who dote upon her and Mary when they enjoy their short-lived lovers' honeymoon, in one of the book's few respites from gloom, on the tropical island of Tenerife.

How then, given all the bad news they bring, have the essays in this collection paradoxically revived my love for this book? Conspicuous in all of the pieces in this volume is a level of emotional seriousness and personal engagement one seldom sees in academic tomes of this nature. This seriousness manifests itself at times in sheer polemical vehemence: witness the gripping forensic battle waged against one another by Jay Prosser and Judith Halberstam, who in successive essays here take up starkly opposing positions on the ambiguous question of Stephen Gordon's psychosexual makeup. (Prosser, himself a female-to-male transsexual, views Stephen as a transsexual *avant la lettre*, a biological female craving the physical sex change she cannot have, while Halberstam, an ardent proponent of "female masculinity," categorizes her as transgressive butch—as someone who wants the right to look and behave like a man without actually becoming one. Needless to say, as on the streets of San Francisco—the Gomorrah-like little burg in which I currently reside—the libidinal back and forth here becomes mind-boggling pretty fast.) Elsewhere in the volume emotional engagement takes the form simply of vibrant and forceful ratiocination— as in Trevor Hope's erudite reflections on the role of fetishism in the novel, or Julie Abraham's stunning meditation on *The Well*, homosexuality, and the symbolic role of cities in modern life.

Yet precisely because of this seriousness I find myself forced to acknowledge once again *The Well's* uncanny rhetorical power—a power unaffected by its manifest failures as a work of art—to activate readerly feeling at an extraordinarily profound level. As virtually every contribution to this volume shows, *The Well of Loneliness* forces us to confront—over and over and with a sometimes astonishing corporeal immediacy—our deepest experiences of eros, intimacy, sexual identity, and how our fleshly bodies relate to the fleshly bodies of others. Something in the very pathos of Stephen Gordon's torment—something in the very magnificence of her confusion—provokes an exorbitant emotional identification in us. Whoever we are, we tend to see ourselves in her.

I find a clue to my own most primitive responses to this novel in the remarkable "Judgment" delivered by Sir Chartres Biron, presiding magistrate at the 1928 obscenity trial that resulted in *The Well's* banning by the British government. This long and painful peroration—confident, pettifogging, and mindlessly cruel—has in spite of its well-tempered stupidity the strange virtue of spotlighting precisely those passages in *The Well of Loneliness* that give the book, for me at least, its ultimate force: Sir Chartres quotes them all. And they are stirring indeed. One hears in the coils of his central assault (an assault that made Hall in the courtroom cry out in protest) all of the book's primal sentiments: stark, unadorned, viciously recast as evidence of "the most horrible, unnatural and disgusting obscenity," yet all the more noble-sounding for the hostility of the context in which they are bruited.

> When this mother [Lady Anna] announces her intention [to send Stephen away from Morton as a punishment for the scandalous affair with Angela Crossby], it says: "Then, suddenly, Stephen knew that unless she could, indeed, drop dead at the feet of this woman in whose womb she had quickened there was one thing which she dared not let pass unchallenged"—what is it that she dare not let to go unchallenged?—"and that was this terrible slur upon her love. And all that was in her rose up to refute it; to protect her love from such unbearable soiling. It was part of herself, and unless she could save it she could not save herself any more. She must stand or fall by the courage of that love to proclaim its right to toleration." "This terrible slur upon her love"—what does that mean? Then again, addressing her mother, "She held up her hand, commanding silence, commanding that slow, quiet voice to cease speaking, and she said: 'As my father loved you, I loved' "—this practitioner of unnatural vice.—" 'As a man loves a woman that was how I loved—protectively like my father. I wanted to give all I had in me to give.' " I am asked to say that this book is not a defence of these practices. What does it go on to say? What is the result of these horrible practices? "It made me feel terribly strong . . . and gentle. It was good, good, *good*"—repeated three times, the last "good" emphasized in order that one may make no mistake about what is meant in this book. [. . .] She writes to her mother in these terms: "You insulted what to me is natural and sacred." "What to me is sacred"? Natural and sacred! Then I am asked to say that this book is in no sense a defence of unnatural practices between women, or a glorification of them, or a praise of them, to put it perhaps not quite so strongly. "Natural" and "Sacred"! "Good" repeated three times. (43–44)

Elsewhere, notes this able embodiment of British justice, "the actual physical acts of these women indulging in unnatural vices are described in the most alluring terms; their result is described as giving these women extraordinary rest, contentment and pleasure" (43).

"It was good, good, *good*." ("Repeated three times, the last 'good' emphasized in order that one may make no mistake about what is meant in this book.") Make no mistake indeed; Radclyffe Hall was the first modern writer to say love between women was good—and to do so so simply and directly and courageously. "Extraordinary rest, contentment and pleasure"? No argument there: I myself have found this to be the case. It matters little in the end, perhaps, what sort of "woman" (invert, lesbian, bisexual, transsexual, asexual, polysexual, natural, warped, pretty, or honky-tonk) one thinks oneself to be in the midst of such rest, contentment, and pleasure, or indeed what sort of "woman" one imagines one's partner to be. The joining up is what counts (has always counted), the putting of one and one together to make two. Hall dared to put it in writing. *The Well of Loneliness*? Embarrassing, yes. Adolescent, yes. Lumbers along grotesquely. Morbid. Dumb. A sacred monster from every (obtuse) angle. Ugh! Pooh! Ahem! But also the first and most unflinching celebration of that form of human erotic joy that just happens to be one's own. And there's nothing for it in the end but a (slightly teary) round of applause. Damn wicked Sir Chartres and all the rest of them! Good old Maimed One! The hell with being tasteful and artsy and a great writer! I love her so much, and good, good, *good* it will always be.

Note

1. Radclyffe Hall, *The Well of Loneliness* (1928; reprint, New York: Anchor Books, 1990). All parenthetical page citations are to this edition.

Contributors

JULIE ABRAHAM teaches twentieth-century literature, women's studies, and lesbian/gay/queer studies at Emory University. She is the author of *Are Girls Necessary? Lesbian Writing and Modern Histories* (New York: Routledge, 1996) and is working on *The City of Feeling*, a study of homosexualities and cities to be published by the University of Minnesota Press. She reviews for *The Nation* and *The Women's Review of Books*.

TERRY CASTLE is Walter A. Haas professor in the humanities at Stanford University. Her most recent books include *The Apparitional Lesbian: Female Homosexuality and Modern Culture* (New York: Columbia University Press 1993), *The Female Thermometer: Eighteenth-Century Culture and the Invention of the Uncanny* (New York: Oxford University Press, 1995), and *Noël Coward and Radclyffe Hall: Kindred Spirits* (New York: Columbia University Press, 1996). She is currently working on a historical anthology of lesbian literature.

SARAH E. CHINN is assistant professor of English at Hunter College, CUNY. She is also the author of *Technology and the Logic of American Racism: A Cultural History of the Body as Evidence* (New York: Continuum, 2000) and has published articles on queer theory and U.S. literatures and cultures in *Discourse, Pre/text*, and *Minnesota Review*.

LAURA DOAN is author of *Fashioning Sapphism: The Origins of a Modern English Lesbian Culture* (New York: Columbia University Press, 2001). Her research interests in the cultural impact of sexology have culminated in two edited projects with Lucy Bland, *Sexology Uncensored: The Documents of Sexual Science* and *Sexology in Culture: Labelling Bodies and Desires* (Chicago: University of Chicago Press, 1998). She is reader in women's studies at Manchester University.

KIM EMERY is an associate professor at the University of Florida, where she teaches courses in U.S. literatures and culture, queer theory, critical pedagogy, and lesbian/gay studies. Her work on Pragmatism and lesbian possibility has also appeared in *The Journal of the History of Sexuality*. She is author of the forthcoming *The Lesbian Index: Pragmatism and Lesbian Subjectivity in the Twentieth-Century United States* (Albany: State University of New York Press, 2002).

JUDITH HALBERSTAM is full professor of literature at the University of California at San Diego. She is author of *Female Masculinity* (Durham, N.C.: Duke University Press, 1998) and co-author with Del LaGrace Volcano of *The Drag King Book* (London: Serpent's Tail, 1999). Halberstam is currently working on a project on queer subcultures.

CLARE HEMMINGS is lecturer in gender studies and gender theory at the London School of Economics. She has published a range of articles on sexuality and gender, most recently, "Waiting for No Man," in Sally R. Munt, ed., *Butch/Femme: Inside Lesbian Gender* (London: Cassell, 1998). She is the coeditor of *The Bisexual Imaginary: Representation, Identity, and Desire* (London: Cassell, 1997), and guest editor of "Stretching Queer Boundaries: Queer Method and Practice for the 21st Century," *Sexualities* 2 (4): November 1999.

TREVOR HOPE teaches comparative literature at Cornell University. He is the author of essays on feminist and queer theory appearing in the journals *Differences* and *Diacritics* and in Naomi Segal, Mandy Merck, and Elizabeth Wright, eds., *Coming Out of Feminism?* (Oxford and Malden, Mass.: Blackwell, 1998). He is currently at work on a study of Radclyffe Hall and degeneration.

SUSAN KINGSLEY KENT is professor of history at the University of Colorado, Boulder. She is the author of *Sex and Suffrage in Britain, 1860–1914* (Princeton: Princeton University Press, 1987), *Making Peace: The Reconstruction of Gender in Interwar Britain* (Princeton: Princeton University Press, 1993), and *Gender and Power in Britain, 1640–1990* (New York: Routledge, 1999). She is currently working on a book about loss and identity in interwar Britain.

JODIE MEDD has recently completed a Ph.D. at Cornell University, with a dissertation entitled "Extraordinary Allegations: Scandalous Female Homosexuality and the Culture of Modernism." She is currently assistant professor of English at Carleton University in Ottawa, Canada.

SALLY R. MUNT is reader in media studies at the University of Sussex. She is author and editor of several books in lesbian and gay studies, *Heroic Desire: Lesbian Identity and Cultural Space* (New York: New York University Press, 1998), *Butch/Femme: Inside Lesbian Gender* (Washington, D.C.: Cassell, 1998), and, with Andy Medhurst, *Lesbian and Gay Studies: A Critical Introduction* (Washington, D.C.: Cassell, 1997).

JAY PROSSER is lecturer in American literature at the University of Leeds. He is author of *Second Skins: The Body Narratives of Transsexuality* (1998) also published by Columbia University Press.

VICTORIA ROSNER is assistant professor of English at Texas A & M University. Her essays have appeared in journals including *Feminist Studies, a/b: Auto/Biography*, and *Tulsa Studies in Women's Literature*. She is currently at work on a book entitled *Interior Designs: Modernism and the Reconstruction of Private Life*.

JEAN WALTON is associate professor of English and women's studies at the University of Rhode Island. She has published on psychoanalysis, race, and sexual difference in *Critical Inquiry, Discourse*, and *The Lesbian Postmodern*, and coedited the *Queer Utilities* special issue of *College Literature*. She is author of *Fair Sex, Savage Dreams: Race, Psychoanalysis, Sexual Difference* (Durham, N.C.: Duke University Press, 2001).

JOANNE WINNING is lecturer in twentieth-century literature at Middlesex University, London. She is author of *The Pilgrimage of Dorothy Richardson* (Madison: University of Wisconsin Press, 2000) and editor of Bryher's *Two Novels: Development and Two Selves* (Madison: University of Wisconsin Press, 2000). Previous publications include *The Crazy Jig: An Anthology of Lesbian and Gay Writing from Scotland* (Edinburgh: Polygon Press, 1992). She is currently working on the first full-length study of lesbian modernism, which examines the literary, artistic, and editorial work of figures such as Virginia Woolf, Djuna Barnes, H.D., Bryher, Romaine Brooks, and Gluck.

Suggested Readings

Backus, Margot Gayle. "Sexual Orientation in the (Post)Imperial Nation: Celticism and Inversion Theory in Radclyffe Hall's *The Well of Loneliness*." *Tulsa Studies in Women's Literature* 15, no. 2 (Fall 1996).

Baker, Michael. *Our Three Selves: The Life of Radclyffe Hall*. New York: William Morrow, 1985.

Barale, Michèle Aina. "Below the Belt: (Un)Covering *The Well of Loneliness*." In Diana Fuss, ed., *Inside/Out: Lesbian Theories, Gay Theories*. New York: Routledge, 1991.

Benstock, Shari. "Expatriate Sapphic Modernism: Entering Literary History." In Karla Jay and Joanne Glasgow, eds., *Lesbian Texts and Contexts: Radical Revisions*. New York: New York University Press, 1990.

Brown, Beverley. "'A Disgusting Book When Properly Read': The Obscenity Trial." *Hecate* 10, no. 2 (1984).

Breen, Margaret Soenser. "Narrative Inversion: The Biblical Heritage of *The Well of Loneliness* and *Desert of the Heart*." *Journal of Homosexuality* 33, nos. 3/4 (1997).

Brimstone, Lyndie. "Towards a New Cartography: Radclyffe Hall, Virginia Woolf, and the Working of Common Land." In Elaine Hobby and Chris White, eds., *What Lesbians Do in Books*. London: The Women's Press, 1991.

Brittain, Vera. *Radclyffe Hall: A Case of Obscenity?* London: Femina Books, 1968.

Buck, Claire. "'Still Some Obstinate Emotion Remains': Radclyffe Hall and the Meanings of Service." In Suzanne Raitt and Trudi Tate, eds., *Women's Fiction and the Great War*. Oxford: Clarendon Press, 1997.

Castle, Terry. *Noël Coward and Radclyffe Hall: Kindred Spirits*. New York: Columbia University Press, 1996.

Cline, Sally. *Radclyffe Hall: A Woman Called John*. London: John Murray, 1997.

de Lauretis, Teresa. "Perverse Desire: The Lure of the Mannish Lesbian." *Australian Feminist Studies* 13 (Autumn 1991): 15–286.

———. *The Practice of Love: Lesbian Sexuality and Perverse Desire*. Bloomington and Indianapolis: Indiana University Press, 1994.

Dickson, Lovat. *Radclyffe Hall at the Well of Loneliness*. New York: Charles Scribner's Sons, 1975.

Faderman, Lillian and Ann Williams. "Radclyffe Hall and the Lesbian Image." *Conditions* 1 (1977).

Franks, Claudia Stillman. *Beyond 'The Well of Loneliness': The Fiction of Radclyffe Hall*. Amersham, England: Avebury, 1982.

———. "Stephen Gordon, Novelist: A Re-evaluation of Radclyffe Hall's *The Well of Loneliness*." *Tulsa Studies in Women's Literature* 1, no. 2 (Fall 1982).

Gilbert, Sandra M. and Susan Gubar. *No Man's Land: The Place of the Woman Writer in the Twentieth Century*, vol. 2, *Sexchanges*. New Haven: Yale University Press, 1989.

Gilmore, Leigh. "Obscenity, Modernity, Identity: Legalizing *The Well of Loneliness* and *Nightwood*." *Journal of the History of Sexuality* 4, no. 4 (1994).

Glasgow, Joanne. "What's a Nice Lesbian Like You Doing in the Church of Torquemada?" In Karla Jay and Joanne Glasgow, eds., *Lesbian Texts and Contexts: Radical Revisions*. New York: New York University Press, 1990.

Hall, Radclyffe. *The Well of Loneliness*. 1928, reprint. New York: Anchor Books, 1990.

Hamer, Emily. *Britannia's Glory: A History of Twentieth-Century Lesbians*. London: Cassell, 1996.

Hennegan, Alison. "Introduction." In Radclyffe Hall, *The Well of Loneliness*. 1928; reprint, London: Virago, 1982.

Henson, Leslie J. "'Articulate Silence(s)': Femme Subjectivity and Class Relations in *The Well of Loneliness*." In Laura Harris and Elizabeth Crocker, eds., *Femme: Feminists, Lesbians, and Bad Girls*. New York: Routledge, 1997.

Ingram, Angela. "'Unutterable Putrefaction' and 'Foul Stuff': Two 'Obscene' Novels of the 1920s." *Women's Studies International Forum* 9, no. 4 (1986).

Inness, Sherrie A. *The Lesbian Menace: Ideology, Identity, and the Representation of Lesbian Life*. Amherst: University of Massachusetts Press, 1997.

MacPike, Loralee. "Is Mary Llewellyn an Invert? The Modernist Supertext of *The Well of Loneliness*." In Elizabeth Jane Harrison and Shirley Peterson, eds., *Unmanning Modernism: Gendered Re-Readings*. Knoxville: The University of Tennessee Press, 1997.

Marcus, Jane. "Sapphistory: The Woolf and the Well." In Karla Jay and Joanne Glasgow, eds., *Lesbian Texts and Contexts: Radical Revisions*. New York: New York University Press, 1990.

McNaron, Toni. "A Journey into Otherness: Teaching *The Well of Loneliness*." In Margaret Cruikshank, ed., *Lesbian Studies Present and Future*. New York: The Feminist Press, 1982.

Madden, Ed. "*The Well of Loneliness*, or The Gospel According to Radclyffe Hall." *Journal of Homosexuality* 33, nos. 3/4 (1997).

Martinez, Inez. "The Lesbian Hero Bound: Radclyffe Hall's Portraits of Sapphic Daughters and Their Mothers." In Stuart Kellog, ed., *Literary Visions of Homosexuality*. New York: Haworth, 1983.

Newton, Esther. "The Mythic Mannish Lesbian: Radclyffe Hall and the New Woman." In Martin Duberman, Martha Vicinus, and George Chauncey Jr., eds., *Hidden from History: Reclaiming the Gay and Lesbian Past*. *Signs* 1984; reprint, New York: New American Library, 1989.

Ormrod, Richard. *Una Troubridge: The Friend of Radclyffe Hall*. New York: Carroll & Graf, 1985.

O'Rourke, Rebecca. *Reflecting on The Well of Loneliness*. London and New York: Routledge, 1989.

Parkes, Adam. "Lesbianism, History, and Censorship: *The Well of Loneliness* and the SUPPRESSED RANDINESS of Virginia Woolf's *Orlando*." *Twentieth Century Literature* 40, no. 4 (Winter 1994).

Pouchard, Line. "Queer Desire in *The Well of Loneliness*." In Catherine Belsey and Jane Moore, eds., *The Feminist Reader: Essays in Gender and the Politics of Literary Criticism*. Malden, Mass.: Blackwell, 1989.

Radford, Jean. "An Inverted Romance: *The Well of Loneliness* and Sexual Ideology." In Jean Radford, ed., *The Progress of Romance: The Politics of Popular Fiction*. London: Routledge, 1986.

Rolley, Katrina. "The Treatment of Homosexuality and *The Well of Loneliness*." In Paul Hyland and Neil Sammells, eds., *Writing and Censorship in Britain*. London and New York: Routledge, 1992.

Rosenman, Ellen Bayuk. "Sexual Identity and *A Room of One's Own*: 'Secret Economies' in Virginia Woolf's Feminist Discourse." *Signs* 14, no. 3 (Spring 1989).

Ruehl, Sonja. "Inverts and Experts: Radclyffe Hall and the Lesbian Identity." In Rosalind Brunt and Caroline Rowan, eds., *Feminism, Culture, and Politics*. London: Lawrence and Wishart, 1982.

Rule, Jane. *Lesbian Images*. Garden City, N.Y.: Doubleday, 1975.

Scanlon, Joan. "Bad Language vs. Bad Prose? Lady Chatterley and *The Well*." *Critical Quarterly* 38, no. 3 (1996).

Souhami, Diana. *The Trials of Radclyffe Hall*. London: Weidenfeld & Nicolson, 1998.

Stimpson, Catharine R. "Zero Degree Deviancy: The Lesbian Novel in English." *Critical Inquiry* 8, no. 2 (Winter 1981).

Troubridge, Lady Una. *The Life and Death of Radclyffe Hall*. London: Hammond Hammond, 1961.

Whitlock, Gillian. "'Everything Is Out of Place': Radclyffe Hall and the Lesbian Literary Tradition." *Feminist Studies* 13, no. 3 (Fall 1987).

Index

Abbot, Berenice, 92

Abraham, Julie, 24, 336–54, 400

Addams, Jane, 91

Allen, Mary, 149, 159

Anderson, Margaret, 92, 337

Antoinette, Marie, 301–2

Asquith, Margot (Lady Oxford), 279–80, 293

Atwood, Clare, 149

Backus, Margot Gayle, 21, 303

Baker, Michael, 147, 149–51, 159, 363

Barale, Michèle Aina, 20

Barnes, Djuna, 18, 337; *Ladies Almanack*, 374; *Nightwood*, 19

Barney, Natalie, 90, 92, 102, 149, 323–24, 337, 374–75

Batten, Mabel Veronica, 79–80, 82, 310

Bennett, Arnold, 5–6, 56, 70, 163, 382

Benstock, Shari, 323–24, 373, 388

Berlant, Lauren, 235

Bersani, Leo and Ulysse Dutoit, 118, 120

Birkett, Norman, 39–40

Biron, Sir Chartres, 1, 39–49, 364, 400–2

Bisexuality, 22, 157, 180

Bloomsbury group, 81, 94

Borden, Mary, 220

Bower, Brady, 219

Breen, Margaret Soenser, 21

British Journal of Inebriety, 8, 72–3

British Medical Journal, 165

Brittain, Vera, 14–15, 58–60, 86, 181

Brooks, Romaine, 149, 337

Broucek, Francis, 211

Brown, Beverley, 373

Bryher (Winifred Ellerman), 3, 375

Buck, Claire, 233

Butch identity, 89, 139, 154, 184–86, 208; in *The Well*, 23, 139, 208

Burgess, Ernest, 337

Bushel, Judge Hyman, 361–62, 364, 366–68

Butler, Judith, 20, 208, 211–12, 265

Cape, Jonathan, 3, 4, 6, 11–12, 39, 41, 71, 358–60

Cardozo, Justice Benjamin, 365

Carpenter, Edward, 22, 94–95, 165–74

Carrington (Dora), 81

Castle, Terry, 2, 18, 25, 149, 302, 394–402

Cather, Willa, 92

Catholicism, *see* Christianity

Chauncey, George, 129

Chicago School, 338–40, 344, 346

Chinn, Sarah, 24, 300–15

Christianity, 21, 23, 85, 87, 200–5, 210, 233, 242

Cixous, Hélène, 194

Class, 9, 139, 258

Cline, Sally, 10, 281

Cockburn, Judge Chief Justice, 41

Colette, 102, 323

Comaroff, Jean, 225

Conditions, 15

Connolly, Cyril, 67–69, 169, 397

Cook, Blanche Wiesen, 15, 356

Cory, Donald, 87

Country Life, 67

Coward, Noël, 149

Craig, Edy, 149

Crisp, Quentin, 265

Cross-dressing, 9–10, 89–90, 99, 146–47, 158

Daily Express, 8, 10–11, 13, 358

Daily News and Westminster Gazette, 65–67, 397

Daily Telegraph, 65, 375

Darwin, Charles, 169, 203, 256, 265

Dawson, Margaret Damer, 149

Dean, Carolyn, 225

Dekoven, Marianne, 373

de Lauretis, Teresa, 20, 109–25, 137–38, 155–57, 208, 355

Dell, Floyd, 336, 338–40

DeQuincy, Thomas, 307

Dett, Nathaniel, 278

Dexter, Mary, 329

Dillon, Michael, 141–42

Discovery, 237

Doan, Laura, 22, 162–78

Douglas, Alfred, 207

Douglas, James, 1, 2, 4, 6, 8–13, 36–38, 73, 232–33, 267–68, 358, 397

Duncan, Isadora, 92, 323

Eastman, Crystal, 92

Edis, Robert, 320

Eliot, T. S., 306

Ellis, Havelock, 22, 399; "Commentary," 2–4, 6, 35–36, 51, 53, 55–56, 58, 61, 71–72, 80, 102, 130–31, 162–63, 316–17, 319, 340; *Sexual Inversion*, 96–97, 100, 110, 132–33, 135, 163, 166–67, 174, 182–84, 186, 188–89, 336, 374

Emery, Kim, 24, 355–71

Evening Standard, 11, 56, 378, 382

Faderman, Lillian, 2, 15–16, 22, 377

Farwell, Marilyn, 181

Feinberg, Leslie, 185

Female masculinity, *see* Masculinity

Feminism, 94; and *The Well; see also*
    Lesbian feminism
Femme identity, 179–94; in *The Well*,
    21–22, 179–83, 185–94
Ferenczi, Sándor, 141, 234
Fetishism, 117–19
First World War, 216–19, 223, 225–26,
    232–42, 263–67, 327–30; in *The Well*,
    216–17, 220–24, 227–29, 232–35,
    237–45, 263–66, 327–30
Flanner, Janet, 337
Forster, E. M., 4, 80, 165, 209, 376;
    Maurice, 80
Foster, Hal, 225, 228
Foucault, Michel, 129, 132, 145, 164, 242,
    257, 374
Freewoman, 94
Freud, Sigmund, 81, 97, 109–11, 116–18,
    155, 181–82, 225, 235, 237, 247, 265
Friede, Donald, 361
Fussell, Paul, 225

Galsworthy, Mrs., 281
Gilbert, Sandra and Susan Gubar, 18,
    130, 163, 320, 327, 330–31
Gilman, Charlotte Perkins, 91
Gilman, Sander, 309
Gilmore, Leigh, 19, 357, 365–66
Glasgow Herald, 5, 57
Glasgow, Joanne, 149–51, 200
Goldman, Emma, 100
Gordon, Taylor, 278, 279–82, 285–87, 293
Gordon, W. R., 9, 65–67, 397
Grahame, Robert Cunningham, 281
Graves, Robert, 223
Greville, Ursula, 281
Gullace, Nicoletta, 218

Halberstam, Judith, 22, 137, 139, 145–61,
    379, 400
Hall, Radclyffe, 2, 12
    as invert, 145, 147–51, 156–57, 159,
        162–3, 378; in *Ladies Almanack*,
        374; letters, 22, 145, 149–51,
        156–57, 316; life of, 79–80, 200,
        281–82, 289, 310, 327; life of
        compared to *The Well*, 81–82,
        102, 138, 206; at the obscenity
        trial, 45
    works: *Adam's Breed*, 4, 52, 61, 72,
        281; "Author's Note" to *The Well*,
        317; "Career of Mark Anthony
        Brakes," 289–92; "Miss Ogilvy
        Finds Herself," 134, 146–48,
        238–39, 241, 246–47, 249; *The
        Unlit Lamp*, 90, 92–93, 99
Hallet, Nicky, 374
Hamer, Diane, 110–11
Hari, Mata, 323
Harlem Renaissance, 291
Hartley, L. P., 4–5, 50–51, 363
H.D. (Hilda Doolittle), 375
Hegel, 172
Hemmings, Clare, 23–24, 179–96
Hennegan, Alison, 164
Henson, Leslie J., 21
Hirschfeld, Magnus, 220, 337
Holmes, Oliver Wendell, 365–66
Homosexuality, 68, 95, 131, 133, 142,
    211–13; and effeminacy, 377; and
    cities, 336–51
Hope, Trevor, 23, 255–73, 400

Intermediate sex, 165–66, 168–70, 173,
    240

Jacob, Naomi, 6

Jay, Karla, 89

Johnson, J. Rosamond, 278–79, 281, 287

Johnson, James Weldon, 278

Johnson, Samuel, 306

Jones, Ann Rosalind, 308

Joyce, James, 93

Joynson-Hicks, William, 6, 359, 375, 378

Kent, Susan Kingsley, 23, 216–31, 399

Kerr, Robert, 320

King, Richard, 7, 63–64

Kinsey, Alfred, 351

Knopf, Alfred, 359

Knopf, Blanche, 360

Krafft-Ebing, Richard von, 22, 84;
    Psychopathia Sexualis, 78, 95–96,
    132–33, 135, 167, 174, 305, 306–7, 309,
    311; cited in *The Well*, 82, 100, 131,
    166, 168, 242, 302, 322

Lacan, Jacques, 111, 116, 121, 225

Lancet, 71, 163

Laplanche, J., and J. B. Pontalis, 115,
    120–21

Lawrence, D. H., 78, 93, 165; *Lady
    Chatterley's Lover*, 19

Lawrence, Margaret, 5

Leavis, Q. D., 6

Lee, Hermione, 382

Lesbian feminism, 89–90, 101, 130; *see
    also* Feminism

Lesbian, mannish, 89–91, 109–25

Lesbianism, 24, 87; sexuality of, 110, 119,
    300–1, 309, 373; in the USA, 355, 357

Leslie-Jones, Veronica, 384

Lewis, Helen Block, 206

Life and Letters, 8–9, 71–72

Liverpool Post and Mercury, 62

Louise, Marie Thérèse (Princesse de
    Lamballe), 301

Lowther, Toupie, 147–49, 327–28

Lyon, Phyllis and Del Martin, 16, 87

MacCannell, Dean, 311, 312

McClintock, Ann, 308

McNaron, Toni, 15

MacPike, Loralee, 20

Madden, Ed, 21

Mannin, Ethel, 4

Marcus, Jane, 19

Martinez, Inez, 16

Masculinity, 159, 217–21; female mas-
    culinity, 22, 145–46, 148, 151, 154;
    masculinity complex, 111, 155; in
    Stephen Gordon, 90–91, 114–15, 130,
    138, 148, 155, 216–17, 220, 244

Marx, Karl, 172

Maugham, Somerset, 278, 281

Medd, Jodie, 23–24, 232–54, 399

Melancholy, 265; in *The Well* 23, 155,
    209

Miller, Nancy K., 14

Millet, Kate, 14

Mills, Florence, 281

Minow, Makiko, 373

Modernism, 277, 306, 372–77, 388; and
    The Well, 14, 19–20, 24–25, 306, 318,
    372–77, 388

Morning Post, 3, 57–58

Morrell, Ottoline, 372

Morrison, Toni, 289

Mulvey, Laura, 181, 184

Munt, Sally R., 23, 184–86, 199–215, 399

Nation and Athenaeum, 5, 13, 52–54, 237, 358

Nestle, Joan, 119–20, 180, 184

New Statesman, 67–69, 237, 397

New Woman, 91–92, 98–100

New York Times, 358–59

Newton, Esther, 2, 16–17, 20, 22, 89–108, 115, 122, 130, 137, 149, 154, 171, 179, 322, 356

North Mail and Newcastle Chronicle, 60–61

O'Leary, Con, 61

O'Rourke, Rebecca, 14–15

Obscene Publications Act of 1857, 1

Obscenity, 1, 18, 39–49, 70, 365–66, 376

Owen, Wilfred, 220, 223

Parkes, Adam, 19, 163, 245, 249, 381

Park, Robert, 24, 338–51

Peabody, George, 279

Peirce, C. S., 365

People, 13, 69

Perverse desire, 110–11, 116, 119

Popular Pictorial, 378

Pouchard, Line, 20

Pound, Roscoe, 365

Probyn, Elspeth, 318

Prosser, Jay, 22, 129–44, 379, 400

Psyche, 237

Psychoanalysis, 20, 23–24, 55, 141, 234–37, 247; and lesbianism, 109, 115; in *The Well*, 141, 155

Race, 21, 24, 277–78, 282–84, 286–88, 291–95, 297–98, 310, 399

Radford, Jean, 17, 164, 234, 308, 379

Raitt, Suzanne, 381

Regina vs. Hicklin, 361, 364–67

Rhys, Jean, 194

Rich, Adrienne, 123, 372

Richardson, Dorothy, 375; *Clear Horizon*, 375, 384–87; *Dawn's Left Hand*, 375, 384; *Pilgrimage*, 383–84, 387–88

Rivers, W. H. R., 235, 237

Roof, Judith, 181

Rosenman, Ellen, 7

Rosner, Victoria, 24, 316–35

Rousseau, Jean-Jacques, 172

Rubin, Gayle, 139

Ruehl, Sonja, 17, 164

Rule, Jane, 16, 77–88, 356

Sackville-West, Vita, 80, 97, 149, 219, 377, 381

Said, Edward, 305, 307

Sand, George, 90

Sanger, Margaret, 92

Santher, Eric, 225

Sassoon, Siegfried, 165, 220, 223

Saturday Review, 5, 50–51, 237, 358

Scanlon, Joan, 19

Scott, Bonnie Kime, 164, 377

Sedgwick, Eve Kosofsky, 151

Sexology, 129–33, 135, 141–42; in *The Well*, 22, 130–31; *see also* Carpenter, Edward; Ellis, Havelock; Krafft-Ebing, Richard von; Ulrichs, Karl Heinrich

Sexual inversion, 62, 129, 131–35, 145–6, 148; in *The Well*, 5, 23–24, 51, 53, 62, 68, 72, 81–83, 129, 134–35, 208, 244–45, 264–65, 302, 311, 364, 397;

Sexual inversion (*Continued*)
  see also Carpenter, Edward; Ellis, Havelock; Krafft-Ebing, Richard von; Ulrichs, Karl Heinrich
Shame, 23, 199–213
Shell shock, 23, 223, 226–27, 234–39, 244–46, 249
Showalter, Elaine, 225, 239
Silverman, Kaja, 116
Simmel, Georg, 339
Sinfield, Alan, 377–78
Smith, Helen Zenna, 220
Smith-Rosenberg, Carroll, 16
Souhami, Diana, 10, 281
Souline, Evguenia, 149–50, 155–56
Spectator, 237
St. John, Christopher (Chrisabel Marshall), 149
Stein, Gertrude, 18, 92, 97, 323, 337, 375
Stimpson, Catharine, 15, 17, 114, 130, 200, 356
Stone, Martin, 235
Strachey, Lytton, 81
Sunday Chronicle, 13
Sunday Express, 1, 5, 10–12, 358, 378, 397
Sunday Times, 55, 358
Symonds, John Addington, 336

T. P.'s & Cassell's Weekly, 61, 378
Tatler, 7, 10, 63
Terry, Ellen, 149
Thiele, Beverly, 171
Time and Tide, 58–60
Times Literary Supplement, 4–5, 51–52
Toklas, Alice B., 100
Tomkins, Silvan, 203–4, 206

Transsexuality, 15, 18, 22, 130, 132–34, 137–42, 148, 152, 158
Trefusis, Violet, 381
Trodd, Anthea, 6
Troubridge, Una, 79–80, 82, 100, 102, 145, 147–48, 150, 159, 180, 206, 219, 281–82, 289, 316, 388; in *Ladies Almanack*, 374
Truth, 69–71

Ulrichs, Karl Heinrich, 78, 133, 174; cited in *The Well*, 82, 100, 131, 321

Van Vechten, Carl, 278
Vicinus, Martha, 217
Vivien, Renée, 102, 323, 337

Walker, Lisa, 180, 189
Walker, Mary, 90
Walton, Jean, 24, 277–99, 399
Warner, Sylvia Townsend, 18
Well of Loneliness, The
  characters: Adolphe Blanc, 295; Anna Gordon in, 181, 203, 321, 395; Angela Crossby in, 43–44, 85, 179–81, 205; Collins in, 85, 99–100, 139–40, 202, 257–60; Jonathan Brockett in, 221; Martin Hallam in, 22, 166, 170–73, 183–84, 193; Mary Llewellyn in, 21, 22, 44–47, 85–87, 102, 166, 170–73, 179–83, 185–94, 308; Philip Gordon in, 260–62, 303, 320–21; Puddle in, 395; Roger Antrim in, 204, Valérie Seymour in, 47, 134, 282, 324–25, 349, 374

reception: censorship of, 8, 12, 13, 18–19, 24, 35–38; 39–49, 358–61; 366; early reviews of, 2–13, 50–73; and feminist criticism, 13–21, 77–125, 355–56, 373; obscenity trial of in England, 1, 19, 22, 39–49, 80, 375; obscenity trial of in the USA, 24, 358–68; publication history of, 6, 12, 14–15, 359–60; and queer theory, 20–21; US/UK differences, 25

Stephen Gordon in: 57, 59–61, 63–66, 68; body of, 9, 77–78, 81, 98, 112–15, 134–35, 137–41, 155; cross-dressing of, 9–10, 99, 158; as a lesbian, 52, 98, 130; masculinity of, 90–91, 114–15, 130, 138, 148, 155, 216–17, 220, 244; as a sexual invert, 23–24, 51, 53, 82–83, 129, 134–35, 152; shame of, 202–5, 238, 363

themes: 22; butch in, 23, 139, 208; Celticism in, 21, 303; Christianity in, 21, 23, 85, 87, 200–5, 210, 233, 242; class in, 9, 139, 258; Englishness in, 304; femme in, 21–22, 179–83, 185–94; masculinity in, 2, 15–17, 22, 67, 85, 101; gender in, 18, 60, 102, 308, 320–21; lesbianism in, 5, 16–18, 78, 87, 114, 148, 397; London in, 340–41, 347, 350; melancholy in, 23, 155, 209; mirror scene in, 112–14, 137–38, 153–55, 158, 379; and modernism, 14, 19–20, 24–25, 306, 318, 372–77, 388; Morton in, 302–4, 318–26, 329–32; and nation, 21, 23–24, 234–35, 263–64; Oratava in, 24, 304, 306–12; Paris in, 323–25, 337–38, 340, 342, 347, 349–51; primitivism in, 304–5, 309, 311; race in, 21, 24, 277–78, 282–84, 286–88, 291–95, 297–98, 310, 399; sexual relationships in, 43–48, 85, 300–1, 309; sexology in, 22, 130–31; sexual inversion in, 3, 5, 51, 62, 68, 72, 81–83, 208, 244–45, 264–65, 302, 311, 364, 397; shame in, 23, 199–213; transsexuality in, 18, 22, 130, 134, 137–41, 148, 152, 158; and war, 23, 216–17, 220–24, 227–29, 232–35, 237–45, 263–66, 327–30; and wounds, 120, 220, 223–24, 239, 242–43, 259, 263–64, 267; writing style of, 5, 19–20, 53–54, 57, 59

Weeks, Jeffrey, 169
Wells, H. G., 384
West, Rebecca, 1
White, Morton, 365
Whitlock, Gillian, 6, 18, 164
Whitman, Walt, 170
Wilde, Oscar, 38, 71, 151, 207, 302, 377–78
Wilder, Frances, 94–95, 97
Williams, Ann, 15
Winning, Joanne, 25, 372–93
Wirth, Louis, 337
Wittig, Monique, 18
Women Police Service, 159
Women Police Volunteers, 159

Women's Auxiliary Police Force, 146

Wooley, Mary, 91

Woolf, Leonard, 4, 52–54, 81, 358, 363

Woolf, Virginia, 1, 5–7, 18, 80–81, 93–94,
    98, 372–73, 375–77, 381, 383, 387, 397;
    Orlando, 18–19, 80, 90, 99, 375, 377,
    380–83, 388; *A Room of One's Own*,
    19, 318

Wylie, I. A. R., 7–8, 55

Yorkshire Post, 13

Young, Allan, 89